OUR LIVES BEFORE THE LAW

OUR LIVES BEFORE
THE LAW

CONSTRUCTING A FEMINIST
JURISPRUDENCE

Judith A. Baer

PRINCETON UNIVERSITY PRESS

PRINCETON, NEW JERSEY

PUBLISHED BY PRINCETON UNIVERSITY PRESS, 41 WILLIAM STREET,
PRINCETON, NEW JERSEY 08540
IN THE UNITED KINGDOM: PRINCETON UNIVERSITY PRESS,
CHICHESTER, WEST SUSSEX

LIBRARY OF CONGRESS CATALOGING-IN-PUBLICATION DATA

BAER, JUDITH A.

OUR LIVES BEFORE THE LAW : CONSTRUCTING A FEMINIST
JURISPRUDENCE / JUDITH A. BAER.

P. CM.

INCLUDES BIBLIOGRAPHICAL REFERENCES AND INDEX.

ISBN 0-691-03316-1 (CLOTH : ALK. PAPER)

ISBN 0-691-01945-2 (PBK. : ALK. PAPER)

1. FEMINIST JURISPRUDENCE. 2. WOMEN—LEGAL STATUS,
LAWS, ETC.—UNITED STATES. I. TITLE.

K349.B34   1999

340′.082—dc21   98-55309

THIS BOOK HAS BEEN COMPOSED IN JANSON

CHAPTER 5 OF THE PRESENT WORK APPEARED AS PART OF THE
AUTHOR'S ESSAY, "WOMEN'S RIGHTS AND THE LIMITS OF
CONSTITUTIONAL DOCTRINE," 44 *WESTERN POLITICAL
QUARTERLY* (1991): 828–852.

THE PAPER USED IN THIS PUBLICATION MEETS THE
MINIMUM REQUIREMENTS OF ANSI/NISO Z39.48-1992 (R1997)
(PERMANENCE OF PAPER)

http: //pup.princeton.edu

PRINTED IN THE UNITED STATES OF AMERICA

1 3 5 7 9 10 8 6 4 2

IN MEMORIAM

THE WOMAN IN THE HOUSTON MORGUE
JANUARY 20, 1993

SHE WAS IN HER TWENTIES,
LEFT A SMALL CHILD,
AND WAS A VICTIM OF
DOMESTIC VIOLENCE.

OUR POLITICS MUST HAVE AS
ONE OF ITS GOALS
AN END TO THIS KIND
OF KILLING.

Jane Rule

CONTENTS

PREFACE

THIS BOOK was born out of anger and hope. The anger comes from my observations of the lives women live and from the failure of contemporary feminist scholarship to deal with the conditions women endure. The hope comes from my belief that theory can explain situations and practice can improve them. These beliefs persist in the face of considerable evidence to the contrary. But acting on them has worked for me often enough to inspire these efforts to reground and redirect feminist jurisprudence.

This is a contrarian book. I reject much of the conventional wisdom about feminism and American society. I believe that the worst mistake feminists have made is to be too nice. The effort to be nice has corrupted and weakened both feminist theory and feminist practice. Far from bashing men, we have labored to avoid offending them. We have too often pulled our punches when discussing male aggression, male irresponsibility, male indolence, and male privilege. We have wasted time and energy criticizing feminists who refuse to moderate their message. Far from trashing full-time homemakers, pink-collar workers, or any women who lead lives different from those we want for ourselves, we have been so eager to praise women for the work they do that we have let it stay women's work. This kind of accommodation may or may not be good politics, but it is never good scholarship. The desire to please must not master the pursuit of truth.

Feminist failures of nerve arise partly from the fact that feminists tend to come from at least one of two groups of people who are trained in kindness, tolerance, acceptance, and guilt. These groups are women and liberals. (And I venture a guess that male feminists are even more likely than women to be present or former liberals.) As critical as feminists are of both gender stereotypes and liberalism, we too often act like lady liberals. Femininity and liberalism share certain habitual attitudes. Guilt is one; another is what might be called asymmetrical solicitude.

Liberals learn to respect other people's points of view, but not to expect these others to reciprocate. Feminists often behave the same way. They extend to their opponents the rights to act and the immunities from interference which are central tenets of liberalism, but they hesitate to claim these benefits for themselves. For example, supporters of the proposed Equal Rights Amendment and of reproductive freedom have gotten frequent reminders that many women disagree with them, that they do not speak for all women. Anti-ERA and antichoice women do not hear similar admonitions, although the same applies to them. Habits of courtesy, deference, and self-criticism have muted the feminist message and have encouraged us to reserve our fiercest criticism for one another.

Our Lives Before the Law, the title of this book, is a reminder that feminist theory is about women's lives. But much of the feminist theory published in the last twenty years rings false in the context of my own life. I had truculently called myself a feminist since I learned the word, but it took the revitalized women's movement, coinciding with my entry into graduate school, to teach me I was not alone. In the early years of the modern women's movement, author after author analyzed, criticized, and rejected current gender role expectations. This message was wonderfully liberating for at least one apprentice scholar who, like successful students everywhere, had learned too well to accept received wisdom. Modern feminism taught me that individual experiences, though personal in impact, are not unique in kind, and that theory can help make sense of them. Already a scholar and a feminist, I became a feminist scholar. I learned to unite the personal with the professional—as I do here—in a way that the traditional academic disciplines discouraged but feminist academics encouraged. Feminist solidarity kept me going through graduate school, a long hard job search, getting fired, and the struggle to rebuild my career.

But feminist theory changed. By the early 1980s, much of what I read sent disturbing messages about the issues I confronted. "The Compassion Trap," " 'Kinder, Kuche, Kirche' as Scientific Law," and "Funeral Oration for Traditional Womanhood" gave way to a "different voice," an "ethic of caring," and "women's ways of knowing." Feminist authors who continued to emphasize male domination and female oppression were accused by other feminists of demonizing men and denigrating women. Feminist theory resonated less and less with my experience.

In my thirties, I was denied tenure at a university at the same time a male colleague of no better qualifications received it. Like many crime victims, I talked about what had happened to me—and was told to shut up. "Don't dwell on it"; "Don't feel sorry for yourself"; and, worst of all, "If you can behave like this, the decision must have been right." And now some feminist authors implied that being wronged was a shameful sign of personal weakness, to be closeted with other skeletons. Nobody seemed to notice that shutting up about it leaves institutions free to do it again, just as shutting up about rape lets rapists get away with it. On second thought, maybe that was the point.

In my forties, my career reestablished, I found myself under more pressure to conform to traditional gender roles than I had been since I left my parents' 1950s home. Single and child-free, I lived like many middle-class professional men until I moved to the heart of Texas. Whether because of the region (more South than West), my advancing age (increasingly identifiable with my students' mothers and the "sandwich generation"), or whatever, my exemption from women's work expired. Women seemed continually to be approaching me with a sign-up sheet in hand. I am, of course, free not to sign up, but I am not free from the expectation. I must choose between doing chores and being perceived as unhelpful in ways that men need not choose. Women have the right to say no; men have an immunity from being asked.

My efforts to make sense of these experiences have led me back to an incident that seemed trivial at the time but lingered as an irritant in my memory. On a spring day in 1980, I played hooky from the Brookings Institution to visit the National Zoo. As I walked down a path, I heard loud, persistent wails of "Mommy!" Since I was not the person addressed, I let the child's cries fade into background noise. I soon became aware of a man standing nearby, shouting, and of bystanders who seemed hostile toward someone. A young woman holding a sobbing toddler appeared at about the time I realized I was the target of the group's disapproval. The mother, the man, and I apologized to one another for our respective misunderstanding of the situation. The hostile faces in the crowd turned friendly and sheepish. The child stopped crying. "You don't have kids, do you?" a woman bystander asked me as I approached the next exhibit.

No, I don't. "Mommy" does not refer to me; the word broadcasts on a frequency I never receive, any more than it did for that man. But strangers could reasonably connect me with a little girl who, for a terrifying moment, couldn't find a mother who didn't know she was lost. To me, I am no one's mommy. But to those people that day, I was anybody's and everybody's bad mommy. I was free not to have children, to forgo the rewards and responsibilities of motherhood. But I am not free of the expectation that I bear these responsibilities or of the judgment that I neglect them. Strangers' expectations impinge on me, much as wolf whistles and similar harassments impinge on women. Perhaps, as women age, we change from universal sex objects into universal mothers. We are available, vulnerable, responsible in ways that men are not.

Here again, feminist theory has failed me. Its legitimization of gender difference and valorization of female caregiving has not encouraged a critical approach to society's assignment of burdensome tasks. Many feminist authors worry that women will have to suppress their "femininity" and act like men in order to achieve equality. I respect their feelings, but my experience has been just the opposite. I am expected to act "feminine" against my own inclination and preference.

I don't need to read feminist theory to know that "women's work" is vital, and that society devalues it. My experience confirms both these generalizations. A professor who preferred teaching and mentoring to research and writing would have trouble in my publish-or-perish department. But so do I, as a woman professor whose priorities fit the institutional standards.

Nurturance is demanded of me beyond my ability to give. These demands stifle the spontaneous empathy which is at the core of human relationships. I may be in a minority; more women may want to be valued for their conventional contributions than to be free of the demand to perform them. But why can't feminist theory serve the needs of different women?

My approach to feminist theory is not the only contrarian feature of this book. I am equally critical of two aspects of the mainstream political discourse of the late 1990s: the increasingly idealized concepts of "family" and "community." Women need communities and families as much as men and children do. But communities and families may need women too much. They seem to depend heavily on sacrifices by women. Every December since I learned to read, I have come upon descriptions of cozy family Christmas celebrations in various ethnic and regional communities. Diverse as these are, they seem to have one thing in common: women get run off their feet. Social discourse about the decline of volunteerism, civic associations, and other components of community does not always notice the historic dependence of these activities on women's efforts. It may take a village to raise a child; but if we are not careful, it will be a village of busy women and unencumbered men.

Communities enforce conformity, create outsiders, and reinforce gender roles. Ever since I moved to College Station, the word "community" has stood between me and things I want to do. Sometimes I win; sometimes I lose; but I have gotten used to being advised not to invite a certain speaker, use a certain word, or write a certain letter to the editor because it will offend the community. My volunteer advisers often hasten to assure me they are really on my side. Needless to say, the community does not reciprocate their tolerance and accommodation. Even as they hold people in, "community" and "family" leave people out. Communities have outsiders, not all of whom volunteer for the position. Because I have a birth defect (a crippled hand), I've learned how easy it is to acquire outsider status and how hard to get rid of it. Because I am a middle-aged, single adult who lives alone, the social rhetoric of the 1990s threatens to exclude me from the scope of public discourse. The unit of political discussion is the family, not the person. Increasingly, I wonder where and even whether my life fits in this scheme.

"Family values" discourse may marginalize me, but it doesn't bore me. My family of origin gave me a critical perspective on the rosy-glow, soft-focus image of the family. This image doesn't describe a home where the largest person is also the biggest baby. My alcoholic, mentally ill father used his hands and his words as weapons against my mother, my brothers, and me. Nobody stopped his abuse, because the family values of the 1950s put the father at the head of the family and shielded families from public scrutiny. Things have improved in the last forty years; resources like women's shelters exist now that were undreamed of in the 1950s. But abusers still get away with it. The feminists, liberals, communitarians, and conservatives who stumble over one another in their rush to reassure everyone that most families are OK, and bad families are the exception, do not facilitate efforts to hold abusers to account. It is not fashionable to suggest that internal forces may encourage family pathology. If patriotism was once the last refuge of the scoundrel, familism may have taken its place.

So my critical, contrarian approach extends both to feminist jurisprudence and to the culture that produced it. It also extends both to what is said in any culture, theory, or jurisprudence, and to what is left unsaid. I am critical of and skeptical about one idea, in particular, that is embedded in contemporary Western culture, both inside and outside of feminist theory. That concept is individual responsibility. I am intrigued by the way society apportions it, among individuals, institutions, and the state. But the fact that I question it does not mean I deny it. This book is my act of personal responsibility. I have written it out of my conviction that truth is a commodity of which the supply exceeds the demand.

ACKNOWLEDGMENTS

NO ONE can write a book alone. At least, after twenty years of trying, I know I can't. I owe debts to a number of individuals and institutions. Several chapters began as convention papers and later became journal articles, while some ideas were first expressed in book reviews. Susan Gluck Mezey, Karen O'Connor, C. Neal Tate, Sanford Levinson, G. Alan Tarr, Leslie Friedman Goldstein, Garry Jennings, Sue Davis, and Jan Leighley gave me opportunities to try out my ideas before academic audiences. Along the way to publication, I had the help of several present and former professor-editors: Sarah Slavin, Rita Mae Kelly, Dean Mann, MaryJo Wagner, and Edward Portis. The anonymous reviewers they wisely selected provided valuable criticism. (I also acknowledge, if with less grace, the contribution of reviewers for journals that rejected my articles.) I thank the *Journal of Politics*, *Women and Politics*, *NWSA Journal*, the *Political Research Quarterly*, and Rowman and Littlefield for granting me permission to reprint parts of these articles or reviews in this book.

I am lucky to teach at a university that is research-friendly in the best sense. Texas A&M University welcomed a stranger into its village and facilitated a project that bewildered some of its best minds. The political science department provided fertile intellectual ground and excellent support services. Charles Johnson, the department head, and Bryan Jones, his predecessor, deserve much of the credit. So does Marcia Bastian, whose ability to create order from chaos extended even to transferring a draft of the entire manuscript from one software program to another. Avis Munson got the final version of the manuscript ready for the publisher; I could not have done it without her. My graduate assistants provided indispensable help. Joseph Fults worked with me on this project for more than four years. Joey's diligent, meticulous work, his familiarity with the law libraries of central Texas, and his resilient pickup truck have made my life much easier. Ashley Brian Coffield, Rachel Gibson, Kimberly McGar, and Sahar Shafqat helped compile the bibliography. Jeanine Harris and Joshua May have taken over since I returned from my year in Washington, D.C.

I completed the first draft of this manuscript at the Woodrow Wilson International Center for Scholars, where I held a fellowship in 1995–96. Fellows and staff persevered through furloughs and blizzards to sustain a community of scholars. Bruce Ackerman, Bernard Crick, David Danelski, and James Henretta have been superb critics and interlocutors. Betty Friedan, who gets her share of criticism in the text, has inspired me with her life's work and educated me through her seminars at the Center. Charles Blitzer and Vicki Bear Dodson devote extraordinary care and energy to maintaining an institution that honors its namesake, our scholar-president. Judithe Registre, my student intern, commuted from American University to the Center to the Library of Congress more times than she or I care to remember. Zdenek David and Linda Worden in the library, Janet Culbreth in the computer center, and Lindsay Collins at the reception desk made daily life easier. George Bowen and Pat Wood dealt heroically with a series of computer glitches. Without Ann Sheffield, Denise Leibowitz, and Arlyn Charles in the Fellowships Office, I would not have been at the Center at all.

I am grateful also for earlier assistance that made a yearlong fellowship possible. At critical points, I was able to think, read, and write. The combined assistance of the American Philosophical Society and the American Council of Learned Societies allowed me to forgo teaching in the summer of 1990 and produce the convention paper that turned into Chapter 4. At Texas A&M, the College of Liberal Arts gave me a Faculty Development Leave for the spring 1993 semester; the university awarded me a Scholarly and Creative Activities Research Award the following year. When I used some of that time to inconvenience my employers by making a successful fellowship application, they cheerfully released me for a year and provided additional support.

Princeton University Press has been an ideal publisher. Ann Himmelberger Wald offered me a contract, left me in peace to write, and guided the project at every stage. When Ann became editor in chief, Kristen Gager saw the manuscript through the final stages. Susan Ecklund proved to be a masterful copy editor.

My mother, Dorothy, and my brothers, Steve, Tom, and Chris, continue to be an important part of my life. For forty years, Tom has provided help I cannot adequately acknowledge. He has told me how men talk among themselves about women. I have not always welcomed his candor when it was offered, but our conversations have educated me about the world I presume to interpret. My second generation of cats, Ariel, Zoe, and Dulcie, divert me from work and make me laugh. I suspect they often laugh at me, but I love them anyway.

The dedication of this book reflects another part of my life, my experience as an aspiring mystery writer. In 1993, the Houston chapter of the Mystery Writers of America arranged a guided tour of the Forensic Sciences Center. The busy professionals at the center were far more generous with their time and their information than we had any right to expect. They allowed us into the room where bodies are held after autopsy and answered our questions about the woman I describe. Covered by a sheet, she lay on a table. Experts tell us the faces of the dead are expressionless, but in her face I saw resignation, a sense of having known this would happen. I dedicate this book to her memory in the spirit of the inscription above the entrance to the building. Translated from the Latin, it reads, "Here, the dead teach and help the living."

JUDITH A. BAER
College Station, Texas
October 1998

PART I

LAW THROUGH WOMEN'S LIVES

ONE

INTRODUCTION

WOMEN ARE more vulnerable and more responsible than men, but they are less free. Like men, women are vulnerable to state and corporate power. But women are also more vulnerable to private violence: as girls, as adults, even in old age. Like men, women are responsible for meeting their own needs. But women are also more responsible for meeting others' needs: for maintaining, nurturing, satisfying (sexually and otherwise), and—the all-purpose term—caring. Even where women enjoy equal formal rights with men, special risks and obligations weaken and compromise women's rights. "So long as we live, there can be no escape from the struggle for power," read the opening words of a classic work of modern political theory.[1] This statement applies to all adults. But for women, it leaves out a huge chunk of reality. So long as we live, there can be no escape from the threat of abuse or the demand for care.

Women's vulnerability is an unpopular subject these days. She who speaks of battering, rape, pornography, and the whole spectrum of violence against women risks being branded a male-basher, a woman-slanderer, or both. The subject of personal responsibility, by contrast, is all the rage. If the government is not quite "a machine that would go of itself," nor the economy quite ruled by an "invisible hand," our public discourse is shaped by traditional notions of these institutions as homeostatic, presumptively impervious to deliberate change; individual behavior becomes the only variable left.[2] Conservatives want more *individual* (as opposed to institutional or collective) responsibility; communitarians call for more individual *responsibility* (as opposed to freedom); and liberals, more receptive to other arguments than creative with their own, seek a middle ground. No one notices that women already have a disproportionate share of responsibility. Feminist theorists, within and outside these groups, have failed to make them notice. This book represents my attempt, as scholar, activist, and human being, to make sense of women's condition and feminist responses to it.

The "second wave" of American feminism, which began in the 1960s, has improved the general situation of American women. The feminist movement has benefited women of every race, class, age, and lifestyle. Antidiscrimination laws have helped women leave the female job ghetto of clerical work, service, and teaching for technical, mechanical, and professional

work; the gap between women's and men's incomes is narrowing; and fertility control has allowed women who might once have been exhausted by
pregnancy and childbirth to reach a healthy, active old age. These are only
a few of the gains attributable in part to the feminist movement.

Feminists get little credit for their contributions to these changes. But
we get plenty of blame for problems we didn't cause, like divorce "reform,"
which can work against women's interests, and the decline, breakdown, or
destruction of the family, whatever these phrases mean. Receiving unde-
served blame while being denied due credit is itself a cause for anger. But
feminists know at least as well as their critics do that, however much feminism has accomplished, it has not been enough.

Feminism has not improved all women's lives. Male violence against
women continues.[3] American women are more likely to be poor than at
any time since the Great Depression. The "feminization of poverty" of
the 1980s came close to creating an underclass of women and children.
Feminism has helped some women (physicians, judges, the ambitious)
more than it has others (displaced homemakers, domestic workers, the
homeless). Women still work harder than men for less reward; this disparity
cuts across boundaries of race and class, age and lifestyle. All but the most
comfortable American women now face the double burden that poor,
working-class, and rural women have always had: the "two roles," the "second shift," the domestic duties waiting for them after their paid workday
is over, while men enjoy leisure.[4] "The problem that has no name" has
become the problem that won't go away.[5] Some of these predicaments may
be beyond feminists' power to change; but as long as they exist, we cannot
proclaim victory.

Feminists like me—white, middle-class, educated—are often told how
privileged we are. Such comments can be toxic, smothering anger with
guilt. But the description is accurate. As a professor in a major research
university—my ambition ever since I wrote my honors thesis at a presti-
gious liberal arts college—I am better off than most of the world's people,
let alone the world's women. Many feminists are similarly fortunate. But I
see little evidence that privileged women "enjoy" their situations in any
but the most limited sense of that word.

In his novel *The World According to Garp*, John Irving creates the Ellen
James Society, a group of feminists who cut off their tongues in solidarity
with a young rape victim whose attacker similarly mutilated her.[6] The
world of American women in the 1990s often resembles a vast Ellen James
Society in which the comfortable imitate the material conditions of the
deprived. A poor woman may go hungry to feed her children, or even go
hungry with them. An affluent woman may go hungry to stay slim, or even
starve herself in anorexia. A working-class woman may hold down two or
three paying jobs, work overtime when she can get the hours, and come

home to unpaid work. A middle-class woman with no dependent family and one paying job may burden herself to exhaustion with the local make-work that outlasts the full-time homemakers it once kept busy, and with the endless demands of others for help and support. Disadvantaged women get no more benefit from advantaged women's self-deprivation than Irving's Ellen James got from healthy women's self-mutilation. This phenomenon, from which feminists are not immune, suggests that improvements in people's economic situations—necessary and desirable as they are—will not suffice to lighten women's burdens.

It is easy to say—I have often longed to say—that the women I describe bring their situation on themselves, that nobody forces them to deprive themselves or cater to others. But we can describe this behavior as voluntary only if we ignore the limits imposed by the range of choices open to these women. Many would suffer serious consequences if they rejected gender role norms. A woman's failure to conform to society's standard of appearance may cost her a relationship or a job. A woman's refusal to do the chores or provide the nurturance that society expects of her may cost her friendships. Some women claim to be content with their lot, and may actually be. But women are expected to conform to the norms of "feminine" behavior whether they want to or not.

Quite often, women impose these expectations on one another. This aspect of socialization is nothing new. Since children are women's work, we would expect women to transmit gender roles as they transmit other values. Mothers, teachers, supervisors, friends, classmates, and coworkers have been showing and telling us how to behave as far back as anyone can remember. What has changed in the last twenty years is the role of feminists in this socialization process. In the 1960s and 1970s, feminists were trenchant critics of conventional feminine roles. But by the 1990s, much feminist writing could be read as efforts to socialize women into these roles.

Duty and Danger: Woman's Condition

The association of women with care is so embedded in our culture that it has come to seem natural, even to some feminists. Natural or not, the traditional roles are easy to acquire. By precept and example, women learn what society expects of them. Caregiving women are there for girls to imitate, much as mother's high heels and lipstick are there to be tried out. The old "nature versus nurture" controversy does not exhaust the range of plausible explanations for women's situation. The special threats and demands women face follow from the human responsibility for self-preservation.

Every human being must have security and sustenance. *Homo sapiens*, like every other species, must reproduce. Meeting these basic needs has often become a legally imposed duty for both men and women. For example, in the nineteenth century all the states had vagrancy laws that obliged any adult who had no means of support to seek employment.[7] Where men and women differ is in how society allows them to meet these needs.

In every society we know of, these imperatives have been structured by men. The arrangement has reversed the classic formula for sharing cake in which A cuts and B chooses. Men (some men, anyway) have done both the cutting and the choosing. They have enjoyed the dual privilege of dividing life into certain kinds of activities, rights, and duties, and of deciding which portions they will take. Women have been stuck with what men left. Ideas of gender difference derive from this male privilege; male dominance consists of this power to categorize, apportion, and assign.

In modern industrial societies, life has been structured by (a tiny minority of) men, for both men and women, around the (artificially created) dichotomy of the public and private spheres. Men preserve themselves in the "public" realm of paid work and political activity. Women, most of whom have been unable to earn a living wage and/or to participate in public life, have been forced to concentrate their energies within the "private" sphere of marriage and family. Outside marriage, women's lot has been precarious; within it, their labor (formerly) ensured (marginally) that their needs would be met (minimally).

The distinct sex-role expectations that men and women face, however secure their economic status, have emerged from these socially mandated means of preserving the self. In Adrienne Rich's words, "Women have been forced to marry because it was necessary, in order to survive economically, in order to have children who would not suffer economic deprivation or social ostracism, in order to remain respectable, in order to do what was expected of women."[8] Except for slaves, few American women have been coerced into relationships with specific men chosen for them by others. But most women have had to choose between marriage to someone in the pool of acceptable husbands and impoverished, dependent, or disparaged spinsterhood. In this century, welfare has been an (increasingly uncertain) option, but qualifying for this "substitute man" requires a baby.[9]

Women have accepted the domestic role to ensure their economic survival. Where survival depends on marriage, women must conform to men's expectations in order to compete in the marriage market. The practice of female genital mutilation, common in parts of Africa, provides an extreme example of this coercion. Women cannot survive unless they marry, and men will not marry them unless they undergo the procedure.[10] Once married, women must conform to the demands of the wife's role, however defined. The reproductive imperative may not always play out the way Rich suggests; the lack of accessible female contraception and the duty to submit to a husband's sexual demands can make motherhood compulsory.

Men do not get off scot-free, either. They are forced into the provider role, and earning a living tends to involve a certain degree of submission and coercion. But there is a qualitative difference between work responsibility and family responsibility. Work is rarely a total relationship; you get time off.[11] Marriage and motherhood (at least while children are young) pervade every aspect of a woman's life. Whatever else women do, wherever else they go, the domestic role locates them "at home, the place women experience the most force," where they "have no privacy to lose or to guarantee."[12] This role requires that women provide the care tradition associates with them. Outside the home, the "pink-collar" job ghetto has channeled most women into additional nurturing roles.[13] Even women who escape into "male" jobs find themselves expected to bring the woman's role with them. The physician must be as solicitous of the patient as the ideal nurse; the college professor, as accessible to the student as the model schoolteacher.

Responsibility, like other things, floats downhill. I could give many concrete examples of this process of distribution, but two will suffice. In 1995, the ABC News program *20/20* reported several deaths of people who ate ground beef contaminated by *Escherichia coli* bacteria. The segment warned consumers to cook ground meat thoroughly to kill the bacteria.[14] The report implied, by omission, that sellers have no obligation to get poisoned meat off the market. One huge American industry thereby relieved another of responsibility for the quality of its product.

This story fits nicely into sociologist William Ryan's dichotomy of exceptionalistic and universalistic solutions. Americans' preference for the former over the latter is old news. What Ryan called "blaming the victim" is so entrenched in public discourse that the mother of one of the dead children used the phrase on camera.[15] The program's limited repertoire of exceptionalistic solutions is equally striking. No one suggested we stop buying the stuff. A boycott could be a good capitalist strategy. A precipitous drop in sales might induce the beef industry to clean up its act and its hamburger. At least, the market is supposed to work that way. But no; collective action is no more conceivable than corporate responsibility. The solution is privatized. And we know who does most of the cooking.

A similar message emerges from a commercial appearing on KTRC-TV, the CBS affiliate in Bryan, Texas. A middle-aged white man is sitting up in bed in a large, comfortable room. A smiling woman, followed by a little girl, carries in a tray. A voice-over intones, "St. Joseph's Hospital has thousands of recovery rooms all over town." The unseen male narrator extols the benefits of recovering at home after a shortened postoperative hospital stay. The spot presumes a family ready and able to care for the patient. Never mind that many people live alone; or provide rather than receive care in their households; or require more complicated nursing care than meals served in bed. Once again, women are given responsibility while men, institutions, and government are let off the hook.

Power and privilege confer the ability to impose responsibilities upon others and refuse them for oneself. Women are responsible for dealing with sexual violence, but men are not responsible for stopping it. Unmarried teenage mothers are to blame for most of our social ills, but middle-class parents do the best they can. This phenomenon is not always or exclusively gendered. Law excuses children from some responsibilities but enforces the power of family and school to impose others. "Perhaps the most important and least appreciated norm governing the lives of young people is that," as a result of this triple jurisdiction, "they are in every aspect of their presence, demeanor, and appearance *accountable*."[16] The Personal Responsibility Act of 1996 pulls the safety net out from under the poorest Americans, but a disgraced president is absolved of responsibility for his crimes because his successor feels he has "suffered enough." The less power, privilege, and freedom a person has, the more responsibility he or she bears.

The Valorized, The Victim, and The Vilifier: The Failures of Feminism

In the early years of the modern women's movement, author after author analyzed, criticized, and rejected current gender role expectations. But as the political climate became more conservative, feminism tagged along. Some feminist scholars seemed to abandon feminism's historic promise "to question everything."[17] This retreat was not total. Feminists have not tried to drive women back into the female job ghetto, and feminists have produced incisive critiques of the beauty-through-torture craze to which many women have martyred themselves.[18] But feminists are no longer united in their commitment to challenging entrenched gender roles and freeing women from conventional expectations.

Feminist scholarship revived the notion of gender differences that was so destructive to women in prefeminist times. Influential works proclaim a "different voice," an "ethic of caring," "women's ways of knowing," and other female traits which these authors cannot convincingly distinguish from traditional "femininity," no matter how hard they try.[19] Since no one has yet succeeded in identifying certain traits as female without excluding other traits as not female, writings like these prescribe as well as describe. Feminist critics of the notion of female-specific theory are dismissed as evidence that "some women within patriarchy can learn to speak, reason, and write from the side of the masculine."[20]

Many feminist scholars argue that society is built around men's needs for separation and autonomy, and that women's needs for caring and connection are devalued. These theorists have got something right. Women are expected to provide care, and society does not value care. But these theorists emphasize the second part of this formula and neglect the first. By valorizing care, nurturance, and responsibility, the difference approach reinforces rather than questions the extra burdens women bear in our society. Feminist theory must support women who chafe against traditional expectations as well as women who fulfill them.

Difference-focused feminism does not monopolize, or even dominate, feminist scholarship. Several widely read theorists emphasize society's institutionalization of male supremacy rather than any notion of gender difference. The most prominent of these scholars dismisses the difference approach as "affirming the perspective that has been forced on women."[21] These feminists have produced strong angry theory, incisive analyses of male power in its various manifestations.[22] But the critical response to this work is almost as disturbing as the feminist revival of gender difference. As Chapter 3 will show, feminist theorists who denounce women's oppression are often read, even by other feminists, as if they were denigrating women's character.[23] It has become almost impossible to write about violence against women without being accused of either male-bashing or reducing women to the status of victims.[24] These accusations, made by authors who call themselves feminists, get widespread media attention; these critiques frequently become better known than what they criticize. Feminist theory must address all forms of aggression against women and put responsibility on the aggressor, not the sufferer.

Meanwhile, insider scholarship and mainstream politics continue, evincing little feminist influence. Presidents send troops abroad to restore "democracy" to countries where half the adult population cannot vote. Communitarians seek to privilege responsibility equally with rights, without noticing how society has distributed these commodities along gender lines. Liberals and conservatives call for increased government respect for religion, without noticing the sexism embedded in much religious theory and practice.[25] Even discourse on the abortion issue threatens to become gender-free. After the 1992 election, the *New York Times* discovered a majority "compromise" position: "discourage abortions but don't ban them." This new consensus was accompanied by no awareness of any feminist position. Feminist theory belongs in all public discourse.

An Introduction to Feminist Jurisprudence

This book represents my attempt to help rectify the mistakes feminist theory has made and to help integrate it into political theory and practice. My efforts at reconstruction and redirection have focused on my own subfield, public law. Feminist jurisprudence is part of the "flowering in feminist thought" that has characterized the 1980s and 1990s.[26] Legal scholars have built on feminist contributions in other academic disciplines, on prefeminist theory, and on minority critiques of scholarship. Feminist jurisprudence shares with its cognate fields a basic organizing premise: that the discipline to which it reacts has a fundamental male bias. Men founded and developed the discipline, long monopolized it, still dominate it, identify its chief concerns in ways that come out of their experience and reflect their interests, and select and socialize its practitioners to carry on the male tradition.

Feminist jurists have already turned out far more work than any critic could review, and the output shows no sign of diminishing. These scholars have been as contentious as they are productive. Their analyses of law, and their critiques of one another's work, have enhanced and enriched legal theory. But reading this work illuminates the roots and sources of feminist theory's failure to respond to feminist problems. This new specialty has made grave errors of both commission and omission. The errors of commission, which pervade some of the most widely read works, include theory that is unsound, unoriginal, and retrograde. The errors of omission consist, first, of an incomplete understanding of what it is that feminists are criticizing; second, of emphasis on what is said to the exclusion of what is not said, but presumed; and, third, paradoxically, of feminist jurists' almost exclusive focus on women.

The first and second errors have plagued authors on both sides of a significant ideological conflict among feminist legal scholars: explanations of male bias in terms of gender difference versus explanations of male bias in terms of male dominance. Both groups criticize an implied conventional or standard jurisprudence. This includes, but is not limited to, some ideas loosely associated with liberalism, particularly its emphasis on individual rights. The feminist critics agree that this jurisprudence is untrue for women, but they do not agree on how or why. Scholars who emphasize gender difference argue that the theory depends on assumptions about human beings which are true only about men. Carol Gilligan, for instance, asserts that women's moral reasoning lacks the rights orientation and oppositional emphasis built into liberal theory. Jurists who emphasize male dominance hold that the theory presumes an autonomy that male supremacy denies to women. Catharine MacKinnon, for instance, argues that male dominance relegates women to a position in which a right is "an injury got up as a gift."[27]

This book will show that I am firmly on the side of the dominance jurists. Difference feminism is feminism in name only. Although it is often called a "second stage" of feminism, it is in fact a step backward.[28] It represents a failure of nerve. While difference feminists strive to distinguish their arguments from old and hackneyed antifeminist difference theories, they fail. Difference feminism is not a progression. It is a regression.

My primary concern in this book, however, is not what sets these two groups of theories apart but what they have in common. I argue that both varieties of jurisprudence fail to understand what they purport to criticize. Neither group of feminist scholars perceives that the standard theory is asymmetrical, both in general and in particular. The theory propounds individual rights; it presumes individual responsibility. Rights are so insecure they must be defended; responsibility is so basic it can go unmentioned. Conventional jurisprudence is also asymmetrical in its application to women. The rights component has never been consistently applied to women, but the responsibility component has.

Feminists are not the only scholars who have read liberal theory as a theory of rights. Communitarians, like Mary Ann Glendon and Amitai Etzioni, exhort Americans to concentrate less on rights and more on responsibilities. Etzioni, for instance, criticizes people who assert rights to health care and housing without noticing that these rights must be asserted precisely because they do not exist.[29] This reading is akin to a historian's concluding that support for slavery in the United States was greater in 1830 than in 1780, or that opposition to women's suffrage increased from 1850 to 1900. Primary sources, read in isolation, might convey these impressions. But the greater prevalence of pro-slavery and antisuffrage writing at the ends of the respective time frames indicated that the status quo needed more defense than it had fifty years earlier, not that it was more popular. Both feminist and communitarian critics of liberalism concentrate too much on what is said and too little on why it has to be said. This second major failure of understanding has frustrated the progress of feminist theory.

I explore the roots and ramifications of the third feminist error of omission: the tendency to react to the historic exclusion of women in and from theory by making women the exclusive and isolated subject of theory. All too often, the feminist response to a conventional theory that confuses the male with the universal is a theory that confines itself to the female and the particular. Whereas conventional theory falsely claimed to be universal, feminist theory does not even try to be. We have ended up with sun and moon, with supposedly general theory that is in fact male, and explicitly specific theory that is exclusively female. This focus on women is a necessary corrective of male bias; but it makes it easy to confuse analyses of women's situation with descriptions of women's character. Feminists who discuss what men, institutions, and the state do to women are therefore read as if they were denying women's agency and autonomy.

Two Stories

I can illustrate my main concerns about feminist theory by analogy with stories from two magazine articles published in the spring of 1993, when I was writing yet another draft of this book. The first story is not about feminism or jurisprudence, but it is a powerful illustration of the problems besetting feminist scholarship. A *New Yorker* article discussed the controversy in the Black Studies Department at the City University of New York. CUNY had dismissed Leonard Jeffries from his position as department chair after he made an anti-Semitic speech. (He sued, but lost.) The piece draws a series of contrasts between Jeffries and his successor, Edmund Gordon. Illustrated by a caricature of the two men, the article describes Jeffries's flamboyant and eccentric behavior in class, attended by an "entourage" composed only partly of students; characterizes Jeffries's academic record as "astonishingly meagre"; and quotes a colleague as saying, "Just knowing he's down the hall makes discussion of race and ethnicity loaded." Gordon, a distinguished scholar in his seventies, emerges as the archetypal professor. His "gentle demeanor and his faith in rational discourse make him seem more conservative than he really is"; his response to the accusation that his marriage to a white woman unfits him for black leadership is that it is "none of your business." The article suggests that Gordon follows the conventions of academic behavior, but Jeffries does not.[30]

That implication raises difficult questions. First, does Jeffries's failure to conform explain the punishment he received? It is not clear how far he departs from actual, as opposed to ideal, academic standards. His professional style is aberrant, and his attack on Gordon violates one of the most precious of academic conventions: respect for individual privacy. But Jeffries is not the only marginal scholar ever to become a department chair in a major university; or the only teacher ever to surround himself with dubious admirers; or—by a long shot—the only academic ever to propound racist theories.

A second pertinent question is to what extent academic conventions reflect racial bias. It is a historical fact that these conventions were developed by white men for white men. To be an academic in North America is to have learned to act like a white man. Is it racist, then, to expect a black man to conform to these standards? If so, what does this argument imply about Gordon? The idea that there is something Caucasian about scholarship could be a racist insult to scholars who are not Caucasian. After all, academic behavior is not natural to anybody, of any race. Third, why does the article imply a dichotomy: why does it set in opposition two scholars, two styles, two political positions? And, finally, why is it two *minority* perspectives that are juxtaposed?

My second story involves two disabled feminists. Writing in *Ms.*, Ynestra King attempts to build feminist theory from the standpoint of disability. King's success is compromised by the fact that she manages to disprove her thesis that disability is "a tragedy of nature" rather than "a socially constructed condition." But her venture into this fresh and fertile theoretical territory, and the critical reaction to her piece, are provocative and instructive.

King, whose legs are partially paralyzed, reports an incident in which an able-bodied friend introduced her to a quadriplegic in a breath-operated wheelchair because "she's disabled, too." King writes, "To suggest that our relative experience of disability is something we could casually compare . . . demonstrates the crudity of perception about the complex nature of bodily experience."[31] Among other things, King's conclusion is difficult to dispute. But a critic, "far more disabled than King," called this "tirade" a "bitter, self-pitying insult, . . . a pathetic attempt to see herself as superior to 'others.' "[32] King's critic does what she (correctly) accused King of doing: dividing a minority group by separating herself from another member of it. The oppositions and juxtapositions are analogous to the treatment of Jeffries and Gordon in the article about City College. What goes unanalyzed, in both situations, is the role played by the majority group.

King's resistance to classifying herself with the quadriplegic became an issue only because the able-bodied friend classified them together. King's experience was similar to that of any outsider who is "told that he will have an easier time of it among 'his own,' and thus learn[s] that the own he thought he possessed was the wrong one, and that this lesser own is really his."[33] King was forced to react to a label imposed on outsiders by an insider, whose own self-distancing from both outsiders was rendered immune from scrutiny. King, her new acquaintance, and her critic were trapped within the majority's definition of the situation. Not only is disability a social construction, but the able-bodied, not the disabled, construct it.

King's critic, for her part, borrows from this same majority culture the most negative, humiliating label society has for the disabled. Accusing a disabled person of self-pity is like calling a feminist strident. These labels are designed to shut people up, to keep others from listening to them, to discredit them. When members of minority groups apply these labels to one another, they allow the majority to interpret their world for them. The majority makes the rules, defines the terms, sets the boundaries, and provides the language. To the extent that any "outsider" theory remains unaware or uncritical of this phenomenon, conventional theory will control minority response.

Feminist critiques of conventional thought confront the same problems minority critiques do. The fact that our academic disciplines are the creation of white, male Europeans is incontrovertible, but so is the fact that women of all races have become full participants in these fields. The behavior of scholars has been a far more formidable barrier to women's advancement than the content of scholarship. Women often encounter expectations different from, higher than, or in addition to those imposed upon men; some of these expectations are imposed by other women. The emphasis tends to be on opposing different "outsider" viewpoints, rather than opposing them to the conventional perspectives they challenge. And, within feminist theory, this concentration on women stays within the terms and boundaries set by conventional "insider" theory.

Conclusion

This introductory chapter and the next three constitute Part I of the book. Chapter 2 explores the underlying premises of feminist theory and jurisprudence. Chapter 3 narrows the focus in order to concentrate on jurisprudence and to subject some important developments in the field to more thorough analysis. Chapter 4, which examines epistemological issues in feminist theory, provides a link between Part I and Part II. About halfway through the chapter, I shift from critiques centered inside feminist theories to critiques centered outside of it: on law, that which the theories criticize. The assertion that legal method is male-biased must be evaluated not only on its own terms but also with reference to actual legal method. My analysis of one type of legal reasoning, constitutional interpretation, shows interpreters combining the rational and the emotional, the abstract and the concrete, and other aspects of reasoning often dichotomized as "male" and "female" in ways that undermine core premises of feminist epistemology. At the same time, this analysis supports the feminist premise of male bias in method. I argue that the absence of jurisprudence may be as powerful a source of law's male bias as the presence of jurisprudence: one way to make law male is to exclude certain subjects from its scope.

Part II applies the themes and theses of Part I to analyses of specific areas of law relevant to gender. These chapters study law's role in assigning rights and responsibilities to men and women, and fashion a feminist response, through an exploration of three issues: the constitutional law of equal protection; reproductive rights; and fetal protection policies. All three topics present crucial theoretical problems in gender theory—equality, rights, and duties, respectively—and all three combine the themes of vulnerability, responsibility, and freedom. For example, the observation that men have been the primary beneficiaries of the Supreme Court's inclusion of sex discrimination within the scope of the Fourteenth Amendment has become hackneyed by now; Chapter 5 clarifies some of the racial and gendered implications of constitutional theory by analyzing the doctrinal developments that contributed to this result. Chapter 6 uses imaginative and counterfactual reasoning to locate reproductive choice in the context of society's distribution of rights and responsibilities. Chapter 7, exploring the issue of fetal protection, finds political discourse "impoverished" in ways that neither liberalism nor its critics have perceived.

These chapters give the lie to the familiar assertion that women's situation is beyond the power of law to change, that sexual inequality results from the legally unreachable behavior of individuals. While it is true that law cannot prevent women from increasing their own vulnerability and responsibility at the expense of their freedom, this book shows how law legitimizes and reinforces male supremacy. So, regrettably, does much feminist theory. Chapter 8 asks, among other questions, how a feminist law can accept its limited power to change society but still promote rather than frustrate social change. The final chapters will pull all of these themes together and work toward a reconstructed jurisprudence that will rectify the errors of conventional jurisprudence while avoiding the errors of the feminist critiques. A primary aim of this jurisprudence is to redistribute rights and responsibilities among women, men, institutions, and government.

TWO

IS LAW MALE?

THE FOUNDATIONS OF FEMINIST
JURISPRUDENCE

> He who before followed behind as the worker, timid and hold-
> ing back, with nothing to expect but a hiding, now strides in
> front, while a third person, not specifically present in Marx's
> account of the transactions between capitalist and worker
> (both of whom are male), follows timidly behind, carrying
> groceries, baby, and diapers.
> *(Nancy C. M. Hartsock)*

THE IDEA that conventional thought has a fundamental male bias is at the core of feminist theory. The historical fact that conventional theories have primarily been the product of male minds, thinking in male supremacist societies, makes this premise highly plausible on its face. What is plausible is also demonstrable. Feminist scholars have shown that Nancy Hartsock's insight about one Western political theory holds for Western jurisprudence in general. "Day one of taking gender into account" was the day theory was structured around the idea of a person with no household responsibilities, no necessary close personal ties, and the ability to earn a living.[1]

Feminist scholars reason from the organizing premise of male bias to two related propositions. First, reality is so distinctively gendered—so different for men and women—that theory developed by men is ill adapted to women. Second, the corrective for male-centered theory is for women consciously to produce theory as women, to "think from" or "think through" their gendered reality to their theory.[2] This derivative premise implies that the male bias of traditional thought has affected not only what we think but how: that it drives epistemology as it does ideology.

Feminist jurisprudence is to law what feminist history is to history, feminist psychology is to psychology, and so forth. Evidence cited to support the proposition that law is male-biased includes, for instance, the fact that American law "offers extensive protection to the right to bear arms or to sell violent pornography, but not to control over our reproductive lives."[3] Feminist jurisprudence has made creative use of theories of gendered reality and seeks to provide explicit female orientation to counter implicit male orientation. Legal theorists have insisted on "asking the woman question" and building theory through consciousness-raising—"the process through which the contemporary radical feminist analysis of the position of women is shaped and shared."[4] This approach is particularly controversial in law because it challenges the assumptions embedded in phrases like "neutral principles" and "government of laws, not of men" (the alternatives feminist jurists reject). Feminist jurists are not the first to reject law's claim to neutrality—Marxists and the Critical Legal Studies movement were way ahead of them—nor are they the only outsider group to challenge law from the group's own perspective. The hostile reception that such critiques have received from the academy indicates the threat they represent to conventional legal wisdom.[5]

Seeing the World as Male: Conventional Theory and Feminist Response

By the time feminism made its presence felt in academia, most scholars had abandoned the claim that the great ideas of the Western tradition were the products of abstract thought divorced from concrete experience. Postmodernism challenged the notion that there is any such thing as objective truth, unaffected by the position of the observer.[6] Marxists argued that "theories may put forth as a necessary truth that which is in fact merely a historically conditioned contingency."[7] The step from this argument to the assertion that some supposed truths may be the result of physically conditioned contingencies, like the sex of the philosopher, is a short one. Feminists have even turned this kind of insight back on Marxists. Catharine MacKinnon's implication that the strongest determinant of a woman's class position is not her relationship to production but her relationship to a man is an example.[8]

The Male Bias of Traditional Thought

> "Do you believe in penis envy?" Kate heard herself asking.
> "Of course," Dr. Anthony said, as though she'd been asked if she believed in the historical Jesus. "That, and the fear of castration, are essential to the structure of the Oedipus complex."
> (Amanda Cross [Carolyn Heilbrun], *A Trap for Fools*)

Feminist scholars start from the recognized fact that the giants of the Western tradition—the interpreters of our world, at least those whose names and work have survived to the present—have been men. Feminist jurists start from the same observation about law. These scholars have been no more successful than anyone else in explaining why this work has been men's work. But the fact that we do not know *why* theory is a male preserve does not preclude the possibility of starting a worthwhile analysis from the fact *that* theory has been men's work.

The premise of male bias does not insist that these founding fathers of philosophy began their work with the thought: "I am male; I shall construct a theory that only a man could create." The bias appears to result instead from the authors' habit of deriving supposedly universal truths from their individual, and therefore male, viewpoints. Some of these propositions are overtly sexist. Aristotle states that "the relation of male to female is naturally that of the superior to the inferior—the ruling to the ruled."[9] Sigmund Freud's theory of penis envy defined women as deficient men; his contrast between the "infantile" clitoral orgasm and the "mature" vaginal orgasm corresponds far better to men's convenience than to women's experience of their own bodies.[10]

A classic example of sexist jurisprudence is contained in Justice Joseph Bradley's argument in *Bradwell v. Illinois* that a state may exclude women from the legal profession so that they may fulfill their destiny as wives and mothers.[11] This opinion is now of mostly historical interest. It was never binding precedent, only a separate concurrence, and there is an ample supply of opinions no less traditional and far more influential. *Muller v. Oregon*, in 1908, upheld "protective" labor laws that allowed states to limit women's working hours. The unanimous Supreme Court opinion in that case baldly stated that women's maternal functions justified their having fewer rights than men.[12] This ruling, too, is history, but the 1990s have brought draconian "fetal protection" policies that threaten all women, pregnant or not, fertile or not, negligent or not. The supporters of these legal efforts to limit women's employment opportunities, restrict their personal freedom, and subject them to unwanted medical procedures concede these policies' "tremendous implications for the women of this country and how they conduct their everyday lives."[13]

By the time large numbers of women were beginning academic and legal careers, the overt sexism of Aristotle and Freud had fallen out of fashion, no state restricted bar admission to men, and protective legislation was yielding to Title VII of the Civil Rights Act of 1964.[14] But apprentice scholars soon learned that male bias in the disciplines transcended overt sexism. The epigraph to this section suggests that removing the overt sexism from a theory may not leave much theory there. Political science has its own versions of the argument made by the fictional Dr. Anthony.[15] Even if we can remove the explicit sexism in the received theories without destroying them, implicit sexism will remain.

Reconsider the *Politics*, for instance: not its defense of patriarchy but the preeminent place among human activities that Aristotle assigns to philoso-

phy and public life. Aristotle's ranking of human endeavors neither originated nor ended with him. Plato before him, John Locke after him, and
Hannah Arendt later still similarly valued human activities. This hierarchy
elevates government and philosophy, both traditional male preserves, while
it devalues home and family, activities that have been women's sphere.[16]
How much of this theory has to do with the intrinsic value of these activities, and how much with the fact that Aristotle had the time and leisure to
pursue the life of the mind? This privilege distinguishes him not only from
the vast majority of men who have ever lived but also from virtually all
women. The rare exceptions have often been forced to wrench that time
away from demands that male philosophers need not meet. Most women
have had more experience with homemaking and child care than Aristotle
got. Would they have looked at things differently?

Freudian theory, too, is sexist in ways that are not obvious. Dr. Anthony
considers penis envy a necessary part of the development of the Oedipus
complex. If the skeptic asks, "Who needs the Oedipus complex?" the doctor might answer that in Freudian theory the superego develops around
the Oedipus complex and the fear of castration. Giving up the Oedipus
complex would entail giving up the Freudian theory of the person. Penis
envy is thus connected to personality development through a kind of logical
domino theory. Modern Freudians have managed to practice their craft
without recourse to penis envy, but even they depend on what Betty Friedan called "sexual solipsism": a presumption that the male body is the
norm.[17] It did not take long for some of Freud's women students to begin
constructing theories from female physiology: theories, for example, that
posited male "womb envy." But Freud's work got more attention than
theirs. Freud, male bias and all, joined Aristotle as a hero of the intellectual
tradition which aspiring theorists study. As a result, "a problem in theory
became cast as a problem in women's development."[18]

Law is no stranger to this kind of bias. True, *Muller v. Oregon* has been
replaced with the neutral principle that "classifications by gender must
serve important governmental objectives and be substantially related to
these objectives."[19] But, as Chapter 5 shows, more men than women initiate
and win cases under this doctrine. Legislators have rid criminal codes of
some of their worst sexist features. For instance, prosecutions for rape,
renamed sexual assault, no longer require proof of the complainant's resistance or virtue. But the law of self-defense, by requiring proportionate
response and imminent danger, authorizes the experience of a man in a
bar fight with a stranger while excluding that of a woman in an abusive
relationship.[20] Child custody law has progressed from paternal preference
to maternal preference to neutrality. But unstated male bias is evident in
the law's refusal to consider the needs of mothers as primary caregivers.[21]

So the more law changes, the more it remains the same. And law seems
to change more readily in some directions than in others. The same law

of self-defense that remains impervious to battered women who kill their abusers yields to the claims of men who use deadly force against trespassing and harassment.[22] The same family law that has ignored mothers' interests has overturned legal adoptions and handed young children over to fathers who are strangers to them.[23] The forces that change law are no more neutral than the forces that made it.

Feminist Critiques of Male-Centered Theory

Once feminists posited a connection between existing theory and maleness, there ensued a rich and generative intellectual enterprise. Any existing part of the received intellectual tradition may be exposed as male-centered. Consider Thomas Hobbes's statement that "a perpetual and restless desire of power after power, which ceaseth only in death" is part of human nature.[24] Marxists have suggested that Hobbes elevated the greed produced by capitalism to a universal truth. Might Hobbes not also have characterized as universally and inevitably human that which was specifically and contingently male? Or consider liberal individualism, as represented by John Stuart Mill. Does this philosophy, which posits the human being as separate from every other human being, not jar with the facts of human reproduction? Might not Mill's emphasis on conflict between society and the individual stint reality as experienced by women immersed in family life?[25] Or what about a theory based on presumptions like these: "Economic analysis suggests that a parent may, over some range, trade custodial rights for money. Although this notion may offend some, a contrary assumption would mean that a parent with full custody would accept no sum of money in return for slightly less custody, even if the parent were extremely poor. Faced with such alternatives, most parents would prefer to see the child a bit less and be able to give the child better housing, more food, more education, better health care, and some luxuries."[26]

This legal model presumes that individuals aggressively assert their rights, that they will trade, barter, and exchange, that they are rational maximizers. Mothers of young children, however, do not typically behave in this manner when they negotiate with former husbands for custody. (Nor, for that matter, do fathers who relinquish custody "rationally" exchange money for the assurance of their children's welfare.) Trying to explain postdivorce parental behavior in rational-choice terms illustrates the inadequacies of a male-based model to explain the behavior of either men or women.

Ann Scales speaks for many feminist legal scholars when she writes: "Feminists have tried to describe for the judiciary a theory of 'special rights' for women which will fit the discrete, non-stereotypical, 'real' differences between the sexes. And herein lies our mistake: We have let the debate become narrowed by accepting as correct those questions which seek to arrive at a definitive list of differences. In so doing, we have adopted the vocabulary, as well as the epistemology and political theory, of the law as it is."[27]

The article quoted just before this passage is a perfect illustration of the dangers inherent in feminist reliance on "the vocabulary . . . of the law as it is." One possible reaction to that paragraph is that it could only be the product of a male mind. The discovery that the authors were Robert Mnookin and Lewis Kornhauser may be gratifying to the feminist jurist, but the problem of infinite regression frustrates this kind of theorizing. Since all philosophers led individual lives, all ideas can be traced to individual experience. The classics of the received tradition are full of ideas that appear to be contingent on male experience. But if male bias explains everything, sooner or later male bias explains nothing—unless we have a coherent and consistent theory of how men think that is different from our theory of how women think. At present, no such theory exists.

Feminists can argue that certain theories posited as universal truths are in fact gender-conditioned contingencies, but these assertions cannot be shown to be true, any more than a Marxist can show that aggression results from capitalism. We cannot claim to know that female contemporaries of Aristotle or Hobbes would have constructed different theories. Such women would, after all, have been products of a male supremacist society. They would have had to lead very privileged lives to have done philosophy at all; they might have looked at domestic duties from the standpoint of one who has escaped them. Freud, unlike Aristotle or Hobbes, had women students, some of whom enthusiastically adopted his theories. Both liberalism and rational choice have women adherents.

Any claim that traditional theory is ill adapted to women's reality has to deal with the fact that women have produced theory within male-defined disciplines that is every bit as good as what men have done. This statement generalizes from the lives of "women worthies," a practice many feminists condemn as "a great disservice to the rest" of women professionals.[28] But the validity of this admonition depends on what conclusions are drawn. If women worthies are invoked (as they often are) to convey the message "they made it; why can't you?" these feminists are right. But the fact that the pioneers are not "typical" of most women does not render their experience worthless as evidence of what women want to accomplish. The obstacles these women faced consisted not in the dissonance of male-centered scholarship to their reality but in their exclusion by a male-dominated academic establishment.

While it is true that sexist cultures may produce sexist theory no matter what sex the author is, we cannot dismiss the work of women scholars as evidence only that "some women within patriarchy can learn to speak, reason, and write from the side of the masculine."[29] That charge links infinite regression with selective interpretation: when a woman theorist agrees with me, she is thinking like a woman; when she disagrees, she is thinking like a man. And describing women's achievements within conventional disciplines as "masculine" does violence to many women's experiences. (Auto)-biographies of early women professionals record their hunger and thirst for learning and their heroic struggles to acquire knowledge. The women I studied with in the 1960s and 1970s felt a similar eagerness, as my women colleagues do now. If conventional learning is so masculine, how could we want it so badly? To suggest that scholarship is masculine is as sexist as Leonard Jeffries's attacks on Edmund Gordon are racist.[30]

We do not even know whether the classic works were the exclusive product of male minds. Research on art, music, and literature has uncovered instances of work attributed to a man that was actually the work of a woman. One of several possible answers to the old question Why are there no great woman artists? is that "there were, but some man attached his name to their work"; and we should recall Virginia Woolf's statement "Anonymous was a woman." There is one famous instance of a philosopher acknowledging his wife's equal partnership. That author was John Stuart Mill, whose *On Liberty* is a classic of the liberal individualism that feminists challenge! Yet, in dedicating the book to the memory of Harriet Taylor Mill, he wrote, "Like all that I have written for many years, it belongs as much to her as to me." How do we know that other classics do not similarly belong to women?

The realization that conventional scholarship may not be as male-centered as it appears does not vitiate the effort to create women-centered theory. The only way to judge whether feminist scholarship can make a contribution to our knowledge is to try it and evaluate the results. The evidence demonstrates that women scholars, studying women's experiences, have added to our knowledge. We know so much, in the 1990s, that we had no idea of in the 1970s, that we can justify doing this kind of scholarship. What we cannot and should not do is to accept its premises uncritically and unreflectively.

Why Does Maleness Matter? Feminist Theory and Gendered Reality

Feminist scholars assert both that conventional theory is male-biased and that woman-centered theory is a necessary corrective to this bias. Both positions need the premise of gendered reality. This awkward phrase is as close as I can come to an accurate characterization of the various theories subsumed under this heading. The idea of a distinctively gendered reality includes, but is not limited to, notions of gender difference. Feminist theorists do not agree on whether gendered reality originates in differences between women and men or whether it is imposed from outside—or both. For their part, those feminists who accept the idea of gender differences do not agree about what the important differences are or about what produces them (the old "nature versus nurture" controversy)—or both. Feminist scholars do share a conviction that any inquiry that fails to take gendered reality into account produces theories that are seriously deficient as explanations of whatever they purport to explain. These feminist theories also share a parallel structure. Each argues, first, that a set of ideas that has been presumed to be universal is in fact contingently male; and, second, that something makes the thought system inapplicable to women. None of the important feminist theories of gendered reality defends either of these arguments convincingly.

Starting from Biology

The female body provides the starting point for much feminist theory, as the male body has for much conventional theory. Like their intellectual predecessors, the feminists tend to start with the genitals; but no organ occupies a place in feminist theory parallel to that of the penis in Freudian theory. The French psychoanalytic theory called *ecriture feminine* is instructive. For Luce Irigaray, who is widely read in North America, the labia, not the clitoris or vagina, occupy a place analogous to that of the penis in Freudian thought. "A woman . . . touches herself constantly without anyone being able to forbid her to do so, for her sex is composed of two lips which embrace continually. Thus, within herself she is already two—but not divisible into ones—who stimulate each other." But "in order to touch himself, a man needs an instrument: his hand, a woman's body, language."[31]

The relevance of this theory of sexuality to jurisprudence is that Irigaray, like other members of the "Psych-et-Po" (psychoanalysis and politics) school of French feminism, maintains "that the projection of male libidinal economy in all patriarchal systems—language, capitalism, socialism, monotheism—has been total; women have been absent."[32] One commentator explains, "To have a penis is to be the sort of person who would think up such ideas as the principle of identity and the principle of noncontradiction."[33] Law, like other man-made systems, is constructed around the ideas of separation, dichotomy, linearity, subject-object distinction. *Ecriture feminine* goes beyond the critics who find implicit male bias in Freudian theory to find it in all social institutions.[34]

Ecriture feminine liberates psychoanalytic theory from male supremacy, and it presents a provocative argument that the implications of psychoanalytic theory extend far beyond the individual psyche into social institutions. Two early psychoanalysts, Karen Horney and Clara Thompson, accomplished the first task (to an apathetic or hostile reception); several contemporary psychoanalysts, Jacques Lacan and his followers, the second (to an enthusiastic international reception).[35] Irigaray and her fellow Psych-et-Po feminists do both, and they provoke their readers to think about polity in new ways.

While feminist psychoanalytic theory rejects the sexism and the narrow individual focus that characterized earlier work, the feminist writers have not corrected the other characteristic errors of psychoanalytic theory. It depends on facts that do not interpret themselves; one has to start with a theory in order to make much intellectual use of anatomy. No psychoanalytic theory convinces anyone who is not predisposed toward psychoanalytic theory in general; acceptance of its logic depends on acceptance of its basic premises. Psychoanalytic theory is hard to refute, but it is equally hard to defend. The premise that the body is the central determining factor in either personality or politics is far from an obvious truth. The similarity between the way separation and dichotomy work in patriarchal idea systems and the way the penis works in the male body does not constitute evidence of any causal or intellectual connection. Even if we must start with the body, why emphasize the genitals—a choice that builds gender difference into the theory?[36] We could start just as plausibly with the hands (whose opposing thumb and fingers speak of separation, linearity, and dichotomy as much as the penis does), the neuromuscular skeleton (which sets us upright on two limbs), or the eyes (which look outward, at objects)—in both women and men.

Some feminist theory starts with physiology rather than anatomy. Robin West, for instance, maintains that American jurisprudence is hostile to women because it is based on the assumption that a human being is separate from all other human beings. This "separation thesis" is "a cluster of claims" that, "while usually true of men, are patently untrue for women." Instead, "Women are essentially, necessarily, inevitably, invariably, always, and forever . . . connected to life and to other human beings during at least four recurrent and critical material experiences: the experience of pregnancy itself; the invasive and 'connecting' experience of heterosexual penetration . . . ; the monthly experience of menstruation, which represents the potential for pregnancy; and the post-pregnancy experience of breast-feeding."[37]

For West, as for Irigaray, social institutions depend on supposedly universal truths that are, in fact, contingent on being male. Unlike Irigaray, West builds a bridge from physical differences to existential reality that avoids the arbitrariness of the arguments from anatomy. West relies on facts that do not have to be subjected to the kind of intricate, subjective interpretation that psychoanalytic theory gives to the genitals. The four functions she emphasizes are exclusively female, and three of them involve the kind of physical connection between bodies she is talking about. These

functions denote experiences that no man has, and that only women have.
If we accept the idea that our experience affects our existential reality, the
sexes may, indeed, be different in the ways West describes. But the appearance of clarity is deceptive. West's use of physiology is as problematic as
Irigaray's use of anatomy.

Everyone knows that childbirth, menstruation, heterosexual penetration, and breast-feeding happen only to women. The difficult question is
what, if anything, follows from these facts. We need not believe that the
exclusively female material experiences are trivial in order to question
West's inference that they are more critical than the experiences which
men and women share. Do we know, for instance, that menarche has a
greater effect on personality than does the transition from elementary to
secondary school, or that having sex with a man changes a woman more
than leaving home, going to college, or getting a job? West commits the
same error that psychoanalytic theorists have made; she presumes that what
is different about men and women is what is most important.

Nor are West's interpretations of her critical material experiences the
only possible ones. The connection she posits between menstruation and
fertility, for instance, is a connection made by the intellect. It is not at all
clear that women's concrete experience of menstruation has much to do
with material connection to other human beings, or even that the primary
significance of menstruation is biological. For Christine Delphy, a French
feminist critic of Psych-et-Po, the primary meaning of menstruation is social and political: "I do not have the right to have my periods. . . . The
society is materially understood and made for a population without periods.
To have a period away from home is to be in a situation which is, if not
dramatic, at least extremely embarrassing."[38] We could similarly reinterpret
West's other critical material experiences: breast-feeding means restrictions on a woman's mobility; or pregnancy means limited freedom. These
constructions of experience are no better than West's are, but she gives us
no grounds for preferring her interpretations to others.[39]

West's assertion that legal theory depends on the separation thesis seems
plausible, much as Irigaray's connection between Western institutions and
"male libidinal economy" does. Yes, human beings are physically distinct
from one another, and, yes, liberal theory emphasizes separation. It is
intriguing to speculate about the theories human beings might have
produced if we were normally born in litters or pairs; but we should remember that physically separate people have produced theories that emphasize connection. Even if liberal theory entails physical separation, the
converse is not true.

Liberal theory does not need the separation thesis. Why must a person
be physically separate from all other people in order to assert rights? Could
not individual autonomy follow from a human being's ability to exercise

reason and will independently from other human beings; or from each human being's intimate knowledge of his or her own needs and interests; or just because, as what Jefferson called a self-evident truth? West's major premise cannot be dismissed as false, but neither can it be accepted as true.

Starting from Culture

Some familiar theory posits links between physical differences and socialization. The "object-relations" psychoanalytic theory of Nancy Chodorow emphasizes the relationship between learned gender difference and the fact that "women mother." For Chodorow, the *social* assignment of child rearing to women affects boys and girls differently because of the *physical* differences between the sexes. Girls, mothered by someone whose body is like theirs, grow up to seek connection; boys, mothered by a person with a different body, seek separation. Chodorow ends up about where West does, but by a less direct route. Women's personalities differ from men's, but nurture and nature have equal importance in establishing this difference.[40] Carol Gilligan built on Chodorow's object-relations theory in her study *In a Different Voice*, a germinal feminist work.

Chodorow's thesis starts with the fact that infants and children in Western culture typically have one woman as primary caregiver and socializer. "Mothering" affects boys and girls differently because the reciprocal relationship between mother and child differs with the child's sex. A mother perceives a daughter as like her but a son as different. A girl sees herself as simlar to the mother, while a boy perceives that he is different from the mother. Thus, a girl's most significant relationship is with a person similar to her, while a boy relates to someone different from him. Attachment is built into a girl's development, while a boy's experience emphasizes separation.[41]

The facts Chodorow emphasizes are not subject to dispute. Yes, women take care of children. Yes, girls' bodies are more like those of their caregivers than boys' bodies are. But the theory that Chodorow constructs from these facts discounts equally important facts. What would have to be true for male and female personalities to develop as Chodorow posits? Children would have to become familiar with adult bodies at an early age. They probably do. Even in households where nudity is discouraged, the differences in size between children and adults facilitate immature observation. Cradled in adult arms, infants are close to breasts, beards, and voices; held in laps, they are near genitals. Toddlers are more or less at crotch height to adults, and have a convenient vantage point.

So the little boy perceives that his mother's body looks, sounds, feels, and smells different from his own. To that extent, the theory works. But does the little girl perceive her mother's body as similar to hers? The mother has breasts and pubic hair (not to mention body hair in general; shaving the legs is not a universal female custom), both of which the little girl lacks. Adults' bodies look, sound, feel, and smell different from children's bodies, even those of the same sex. How do we know that children think sex differences are more important than age differences?

The difficulty with theories based on childhood perceptions is that they focus on the physical characteristics that adults consider important: sexual distinctions rather than those based on age. We do not really know that children perceive things this way. Children may see themselves as little and weak, surrounded by big, strong adults. Children's psychosexual development may depend as much on adult-child differences as on male-female differences. If it does, Chodorow's psychology of sexual differences is as questionable as Irigaray's anatomy or West's physiology.[42]

Starting from Power

So far, the ideas of gendered reality I have discussed have also been ideas of gender difference. But some feminist theorists hold that the crucial gendered realities are differences in men's and women's positions in society. This school of feminist jurisprudence shows the influence of Marxist scholarship and the Critical Legal Studies movement. The emphasis is not on sexual differences but on what Catharine MacKinnon calls "power in its gendered forms." MacKinnon contrasts the "difference" approach with her own "dominance" approach. She presumes that male bias in law results not from differences in male and female character but from men's subjection of women. MacKinnon's typology expresses the crucial difference between the two approaches.[43]

Feminist analyses that start from power apply concepts of subjection and exploitation derived from the work of their intellectual ancestors. These feminists agree that male dominance is the source of gender difference, but they explain this dominance in different ways. MacKinnon locates it in men's sexual exploitation of women, while Nancy Hartsock traces it to women's assigned tasks (by men) in the sexual division of labor. "Women's activity as institutionalized has a double aspect: their contribution to subsistence and their contribution to child rearing. Whether or not all women do both, women as a sex are institutionally responsible for producing both goods and human beings."[44]

These theories are examples of what is often called "grand theory."[45] They rest on premises one can never know to be true. This embedded uncertainty has not stifled any theorist yet. Marxism is grand theory, too; but even scholars who reject it—as do most American social scientists—borrow its concepts. These theories succeed or fail as analytical tools by what they help us see and what they let us do.

To base theory on gendered power is to start with the documented fact of male supremacy and the historically supported presumption that rulers rule in their own interests. To base theory on gender difference is to start with facts that require intricate interpretation before they can generate any theory at all. The dominance approach is thus attractively realistic. The theory it produces is not without error; like Marxist and critical theory, it seems to leave out important chunks of truth. As Chapter 3 will show, this feminist theory has received extensive criticism. But it is hard to avoid the conclusion that theory based on power is more plausible, on its face, than theory based on difference.

The dominance approach appeals to the student of politics for another reason: it directs our attention outward rather than inward. One cannot discuss women's subjection and exploitation without discussing who and what subjects and exploits women. Instead of concentrating on women's character, dominance theory concentrates on women in relation to society. The tendency of gender difference theory to focus inward may partly explain the curious omission I discussed earlier, the tendency of political discourse to ignore or marginalize feminist concerns.[46] I doubt that people read Irigaray or Chodorow or Gilligan and conclude that gender issues may be excluded from their discourse because women are different. But, to the extent that feminist theory concentrates on gender difference instead of on social and political arrangements, feminist scholars are withdrawing from mainstream discourse. Conceptualizing woman as different is not a way out of marginalization. Conceptualizing woman as dominated and exploited may be.

Is Difference Real? Theory as Truth

Feminist jurisprudence has, then, not one but several explanations of gendered reality. These theories start from different premises, but they are not mutually contradictory. No theory must emphasize biology *or* socialization *or* power, to the exclusion of all other possible sources of gendered reality. Nor do disagreements among these authors mean that one must be right and the others wrong. Any of them could be at least partly right; any or all could be wrong. But none of these theories is new, original, verifiable, or even necessarily feminist. Both separately and together, they fail to accomplish what they promise.

It is obvious that feminists did not invent difference theory. It may be less obvious that feminists did not invent their own particular difference theories. Feminist theorists either accept the basic premises of the works they reject or reason by analogy from the premises of older challenges to traditional theory. For example, feminist psychoanalytic theory rejects the male body as a starting point—but accepts the theory's basic premise that the body is crucial. Similarly, Robin West gets to theory from the body, thereby doing intentionally what she (rightly or wrongly) criticizes liberal theorists for doing. She presumes not only that what differentiates men and women is what is most important about them but also that the body is the most powerful influence on the psyche.

The feminist theorists who emphasize culture and power similarly reason within the boundaries of their intellectual enterprise. Chodorow's object-relations theory accepts psychology's emphasis on childhood experience and sex difference.[47] Theorists who emphasize male dominance tend to reason by analogy from Marxism, Critical Legal Studies, or both. Even when they insist that applying Marxist theory to women's lives distorts rather than illuminates reality, they essentially substitute "gender" for "class" in their own analyses.[48]

These premises are as vulnerable to a charge of unstated male bias as any of the premises that feminist scholars reject. Even if the premises are not male-biased, they may have other defects. No intellectual enterprise can begin by discarding all premises; we have to think within boundaries if we are to think at all. But we need an idea of what those unstated premises are—if not to discard them, at least to examine them. This book argues that fundamental premises *of* feminist theory have gone unrecognized *by* feminist theory.

An additional problem with these theories is that it is not clear how to evaluate them. They are not really hypotheses, and are not subject to proof or disproof in the ordinary scientific sense. They cannot be tested under controlled conditions. We need only imagine an experiment testing Chodorow's object-relations theory by raising children in laboratories where some are, and others are not, mothered by women to perceive how impossible such a venture would be. Biology, culture, and power are too densely and intricately connected to permit the testing of any one factor in isolation from the others.

Another factor that makes gender theories difficult to accept or reject applies particularly to those based on physical characteristics. We have already seen how easy it is to "play" with the theories of Irigaray, Chodorow, or West. For example, the male genitals are not the only possible anatomical explanation for the structure of ideas and institutions; connection to others is not the only social meaning of female physiological functions; sex differences are not the only noticeable physical differences between children and adults. Feminist theorists are no more successful than conventional theorists have been in demonstrating that their interpretations are superior to others—or even in perceiving a need for such arguments.

Difference theories are not based on facts; they are interpretations of facts. The fact does not control the theory; the theory controls what the fact means. Thus, gender differences are not facts but ideas. The meaning of these differences varies according to the particular interpretation at issue. The physical *attributes* of women and men are facts, but the *difference(s)* these attributes make are socially constructed. Gender difference has no fixed meaning.[49]

Thinking as Women: Constructing Feminist Theory

The third premise of feminist scholarship holds that we should ground our theories in our specifically female reality. This premise drives both content and method. "Thinking as women" means both thinking about women (rather than about "human beings" who are in fact men) and thinking like women (rather than like "unbiased, objective" scholars who have been taught how to think by men). This idea follows logically from the postmodernist claim that thought is subjective: grounded in and inseparable from the experience of the thinker.[50] Feminist theorists share a commitment to reasoning from women's specific lives rather than seeking a careful generality.[51]

Specificity and the Possibility of Inclusion

Feminists are not the only scholars who attempt to privilege specificity. Black, Asian, and homosexual theorists, male and female, have made similar claims for their own viewpoints. The literature on disability produced by rather than about the disabled contains the seeds of this kind of theory.[52] If specificity is inevitable, conventional Western scholarship has a white male bias because, up to now, white males have produced this work. "Outsider" scholarship presumes that the way for the excluded to include themselves is to counter the existing implicit specificity with explicit specificity. Drucilla Cornell finds an either-or proposition for feminists: "political activity, if it is to avoid the ever present danger of the masculine-dominated world feminism seeks to dismantle, demands that we write the feminine."[53] This project seems to demand that feminists emphasize the difference between women and men and the similarity among women.

"Thinking as women" is prized by feminist scholars as a means to an end: the construction of *general* theory. But all too often, feminist theory has done what it criticizes conventional theory for doing. It has privileged an individual standpoint as universal. Minority critiques of feminist theory have found many examples of this kind of bias. For example, Paula Giddings, a black scholar, wrote of an early classic of modern feminism, *The Feminine Mystique*: "[Betty] Friedan's observation that 'I never knew a woman, when I was growing up, who used her mind, played her own part in the world, and also loved, and had children' seemed to come from another planet."[54] Friedan, who accused Sigmund Freud of "sexual solipsism," was herself guilty of what Angela Harris calls "white solipsism."[55] Adrienne Rich has documented "the erasure of lesbian existence from so much of scholarly feminist literature."[56] These critiques vindicate Drucilla Cornell's observation that much feminist theory "erases actual differences between women in the name of the norm of the white, middle-class, heterosexual woman who is hailed as Woman."[57] Just as conventional theory has excluded women, feminist theory has excluded minority women. As "majority" feminist scholars accuse conventional theory of male bias, they find themselves accused by minority feminists of white, middle-class, and heterosexual bias. Explicit specificity in feminist theory has privileged some viewpoints and excluded others as much as the implicit specificity of conventional theory has.

But discord between any general theory and specific lives must be demonstrated, not presumed. For instance, Betty Friedan's white solipsism does not render everything she said—about the "happy housewife" image in women's magazines or the use of social theory to discourage women's ambitions, for example—irrelevant for women of color, any more than all of Freudian theory becomes irrelevant for women if they have no Oedipus complex. The appropriate response to "You don't speak for me" is not the self-belittling "Oh, I'm so sorry, I meant to say 'white, middle-class, heterosexual women,' " but the self-critical "Where and how am I wrong?"

A partial solution to the problem of bias is to include as many viewpoints as possible, to read and listen as much as we write and speak, to subject our theory to continual correction and revision. Mari Matsuda calls for a "multiple consciousness" that incorporates "inclusive, dynamic standpoints derived from exposure to diverse viewpoints."[58] But theory is inevitably exclusive, however hard theorists strive to be inclusive. Certain aspects of scholars' lives differentiate us from, and privilege us by comparison with, most other people, even those of the same gender, race, sexual preference, and/or class. We each got the education that made us into scholars; we each have some time and space for thinking and writing. These circumstances make our lives radically different from those of the vast majority of people who have ever lived. We are privileged also by our age, our status as adults. This fact is a crucial part of theories that start from childhood experience; scholars, no longer children, are writing about children.

Inevitably, feminist theorists' search for commonalities in women's lives is skewed toward the perspectives that theorists embody. This bias does not vitiate critiques of what MacKinnon calls "the purported generality, disinterestedness, and universality of previous accounts."[59] But unmasking bias in older theory may be an easier task than keeping bias out of feminist theory. The things scholars have in common may bias us as strongly as do the attributes that divide us.[60]

The self-conscious acknowledgments of viewpoint and correction of bias are essential tasks for feminist scholars and activists. But recognizing that our concerns may not be *universal* does not require us to conclude that they are therefore *unimportant*. To contrast "today's feminist elite" with the "real concerns of women," for instance, is to fall into the "lady liberal" trap I described in the preface.[61] The fact that feminist scholars are not typical of all or most women does not make feminists' concerns less real, or less important, or less "women's" than those of any other women.

Beyond Specificity: Asking the Human Question

"Asking the woman (or minority) question," is imperative, but it is not enough. An inherent danger in writing from specific viewpoints is to write *only* from specific viewpoints. Asserting that one's individual perspective has been left out of that which is assumed to be typical is different from writing from a perspective that one assumes to be typical. Feminist critiques of traditional theory have done the former, but the theory they criticize has done the latter. Minority critiques of feminist theory have adopted an analogous stance; the authors write as minority women, not as women or human beings. The message has been "My specific experience makes your theory wrong for me," not "My specific experience makes your theory wrong for both of us."

So there is liberal theory, and then there are feminist critiques of it; or there is feminist jurisprudence, and then there are minority critiques of it. Which is the sun, and which the moon? By criticizing the existing theory, the outsider gives it primacy, forcing herself to define her own viewpoint in relation to what is being criticized. The danger lies not in doing this—some of it is a necessary corrective to unrecognized bias—but in doing nothing else.

An excellent concrete illustration of the limits and dangers of "sun versus moon" theory comes from the case law of sexual harassment. The Equal Employment Opportunity Commission and the federal courts have ruled that this type of conduct violates Title VII. Sexual harassment includes behavior "that, while not affecting economic benefits, creates a hostile or offensive working environment."[62] This law does not interpret itself, and the courts have made heavy weather of construing it.

While it is true that one worker's hostile environment may be another's idea of fun, the actual cases suggest that these interpretive difficulties are more apparent than real. Supervisors call subordinates "bitch," "cunt," "fat ass," or "dumb fucking broad." An IRS agent stalks a colleague until, she says, "I was frightened." A company president asks a manager to "go to the Holiday Inn" with him to discuss a salary increase.[63] Every appellate court that has construed "hostile environment" since 1991 has ruled at the very least that such allegations permit the suit to go forward. Indeed, the three most recent leading cases all ruled for the plaintiff. The difficulty has arisen in deciding whose perspective to adopt in determining whether conduct creates a hostile environment.

In a 1993 case, *Harris v. Forklift Systems*, the Supreme Court unanimously adopted the "reasonable person" standard. "So long as the environment would reasonably be perceived, and is perceived, as hostile or abusive," wrote Sandra Day O'Connor, sexual harassment existed.[64] The "reasonable person" standard originated in tort law, where it was once "reasonable man." This historical fact disturbed two appellate panels in the Ninth Circuit, both before and after *Harris*. In 1991, *Ellison v. Brady*, the IRS case, suggested that "from the alleged harasser's viewpoint," he "could be portrayed as a modern-day Cyrano de Bergerac wishing no more than to woo Ellison with his words." Instead, "We adopt the perspective of a reasonable *woman* because a sex-blind reasonable person standard tends to be male-biased and tends to systematically ignore the experiences of women."[65] Three years later, *Steiner v. Showboat Operating Company*, the "dumb fucking broad" case, reaffirmed *Ellison* without perceiving any conflict with *Harris*, the binding precedent. *Ellison*'s identification of "reasonable person" with "reasonable man" is accurate history, but its implicit identification of "man" with "harasser" gives up too much. Its juxtaposition of "person" and "woman" inevitably suggests that people are men, and women are something other than people. Like much feminist theory, these cases bring confusion and rigid dichotomization where none need exist.[66]

Two feminist theorists ask: "Why is it, just at the moment in Western history when previously silenced populations have begun to speak for themselves and on behalf of their subjectivities, that the concept of the subject and the possibility of discovering/creating a liberating 'truth' become suspect?"[67] Suppose women, whatever their race, class, or sexual preference, did what men have been doing: wrote theory *as human beings*? Suppose lesbians, women of color, and disabled women wrote theory *as women*, without adjectives? Whether or not "objective" truth is possible, we can distinguish among ways of getting at (partial or subjective) truth. For instance, imagine theory that neither ignored pregnancy and childbirth nor argued that they render standard theory inapplicable to women but treated them as common human experiences. Or imagine feminist theory that dealt with body image from the perspective of women who, because of race or disability, can never conform to "mainstream" standards. How might such theories construe the politics of the body?

One thesis that stops just short of transcending specificity is Angela Harris's critique of "gender essentialism—the notion that a unitary, 'essential' woman's experience can be isolated and described."[68] This essentialism, Harris insists, ignores racial differences. She points out that women of color typically describe themselves as "black," "Asian," and so forth, but white women almost never describe themselves in racial terms. Race is a crucial part of the identities of women of color (in Europe and North America, at least), but not of white women. Therefore, no "unitary" description of women is possible, and the essentialist premise is false.

It is hard to argue with Harris's conclusion about the importance of racial identity to women of color. But can we infer its nonimportance to white women from their relative indifference to it? How can being Caucasian be unimportant if being any other race is so important? Peggy McIntosh has suggested that the freedom *not* to think about race is an important part of white privilege.[69] Does self-image (who we think we are) necessarily define self (who we really are)? Harris verges on a powerful generalization from a minority perspective: a generalization that challenges feminist premises about identity and experience. If race is crucial to everyone's experience, whether or not everyone is conscious of race, Harris is still right: no essential woman's experience exists because women differ with respect to this core attribute. But her emphasis on racial differences reaffirms the dominant relationship between unitary theories and minority critiques, instead of challenging it.[70] Theory that does not fit minority or marginalized women should be retheorized, not merely specified.[71]

Minority and Margin: Thinking from the Outside

My perspective on feminist theory is that of a white, middle-class, heterosexual woman. I usually recognize myself in what I read. When it jars with my experience, the dissonance comes not from my race or sexuality but from the body in which I live and the family in which I grew up. These experiences have sharpened my critical scrutiny even while my childhood emotions have faded. Disability and family pathology are commonly seen as exceptions to rules, deviations from norms: experiences that provide "outsider" perspectives. But I have suggested that treating "deviant" experiences as if they were usual or common—whether they are or not—may lead to important new insights about general theory.

My approach to issues of responsibility has been shaped by the fact that something bad happened to me that I did not do to myself. This knowledge has made me impervious to the victim-blaming that has captured so many of the best minds of my generation. When a legislator composes a little jingle about welfare recipients—"We have a hobby; it's called breeding / Welfare pays for baby feeding"—I hear the ridicule before I hear the reason for it.[72] When conservatives talk about ways to "restigmatize" unwed motherhood or divorce, I wish I knew as little about stigmatization as they do.[73] When pundits bemoan "the decline of shame," they may mean the shame once felt by single mothers; but I think of the disabled children I have heard about who are not teased in school. Who, forty years ago, envisioned either change in attitude? When fetal rights activists propose oppressive restrictions on pregnant women to prevent birth defects, I perceive the contradiction between this solicitude and social attitudes toward people with birth defects.[74]

Disability does not, always and everywhere, make a person an outsider; but a disabled person can become an outsider at any time, in any place, in any context (for example, when the group decides to have lunch at the local Salad Bar from Hell). Disability does not confer a shared identity in the same way or to the same extent that other kinds of marginality can. While Ynestra King's essay offended some readers, her argument that differences among the experiences of disabled people militate against group identification—an identity all too easy for the able-bodied to impose from outside—is valid.[75] Neither disability nor family pathology creates a distinct minority; they marginalize, but not quite as race, gender, and sexual orientation do. These attributes provide perspectives that let us reconsider the connections between groups and individuals, personhood and identity, margin and center.

I did not share Paula Giddings's feeling that *The Feminine Mystique* came from another planet. But the popular comic strip *Cathy* provides daily evidence of the gulf between my attitude toward my body and the attitude that is presumed typical. The humor of Cathy's obsession with her weight, her diet, her clothes, her hair, and her bathing suit does not depend on exaggeration. Both scholarly studies and casual observation suggest that the artist, Cathy Guisewite, has accurately captured a widespread cultural phenomenon.[76] But it has nothing to do with me. I learned not to let my body monopolize my attention, to save my sanity by finding other things to think about. I learned this lesson without anyone teaching it to me, long before I had enough command of language to say what I knew. As a teenager, I was at war with my parents over my failure to be obsessed about my appearance the way adolescent girls are expected to be. As an adult, I am often both the only overweight woman in a group and the only woman who does not call herself fat.

Some feminist theory has made me feel the way I feel about *Cathy* and Giddings felt about *The Feminine Mystique*. Susan Bordo's excellent book *Unbearable Weight* discusses the impact of her twenty-five-pound weight loss on her "efficacy as an alternative role model for [her] female students." She no longer "demonstrate[s] the possibility of confidence, expressiveness, and success in a less than adequately normalized body."[77] What strikes me as bizarre is not Bordo's factual account (how would I know?) but her interpretation of what her image had been. My experience, both as a disabled person to whom others relate and as a person who relates to other disabled people, confirms the insights of research that the "different" body is seen as the rejected "Other," the object not of identification but of differentiation.[78] Bordo's self-description puzzles me, too. When between one-third and one-half of adult Americans are overweight, how abnormal can twenty-five extra pounds make you? Is Bordo confusing a norm, which, by definition, some people meet, with an ideal, which may be unattainable? If the latter interpretation is correct, it is an example of retheorizing from a marginalized identity, just as Angela Harris's insight about the meaning of racial identity to minority women forces us to revise any "essentialist" concept of women or human beings. Thinking from disability may allow us to perceive that dissonance between ideal and reality, rather than perpetual striving toward a norm, is the common situation of women.

Not all disabled people think alike, as the exchange between Ynestra King and her critic showed. Some disabled people embrace the concept of individual responsibility. Some disabled women are as preoccupied with their looks as anyone else. (And class privilege affects my attitude; I can get away with being casual about my appearance.) Nor am I arguing that *only* disabled women can perceive these difficulties with mainstream theory. The point I am making here is, rather, that this "exceptional" perspective reveals what "normals" may not perceive and helps retheorize general theory to make it inclusive.

Growing up in an unhealthy family does not confer minority or "outside" status. But, like disability, the experience puts us to some extent outside, whence we may get at part of the truth about what is presumed normal. We hear that "all families are dysfunctional," just as we hear that "everybody's handicapped in some way" (though not on the playground or in the Social Security office). But discourse about the family tends to juxtapose rule and exception. The following, from a review essay by Jean Bethke Elshtain, is typical: "Some families are rotten and the children in those families should be spirited to safety as quickly as possible. But truly rotten families are, thank God, few and far between. More commonly we have good enough families or almost good enough ones." There is no way Elshtain or anyone else can verify or refute this categorical assertion. There are just too many families out there. The statement is a premise, not a conclusion.

If most families are adequate, it is easier to confuse an ideal ("haven in a heartless world") with a norm.[79] If families are either good or bad, and the bad ones are the exception, it is easier to dismiss the reports of children as exaggerations or even lies (as happened to me; I got the message, and shut up). If we base our thinking about families on our knowledge of adequate ones, it is easier to explain away family pathology in terms of individual circumstances. If we label families rather than characterizing behavior within families, it is easier to maintain a boundary between rule and exception and to define society's task as *either* taking the children away (as if there were places to put them) *or* letting the family be.

I hope my family was unusual. My father was, after all, hospitalized during my childhood. But in our crowded neighborhood my ears told me that verbal abuse, at least, was not confined to our home; yet the other parents were not mentally ill. Forty years later, research has shown that any family is vulnerable to domestic violence; abuse occurs within families of every demographic description; and no income, education, race, religion, or any other factor confers immunity. So it might make sense to consider whether pathogenic factors exist not within specific families (we know they do) but within the institution of the family itself. Family life isolates parents. It gives them enormous power with minimal accountability (if lots of advice) and enormous responsibility with minimal help. This "privacy" is sanctioned by law.[80] Even if these factors do not encourage the abuse of children, they certainly permit the abuse of power. Emphasizing a dichotomy between "normal" and "deviant" families marginalizes the experience of abuse by explaining it in terms of unusual individual circumstances, and by implying that experiences like mine are not "typical" and therefore are irrelevant. In fact, one might conclude that disability and family pathology are similar marginalizing aspects of identity because they leave a huge part of human experience out of the equation. By doing so, they constrain the truths at which we can arrive.

Is Universality Possible? Unanswered Questions

Postmodernism holds that knowledge is subjective, inevitably influenced by the experience of the thinker. Essentialism holds that an identity and experience shared by the members of a group can be discovered and described. While these two positions do not contradict each other outright, their coexistence is problematic. The postmodernists' insistence that attributes like gender, race, and class affect knowledge is not fully compatible with the gender essentialists' search for a female identity that transcends race and class. Not surprisingly, both postmodernism and essentialism have aroused considerable disagreement among scholars, feminist and otherwise. I do not label myself either a postmodernist or an essentialist. However, my rejection of the labels does not imply my rejection of the arguments.

No consensus exists within feminist theory about the possibility of locating a common essential identity. Angela Harris's argument about race persuades me that no such shared identity is possible now. Everything is about race, everything is about class, and everything is about gender. Although certain experiences, situations, and statuses seem to be shared by all or nearly all women (and by no men), the ways in which gender affects women's lives are so differentiated by race and class that we do not yet know if anything remains when all the important differences are recognized. Still less do any of us know the relative importance of any such essential identity compared with the factors that differentiate women.

But what is problematic in theory is mediated by practice. Both post-modernists and essentialists act on their premises to produce scholarship that enhances our understanding. This discontinuity between theory and practice is not unique to feminist scholarship. Physics, for example, incor-porates two incompatible explanations of how light is transmitted from luminous bodies to the eye. Wave theorists and particle theorists dispute one another endlessly—while conducting studies that steadily advance knowledge. The combination of mainstream theory and minority critiques that feminist scholarship has now may not move us toward commonality. But, to the extent that postmodernism and essentialism stimulate inquiry rather than stifle it, the tension between them does more good than harm.[81]

Conclusion

This chapter has identified three organizing premises of feminist theory: that conventional theory is male-biased; that reality is gendered; and that female-specific theory is a necessary corrective. None of these premises can be accepted without qualification. Nor can they be rejected outright, because the scholarship these premises have stimulated demonstrates their generative force. They have inspired valuable and edifying theory. But each premise appears also to encourage characteristic and recurring errors. Feminist critiques of conventional theory are not always clear about what it is they are criticizing or what they mean when they say it is male-biased. Feminist efforts to construct theory from women's experience tend toward both overinclusion and underinclusion. Like men who presume to speak for "humankind," too many white, heterosexual feminists presume to speak for "women." But most feminists claim *only* the right to speak as women, not the right to speak as human beings. Feminist theories of gendered reality are not always distinguishable from prefeminist or even antifeminist theories. So far, feminist theory is hampered by its focus on doubtful and dangerous presumptions of gender difference and its failure to move from a female to a human stance.

THREE

WHAT MAKES LAW MALE?

GENDERED JURISPRUDENCE AND
FEMINIST CRITIQUE

Women are actually or potentially materially connected to
human life. Men aren't.
(Robin West)

The difference is that men have power and women do not.
(Catharine MacKinnon)

FEMINIST jurists agree that law is male, that legal theory must come from women's lives, and that legal reality is gendered. We disagree among ourselves about what makes law male, how to derive theory from experience, and what about law is gendered. While feminist jurisprudence is far too rich and diverse to be contained within neat categories, two distinct theories of the source and nature of law's maleness emerged in the 1980s. Catharine MacKinnon—who is definitely not a disinterested critic—labels these approaches "difference" and "dominance" theory.[1] Difference theory maintains that law disadvantages women because it derives from male thought and experience. Dominance theory asserts that male bias in law results from men's subjection of women.

These categories are not mutually exclusive. Difference jurists do not deny that men have power over women, nor do dominance jurists deny the existence of gender distinctions. What unites these groups of scholars is no less important than what divides them. One shared concern of difference jurists and dominance jurists is a basic distrust of a particular aspect of "traditional male" jurisprudence: liberalism's emphasis on autonomy, individual rights, and abstract justice. While feminist jurists do not reject this outright, they find it—for different reasons—untrue for women.

Feminist jurists' contribution to scholarship goes far beyond their critiques of liberal theory, which goes far beyond what feminist jurists criticize in it.[2] But a focus on feminist responses to conventional rights theory encourages a fresh approach to feminist jurisprudence. Feminist jurists' understanding of the social context of the theory they criticize, and of its relationship to women's lives, is incomplete. Feminist theorists have failed to perceive two important points. First, liberal theory not only posits individual rights but also presumes individual responsibility. Second, the explicit rights theory has not been consistently applied to women, while the implicit responsibility theory has. These failures of understanding have led to misinterpretation of the nature and sources of male bias in law. They have made feminist jurisprudence itself vulnerable to misinterpretation. Finally, they have encouraged a preoccupation with women that pulls feminist concerns out of mainstream discourse and lets men, institutions, and government off the hook.

Character and Situation Jurisprudence

The dichotomy between difference and dominance is a subspecies of a hardy perennial in feminist theory. It grows nearly everywhere and in a variety of types. It has juxtaposed theories that posit crucial gender differences against theories that posit male dominance. The former stress women's relationships to others; the latter emphasize women's separation from others. Robin West distinguishes "cultural feminists," for whom "the important difference between men and women is that women raise children and men don't," and "radical feminists," for whom "the important difference between men and women is that women get fucked and men fuck." The historian Karen Offen has juxtaposed "relational feminism" and "individualist feminism."[3] These dichotomies evoke the division between "egalitarian feminism" and "social feminism" that antedated the Nineteenth Amendment. Egalitarian feminists emphasized women's autonomy and worked for equal rights, whereas social feminists emphasized women's family role and worked for protective legislation.[4]

While MacKinnon's typology of difference and dominance accurately describes the contrasts between the two schools of thought, her modifiers complicate rather than clarify. To speak of gender "difference" is to sentence oneself to a perpetual struggle against connotations. Jacques Derrida asserts that when we use dichotomies—male/female, soul/body, mind/matter, and so forth—"the two terms are not simply opposed in their meanings, but are arranged in a hierarchical order which gives the first term *priority*." If Derrida is right, the concept "difference" cannot be neutralized; it is intrinsically biased. Whether Derrida is right or wrong about difference in general, he is right about the semantics and history of gender difference. The etymology of the two common English sets of antonyms—"man" and "woman," "male" and "female"—inevitably privileges the former term.[5] The word "dominance" also has an inconvenient history. Male dominance is a historical fact; but scholar after scholar, moving beyond the books to women's records of their own lives, has found that women have enjoyed more autonomy and less subjection than male-centered research implies.

To speak of dominance may seem to bias efforts to construct theory by begging an important question.[6]

My way out of these difficulties is to do some renaming. I speak of gender "distinction" rather than gender "difference." I refer to the theories that emphasize gender difference as theories of women's "character." Similarly, while the implication that *dominance* is a universal feature of women's lives is contentious, the assertion that women's *situation* has been a subject one is incontrovertible. Therefore, I refer to the theories that emphasize dominance as theories of women's "situation." Character theory's emphasis on essential gender distinction mirrors liberalism's emphasis on essential human nature. Situation theory's emphasis on male dominance mirrors Marxism's emphasis on class struggle. Character theory (jurisprudence) holds that what makes law male is the fact that men created it for themselves. Situation theory (jurisprudence) holds that what makes law male is the fact that men use it to subordinate women.

These two distinct conceptions of the male bias of law support two distinct interpretations of the male bias of rights theory. Character jurists assert that this theory is male-biased because it rests on assumptions about human beings which are true only about men. Situation jurists assert that it is male-biased because it presumes an autonomy that male supremacy denies to women. Character jurisprudence unmasks male bias in law and explains how women are penalized for behavior, responses, and modes of thought that differ from men's. But this theory fails to liberate itself from entrenched social obligations that arise from traditional gender roles. Situation jurisprudence, for its part, has shown how law and jurisprudence facilitate men's subjection of women. But this school of feminist theory often fails to get its arguments across because its understanding of the relationship between the male theory it rejects and the women's lives it analyzes is incomplete.

Character Theory and Jurisprudence

The organizing premise of character jurisprudence is that women share some distinctive features that make male-centered theory wrong for them. I have already discussed the impossibility of empirically verifying theories of gender distinction. If we theorize about character at all, we must accept this uncertainty.[7] But there is a difference between demanding proof of the unprovable and demanding lucid argument, supported by reliable evidence. We need not adopt a "crude verificationistic model of science" in order to reject some of the uses to which unprovable theory can be put.[8]

Feminist theorists must confront the unsavory history of character theory. The product of a male supremacist society, this theory has rationalized and validated that male supremacy. Society is prior to theory, not theory to society. Character theory has been used to oppress women, to limit their freedom, and to force them to conform to theoretical models of "feminine" personality and behavior. Legal institutions used the theory of *Muller v. Oregon* to keep women out of good jobs; psychotherapeutic institutions used Freudian theory to "fix" women's psyches; educational institutions used social science to channel girls into conventional female roles and occupations.[9] These theories of women's character were used not to expand possibilities but to restrict them; women were coerced on the basis of ideas not known to be valid. The tasks confronting feminist character theory are, first, to offer a convincing explanation of whence these personality differences arise, and, second, to show that these differences are healthy for human beings.

Character jurisprudence has a mature theory of gender distinction, derived primarily from the work of Nancy Chodorow and Carol Gilligan.[10] As we saw in Chapter 2, Chodorow's object-relations theory is not without serious defects. Gilligan and Chodorow do not agree on every detail, but together they present a coherent explanation of how women's character differs from men's, how things got that way, and how these gender distinctions make law ill adapted to women. These are works that no scholar can ignore, and from which every reader can learn. But ultimately the theory undermines the sexual equality it claims to promote.

Man's Separation, Woman's Connection: The Different Voice

Carol Gilligan's book *In a Different Voice* asserts that women derive from their life experience a morality fundamentally distinct from that of men. While men's moral development emphasizes "rights and noninterference," women's psychology is "distinctive in its greater orientation toward relationships and interdependence," valuing "attachment" to others over "separation" from them.[11] Gilligan relies on data she herself generated in studies conducted during the 1970s. This material shows women doing their moral reasoning differently from men, and being devalued for it.

Gilligan's signature passage recounts the different responses of two eleven-year-olds, Jake and Amy, to this classic dilemma: Heinz's dying wife needs a drug that he cannot afford to buy. The druggist refuses to lower the price. Is Heinz justified in stealing the drug? Jake's unequivocal "yes," advocating a principled decision to break a rule, fits onto the highest level of Lawrence Kohlberg's "stages of moral development," the dominant paradigm in the field when Gilligan wrote. But Amy said, "If he stole the drug, he might save his wife then, but if he did, he might have to go to jail, and then his wife might get sicker again, and he couldn't get more of the drug. . . . They should really just talk it out and find some other way to make the money." Amy perceives "not a math problem involving humans but a narrative of relationships that extends over time." For Gilligan, Amy's solution epitomizes women's different voice. "The standard of moral judgment that informs their assessment of self is a standard of relationship, an ethic of nurturance, responsibility, and care."[12]

Gilligan's model of moral development, like Kohlberg's, is dynamic rather than static. The ethic of care includes three distinct moral stages. As women mature, "an initial focus on caring for the self" is succeeded by a "transitional phase" in which "the good is equated with caring for others." This stage, in its turn, gives way to a "third perspective," which "focuses on the dynamics of relationships and dissipates the tension between selfishness and responsibility through a new understanding of the connection between other and self."[13]

But Gilligan's ethic does not get equal respect with Kohlberg's scheme. The cues that Amy's interviewer (whose sex goes unspecified) gives her epitomize society's response to this ethic of care. By making it clear that Amy is not giving the right answer, the interviewer shows how society punishes women for not being like men. Negative cues like these may begin or accelerate a developmental pattern so familiar to researchers that they have a name for it: "the fall."[14] Gilligan's own longitudinal study, showing how confident eleven-year-olds, girls like Amy, become timorous sixteen-year-olds, is only one illustration of the common decline in girls' self-image during puberty and adolescence.[15]

Robin West was one of the first feminist legal scholars to build on Chodorow and Gilligan. "Virtually all modern American legal theorists," she writes, accept "the 'separation thesis' of what it means to be a human being: a 'human being,' whatever else he is, is physically separate from all other human beings." West's "he" is deliberate: "The cluster of claims that jointly constitute the 'separation thesis,' . . . while usually true of men, are patently untrue of women." Women are "connected to life and to other human beings during at least four recurrent and critical material experiences: the experience of pregnancy itself; the invasive and 'connecting' experience of heterosexual penetration, which may lead to pregnancy; the monthly experience of menstruation, which represents the potential for pregnancy; and the post-pregnancy experience of breast-feeding. If by 'human beings,' legal theorists mean women as well as men, then the 'separation thesis' is clearly false."[16]

West's "connection thesis" has not survived critical scrutiny. The experiences West identifies are insufficient bases for theory. One difficulty is logi-

cal: How can you be connected to other people without their being connected to you? Another problem is chronological: the experiences West
identifies as critical normally do not occur before the second decade of a
woman's life. Therefore, a woman's formative years are not influenced by
the experiences that West sees as crucial to women's sense of self. A third
serious error is West's implication that these critical material experiences
are common to all or virtually all women. This is patently incorrect; even
menstruation, the most common of the four, occurs for only about half a
woman's life span. If by "women" West means those for whom her connection thesis is true, then women who do not perform any, some, or all of
these functions are not women.

Obvious as the defects of West's character jurisprudence are, her article
was widely read, extensively cited, and approvingly quoted for several years
after it appeared in 1988. Friendly critics refused to take some of West's
extreme positions at face value, suggesting, for instance, that perhaps she
meant to say that the *possibility* of the critical experiences materially connects women to human life.[17] But West does not have a theory of how such
a connection works. This favorable response to an obviously flawed thesis
is a measure of how receptive feminist scholars have been to character
jurisprudence.

The influence of Gilligan and Chodorow on feminist legal theory has
been pervasive and profound. Character jurists agree, first, that there is a
distinctive female morality which emphasizes connection rather than separation; and, second, that society's exclusion of this morality from public
discourse has made law a preserve of values contingently associated with
men. These conclusions pose a challenge not only to psychological theory
but also to the philosophy of liberal individualism and to law based wholly
or partly on that philosophy.

The "caring and connection" thesis became, and has remained, popular.
Gilligan's book is one of the few academic works to become a best-seller.
The prevalence in public discourse of statements beginning "this world
would be a better place if men . . ." or "it would be a shame if feminism
meant that women . . ." provides ample evidence of the appeal of this ethic.
Its popularity is easy to understand. Gilligan's words and those of her subjects resonate with everyday experience and observation. Her critique of
psychology for taking as human that which is in fact male, and devaluing
women for not fitting in, has implications that go far beyond her field and,
indeed, beyond scholarship in general. We know that care, nurturance, and
connections are essential for individuals and for society. We also know that
society depreciates these attributes. Gilligan's demand that theory be revised to include women was interpreted as a powerful feminist statement;
her defense of an ethic of care was seen as socially healthy.

The appeal of character theory has not protected it from the criticism visited on most scholarship which makes any impression at all. The critical reaction to Gilligan's work, in particular, has been extensive and incisive. Many commentators agree that her thesis is not adequately supported by argument or evidence; her observations about women are not original; and the specific moral orientation she ascribes to women is the product of male dominance rather than female character.[18] West and Chodorow have no more success than Gilligan in providing a sound empirical foundation for a female ethic of care. Chapter 2 showed how easy it is to develop alternative explanations of the significance of the same facts on which these authors rely. The social meanings that West assigns to her critical experiences or Chodorow to her combination of anatomy and sociology are not the only possible interpretations. The conclusions these theorists draw from the facts they emphasize are, therefore, problematic.

So the underlying premises of a female ethic of care and connection are at best dubious and at worst false. The idea itself is far from original. Its proponents have no new observations either about gender or about conventional theory. The critique of liberal individualism which Gilligan permits the reader to infer from her thesis has been made independently of her work. It did not even begin as a feminist critique. Philip Slater in the 1970s and Robert Bellah in the 1980s both argued that individualism encourages people to separate themselves from others in pathological ways and that the "disconnector virtues" destroy intimacy and relationship. Slater specifically labels care, nurturance, and attachment as qualities society attributes to women.[19] These authors go uncited by the feminist character theorists.

What character theory says about men and women is no more necessarily feminist than it is original. The psychiatrist Joseph Rheingold wrote back in 1964 that "*woman is nurturance*" and, that "when women grow up" free of "subversion by feminist doctrine" and "enter upon motherhood with a sense of altruistic fulfillment, we shall attain the goal of a good life and a secure world in which to live it." A few years later, David Bakan, a philosopher, described women as characterized by "communion" with others, while men sought "agency," which "manifests itself in the formation of separations." Gilligan is not even the first woman to write like this; Gina Lombroso, in 1923, labeled women as "alterocentric," while men were "egocentric." Robin West sounds suspiciously like Erik Erikson, who framed the core question of female psychology thus: "How does the identity formation of women differ by dint of the fact that their somatic design harbors an 'inner space' destined to bear the offspring of chosen men, and, with it, a biological, psychological, social, and ethical commitment to take care of human infancy?" Feminist character theory bears a disturbing similarity to earlier theories that range from prefeminist to antifeminist.[20]

West's article anticipates this criticism:

> Women's ethic of care, and commitment to the value of nurturance and intimacy celebrated by cultural feminism, has existed *in spite of* patriarchy's contempt for and under-valuation of these values, not because of their false claim to honor women's separate sphere. While it is of course true that cultural feminism's celebration of women's ethic of care echoes patriarchy's celebration of separate spheres, the former is hardly an apology for the latter. The differences between cultural feminism and patriarchy are all-important ones: patriarchy devalues women, and cultural feminism does not. Patriarchy celebrates women's separate sphere in order to reinforce women's powerlessness. Cultural feminism does not.[21]

It is true that reinforcing the status quo is not the *purpose* of cultural feminism. Whether gender differences are natural or acquired, sexual equality demands that women's contributions be valued equally with men's. The road taken by character jurisprudence is paved with good intentions. But knowing what the theory does not intend to do cannot tell us what it does. The fact of women's caregiving in a society which disparages care cannot prove that the ethic is natural to women rather than forced upon them. Character theorists fail to convince critical readers that gender distinctions in personality or morality rest on anything other than sex-role socialization, which may not be healthy or desirable at all. "Different voices" may well result from old-fashioned social learning: as children grow up, they learn that society expects different things from men and women, and they adopt the behavior that adults approve. These differences may support a character theory, but it cannot be a feminist one.

For all its criticism of liberalism, much character theory implies a typical liberal faith in consensus: if we only let the different voices in, society will incorporate women's needs as well as men's.[22] This faith is not shared by feminist critics of character theory, who have encountered the "care and connection" thesis before. Catharine MacKinnon writes, "It is enlightening that affirming the perspective that has been forced on women is rather widely taken as progress toward taking women seriously."[23] Kathy Ferguson finds "political naivete" in Gilligan's failure to perceive that "the differences she names . . . maintain male privilege and female subordination."[24] Joan Tronto finds similarities between Gilligan's ethic of care and the moral views of members of disadvantaged minorities.[25]

Women's morality may emphasize nurture and care because a male supremacist society forces the duties of nurture and care upon women. Far from being benign, the distinctive moral voice may be an unhealthy adaptation to subjection. Care and nurturance are socially valuable whether or not they are voluntarily provided; but an ethic forced upon women cannot be feminist. We must ask, first, whether familiar descriptions of women are valid when they come from feminists; and, second, whether feminists can celebrate a female ethic without coercing women into assigned roles and positions.

Care and Coercion: The Roots of a Female Ethic

Character theorists do not claim to know whether women's association with care is voluntary in the sense of arising from free will rather than being determined, but they do suggest that the association is voluntary in the sense of being independent of external constraints. Much character jurisprudence moves from the observation that women are devalued for acting like women to the assumption that they would be rewarded for acting like men. Rosemarie Tong suggests that "the truly educated woman— that is, the woman with a mind of her own—will refuse to become a 'man' in exchange for social approval."[26] These arguments make two highly dubious assumptions: that society would fulfill its part in any such exchange, and that women are free to make it.

When women put nurturance aside in favor of asserting rights, society's rewards for this behavior are scant, and its punishments harsh. Consider the case of Ann Hopkins, an accountant at Price Waterhouse who was denied promotion to partnership. Hopkins's superiors had criticized her "macho" and "tough-talking" behavior. They advised her to take "a course at charm school" and to "walk more femininely, talk more femininely, dress more femininely, wear makeup, have her hair styled, and wear jewelry."[27]

"The valorization of justice and the trivialization of care" do not indicate that women's focus on the latter has been voluntary.[28] Women may be punished for either feminine or masculine behavior. In other words, women are punished whatever they do, *for being women*. It is not clear that society has treated women worse for rejecting male behavior than for emulating it. In any case, the vast majority of women do not have the option "to become a 'man.' " The female job ghetto includes numerous occupations where hairstyling, makeup, and charm are requirements. And the comparatively few women who hold "male" jobs might not want to adopt "male" behavior in other areas of their lives even if they could. The same Ann Hopkins who allegedly acted like a man at work had young children at home. Feminist theory must be careful not to imply that a woman must make an across-the-board choice between "feminine" and "not feminine";

a woman may make different choices at different times and in different aspects of her life.

No astute observer would assert that every act of care and nurturance women perform is extorted from them, or that every statement women make about the value of connection and relationships represents the internalization of social expectations. But the character theorists themselves connect the ethic of care to women's traditional roles—and these have been compulsory. Even when law and power have not forced women into domestic or quasi-domestic duties, necessity has done so. The rights-power-autonomy cluster is not fundamental for men, nor is the intimacy-connection-nurturance cluster fundamental for women. These imperatives are derived from the basic responsibility for self-preservation and a male supremacist society's gendered options for meeting this responsibility.

MacKinnon is right: the "caring" perspective has been forced on women. The historical fact of coercion does not prove that women would not have chosen to provide care; or that they had no choice how to provide it; or that providing it was not good for them; or even that they did not want to provide it. (It is possible to learn to like doing something you did not choose to do, as most children discover.) But the coercion does militate against accepting an ethic of care on its own terms. This different ethic represents not what the voice says but what the ear hears.

Feminist Care or Feminine Obligation?

Character theory affirms the contributions women have made to a society that disparages these contributions. The theory reminds us of the social importance of care and shows how society's devaluing of care denigrates women. Feminist theorists' valorization of care is, therefore, a healthy development. Society should value essential work and the people who do it.

But character theory goes beyond valorizing care; it valorizes care as specifically female. This linkage of women and caring bears a heavy burden of justification, for several reasons. First, the idea that the status of *any* activity can be improved by associating it with women is ahistorical. Example after example exists of exactly the opposite relationship: the status of occupations falling with the entry of women and rising with the entry of men.[29] Second, we do not know whether women's association with care arises from female predilection or social coercion. Third, we do not know whether an ethic of care is good for women. Finally, we lack a clear understanding of what an ethic of care would replace.

Could a voluntary female ethic of care ever exist? This question suggests a broader question: Can feminist theory accomplish what Drucilla Cornell defines as its primary task—identify "a feminine 'voice' and a feminine 'reality' "—without implicitly labeling what it excludes as not feminine?[30] For that matter, can we identify any attribute as typically or essentially "X"—whether X is "human," "female," "male," "Asian," "Jewish," or whatever—without implying that the lack of this attribute is "not-X?"

The history of such labels strongly favors negative answers to these questions. Identifying attributes as typical of any group without creating pressure on group members to either embrace or reject these attributes seems no more possible than discussing difference without implying inferiority.[31] In Joan Scott's words, "meanings are constructed through exclusions"; to define attributes as "feminine" implies that the absence of these attributes is other than "feminine."[32] Labeling certain attributes as "X" typically creates either a positive model of "X-ness" to which people within the group are expected to conform or a negative model from which they must distinguish themselves. Chapter 1 provides concrete instances of the difficulty, if not impossibility, of assigning attributes to groups without creating coercion. Edmund Gordon was criticized by other blacks for his alleged failure to conform to a positive model associated with black identity; Ynestra King was criticized by another disabled woman for allegedly conforming to a negative stereotype associated with disability. Cornell argues that feminists must write the feminine lest we be stuck with the masculine.[33] But if we write the feminine, we will be stuck with the feminine—which may be even worse.

Would a value system centered around care and connection be good for women? Some quotations from Gilligan's subjects suggest otherwise. Emily, for example, decides not to go to a medical school far from home because her parents would be hurt by her inaccessibility. They have no unusual needs, just "a right to see me a certain way, at certain times." Emily claims no equivalent right for herself; "my motivation was sort of selfish."[34] Emily's parents have no obligation to free her to venture forth. Women like Emily do not assert rights for themselves against other people at the same time they grant other people rights against them. True, Emily's ethic of care places her at the intermediate rather than the final stage of Gilligan's scheme of moral development. But Emily will make this decision only once. If crucial life decisions come at a point in a woman's moral development when she still perceives her own interests as "selfish," the ethic of care represents a serious danger to women's autonomy. Even at the highest stage, the people to whom Gilligan's subjects have obligations rarely have obligations toward them.[35]

The asymmetry of the ethic of care becomes clearer if we look beyond issues of gender. Not all cultures restrict this ethic to women. Caroline Alexander, an American classicist who taught at the University of Malawi for three years, recalls a negative side to these obligations:

The economic disparity between a European and a Malawian professional is compounded by the latter's inescapable obligations to his family. These kinship responsibilities are often taken by Europeans as indicative of the more humane and caring nature of traditional African culture, but in practice they can foster attitudes as vicious and self-regarding as any in the West. Once a village man or woman has "made good"—which is to say, is salaried—he or she will be expected to meet whatever financial demands are made by a needy or greedy relative, no matter how tangential the lives of the two parties may have been up to that point. Relatives descend expecting to be housed and fed; they may come from many miles away for loans or gifts. Anyone who denies such requests will be looked on askance by the rest of his family, and his life will be made extremely unpleasant. The new salary is bled away as the obligations become too many to meet.[36]

The obligations faced by "Emilys" in Boston are as unilateral as those of professionals in Malawi. Gilligan's subjects internalize the duties imposed on them. Alexander points to a problem that character theorists ignore. The attitudes she describes as "vicious and self-regarding" are not those of people who refuse to provide nurturance but of people who expect it. It would be useful to know as much about what people demand of one another as we do about what some people demand of themselves.

The difficulty with Gilligan's work may be inherent in the study of psychology. By focusing on individuals' accounts, she misses the extent to which individuals are constrained by outside expectations. This focus on the self is not surprising, because it conforms to ordinary language usage: my "ethic" is the set of principles by which I govern myself. *In a Different Voice* does apply the ethic of care to men; it is not quite an ethic of unilateral female obligation.[37] But to the extent that this ethic is applied primarily to women's conduct, it focuses on what they should do, not on how others should act toward them. It says "I should," not "I am entitled to."

Other character theorists have been less careful than Gilligan to avoid the trap of single-sex duty. Some of them extend the ethical component of distinction theory in a way that tends to absolve everyone else of responsibility. Nel Noddings posits an "ethic of caring" that "locate[s] the very wellspring of ethical behavior in human affective response." Noddings writes, "The one-caring has one great aim: to preserve and enhance caring in herself and in those with whom she comes in contact." Noddings labels this ethic "feminine," and her "one-caring" is always "she."[38]

Jean Bethke Elshtain, Elizabeth Fox-Genovese, and Sara Ruddick—respectively, a political scientist, a historian, and a philosopher—derive unilateral female obligations from the maternal role. Elshtain calls on "the reflective feminist" to "be as concerned with children as she is with female subjects."[39] Fox-Genovese criticizes feminists for slighting "the real concerns of women"; both the text and the jacket art of her latest book suggest that these "real concerns" are children.[40] Ruddick's "maternal thinking" represents a voice as different as Gilligan's moral theory. Ruddick's "woman's politics of *resistance* is composed of women who take responsibility for the tasks of caring labor and then find themselves confronted with politics or actions that interfere with their right or capacity to do their work. In the name of womanly duties that they have assumed and that their communities expect of them, they resist."[41] This character theory assigns women the whole spectrum of obligation, from raising children to securing world peace.

Things get even worse when we move from academic publications to books designed for the general public. Suzanne Gordon lambastes "equal-opportunity feminism" and lauds "transformative feminism." The former is exemplified by a banker who "does not exude much warmth," a scientist who discourages her students from confiding in her, and the (documented) failures of professional women to support the efforts of working-class women to improve their status. Class bias is no more acceptable among feminists than anywhere else, but Gordon nowhere explains why these women owe other people more than their male counterparts do. Feminism is, after all, as much a movement for equality between women and men as for equality among women. Gordon would deny to women much of the freedom that men enjoy to decide how much sympathy and help to give. Transformative feminism demands more of women than it does of men. It is not equality, but another second shift, another double burden.[42]

A prefeminist character theory, inadequately supported, logically defective, and disguised with a few new adjectives, leaves women where they have been all along: deprived of rights and burdened with obligations. If women are different from men, they do not need and should not want the rights and privileges that men enjoy; if the most important things women do are the things men cannot do, it makes sense to confine women to their traditional functions. It's not male supremacy or, worse yet, patriarchy; it's everybody doing what's best for him or her. For example, if "men, in order to develop, must separate or deny their attachment to their mothers; women do not need to do either of these things in their development," does this justify social arrangements whereby daughters care for aged mothers while sons need not?[43]

Emphasizing gender differences has served a crucial function in traditional theory; it has rationalized the sexual division of labor produced by a male supremacist society. Nothing in the allegedly new, allegedly feminist theory assures us that it can lead to change in this assignment of roles, or that there can be any such thing as a voluntarily adopted female ethic of care. Character jurisprudence lends itself to uses that retard rather than advance sexual equality. The fact that character theory is written by women for women cannot save it. There is, after all, no shortage of complaints from men about the sex-role expectations they confront, expectations which originate in male-dominated society. And there is nothing new about women imposing obligations on other women. That law has been a male preserve is an incontrovertible truth. That this same male-developed law ignores or discounts women's reality is at least plausible. But character theory has not given rise to a woman-centered jurisprudence that avoids the errors of the male tradition it claims to replace.

Justice Reconsidered: Gender Disadvantage and Gender Privilege

It is a tenet of feminist scholarship that the "female" ethic of care and the "male" ethic of justice are interdependent. Kathy Ferguson argues that "men are able to sustain an identity of separation and independence, and a morality that stresses autonomy and rights, in part because women are weaving the web of sociality on which men depend even as they devalue it in their theories and their institutions."[44] Feminist critics of liberalism protest that its idea of the individual's relation to the state presupposes women's assignment to the "private" sphere.[45] We have seen that the ethic of care is forced on women, whether or not they would choose it. Men *may* "do justice" because women *must* "do care." Privileged people—men—get to choose. They choose justice, rights, autonomy, separation over care, nurturance, connection. Subjugated people—women—have duties assigned to them. They are assigned care.

Do men renounce care because it is not rewarded? Aside from the obvious chicken-and-egg problem this question presents, it is not generally true that people engage only in activities that bring tangible benefits. I know of no extrinsic rewards attached to watching football games on television, for instance. Nevertheless, this activity is so popular among men that some men may even prefer it to caregiving.

If justice is a choice and care is a duty, what does this suggest about the relative merits of the two ethics? Not that justice is more valuable than care; or that caregiving is without intrinsic rewards for the caregiver (but if they're so great, why don't men want more of them?); or that feminist theory should abandon care and embrace justice. Not even that women would necessarily choose justice over care if they could choose. But if people who can choose adopt the ethic of justice, maybe something about that ethic makes it desirable. Feminist theory, like outsider theory in general, emphasizes out-group disadvantage and the need to mitigate it. We might learn as much from examining in-group privilege and the possibility of sharing it. It is time to suggest that an ethic of rights may be more rewarding, more valuable, more fulfilling, more interesting, and even more fun than an ethic of care.

This suggestion may give rise to several objections. First, while the choice of justice over care may be good for individuals, it has had serious consequences for society. Sara Ruddick's vision of a woman's politics of resistance suggests the virtues of bringing an ethic of care and connection to a sphere in which an ethic of rights and autonomy has prevailed. The lessons caregivers learn include the resilient humor Ruddick associates with maternal thinking and the fact that punishment is only one way, and not always the best way, to influence behavior. These insights belong in public life.

A second objection to preferring justice to care is that drawing conclusions about the relative desirability of value orientations from male preferences may beg the question of gender difference. If women are unlike men, women might not make the same choices that men have made. But we have yet to encounter a convincing argument for the kind of gender distinctions that would entail gender-specific ethics; the question will have to stay begged. We do know enough about power to distrust assertions that an ethic forced upon subject people is one they would choose.

Let us assume, for the moment, that the ethic of rights is not "male," and consider its merit for individuals. To be able to do as we think best, even if others disagree; to claim limits on what may be demanded of us; to question rules—even, like Heinz, to claim exceptions to rules; to weigh competing claims—even, unlike Emily, to decide that our own needs outweigh those of others: these privileges may have more intrinsic value than character theorists are willing to recognize. What would such choices mean for women? To be free to grant or withhold help; to encourage or discourage the confidences of others; to pursue one's own interests concurrently with or separately from the interests of children, students, associates, subordinates, or anyone else; and to make these choices without guilt: is this not an improvement over what the ethicists of care, the maternal thinkers, and the transformative feminists offer us?

Rights, noninterference, and autonomy cannot, *by themselves*, make a complete ethic. Care has to come in somewhere. But to bring care in as female is to renounce for women both the privilege to choose and the choice the privileged have made. The autonomy privileged by rights theory can be and has been abused; choices are often made "selfishly." But rights and autonomy enable more than selfish behavior. They have enabled people to create theory (not to mention literature, art, and science); to participate in public life; to work for ideals. Assuming an ethic derived from women's place in sexist society will not enable feminists to change the world; claiming the privileges associated with men's place, may.

But that possibility raises a third, and more serious, objection to a feminist valorization of justice. While a legal system based on sexual equality must reject a female ethic of care, it must also take into account the fact that care remains women's province. Even if caregiving is not good for the caregivers, even if they do it because they have to, the law must not only stop punishing them but start rewarding them. Feminist jurists must claim as a crucial task the rewriting of laws that put women at a disadvantage because of family responsibilities or ignore the emotional needs that arise from caregiving. Stingy maternity leaves, and child custody laws that ignore the fact that women mother, have no place in a feminist jurisprudence. This revision is a difficult task, because law must reward the performance of these duties without reinforcing the maldistribution of responsibility, and facilitate women's giving up unfair burdens without coercing them into doing so. But character theory does not help us do either. It ultimately endorses the validity of the male division between justice and care, and accepts the patriarchal assignment of care to women.

Feminist theorists must stop holding one another back with demands for femininity. Suzanne Gordon's demand that we attend to the needs of subordinates, Jean Bethke Elshtain's demand for solicitude for children, and Elizabeth Fox-Genovese's demand for attention to the "real" concerns of women must all be recognized as what they are: the familiar socialization of women by women into conventional gender roles. Character jurisprudence is not progression; it is regression.

Beyond Sameness and Difference

This analysis of character jurisprudence can help repair "the deep split among American feminists between 'sameness' and 'difference.' "[46] The dichotomy is false. Feminist jurists need not—indeed, we must not—choose between laws that treat men and women the same and laws that treat them differently. We already know that both kinds of law can be sexist. Our gender-neutral law of reproductive rights treats women worse than men, but so did "protective" labor legislation. Conversely, both gender-neutral and gender-specific laws can promote sexual equality. Comparable worth legislation would make women more nearly equal with men. So have affirmative action policies.

Women can have it both ways. Law can treat men and women alike where they are alike and differently where they are different. For example, the Supreme Court correctly ruled in *Cal. Fed. v. Guerra* that there is no contradiction between the Pregnancy Discrimination Act of 1978 and the California statute that mandates unpaid maternity leaves of up to four months.[47] To the extent that pregnancy is like other temporarily disabling conditions, the PDA treats it as such. To the extent that it is different—it produces a baby—the state law treats it as different. The same principle would permit surrogacy contracts while giving the biological mother the right to abrogate the contract after childbirth. Allowing the practice would treat surrogate mothers like sperm donors to the extent the two are alike: entrepreneurs in a capitalist economic system. Letting the mother back out recognizes the nature and extent of a woman's difference from a man.[48]

The insight that character theory is based on sexist role expectations militates against any acceptance of gender-specific laws based on women's physical or social functions. Whatever good these laws may do, they also reinforce unjust social arrangements. The need for policies that recognize the contributions of mothers, caregivers, and nurturers can be met by gender-neutral laws. The need for policies that compensate women for the disadvantages they incur from performing their socially assigned functions can be met by sex-specific ameliorative legislation. The need for policies that authorize the female view of the world can be met at least in part by a radical rewriting of equal protection doctrine. The problem is not how neutral you make it but how you make it neutral.[49]

Feminist jurists should think about care and justice not as women but as human beings. We should transcend specificity and aspire to universality. Sexual equality does not lie in women's valorization of care but in women's breaking up the male monopoly on justice and giving up the female monopoly on care. That accomplishment would create a different voice for women and men.

Situation Theory and Jurisprudence

Situation theory does not so much reject the premises of character theory as demote them. Character theory starts with people, and fails to understand power. Situation theory starts with power, and is accused of misunderstanding people. The central fact of situation theory is men's power over women. The central fact of situation jurisprudence is law's status as an instrument of this power.

Like character jurisprudence, situation jurisprudence criticizes older theory, particularly rights theory. Situation jurists assert that liberalism presumes an autonomy that sexist society denies to women. As Wendy Brown puts it, "One trouble with rights is that they isolate individuals in theory when they are not independent of one another in reality."[50] Catharine MacKinnon questions "the liberal idea of the private [in which] consent tends to be presumed." MacKinnon asserts that this premise, applied to women, is a lie. "Feminism confronts the fact that women have no privacy to lose or to guarantee."[51]

Why not? This question gets to the core of MacKinnon's theory of the state: her locating the source of women's subordination in their assigned sexual (not reproductive or nurturing) function. Men fuck and women are fucked, both literally and figuratively. "Fuck" is the only "English verb that *elides the distinction between rape and intercourse, love and violation.*"[52] And elide the distinction is exactly what MacKinnon does. "Rape and intercourse are not authoritatively separated by any difference between the physical acts or amount of force involved but only legally, by a standard that centers on the man's interpretation of the encounter. . . . Perhaps the wrong of rape has proved so difficult to define because the unquestionable starting point has been that rape is defined as distinct from intercourse, while for women it is difficult to distinguish the two under conditions of male dominance."[53] The elided distinction is irrelevant to the function of sex in male supremacist society.

What is that function? Not reproduction, because then sex "would not happen every night (or even twice a week) for forty or fifty years, nor would prostitutes exist." Certainly not mutual gratification, pleasure, or recreation; in that case, rape would not exist. Not relief of men's desire; they can masturbate. Instead, sex is the means by which men exert power over women, and the model and metaphor for that power. Women's function is to be men's sexual outlets. It makes sense, therefore, that a male supremacist state would have recognized a right to choose abortion, which "facilitates women's heterosexual availability," but not a right to choose jobs involving reproductive hazards; "fertile women are apparently not real persons."[54]

One weakness of "grand theories" like MacKinnon's is that, while they can explain concrete results, they can rarely explain why one thing happens and not another. MacKinnon's reading of abortion law and fetal protection policies fails to explain why these results were preferred to the alternatives. Allowing abortion does facilitate women's heterosexual ability, but prohibiting abortion facilitates women's heterosexual accountability. Why prefer the first to the second? Fetal protection rules did limit women's autonomy, but forcing women to choose between decent salaries and safe working conditions is a clear example of symbolic fucking disguised as freedom. Why prefer direct coercion to coercively structured choice?

MacKinnon hammers home the point *that* law is male, but she is less persuasive on *how* law is male, and on *why* its maleness takes some forms rather than others. Her analysis of pornography, for example, assumes that the vigor and prevalence of this mode of expression are due to the First Amendment. She misses the way pornography thrives in spite of court decisions excluding certain kinds of utterances from the First Amendment and statutes which look strict on paper. Thus, she attributes to liberalism a phenomenon that has at least as much to do with capitalism. But this is a new version of an old criticism which has not stifled any grand theorist yet. MacKinnon's theory cannot explain everything, but it can explain a lot. Her explanation of women's subjection in terms of their use as sexual outlets fits within my framework: women's sexual function can be understood as one manifestation of the male power to create categories and to assign roles and functions within them.[55]

The idea that women's sexual function is the source of their subjection explains a great deal of the reality "out there." MacKinnon recounts numerous instances of rape, battering, pornography, sexual harassment, and other oppressive sexual practices.[56] She draws on everyday speech: " 'We had sex three times' typically means that the man entered the woman three times and orgasmed three times."[57] "Sex" does not refer to the woman's experience, or to homosexual relations, or, for that matter, to the ways people can gratify desire without a penis entering a vagina. This quirk of usage may help explain the prevalence of sniggering speculation about what homosexuals "do" (isn't it sex?), not to mention the difficulties people encounter in avoiding conception (do they lack imagination?).

Women who agree on little else share a perception of sex as men's exertion of power over them. An activist in Operation Rescue says, "The idea [of abortion] is that a man can use a woman, vacuum her out, and she's ready to be used again." A NOW chapter advises feminists, "If your husband or lover is anti-choice and thinks the government has a right to control women's bodies, then control his access to your body. 'Just Say No' to more sex until all women are free to control their own lives and bodies."[58] These statements may repel, the first for its crudity and the second for its similarity to the "pussy power" rhetoric of the 1960s.[59] But consider what both statements reveal about women's lives. While the pro-choice activist is more optimistic than her adversary about the prospects for changing this reality, both women agree that sex is something men make women do. The notion of sex as an activity women choose and enjoy is missing; would a woman who likes sex deprive herself to punish her lover? The fact that women can speak this way to one another, and be understood, supports MacKinnon's thesis. MacKinnon tries to break the connection between gender difference and women's character by concentrating on the connection between difference and "power in its gendered forms."[60] If her analysis of women's subjection is correct, so is her critique of liberal rights theory. It is not wrong for women; but it is not right enough to destroy gendered power, and it is used to allow men to sustain this power.

But MacKinnon's analysis leaves out too much of women's lives. She captures the objectification, the danger, and the vulnerability, but she misses so much of the work, the demands, the domestic burdens. MacKinnon's focus on vulnerability gives short shrift to the *responsibility* women bear. Sex is not the only service women provide, or even necessarily the most important one. It's not only the lying down that oppresses but the jumping up: the expectation that one is available to meet others' needs is a crucial component of women's situation. Gendered power does not stop with sexuality.

Getting the Reader Right: Situation Theory and Its Critics

Like character jurisprudence, situation jurisprudence has serious defects and has been thoroughly criticized. Unlike character jurisprudence, situation jurisprudence has received criticism that bears little relation to its actual weaknesses and often supports it while claiming to refute it. MacKinnon's work, in particular, has been criticized at least as thoroughly as Gilligan's. MacKinnon's critics reject both her grand theory and the attack on rights theory which she derives from it. This response to her work shows that the generative effect of her theory has been different from what she intended. Instead of replacing character theory with situation theory, the critics have replaced discussion about differences between men and women with discussion of differences among women. MacKinnon's critics have confused jurisprudence with biography. They are wrong in almost everything they say, but right in what they imply.

MacKinnon's responses to these criticisms do not initiate dialogue and advance debate in the classic scholarly fashion. She does not rebut, let alone anticipate, counterarguments. Her *ad hominem et feminam* counterattacks and biographical accounts provide an easy low road out of an argument. For example, she accuses her feminist critics of "collaboration" (with all that word implies) and refers to the battered star of the porno film *Deep Throat* instead of debating the constitutionality of antipornography legislation.[61] Her refusal to rebut is unfortunate, because many of these criticisms rest on correctable misunderstanding.

MacKinnon's critics have found evidence which appears to refute her thesis in the same everyday life upon which she draws to support it. Many feminists have written in terms which make clear the personal nature of their reactions. Any argument that provokes titles like "My Mother Liked to Fuck" or "Catharine MacKinnon, May I Speak?" has hit a nerve.[62] Academics may dismiss these writers as "ranters" and their essays as irrelevant autobiography; critiques which conform to scholarly conventions may get praise for their "nuanced" approach.[63] But the autobiographers and the scholars make the same critique. The tone and context differ, but the content is similar.

The common theme of these critiques—general or personal, scholarly or autobiographical, engaged or detached—is that MacKinnon distorts reality to fit theory. Richard Posner complains that she "depicts the United States as a vast conspiracy of men to rape and terrorize women."[64] Nadine Strossen accuses her of denying women's "sexual agency" and promoting a "victim-centered view of women."[65] Carol Smart reads her construction of "male power as omnipotent" to mean that women "have no consciousness other than that which male power allows them to have."[66] Drucilla Cornell writes, "Feminine *jouissance*, with all of its disruptive force, is denied."[67] Several feminist critics insist that MacKinnon's theory is ethnocentric and/or heterocentric. Angela Harris accuses her of ignoring the effect of race on women's identity.[68] Patricia Cain and Wendy Brown accuse her of ignoring or misunderstanding lesbian sexuality.[69]

All these critics are wrong. Women need not believe in a rapist-terrorist conspiracy to know that they are *vulnerable* to male violence. For example, I need not assume that every man is a potential rapist; but for my own safety I must assume that any man may be. I need not assume that every class I teach, every audience I address, or every conference I attend includes rapists, batterers, or child support delinquents; but I know they may be there. The threat of abuse is not omnipresent, but it cannot be presumed absent.

MacKinnon neither says nor implies that all heterosexual intercourse is rape. To say that it is difficult to tell rape and intercourse apart does not mean that they are the same thing, any more than my difficulty in telling twins apart means they are the same person. MacKinnon does not deny that women can want sex with men or women. Her neglect of *jouissance* is a mistake, because *jouissance* supports her theory. "Sexuality is to feminism what work is to marxism: that which is most one's own, yet most taken away."[70] There is dressmaking, and then there is the Triangle Shirtwaist Company; there is *jouissance*, and then there is *Deep Throat*. Women's erotic capacity is part of what has been "taken away" by male appropriation of female sexuality.

This appropriation is not absolute. Some women have the freedom to learn how to give themselves pleasure, and to teach their partners how to do so. But that freedom does not enable women to decide when, where, how, and with whom. Recognition of *jouissance* would have made it harder for MacKinnon's angriest critics to assert that she denied, dismissed, ignored, or trivialized their experience. But she locates women's subordination not in their individual sexual behavior but in their assigned sexual function. She has a theory of the state, not a theory of sexuality.

Personal accounts offered in rebuttal of MacKinnon's thesis do not refute it and may even support it. Joan Nestle describes her mother, Regina, as "a working woman who liked to fuck, who believed she had the right to have a penis inside her if she liked it and who sought deeply for love but knew that was much harder to find." Nestle's critique would have been stronger if her mother had fucked only when she liked, or got to fuck whenever she felt like it, or liked it every time she did it, or had the freedom to do it without risking injury. Regina did seek out sexual partners. She also paid for her initiative, more than once, with rape and beatings. She was punished for becoming a sexual subject rather than a sexual object. But Nestle's celebration of her mother's vitality is nowhere accompanied by attention to the male violence that met it.[71]

Mary Dunlap took similar exception when she and MacKinnon spoke at a conference in 1985. Dunlap proclaimed, "I am not subordinate to any man! And I have been told by Kitty MacKinnon that women have never *not* been subordinate to men. So I stand here an exception and invite all the other women here to be an exception and stand."[72] This self-description is accurate in the sense that Dunlap, a lawyer, a professor, and a lesbian, leads a different life from those of most women. But does it follow that she never has been or will be subordinate; that no man has ever dominated her in any way; or that refusing subordination has been without cost? Not as a daughter, a student, a worker, a novice professional, or a woman competing and interacting with men? Even if Dunlap is not subordinate to men, she, like Adrienne Rich, "live[s] under the power of the fathers" and has "access to only so much of privilege or influence as the patriarchy is willing to accede to me."[73]

MacKinnon relegated her response to Dunlap to a footnote in *Feminism Unmodified*. "This statement turns a critique of a structural condition into a statement of individual inevitability, an indictment of oppression into a reason for passivity and despair. . . . And any woman's victory over sexism becomes a source of proud disidentification from the rest of her sex and proud denial of the rest of her life."[74] But MacKinnon is in no position to dismiss personal critiques; she has written again and again that theory must be derived from experience.

Suzanne Rhodenbaugh, the author of "Catharine MacKinnon, May I Speak?" writes, "She appears to be saying that, for women, much of the history of sexuality is comprised of the being *done to*, of being exploited and victimized." This, says Rhodenbaugh, "is not my experience of sexuality. . . . I have longed for it, and sought it." But her own story, which includes "having had raped, having been beaten by a husband, [and] having gone through a pregnancy against my will," would fit right into *Feminism Unmodified*. Rhodenbaugh does not praise herself, as well she might, for preserving her sexuality in the face of this violence. She is forthright about the effects of her experiences: "After the rape, I permanently interiorized fear." Yet she follows this revelation with the confusing statement that "I don't believe that experience was in any way part of my history of sexuality."[75] For Rhodenbaugh, MacKinnon is "another voice reducing us, one saying we are creatures mainly acted upon. This feels . . . like new injustice. For, if my history of sexuality includes [all that] has happened to my body and my sexual attention that I did not seek but was subjected to, if such even *characterize* my experience, then presumably as a sexual creature I'm little more than a victim."[76]

Why do critics respond so personally? And why do these critiques appeal to so many women? Dunlap and Rhodenbaugh insist that emphasis on women's victimization entails that women are only and invariably victims: that theorists like MacKinnon insult women by ignoring their agency and autonomy. In criticizing MacKinnon, Dunlap praises herself. The fact that the praise is justified does not turn autobiography into jurisprudence. In context, Dunlap's statement says, "I'm not subordinate." It implies, "If you are, there's something wrong with you, not with anybody or anything else." No structural analysis is possible, because everybody is too busy with self-analysis. Women define themselves in contrast to other women. Applied to sex, these statements are potent silencers because of what fifty years of mass-market sexology has told us about female desire. Personal accounts and professional knowledge may combine to silence women who find that their own *jouissance* has little to do with the conditions of their sexual activity.

Suzanne Rhodenbaugh's aversion to the "victim" label strikes a responsive chord. She does not hold herself responsible for her injuries, although in this time and place rape victims are often made to feel responsible.[77] She implies, rather, that to be a victim is to be something less than an autonomous actor not only in a particular situation but in general. She has a valid point here, but not about MacKinnon. Law does tend to construct and interpret women's lives so that "victim" labels adhere more easily to women than do "actor" labels. The legal response to battered women who injure or kill their abusers reinforces this point. The law of self-defense bends itself to men who violently overreact to annoyance, but not to women who retaliate against chronic violence. At the same time, the law of diminished capacity has expanded to include a "battered woman syndrome" of "learned helplessness."[78] A homeowner who shoots a trespasser is defending himself; a battered woman who kills suffers from a syndrome. Many feminists are uneasy about a jurisprudence that seems to rely on concepts of female passivity.

But the term "victim" is not always and everywhere belittling. The label has been empowering for activists like the actor Theresa Saldana, who founded Victims for Victims after a near-fatal stabbing and fought successfully to keep her attacker in prison. "Victims' rights" identifies an increasingly effective social movement. Why are things so different when the violence against women does not come from strangers?

By Rhodenbaugh's own account, she has been both victim and actor. By any reasonable definition, her history includes both what she did and what was done to her. But she insists that only her agency is characteristic. Yes, she says, I was raped, and yes, rape changed me forever, but rape is not part of my *history*: only what we do really counts, not what is done to us. To characterize her experience is to characterize her. She appears to confuse history with personality, to read situation theory as if it were character theory.

This familiar confusion helps explain why critics often accuse MacKinnon of excluding lesbians and women of color. Once again, she is read as describing women's essence rather than their situation. This misinterpretation is particularly unfortunate in Angela Harris's essay. If Harris had understood MacKinnon better, she might have focused on MacKinnon's disregard of a possible racial distinction that a notorious recent event threw into prominence. When a jury that included several black women acquitted former football star O. J. Simpson of the murder of his ex-wife in October 1995, the verdict appalled and bewildered many white feminists. It was difficult to understand how a jury could discount the combination of DNA evidence and Simpson's history of wife abuse. The verdict suggests that black women may fear public power at least as much as they fear private violence.[79] So, for that matter, may lesbians. The critics' confusion of character theory and situation theory has not only exposed MacKinnon to unjustified criticism; it may also have shielded her from valid criticism. Her failure to perceive that character and situation are different kinds of explanations allows the misinterpretation to continue.

MacKinnon may get the words right, but her words do not get the reader right. Her critics turn the question What has been done to women? into the question What are women like? If we turn situation theory into a type of character theory, we cannot discuss what has been done to women without seeming to diminish them. But how can you be diminished by the fact that somebody hurt you? If we fail to discuss what has been done to women, we leave out a huge part of reality. We limit the insights we can reach about people who do these things and about a society that lets them do it and teaches them how. Critiques of situation jurisprudence fall into the same trap as character jurisprudence: they let men and institutions off the hook while focusing women's attention on themselves. Whereas character jurisprudence threatens to trap women in gender-role expectations, critical reaction to situation jurisprudence threatens to frustrate gender-role change. Character theory has produced an ethic of burden and obligation; situation theory has been read as an insult to women.

The Situation and the Situated

Liberalism glorifies will and choice.
(*John A. Robertson*)

The (con)fusion between women's situation and women's identity pervades public discourse. For example, any negative judgments about traditional female occupations must be worded with exquisite care, lest they be misinterpreted as expressions of contempt for those who perform these tasks. This difficulty is not limited to situations involving women. Consider, for example, the virtual impossibility of opposing the Gulf War in 1991 without being challenged to affirm one's support of the troops fighting it—or the difficulty of criticizing the Vietnam War, then and now, without being accused of disrespect for those troops.[80] Another example of this confusion is the classic 1960s cartoon in which an elderly, shabbily dressed woman wonders if "war on poverty" means "they're going to shoot me." The reaction of many disabled activists to charity drives like Jerry Lewis's annual muscular dystrophy telethon is a similar phenomenon. Those who solicit money for the prevention, cure, or alleviation of a disability are accused, rightly or wrongly, of denigrating the disabled.

Why do we presume these identifications of act and actor, of situation and situated? I submit that the roots of this confusion lie in a combination of two premises embedded in conventional theory: individual responsibility and free will. The idea of individual responsibility is not always easily separable from the (similar, but not identical) notion that people are responsible for what happens to them. MacKinnon's rhetorical question—why, "when a woman spreads her legs for a camera, she is assumed to be exercising free will?"—has an easy answer: "because this is the general assumption we make about adult human acts."[81] And this assumption is not always easily separable from the assumption that we will the consequences of our acts.

The premise of responsibility has several different meanings. The simplest, clearest interpretation is the popular idea that people bring their troubles on themselves. Much contemporary conventional wisdom attributes such problems as poverty, domestic violence, and disease to the actions of those who suffer from them. The woman who advised Linda Marchiano ("Lovelace"), who was kidnaped, raped, beaten, held prisoner, hypnotized, and forced to appear in pornographic films, to "deal with whatever in herself allowed her to let this happen to her" speaks for many others, including some feminists.[82] In 1993, a feminist activist and former prostitute walked out of a roundtable at the University of Minnesota Law School because she felt the academic participants ignored her account of being exploited. They wanted to believe she chose to sell sex.[83]

This premise of agency can degenerate into a kind of magical thinking. No longer a *tabula rasa*, the human mind becomes a *tabula plena* that writes the experience of every other mind in relation to it. For example, Ann Landers published a letter whose author recounted her and her husband's struggles to find work: "[The middle class] have become part of the working poor. People with one or two degrees can no longer find positions that pay well enough to support a family." Although both statistical evidence and expert opinion support this assertion, Landers suggested to the writer, "Your negative attitude may have something to do with all the bad luck you've been experiencing."[84]

Assertions like these are empirical statements (true or false) about cause and effect. A person can be responsible for something if and only if there is "a causal connection between his act and the outcome or, if inaction is the basis of his possible responsibility, it must be the case that he might have so acted that the outcome would have been different." "If you hadn't gone to the frat party in the first place, it wouldn't have happened" is a common example of an attribution of responsibility that satisfies this "minimum condition."[85] In other situations, the minimum condition holds generally, but not universally. For instance, the link between lung cancer and smoking is an established fact, although nonsmokers can get lung cancer. The alleged link between silicone breast implants and devastating illnesses may never be established; but the case against the manufacturers presumes the plaintiffs would not be ill without their choice to have this elective surgery.

But these causal connections do not explain all the ways in which society attributes responsibility. The consumers of nicotine get far more negative input from the government than do the corporations that sell known carcinogens. A book reviewer wonders why "women like Colleen Swanson, an attractive, petite woman who wore a size 32-B bra, feel so bad about themselves that they are willing to do anything to achieve some unattainable ideal," not why companies like the Dow Corning Corporation marketed the inadequately tested implants that Swanson received.[86] We could invoke capitalism as the explanation for these skewed attributions of responsibility; after all, who questions the profit motive? But these attributions are not limited to market contexts, as the "frat party" example shows, as does popular psychology's fascination with "why so many women 'choose' abusive men, not why there are so many abusive men to choose from."[87]

Some familiar allegations about people's responsibility for their situations have no empirical support whatsoever. Links between cancer and anger, stress, sexual repression, or negative attitudes have never been verified; nevertheless, they remain staples of popular psychology. The responsibility thesis is obviously inapplicable to several of the situations previously mentioned; children do not cause their poverty, many Vietnam veterans were drafted, and Jerry Lewis's critics did not give themselves muscular dystrophy.[88] Why does the argument retain its appeal, in the face of overwhelming contrary evidence? The "blaming the victim" approach to social problems is a useful conservative tool. Opposing the changes that might reduce poverty, illness, and abuse is easier when individuals are held responsible for their situations. This belief may serve psychological needs as well as political agendas. A feminist philosopher who has a chronic disabling disease speculates that people who thought she had caused her illness "were all trying to believe that nothing this important is beyond our control."[89]

But we need not go to the extremes of denying that some men were forced to serve in Vietnam or asserting that people cause their disabilities in order to confuse person and situation. The premise of individual responsibility is not always an assertion about cause and effect. It has at least two other important meanings. It is an assignment: whose job is it to do what? As we saw in Chapter 1, self-preservation is assumed to be the responsibility of every adult. Everyday usage suggests that this responsibility extends to dealing with one's own disability ("physically challenged"), victimization ("why didn't she leave?"), illness, poverty, and so forth.

This individual responsibility is as integral to liberal theory as are the individual rights that feminist jurists question. The opening words of Bruce Ackerman's book *Social Justice and the Liberal State* are meant for all adults:

> So long as we live, there can be no escape from the struggle for power. Each of us must control his body and the world around it. However modest these personal claims, they are forever at risk in a world of scarce resources. Someone, somewhere, will—if given the chance—take the food that sustains or the heart that beats within. No one can afford to remain passive while others stake their claims. Nothing will be left to reward such self-restraint. Only death can purchase immunity from hostile claims to the power I seek to exercise.[90]

Robin West reads this passage as a, perhaps the, "liberal legalist phenomenological narrative."[91] Interpreting that narrative, she uses the word "autonomy" no fewer than three times in one paragraph. West has not misread Ackerman. But author and critic alike fail to mention that individual autonomy presupposes individual responsibility as well as individual rights. The latter are propounded; the former is *presumed.* We must say that protecting ourselves is our right; the idea that protecting ourselves is our responsibility is so basic that nobody needs to say it. We could ask What makes life so hard? Why are the resources scarce? Who are these "others" who stake their claims? But conventional theory does not ask these questions.

The story of Heinz's dilemma from *In a Different Voice* illustrates this point. Despite the vast amount of analysis to which the fictional Heinz, and the real Jake and Amy, have been subjected, some important questions have *not* been asked about this vignette.[92] Why does the case ask what Heinz should do, not what the druggist should do? Why do studies of moral development focus on (dis)obedience rather than on charity? Why is legalism questioned, while capitalism is assumed? The dilemma, and the responsibility, are Heinz's, not the druggist's. The case takes the druggist's behavior as a given. Individuals are responsible for preserving themselves, not for helping others. "Individuals," of course, means "men." Women are responsible for both themselves and others.

The third meaning of the premise of individual responsibility is a stance, a perspective, which can be precisely the opposite of an attribution of cause. This last meaning presupposes that a situation belongs not to whoever or whatever is causing it but to the person experiencing it. If a woman is abused, a man is in combat, or a family is poor, they own the situations. The situation of a battered woman may not be her fault in the sense of causation, but it is her fault in the sense of being her misfortune: the abuse belongs to her, not to the abuser or the society in which the abuse occurs. The term "battered woman" itself incorporates this premise; society defines the problem in terms of victims, not in terms of violent husbands and lovers. Book reviewers identify the "key question" of studies of dysfunctional families as Why do some children thrive despite early-childhood trauma?—thereby focusing attention on individuals rather than systems, victims rather than aggressors.[93] These social attributions of responsibility, which conflate situation and situated, make it easy to read statements like the following, from MacKinnon, as negative statements about women:

> Over time, women have been economically exploited, relegated to domestic slavery, forced into motherhood, sexually objectified, physically abused, used in denigrating entertainment, deprived of a voice and authentic culture, and disenfranchised and excluded from public life. Women, by contrast with comparable men, have systematically been subjected to physical insecurity; targeted for sexual denigration and violation; depersonalized and denigrated; deprived of respect, credibility, and resources; and silenced—and denied public presence, voice, and representation of their interests.[94]

All of what MacKinnon says here is true. It is not even exaggerated. But these descriptions of male dominance are read as if they were descriptions of female character. The unexamined premises of individual responsibility obscure the fact that MacKinnon is describing not women but their position in society.

Why is our culture so fixated on those who suffer rather than on those who inflict suffering? Why explain rape, domestic violence, and virtually every other human affliction with reference to situation rather than to cause? Because society condemns aggression less than it condemns weakness. The perpetrators of violence are exhibiting an extreme version of what William Galston calls the "familiar litany" of the virtues of liberal economy: "initiative, drive, determination."[95] The aggression that made Mike Tyson a boxing champion does not distinguish itself from the aggression that made him a rapist—especially since the media excused Mike Tyson the wife-beater while blaming Robin Givens for their failed marriage. Is it surprising that eighteen-year-old Desiree Washington got almost as much public censure for her imprudent visit to Tyson's hotel room as he did for his violence against her? (At professional meetings, hotel rooms are the only places that ensure privacy; wouldn't it be nice if we could presume safety?) As Galston suggests, liberal societies depend on aggression. One form this aggression takes is the exploitation of weaknesses like naïveté, imprudence, ignorance, and gullibility. Although weakness is as essential to liberal economy as aggression—if P. T. Barnum was right, you need at least one-fifth as many suckers as takers—weakness is easier to condemn even when there is no fault to find with the victims.

Women and Men, Rights and Responsibility: Asymmetrical Thinking

Like the model of moral development which Gilligan challenged, the embedded theory opposed by the feminist situation jurists incorporates an assignment of (explicit) individual rights and (implicit) individual responsibility. And these two components of theory affect women's lives in different ways. Women's freedom is a question. Women's responsibility is a fact.

The rights theory which character jurists and situation jurists criticize as hostile to women has never fully applied to them. We have already encountered the feminist argument that traditional rights theory requires the exclusion of women from the group of rights-bearing individuals. Whether or not one accepts this argument, the slightest acquaintance with liberal theory reveals that it incorporates an unresolved "woman question."[96] Liberalism has never decided whether or not its rights apply to women. The use of the generic "man," still common, can mask this question. John Stuart Mill would not have had to write a book arguing that liberalism includes women if his contemporaries had agreed that it does.[97]

What about responsibility? The world may not be as bleak and threatening a place as Bruce Ackerman paints it, but he is right on one point: men and women, we all have to protect ourselves. What differs are the ways in which society allows us to do this. Ethical standards—Emily must accommodate her parents, Heinz must choose between obedience and his wife's life, the druggist need not give medicine to the sick—grow out of these social roles. Men and (maybe) women are free; both men and women are responsible. This asymmetry applies not just to women but to at least one other group: children. People under eighteen may not vote; people under twenty-one may not drink alcohol; and the constitutional rights of minors are truncated—but if they have incomes, they pay taxes.[98] Power includes the ability to grant and withhold rights as well as responsibilities.

Feminists' failure to see conventional jurisprudence whole means that the responsibility component is accepted without question and remains embedded in their own thought. No wonder feminist jurisprudence has concentrated so exclusively on women that it has theories of women only. No wonder character theory's ethic of care can degenerate into an ethic of obligation. No wonder feminist theorists who discuss what happens to women are often accused of denigrating them. This overemphasis on individual responsibility ensures that jurisprudence that focuses exclusively on women will remain trapped in "we're different (no we're not; yes we are)" and "I'm not subordinate (what's wrong with you?)."

Feminist jurisprudence faces three important tasks. First, it must do the opposite of what conventional theory and feminist critiques have done: posit rights and question responsibility. Second, it must develop analyses that will separate situations from the people experiencing them, so we can talk about women's victimization without labeling them as victims. Finally, it must move beyond women and begin scrutinizing men and institutions.

I do not mean to suggest that feminist jurisprudence should abandon the study of women. Without feminist scholars' insistence on drawing theory from women's lives, law would still define situations as men perceive them. We would have no sexual harassment law; our rape laws would be stuck in the 1960s, when the marital exception was universal and resistance and corroboration requirements common; and the battered women's defense would not exist—among other things. But feminist theory's preoccupation with women limits our understanding of women's situation, because women neither create nor sustain their position in society.

In a New Voice: The Future of Feminist Jurisprudence

What if we had feminist psychology which studied women's expectations of others more and their feelings about themselves less? What if we had feminist ethics which studied power at least as much as obedience? What if we had feminist jurisprudence which studied the role of law in constructing and maintaining a society which makes women both vulnerable and responsible? These possibilities require a departure from the focus on women which has characterized feminist theory so far.

One concrete example of the necessary change in focus would be to separate discussion of the value of care from the association of care with women. Another improvement would be to discard the assumption that a woman must *either* accept *or* reject a female ethic in favor of letting her decide when to do care and when to do justice. A third healthy change would be to use the active voice when discussing women's experience, in order to deal with women's subjection without characterizing them as passive. Suppose Suzanne Rhodenbaugh had written, "A man raped me; a man beat me; a man had sex with me without protecting me from pregnancy." These words convey the facts without labeling the victim. If talking about victims makes us uncomfortable, let's talk about victimizers instead: not "women are raped," but "men rape women." This change from passive to active voice puts the emphasis where it belongs: on the subject, not the object.

The obvious problem with writing in this way is that it invites accusations of "male-bashing." We have trouble reading linear sentences without mentally inserting modifiers into them: not often "Only men rape women"—which is true within the conventional meaning of the word "rape"—but words like "all," "most," "sometimes," and so forth. Feminists can qualify the statements—"Well, of course not all men rape . . . ," and so forth—but to qualify is to weaken. A common grammatical confusion occurs whereby "Not all men rape" may become "All men do not rape," but those two sentences do not mean the same thing. The second statement means "No men rape," an assertion as false as its opposite. The passive voice is safer and easier partly because it avoids these complications.[99] But writing in the passive voice invites accusations of *female*-bashing. It focuses attention on women themselves and away from what is happening to them. Efforts to take seriously male aggression against women—to get people to *listen*—are frustrated by a double bind: talking about what men do is interpreted as man-hating; talking about what women suffer is interpreted as self-pitying. If accusations of antimale prejudice are the price of telling the truth and being understood, feminist scholars must be willing to pay that price.

Linear, categorical statements—"men [verb] women"—are untrue for some (most? many? a few?) men. But the real danger in these statements is not overstatement but oversimplification. Feminist scholars must write the blunt sentences, but feminist scholarship cannot stop with them. They will not answer questions like Why do men get away with violence against women? Why don't men prevent pregnancy? Why must women bear children against their will? or Where do men learn to act this way? Answering these questions requires recourse to such abstractions as "culture," "society," "institutions," and "law," and how these combine with men to subjugate women. A regrounded and refocused feminist jurisprudence can escape the traps into which feminist critiques of conventional theory have fallen.

What makes law male? The two types of feminist jurisprudence I have analyzed here help clarify law's male bias. Situation jurisprudence is a better, more generative, more accurate theory than character jurisprudence. But neither theory fully understands that the roots of law's maleness lie in men's division of life into public and private, justice and care, subject and object, rights and responsibility; and in men's assignment of women to specific spheres and duties. Situation jurisprudence perceives the sexist roots of this dichotomy, but it misses conventional theory's division between rights and responsibility; as a consequence, situation jurisprudence is misread. To understand these aspects of law, feminist theory must move beyond What are we like? to Who is doing this to us, and why? Until we devote equal attention to men, institutions, and the state, we will never understand what is male about law. Woman is not the sole proper study of womankind.

FOUR

HOW IS LAW MALE?

GENDERED METHOD AND
FEMINIST RESPONSE

ANGLO-AMERICAN law—like Latin, one of its ancestor languages—was long "spoken and written . . . with totally negligible exceptions only by males."[1] Men wrote the constitutions, enacted the laws in pursuance thereof, argued the cases challenging the laws, wrote the opinions which disposed of the cases, and criticized the opinions which settled the cases which challenged the laws which referred to the constitutions which men wrote. Law's "heavenly chorus" has sung not only "with a strong upper-class accent" but also in a low pitch.[2]

The exceptions to this generalization are no longer negligible. They include almost half the nation's law students, one-tenth of Congress, growing numbers of jurists and judges, and even two Supreme Court justices. However, an observation which Evelyn Fox Keller has made about medicine applies also to law: "Women, or any 'outsiders' for that matter, come to internalize the concerns and values of a world to which they aspire to belong."[3] Women who come to law and jurisprudence work within a male tradition. Law has been a male activity. It is now a male activity in which both men and women engage.

The idea that law is male is the core of feminist jurisprudence. The previous chapter examined different answers to the question What makes law male? But there is more to feminist jurisprudence than ideology. How we think is as significant as what we think; method is no less important than content. Some feminist jurists assert that law, derived from predominantly male ways of thinking, knowing, and living, is intrinsically destructive to women in ways independent of ideology.[4] These scholars have asked not only what makes law male but also how, and in what ways, law is male.

Feminist theory does not make a sharp distinction between arguments about content and arguments about method. The notion of gendered epistemology sometimes elides into the notion of gendered ideology. And the epistemological critique falls into the same traps the ideological critiques did: it is constricted by the conventional theory it purports to reject and only partly understands. In feminist epistemology, as in ideology, the "difference debate" threatens to crowd out more promising subjects of discourse, as theses incapable of verification are disputed endlessly.[5] The previous chapter argued that feminist jurists' incomplete understanding of the theories they criticized trapped character jurists in uncritical acceptance of traditional female obligations and frustrated situation jurists' efforts to get their arguments across. This chapter argues that similar errors have led to notions of "male" and "female" modes of knowledge and thought which display little sensitivity to context and bear little resemblance to how people actually think.

Gendered Thinking: Conventional Epistemology and Feminist Critiques

Whatever else law is, it is thought. It uses reason, a facility often viewed as inherently masculine. Some radical feminist scholars condemn reason as a tool for what Mary Daly calls patriarchy's "gang rape of minds as well as bodies."[6] While few feminists embrace this extreme position, several authors posit gender differences in modes of thought. The Psych-et-Po French feminists associate the dichotomous, oppositional nature of "male libidinal economy" with method as well as content.[7] Evelyn Fox Keller's work on philosophy of science posits gender differences in reasoning, generalizing from her contrast between the research methods of Nobel Prize winner Barbara McClintock and those of her mostly male peers. While McClintock emphasizes "letting the material speak to you," her counterparts seek to "impose an order" on the material according to the Baconian model. Keller suggests that women scientists may seek to cooperate with nature rather than to master it.[8] Carol Gilligan's emphasis on connection over separation has a similar epistemological component. The popular feminist idea of a contrast between "abstract, deductive" male reasoning and "concrete, contextualized" female reasoning has come to jurisprudence from studies like these.[9]

Joan Williams contrasts a "traditional Western epistemology" which feminists characterize as "male" with a woman-centered "new epistemology." The former consists of "a range of long-standing Western verities, some dating to the Enlightenment, and others all the way back to Plato." These verities "celebrated reason over emotion" and posited "an absolute truth accessible through rigorous logical manipulation of abstractions." The "new" feminist epistemology rejects these ideas in favor of "sensitivity to context, and . . . a faith in emotion and intuition as tools of thought."[10] These old and new epistemologies occupy positions symmetrical to those of liberal theory and any given feminist critique: they constitute a loosely defined, generally accepted standard theory and a feminist response to that theory.

While feminist epistemology's debt to character theory is obvious, situation theorists have made important intellectual contributions. Catharine MacKinnon identifies consciousness-raising as feminist methodology.[11] (Consciousness-raising groups were the small, informal women's discussion groups of the 1960s and 1970s in which women analyzed their personal experience in a feminist context.) Feminist standpoint theory emphasizes "the distinctive features of women's situation in a gender-stratified society" as sources of method.[12] These distinctive features include women's responsibility for what a sociologist calls "the world of concrete particulars."[13] Feminist epistemology is not divisible into categories like character jurisprudence and situation jurisprudence. To speak of "character epistemology" and "situation epistemology" would confuse rather than clarify. Whether women think differently from men because their genitals are contiguous rather than separate (*ecriture feminine*), because they were raised by people like them rather than unlike them (object-relations theory), or because women rank below men on the stratification scale (standpoint epistemology), many feminist scholars agree that women think differently from men.

Abstract Separation, Concrete Connection:
The Different Mind

Efforts to garner empirical evidence to support the theory of gender differences in thinking have not been lacking. Carol Gilligan's book, *In a Different Voice*, posited gender differences in moral reasoning. While Gilligan's study convinced few who were not predisposed toward her conclusions,[14] later scholars have built upon her research. The clearest and most complete formulation of a theory of female-specific method comes from a book published four years after Gilligan's. The Fund for Improvement in Post-Secondary Education (FIPSE) Education for Women's Development Project, directed by psychologist Mary Field Belenky, produced a widely acclaimed and extensively cited study of female learning.[15]

Belenky and her associates conducted extensive interviews with women students in six high schools and colleges and women clients of three social service agencies. The respondents, unlike Gilligan's, included women of different ages, incomes, and class, regional, ethnic, and educational backgrounds. *Women's Ways of Knowing* builds on Gilligan's work to argue that two distinct epistemological orientations exist. *Separate knowing* is the methodology emphasized in conventional postsecondary education. It seeks evaluative standards and analytical techniques; its "orientation is toward impersonal rules." It is hard to imagine a better description of legal reasoning. *Connected knowing* reads like Barbara McClintock's method as described by Evelyn Keller. "The orientation . . . is toward relationship";

for example, the poetry reader asks, "What is this poet trying to say to me?" The study concludes, "We believe that connected knowing comes more easily to many women than does separate knowing."[16]

Belenky does not have a theory of gender *difference*, since there is no parallel study of men. Even if there were, a single project is a weak foundation for a theory. Belenky does have a theory of knowledge, which she undermines by her dubious dichotomy; analytical, rule-based knowing connects the knower to the known as much as relationship-based knowing does. The conclusion is so qualified—how many are many?—that it is difficult to accept or reject, or even to discuss or dispute. Nevertheless, the FIPSE study has made a contribution by giving the "new epistemology" the type of concrete context feminist theorists value so highly.

Two Epistemologies

To summarize, feminist scholars' concept of the conventional theory is of a reasoned, dichotomous, oppositional, hierarchical, abstract, and deductive epistemology of separation. The feminist alternative theory is an intuitive/emotional, holistic, noninvasive, concrete, and contextualized epistemology of connection. Feminist critiques of the "old" epistemology have a powerful appeal, and make salient and crucial points. But feminist epistemology makes false claims for itself. It commits some of the same errors it finds in "male" epistemology. The "new" epistemology ignores the social and political context in which thinking and knowing take place. Moreover, in legal method at least, the distinctions between "male" and "female" break down in practice.

Gender Difference and Gendered Power

The overwhelming maleness of law's history lends credence to the assertion that legal reasoning is hostile to women's ways of knowing. So does the powerful emotional resonance that works like Gilligan's, Keller's, and Belenky's have had for female scholars. The law professor who credited *In a Different Voice* with helping her understand "at a new level why I felt so uncomfortable in law school" is not alone. Catharine MacKinnon observes that women lawyers "go dead in the eyes like ghetto children, unlike the men, who come out of law school glowing in the dark." A recent study of law students at the University of Pennsylvania found "there is indeed a gendered academic experience." The research showed that "women and men begin Penn Law School with equally stellar credentials. Holding incoming statistics constant, however, women graduate from the Law School with significantly less distinguished professional credentials."[17] The Socratic method of the law school classroom, in which the instructor refutes everything the student says, is an ordeal for many women students.[18] A student at Harvard Law School, where this method originated, resorts to the same metaphor Mary Daly used: "When I get called on, I really think about rape. It's sudden. You're exposed. You can't move. You can't say no. And there's this man who's in control, telling you exactly what to do."[19] For feminist scholars, it is an easy step from these observations to the idea that law, rather like football, requires skills at which men surpass women.

Efforts to support this "football hypothesis" from personal experience confront at least two obstacles. Any familiarity with legal education or the sociology of the professions will suggest that power relationships are basic to apprentices' feelings of alienation.[20] The knowledge, skills, and outlooks that seniors possess and juniors lack are important components of that power. Legal reasoning does not come naturally to anyone. Men do not like law school, either, or find it easy; a male classmate of the student who talked about rape said, "I think about that class and I get ill."[21] Being a woman is one way not to fit in, but the gender differences in professional socialization appear to mean not that women are uniquely miserable but that men and women are miserable in different ways. The argument that law is an activity designed around "male" abilities ignores women's mastery of the discipline. No longer "tokens" or "woman worthies," women are approaching equality in law school enrollment, as they are in other graduate and professional programs such as medicine. It is intriguing to speculate about how women would perform if they did not feel uncomfortable.

Rejecting the football hypothesis is not a denial that women professionals may confront special difficulties as women. There are many ways in which power and gender can combine to make a lawyer feel like an outsider in her profession, whether or not law is geared to her abilities. She might not be welcome in it; or she might enter it with personal burdens that impede her progress; or discouragement might undermine her self-esteem. Evidence exists to support all three of these possibilities. The Penn study reports that the sexist behavior of peers and professors makes the law school "a hostile learning environment for a disproportionate number of its female students."[22] Robin West's trenchant observation that "women suffer more than men" applies to the legal profession as much as it does anywhere else.[23] The women may be afraid (because of vulnerability to violence), hungry (because of poverty or dieting), or tired (because of domestic responsibilities)—if not all three. And an American Association of University Women study, aptly entitled *How Schools Shortchange Girls*, documents the ways female intellectual development is thwarted from early childhood on.[24]

All of the foregoing explanations are rooted in facts which can be studied. None of these explanations require us to accept the highly problematic notion of intellectual gender differences. Feminist epistemology, like all feminist theory, must be as attentive to the (documented) effects of people's position in society as to the (theorized) effects of body and mind.

The "rape" metaphor expresses a feeling that many women will recognize from their own dealings with men, both public and private. Consider, for example, the following statements: "Name one time when I ————," followed by, "once is not 'always' "; or, "You're contradicting yourself if you demand *both* equality of opportunity *and* maternity leaves"; or, "I challenge you to find support for *Roe v. Wade* in the text of the Constitution, the intent of the framers, or any constitutional doctrine. Go on, convince me." Suppose we encountered analogous statements in a novel where the author expects the reader to figure out which character is speaking. Would any reader have trouble guessing whether the speaker was male or female? The technique is familiar: A uses reason to "set a trap" for B. Once B is trapped, A is free to ignore B's demands, grievances, or feelings (in personal relationships) or is reconfirmed in superior status relative to A (in the classroom).

A similar process is at work in the Mnookin and Kornhauser article quoted in Chapter 2. "Economic analysis," the authors write, "suggests that a parent may, over some range, trade custodial rights for money. . . . Most parents would prefer to see the child a bit less and be able to give the child better housing, more food, more education, better health care, and some luxuries."[25] Most parents faced with this choice are mothers, whose income is usually lower than that of their children's fathers and who usually have been their children's primary caregivers. The rational-choice model the essay applies to parental behavior is based on "public" and traditionally male activities, not on observations of mothers and children. The authors make judgments about women's behavior with a theory drawn from men's experience. The article sets a trap for mothers. "Rape" does not seem an exaggerated metaphor to describe this intellectual imperialism.

But is it law and reason which oppress? Intellectual trap-setting does not threaten us when students (or children, who excel at it) try it. Even when they set logical traps for us, they cannot make us change our behavior to accommodate their wishes. The problem with reason when used by men against women in the preceding examples is twofold. First, the men have the power to refuse to change their behavior, whether the context is personal or public. Second, the men have preset the agenda; theory and doctrine have emerged from the priorities which men have chosen in activities which they have monopolized. It is the uses to which reasoning is put, not the reasoning itself, which is coercive. What makes reason threatening is its use by people with power over us. Emotion, used in the same way, is an equally powerful instrument of oppression.

Gendered power consists not only in the use of "men's" knowledge as an instrument of male supremacy but also in the creation of "women's" knowledge. Several critiques of character theory argue that male supremacist society forces the "ethic of care" on women so that men are free to pursue an "ethic of justice." I suggested earlier that if this interpretation is correct, the ethic men have reserved for themselves may be preferable to the ethic they assign to women.[26] The dichotomy between "male" and "female" epistemology invites a similar conclusion.

Dorothy Smith has suggested that the tasks society assigns to women require certain kinds of thought:

> Under the traditional gender regime, providing for a man's liberation . . . is a woman who keeps house for him, bears and cares for his children, washes his clothes, looks after him when he is sick, and generally provides for the logistics of his bodily existence.
>
> Women's work in and around professional and managerial settings performs analogous functions. Women's work mediates between the abstracted and conceptual and the material form in which it must travel to communicate. Women do the clerical work, the word processing, the interviewing for the survey; they take messages, handle mail, make appointments, and care for patients. At almost every point women mediate for men at work the relationship between the conceptual mode of action and the actual concrete forms in which it is and must be realized, and the actual material conditions upon which it depends. . . . The more successful women are in mediating the world of concrete particulars so that *men do not have to* become engaged with (and therefore conscious of) that world as a condition to their abstract activities, the more complete men's absorption in it and the more effective its authority.[27]

If Smith is right—and her facts are hard to dispute—women's thinking is concrete, contextual, and connected because it must be. "Women's ways of knowing," like their "ethics of care," come from things women have had to do to meet their basic needs. The italicized phrase in the quotation contains a huge implicit concession. If men need not deal with concrete particulars, men have the privilege to choose what they will do. Men have access to the abstract; women, so to speak, are stuck in the concrete. Even women who make it into the professional world of the abstract may be stuck with concrete particulars just as they are stuck with nurturing duties. Women doctors, for example, report that nurses expect them, but not men doctors, to do their own domestic and clerical work; while these expectations may increase equality among women, they decrease equality between the sexes.[28]

If people with the privilege to choose prefer the abstract to the concrete, intellectual work over maintenance work, thought over feeling, logic over intuition—then maybe the traditional male activities are intrinsically more rewarding than their female counterparts.[29] Maybe Plato, Aristotle, John Locke, and Hannah Arendt were correct on that specific point. And if they were, the feminist goal must be not to privilege woman's different perspective but to share the different kinds of work from which the different perspectives arise.

Any viable intellectual method needs both the abstract and concrete components. The physician who is unaware that the patient can't get to the clinic, the experimenter who doesn't know that the survey respondents have difficulty reading the questionnaire, or the author whose manuscript will weigh ten pounds in paperback are at a disadvantage in the practice of their professions. They must either rely on nurses, secretaries, assistants, and editors or deal with the practical problems of their trades. The concrete work is no less noble, no less important, no less worthy than the abstract work. Feminists can and must insist that "concrete particulars" get equal respect with "abstract activities." But sexual equality lies in women's breaking up the male monopoly on the abstract and giving up the female monopoly on the concrete. Feminist epistemology, like feminist ethics, must start with women; but it must also move from the specifically female to the generally human.

Old/New?/Male/Female? The Great Dichotomy

To conclude either that distinctively female ways of knowing exist or that existing intellectual enterprises are hostile to them, therefore, is to ignore the role of gendered power. Any observable differences between male and female epistemological orientations can be better explained by power relationships than by gender-linked attributes. The idea that conventional modes of thought are male-biased has been discredited. But feminist epistemology itself remains to be examined. Is it as original, and as female, as it claims to be? How valid are its distinctions between epistemological orientations, apart from the question of whether these orientations can be linked to gender?

The "new epistemology" may be new compared with Plato, but it antedates feminism. Joan Williams has shown that the critique of traditional epistemology "has been largely developed by men," including Friedrich Nietzsche, Ludwig Wittgenstein, and the American pragmatists.[30] (Williams might have added the legal realists, who maintained that reasoned arguments often justify positions reached emotionally or viscerally.)[31] The same is true of the association between the old and new epistemologies and gender differences. A decade before Gilligan, Philip Slater characterized "rationalism," which he defined as "the inability to perceive wholes," as one of the "disconnector virtues" associated with men. He contrasted this kind of "icy pathology" with the warmth, nurturance, and awareness of "humanity's embeddedness in a larger organic system" associated with women.[32] Feminist epistemology provides neither an original critique of conventional epistemology nor any original method.

A consistent theme in feminist scholarship is that conventional method overemphasizes dichotomization; it divides whatever it studies into sets of opposed and mutually exclusive pairs. Every teacher knows that classification is an indispensable pedagogical tool. Showing what something is not helps to clarify what it is. But the heuristic utility of classification does not explain why distinguishing and discriminating have acquired so much more status in scholarship than have relating and synthesizing. All too often, drawing attention to differences is praised as "nuanced" or "sophisticated"; drawing attention to similarities is disparaged as "lumping together."

Another problem with dichotomous reasoning is the ease with which opposed pairs can be reified. Ideas like "reason" and "emotion," "separation" and "connection," "abstract" and "concrete" start out in the mind and come to stand for something assumed to exist outside it, like "the head" and "the heart." Oppositional reasoning can exaggerate the differences and discount the similarities between the things being opposed. It can oversimplify the complex, making what is multifaceted appear bifurcated. As Slater implies, oppositional reasoning can make the whole difficult to perceive. As Derrida suggests, a dichotomy may inevitably be also a hierarchy in which the first term of an opposed pair is privileged over the second.[33] Any or all of these criticisms of dichotomous reasoning may be valid. But I could have conveyed the sense of that critique by drawing two columns, labeling them "conventional epistemology" and "feminist epistemology," and listing the appropriate adjectives under each heading. This is a dichotomization.

Feminist epistemology does something it criticizes conventional epistemology for doing. Gilligan, for example, finds conventional oppositional thinking in the story of Heinz's dilemma. He must either steal the drug or let his wife die. Amy's solution transcends the dichotomy; her reasoning substitutes connection for the separation the story implies. In questioning the dichotomization built into conventional moral philosophy, Gilligan has built in a dichotomy between men's and women's reasoning. Similarly, Irigaray describes women's psyche in opposition to men's, Keller defines a woman scientist's research methods by contrasting them with prevailing scientific conventions, and Smith juxtaposes concrete particulars against abstract generalities. As long as there are two sexes, dichotomy is built into gender theory. But feminists' critique of oppositional reasoning as male-biased loses credibility if they do it themselves. In general, feminist theory is aware of the inherent dangers of oppositional reasoning. But, in particular, feminist theorists have proved as vulnerable to these dangers as any other theorists.

Consider, for example, the dichotomy between abstract thought and concrete experience so popular in feminist writing. A point I made in Chapter 2 with respect to psychoanalytic theory is true for theory in general, feminist or not.[34] Facts do not interpret themselves. While we claim to derive theory from experience, the human mind cannot make sense of experience without some sort of theory, however rudimentary. Catharine MacKinnon's discussion of "the centrality of sexuality" in feminist theory illustrates the dangers of overreliance on this particular dichotomy. She asserts that this aspect of theory "emerges not from Freudian conceptions, not from Lacanian roots, but from consciousness raising and other feminist practice on diverse issues."[35] The dichotomy implied here between theory and practice is generally false and specifically ahistorical. Theory was prior to consciousness-raising. Guidelines for "CR" groups included topics like "Sex objects—do you feel like one?" and directives like "Discover that your personal problem is not only yours."[36] The feminist theory we have now is more complex and sophisticated than the theory which guided consciousness-raising, but it is misleading to say that theory comes from practice; they reinforce each other.[37]

The tangible costs of this oppositional reasoning become apparent in Part II of this book, which deals with particular legal issues. Chapters 6 and 7 examine, respectively, feminist critiques of conventional rights theory as it relates to reproductive choice and scholarly defenses of fetal protection policies which deny conventional rights to women. These works oppose rights and needs, rights and relationships, and rights and support as if these things were, indeed, mutually exclusive.[38] The insight that negative rights without positive rights can be what MacKinnon calls injuries got up as gifts leads to an unjustified suspicion of negative rights as inherently biased against women's needs.[39] And this confusion, I argue, makes attractive what are in fact profoundly sexist arguments against reproductive freedom and for fetal protection.

Epistemology in Theory and Practice: A Feminist Perspective on Constitutional Interpretation

So far, I have concentrated on feminist critiques of conventional epistemology rather than on the intellectual activities in which men and women engage. I have not yet looked at law to find out how it is male, or at activities identified with women to discover how they are not male. When we turn from theories about decision making to actual decisions, the distinctions between "male" and "female" epistemologies blur. Dichotomies which seem plausible in theory tend to collapse in practice.

Law is a type of thinking. A thinker "engages in a discipline. She asks certain questions ... rather than others; she establishes criteria for the truth, adequacy, and relevance of proposed answers; and she cares about the findings she makes and can act on."[40] This description comes from Sara Ruddick's analysis of *maternal* thinking. Constitutional interpretation has something in common with an activity in which women have always engaged.

Ruddick asserts that reason is a tool which women use to realize their goals in child care and child rearing, activities which are so typically female that everyone knows what we mean when we label them "mothering." Asking questions, establishing criteria by which to assess answers, and acting on findings are intellectual activities. Maternal thinking does not drive out feeling. Excluding emotion in favor of thought is unlikely to constitute one of the "characteristic errors" of the discipline in which the mother engages.[41] The point is, rather, that this activity, commonly seen as an expression of emotional "femininity," is also an intellectual activity. In mothering—of all places!—the dichotomies which feminist theorists love do not hold.

If a "female" activity incorporates certain skills thought of as masculine, could a "male" activity incorporate elements defined as feminine? This is a huge question, impossible to answer about a subject as vast as "the law." The scholar must identify a particular subcategory of law to deal with. I have picked the type of legal reasoning I know most about: constitutional interpretation. I apply to constitutional law some of the arguments developed in feminist critiques of conventional scholarship. In order to separate embedded, implicit sexism from overt, explicit sexism, I have chosen cases which do not present questions of sexual equality.[42]

Primary and secondary sources on constitutional interpretation suggest that it is not only or simply abstract, rational, logical, or oppositional; it combines reason and emotion, abstraction and concretion, separation and connection. Constitutional law is not male-biased in its method. However, certain modes of interpretation reinforce the male dominance that has characterized this discipline. I suggest ways to re-create constitutional theory so that it can be part of a woman-centered jurisprudence.

Constitutional Thinking

Constitutional interpretation is a type of legal reasoning. Characterizations of legal reasoning include Oliver Wendell Holmes's "the processes of analogy, discrimination, and deduction" and Edward Levi's "reasoning by example."[43] According to Lief Carter, "Legal reasoning describes how a legal opinion combines . . . the facts established at trial, the rules that bear on the case, social background facts, and widely shared values."[44] Katharine Bartlett asserts that legal reasoning "unfolds, not in a linear, sequential, or strictly logical manner, but rather in a pragmatic and interactive manner. Facts determine which rules are appropriate, and rules determine which facts are relevant."[45]

What questions, criteria, and rules distinguish constitutional interpretation from other modes of intellectual activity? One way of illustrating this field's particular standards and distinctions is to examine concrete examples of doctrine in the making. I have selected two cases which combine emotional salience with innovative constitutional claims. *DeShaney v. Winnebago County Department of Social Services* rejected the due process claims of a boy whose father beat him nearly to death.[46] *Cruzan v. Missouri Department of Health* upheld the state's power to require continuing treatment for a comatose woman.[47]

The story of Joshua DeShaney and the Department of Social Services is grimly familiar. Melody and Randy DeShaney were divorced in 1980, when Joshua was a year old. The couple agreed that Randy would get custody. Within two years, Randy had moved with Joshua from Wyoming to Neenah, Wisconsin, married again, and separated from his second wife. She initiated DSS's first investigation in January 1982, when she left Randy and filed a complaint with the agency. DSS intervened; Randy denied; and the investigation was dropped.

DSS next heard about Joshua a year later, when he was hospitalized. His doctor suspected abuse and contacted the agency, as state law required. A judge awarded the hospital temporary custody of the boy, but an ad hoc "Child Protection Team" found insufficient evidence to justify permanent removal from the home. Randy got his son back when he agreed to get counseling and put Joshua in a preschool program. Joshua never got to school; but within a month he was back in the emergency room and DSS was back on the case. A social worker, Ann Kemmeter, made monthly visits to the home for the next six months. The case records indicate that she continued to suspect abuse, but they do not explain why DSS did not intervene more aggressively. Kemmeter tried to see Joshua twice more after DSS received a third report from the hospital in November 1983, but both times Randy and his live-in girlfriend informed her that Joshua was too ill to see her.[48]

Kemmeter told Melody DeShaney later, "I just knew the phone would ring someday and Joshua would be dead."[49] But no one from DSS made any effort to contact Joshua's mother in Wyoming until March 1984, when she learned that her son was in a coma as a result of a beating by Randy. Joshua remains severely retarded and will have to spend the rest of his life in an institution. Randy went to prison. Melody sued DSS, alleging that the agency's failure to remove Joshua from his father's custody deprived him of due process of law.

The Supreme Court had never ruled that the Fourteenth Amendment imposes a positive duty on the state to protect a person not in its custody, and it refused to do so now. The justices rejected Melody's claim by a vote of six to three. There were at least two ways the Court could have upheld the claim without creating such a general duty. First, the Court could have adopted the argument in Justice Brennan's dissent: that the state's assignment to DSS of responsibility for dealing with child abuse "effectively confined Joshua DeShaney within the walls of Randy DeShaney's home until such time as DSS took action to remove him."[50] Second, the Court could have limited the positive duty to the protection of children, who are traditionally wards of the state. Neither of these rulings would have demanded a choice between reason and emotion, between natural engagement and acquired detachment.

But the Court did choose, in a way that Plato, Freud, or contemporary feminist theory could explain. Chief Justice Rehnquist's majority opinion declared, "Judges and lawyers, like other humans, are moved by natural sympathy. . . . But before yielding to that impulse, it is well to remember once again that the harm was inflicted not by the State of Wisconsin, but by Joshua's father."[51] Justice Blackmun, dissenting, found the majority's "sterile formalism" out of place in a Fourteenth Amendment case. "Poor Joshua! Victim of repeated attacks by an irresponsible, bullying, cowardly, and intemperate father, and abandoned by respondents who placed him in a dangerous predicament and who knew or learned what was going on, and yet did essentially nothing."[52]

Cruzan asked the Court to decide whether the parents of a thirty-two-year-old woman had the right to decide to discontinue life-sustaining treatment for her. Nancy Cruzan had been in a "persistent vegetative state," kept alive by tube feedings, since an automobile accident in 1983. Before her accident, she had once told friends that she would not want to be kept alive in such a condition. But, when Lester and Joyce Cruzan asked the hospital to stop feeding her, administrators refused to grant this request without court approval. A trial court agreed with the parents, but the Missouri Supreme Court reversed the ruling. The Cruzans obtained certiorari from the United States Supreme Court, which heard oral argument on 6 December 1989.

While Robert Presson, assistant attorney general of Missouri, was addressing the Court, Justice Blackmun asked: "Have you ever seen a person in a persistent vegetative state?" "I have seen Nancy Cruzan herself," Mr. Presson responded. This was obviously not the answer that Mr. Blackmun expected. "You have seen Nancy? Have you seen any others?" he asked.[53]

In June 1990, the Court ruled that the Fourteenth Amendment protects a person's right to refuse life-sustaining treatment through such means as a "living will," but it upheld the state's power to require continuing treatment for Cruzan. The five-justice majority on the second point (a group which did not include Justice Blackmun) distanced themselves, implicitly or explicitly, from Nancy Cruzan. Chief Justice Rehnquist's opinion for the Court said, "The question is simply and starkly whether the United States Constitution prohibits Missouri from choosing the rule of decision which it did." Justice O'Connor's concurring opinion pointed out that the *Cruzan* decision did not resolve this "difficult and sensitive problem. Today we decide only that one state's solution does not violate the Constitution." Justice Scalia showed slightly more awareness of the quandary: "The various opinions in this case portray quite clearly the difficult, indeed agonizing, questions. . . . What I have said above is not meant to suggest that I would think it desirable, if we were sure that Nancy Cruzan wanted to die, to keep her alive by the means at issue here. I assert only that the Constitution has nothing to say about the subject."[54]

What is relevant? What the Constitution provides, what Missouri did, and the reliability of the evidence of Nancy Cruzan's intentions. What is irrelevant? Nancy Cruzan's condition, her parents' feelings, and their relationship with her. The Court majority took pains to separate its decision from the concrete situation which produced the case. This rejection of the emotional, the concrete, the relational, and the personal in favor of the rational, the abstract, the detached, and the generalizable is a common feature of legal thinking.

Legal Feeling

The priorities of *DeShaney* and *Cruzan*—thought over feeling, abstract over concrete, general over particular—have also been described as common features of *male* thinking.[55] But analysis—that is, using one's reason to examine one's emotional response to legal decisions and feminist critiques of them—defeats this implied dichotomy. Everyday experience, in constitutional interpretation as elsewhere, contradicts the idea that reason is nonfemale or emotion is nonmale. Traditionally female activities include thinking, and traditionally male activities include feeling—whether or not these faculties are recognized as such in the contexts in which they appear.

The separation between thought and feeling represented by *Cruzan* has often been a goal for constitutional interpreters. The same Justice Blackmun who sought to combine reason and emotion during oral argument in *Cruzan* also wrote that judges "should not allow our personal preferences as to the wisdom of legislative and congressional action, or our distaste for such action, to guide our judicial decisions in cases such as these."[56] If

Blackmun had substituted "dictate" for "guide" in that last sentence, few readers would have any trouble agreeing with him. I do not mean to suggest that what the justices should have done was to arrange a trip to a Washington hospital, spend a day at the bedside of a patient in a condition similar to Nancy Cruzan's, and vote solely on the basis of the emotions this experience evoked. But contact with such a patient might have guided and improved the judicial search through the texts for the relevant principles. Feelings serve a purpose, and we ignore them at our peril.

What is troubling about *DeShaney* and *Cruzan* is not the justices' refusal to lead with their feelings but their apparent insistence on making a decision in isolation from feeling and experience. Abe Fortas's remark about his argument before the Supreme Court in *Gideon v. Wainwright* is apposite: "What I'd like to have said was, 'Let's not talk, let's go down and watch one of these fellows try to defend himself.' "[57] If the integration of reason and emotion is essentially female, then women have much to bring to constitutional interpretation.

The difficulty with that statement is its implication that emotion is not already there. This implication is false. More than a few examples exist of opinions which partake of the emotional, the individual, and the concrete. Justice Brennan's dissent in *Cruzan*, for example, pointed out that "Nancy Cruzan has dwelt in that twilight zone for six years. She is oblivious to her surroundings and will remain so."[58] Or recall Felix Frankfurter's statement in *Rochin v. California*: "This is conduct that shocks the conscience" compared with Hugo Black's and William Douglas's insistence on literal readings of the Fourth and Fifth Amendments.[59] Between *Rochin* and *Cruzan* lie numerous examples of constitutional feeling, some of them not necessarily recognized as such by their authors.

One area in which judges often prefer to emote rather than to think is in cases concerning the family, especially the relationship of parents and children. The series of cases involving parental notification or consent before a minor's abortion contain examples of an idealized, uncritical view of family relationships. But an even clearer example comes from two 1979 cases which upheld a parent's right to request that a minor child be committed to a state institution. One of the institutionalized children in *Parham v. J.R.* was a six-year-old boy whose mother and stepfather "were unable to control [him] to their satisfaction." They got him admitted to a Georgia institution and eventually relinquished custody of him.[60] The plaintiffs in the companion case, *Secretary of Public Welfare v. Institutionalized Juveniles*, included children committed for such offenses as "making weird noises, refusing to do work, and talking back to teachers."[61]

Some detached, rational, typically "masculine" analysis of these facts would seem to require the thinker to question the relevance to these cases of conventional generalizations about parent-child relationships. But Chief

Justice Burger, writing for the majority, based his ruling on such traditional pieties as "Natural bonds of affection lead parents to act in the best interests of their children."[62] (So *Parham*, a case I contrast with *DeShaney*, has something in common with it after all.) The commitment decisions rest on an idealized concept of the family which does not hold up in reality—especially not the reality of any of these cases, which arise only when the traditional bonds between parents and children break down.

Not even William Rehnquist, who professed disciplined detachment in *DeShaney* and *Cruzan*, is immune from emotion on the job. A few months after *DeShaney*, he dissented in *Texas v. Johnson*. Rehnquist countered the Court's ruling that a state law forbidding the "desecration of venerated objects" violated the First Amendment with an opinion that quoted "The Star-Spangled Banner," "Rally Round the Flag, Boys," and the entire text of John Greenleaf Whittier's poem "Barbara Frietchie." Rehnquist waxed eloquent on the "almost mystical reverence" which "millions and millions of Americans" feel for the flag. "The uniquely deep awe and respect for our flag felt by virtually all of us are bundled off under the rubric of 'designated symbols.' "[63]

A woman scholar's argument that emotional factors have a legitimate place in court decisions may appear to reinforce the "women's ways of knowing" I have sought to dislodge. I am mindful of this irony. But opinions like those in *Rochin*, *Parham*, and *Johnson* seriously weaken any claim that constitutional interpretation excludes emotional reaction in favor of reasoning. Judges invoke emotions when this ploy strengthens their position, as Rehnquist does in *Johnson*, and renounce emotions when this stance is useful, as Rehnquist does in *DeShaney*. Constitutional interpretation does not maintain, in practice, a dichotomy between reason and emotion, between theory and experience, between the general and the individual. To reject reason as somehow "antifemale" (or emotion as "antimale") is to assume oppositions where none need exist. The fact that, at least since Plato's *Republic*, people have constructed theories which organize the psyche in this oppositional way does not prove that the psyche so organizes itself, or that mental activity separates itself into these kinds of divisions. A feminist approach to constitutional law may perform the valuable service of discrediting those traditional dichotomies.

Legal Doing

Law is more than an academic discipline; it is also a manifestation of power. While "constitutional interpretation" can refer to abstract textual exegesis, the term more often means case adjudication or theorizing prompted by such adjudication.[64] This kind of interpretation is a political activity, taking place in a context which has its own rules, as important as the conventions of scholarship. A feminist approach to constitutional interpretation must deal with its political as well as its intellectual meaning.

Justice Scalia's conclusion in *Cruzan* that "the Constitution has nothing to say about the subject" of the right to die arose not only from his reading of text and precedent but also from his conviction that "the Federal courts have no business in this field."[65] Scalia was invoking a theme which pervades the literature on constitutional interpretation: the need for judicial self-restraint. The judge is admonished to forswear "a jurisprudence of idiosyncrasy" in favor of "self-conscious renunciation of power."[66] Though these quotations come from judicial conservatives, the concern for judicial restraint has not been theirs alone. Jurists at all points on the ideological spectrum have insisted that judges do not constitute a "super-legislature" but must defer in ambiguous cases to public officials whose duty it is to enact and enforce law and who are elected by and directly accountable to the people.[67]

Not all constitutionalists agree that "the countermajoritarian difficulty" requires judges to practice restraint; we can as plausibly infer from the presence of a written constitution and of an appointed judiciary that majority rule is not the sole or primary organizing principle of American government.[68] Nor has every jurist who preached self-restraint, consistently practiced it.[69] But deliberate refusal of power is one of the available rules that guides constitutional adjudication. The judge must hold back; must give others' desires priority over his or her own; must assume a secondary, if not a subordinate, role.[70]

This emphasis on "deference" and "renunciation of power" evokes demands which have been and continue to be made of women. The "feminine" role has historically involved a considerable amount of deferring to others. Now, obviously, a judge is not going to act like a woman in a subordinate relationship to a man. But something is going on in this concept of the judicial role which is similar to certain concepts of women's roles. We can think of other public and traditionally male roles in which this kind of self-subordination to the interests of others plays a part: lawyers in relation to their clients, for instance. And, if the practice of judicial self-restraint is sometimes more apparent than real, that gap between appearance and reality hardly distinguishes the judicial from the "feminine" role.

Another aspect of the political context in which constitutional interpretation takes place is appellate judges' need to convince other people of the validity of their position. Frankfurter's "shocks the conscience" language in *Rochin*, for example, may have been at least as much a product of his search for a majority as of any shared judicial emotion. Studies of "judicial strategy," of particular judicial roles, and of specific instances of consensus-building have shown that a classic description of presidential power applies as well to appellate judges: theirs is "the power to persuade."[71] This characterization may hold even more strongly for the judge than for the president, because judges have little recourse to coercion if persuasion fails.

Analyses of judicial decision making which rely on biographical material suggest that successful persuasion appeals to a judge's feelings, to abstractions like collegiality, loyalty, or patriotism, or to a judge's ego and vanity, at least as often as it appeals to the intellect. We can appreciate this point by examining two classic examples of successful judicial persuasion: Felix Frankfurter's attempt to secure a unanimous vote in *Hirabayashi v. United States* in 1943 and Earl Warren's similar accomplishment in the first *Brown v. Board of Education* case in the 1953–54 term.[72]

The initial vote on *Hirabayashi* was eight to one to uphold the curfew imposed by the military on all West Coast residents of Japanese descent. Frankfurter's first effort to win over Frank Murphy invoked his colleague's "desire to do all that is humanly possible to maintain and enhance the *corporate* reputation of the Court." When this appeal to loyalty failed, Frankfurter touched the nerve of Murphy's intellectual insecurities and appealed to his patriotism (in wartime). He wrote a memorandum mentioning (but not specifying) the dissent's "internal contradictions," and he characterized the dissent as an accusation that "everybody is out of step except Johnny," and that the majority was "playing into the hands of the enemy."[73] The dissent became a concurrence.

Warren's quest for unanimity in *Brown* may have gotten some silent help from Frankfurter. The published accounts contain no record of Frankfurter pressing an intellectual advantage in the way he often did or challenging Warren's implication in conference that a vote to uphold segregation was a vote for racism. Warren himself won some goodwill by personally delivering his draft opinion to Justice Robert Jackson in the hospital. With Stanley Reed, the final holdout, Warren appealed to unity and loyalty as Frankfurter had done a decade before: "Stan, you're all by yourself in this now. You've got to decide whether it's really the best thing for the country."[74] The behaviors which Frankfurter and Warren displayed—emotional appeals, personal favors, flattery, and knowing when to be quiet—involve social skills conventionally associated with "femininity." If this kind of analysis were extended to other areas of human activity, we might discover that dichotomies like "masculine"and "feminine" are misleading when used to describe activities: that most human tasks combine skills across gender stereotypes.

Excessive reliance on dichotomization is not the only error which feminists have imitated from the conventional epistemology they criticize. Although feminist epistemology perceives female thinking as concrete and contextual, feminist epistemologists have emphasized the kind of abstract theorizing they associate with male thought at the expense of attention to the concrete context of intellectual activity in building their theories.

This exploration has challenged the notion that men have constructed law the way they have constructed many sports: as an activity whose practices and procedures reward male abilities. Men's historic monopoly on constitutional interpretation has not turned the enterprise into something men can do better than women can. But many women find law a hostile or indifferent habitat, a place where their needs and desires are ignored, trivialized, discounted, or brutalized, a country whose language is difficult for them to learn. While this chapter has rejected gender difference as an explanation of law's maleness, we have yet to account for a legal system that "offers extensive protection to the right to bear arms or to sell violent pornography, but not to control over our reproductive lives."[75]

Constitutional Interpreting

Undergraduate constitutional law texts often include a section on "modes of," "methods of," "techniques of," or "approaches to" constitutional interpretation.[76] These essays convey the message that there are several different ways to "do" constitutional interpretation: the interpreter has various sources available as guides to adjudication. These guides include the constitutional text; the intent of the framers; precedent; existing constitutional doctrine; logic; and the effort to adapt constitutional purposes to changing conditions, which has been labeled the "living Constitution" approach.[77]

None of these approaches necessarily excludes any others. The interpreter can combine a search for original meaning, a textual analysis of the relevant clause or clauses, and an effort to make interpretation responsive to change. The results of such syntheses have been called "purposive analysis," "teleological," "giving effect to fundamental values," "identify[ing] the Constitution's ends or purposes," or "construing the document in terms of constitutional aspirations."[78] But advocates of at least two familiar methods have argued for their primacy. For Hugo Black, textual analysis became a search for binding, absolute, literal meaning.[79] More recently, the search for the "intent of the framers" became a call to "resurrect the original meaning of constitutional provisions and statutes as the only reliable guide for judgment."[80] Some scholars who are not exclusively committed to a single method do reject certain items on the list as illegitimate. Originalist jurisprudence has been countered by pleas to "let the framers sleep."[81]

"I am always amused," Alan M. Dershowitz has written, "by the fact that so many of those who so loudly proclaim a slavish obeisance to the narrow intent of the framers are so much like them in background."[82] Jurists who look to original intent for guidance rather than mandates must still be aware that reference to the sources of original meaning is, inevitably, reference to *male* words, *male* values, and *male* purposes. This male monopoly applies also to text, doctrine, and precedent. Women did not participate in the drafting or adoption of the original Constitution; throughout most of American history, women were excluded from participation in amending or interpreting it. Whatever constitutional theorizing women got to do—and there may have been more than we know about, as has been proved true for art and literature—is lost to us.

Knowing what we know about the human mind, it is virtually impossible to believe that things would have been exactly the same if women had been equal partners from the beginning. We do not need theories of gender difference to recognize how different the lives of men and women are and have been. Contemporary jurisprudence, epistemology, and feminist theory concede the impossibility of "unmediated truth,"[83] the inevitable connection between conclusion and what Benjamin Cardozo called the "stream of tendency, whether you call it philosophy or not, which gives coherence and direction to thought and action."[84] Therefore, several common modes of constitutional interpretation inevitably bias us in a male direction.

From a feminist perspective, some version of a "living Constitution" becomes imperative. Rather than producing "a formula for an end run around popular government," efforts to adapt the text to the times become potential correctives for women's historic exclusion.[85] But flexibility is not a sufficient condition for change. It can work as easily to reinforce male bias as to control it. Within a male-dominated enterprise, we can expect it to work this way. For feminists, the choice between modes of interpretation may be a choice between approaches which permit male bias and approaches which ensure it.

The search for neutral principles does not render constitutional doctrine impartial.[86] Experience demonstrates the truth of Katharine Bartlett's observation that "neutral rules and procedures tend to drive underground the ideologies of the decisionmaker."[87] Individuality affects decision making, however much single-method interpreters try to deny it; and individuality includes gender. Since adjudication is a collegial enterprise, the impact of gender is collective as well as individual. Law has been a language spoken not only *by* males but *to* them, and usually *about* them. This monopoly has been so extensive that a best-seller could describe the Supreme Court in the late 1970s as having "a men's-club atmosphere."[88] Constitutional history has been the history of men speaking to men.

Constitutional interpretation is a discipline which offers ample opportunity to the creative individual mind—so much freedom, in fact, that judges as different as Hugo Black and Robert Bork have been troubled by it. What Roberto Unger has written about one interpretive issue has general application: "The detailed structure of American equal protection doctrine cannot be derived from either the Constitution itself or all [its] general conceptions and commitments. No one who had mastered this intellectual structure together with the constitutional history of the United States and all relevant features of American society and culture could have foreseen that equal protection doctrine would have assumed its present form."[89]

The historic maleness of constitutional doctrine may help explain why it is so difficult to construct plausible constitutional arguments to support women's claims. The lack of fit between constitutional doctrine and reproductive choice, for example, may be due not to defects in the reasoning of *Roe v. Wade* but to defects in the doctrine which produced it. The apparent contradiction between equal opportunity and maternity leave may have similar roots. If women had been authoritative interpreters from the beginning, they might have constructed doctrine that recognized reproductive choice with no violence to history, theory, or logic.[90] But imagining "what might have been" is an exercise of limited value. We need to consider what could be: the possibilities for creating feminist constitutional doctrine, starting from where we are now.

Conclusion: Legal Re-Creating

What are women to law; and what is law, to women? Once, the only role women played in large numbers was that of object—the talked-about, the acted-upon, the dealt-with—by men talking to other men. Early in this chapter, I examined the intellectual imperialism which characterizes much conventional legal analysis of women's behavior. A different approach is suggested by a 1996 article in the Washington, D.C., alternative press.[91] This essay focuses on a high school women's varsity basketball team. It is neither an athletic nor an academic success story. Cardozo High School's "Lady Clerks'" 4–14 record in 1995–96 is a fairly accurate micro-image of the school's performance. What makes the story remarkable is its account of the lives of four members of the team.

They live in one of the worst parts of Washington. Their families, their school, and their neighborhood show the effects of poverty, crime, drugs, and neglect. They are poor, fatherless, and in danger both at school and on the streets. They don't all like one another; the teamwork necessary to play the game takes considerable effort. They have no fans, too little coaching, shabby equipment and facilities; they have no hope of athletic scholarships. One player has a two-year-old son whose father is in prison. She struggles to maintain a C average so she can stay on the team. Another is so tall and heavy that spectators ridicule her. Two more are twins whose mother tried to keep them out of Cardozo. They had to leave their parochial school when their great-grandmother died, reducing the family's income.

For these women, sports and schoolwork are things to "put my head to," but they or their friends "got" pregnant. This distinction between agency and accident does not necessarily conform to the ways legal scholars perceive the world. Nor does the notion of a family with three generations of wage earners. (My great-grandmother's death had the opposite effect on my family's income as was true for the twins; how might these different circumstances affect family relationships?) A feminist jurisprudence needs ideology and epistemology that respect concrete experience like this and incorporate it into scholarly inquiry. If we knew why these teenagers view pregnancy as something that happens to you, we might help them learn otherwise—or come to understand that they are right.

Now, women are "doing law" as well being "done-to" by it. Just as Sara Ruddick found that maternal practice incorporates abilities traditionally associated with men, my analysis shows that constitutional practice incorporates capacities traditionally attributed to women. Law does not ask of women anything that they have not been doing elsewhere. And men, without necessarily realizing it, have been doing in law things that women are expected to do but criticized for doing. Dichotomies between male and female skills have a way of dissolving when we look at what people actually do. The question of the existence of intellectual gender differences, a puzzle that has occupied so much feminist attention, is far from settled. But analysis of actual practices suggests no reason to fear that constitutional interpretation is something women cannot do as well as men can.

Conventional reasoning claims to reject the concrete for the abstract, the contextual for the deductive, the emotional for the intellectual. Legal claims which do not fit into the prevailing rules may be rejected as illegitimate. For example, to demand both equal employment rights and maternity leave appears "inconsistent" and therefore "irrational." A challenge to the rule that only deliberate discrimination can violate the equal protection clause resembles a demand for "result-oriented jurisprudence." A jurisprudence which questions the exclusion of most divorce and child custody law from the scope of constitutional guarantees appears to violate federalism and judicial restraint. A demand for recognition of the right to reproductive choice seems to ask "the woman question" instead of applying "neutral principles." Claims which cannot be rooted in prevailing doctrine can be rejected as substituting emotion for reason. This dissonance between conventional doctrine and women's needs makes it easy for feminists to suspect that the methods which produced the doctrine are male-biased.

But an argument for feminist method need not presume that women think differently from men. It need only presume that men, who once monopolized and continue to dominate intellectual activity, use the rules in their own interests. Feminists are justified in suspecting that methods can frustrate women's claims. In Chapter 5, I show how this process of inclusion and exclusion has worked in equal protection doctrine.

One way for the powerful to use rules is to put certain interests outside their scope. As Deborah Rhode says, the legal system offers far less protection to women's needs, such as reproductive freedom, than to interests which some men confuse with needs, such as access to firearms or pornography. But it is not jurisprudence which privileges these particular "male" claims; to say that the absence of jurisprudence does so may be more accurate. The law books are virtually barren of doctrine on the right to bear arms. This right was such a nonissue for so long that, once it became an issue, the people who cared about it were strong enough to prevent the state from taking it away. Pornography, de facto if not de jure, enjoys a similar liberty.[92] Pornography and firearms do not require a rule-based defense in the way that so many of women's vital interests do. One reason for these disparities may be that pornography and firearms fit nicely into a capitalist economy; you can buy and sell them. But this can only be a partial explanation; abortions are bought and sold, too. The problem is not necessarily that the doctrine works better for men than for women, but that many interests important to the privileged group need not fit into the doctrine at all. Since conventional theory is biased against women in these ways, feminists do not bear the burden of proof that new methods are necessary.

I submit that a feminist jurisprudence is free to reject the conceptual traps of man-made law and to devise new approaches to legal reasoning which consciously employ the emotional, intuitive, and imaginative faculties of the mind. One reason this enterprise is legitimate is that conventional legal decision making incorporates the emotional, concrete, and contextual thinking it claims to reject. If men can do these things covertly, women can do them overtly. Even if the rules of constitutional adjudication were not invented for the express purpose of frustrating claims to sexual equality, they can and do serve that purpose. In Katharine Bartlett's words, rules drive ideologies underground. Since feminist ideology was not present to be driven underground when these rules were developed, feminists are justified in suspecting that the rules will frustrate their claims.

I am not suggesting that feminists should declare legal principles by fiat. I am suggesting that feminists are justified in attempting to reason from preference to conclusion. One way out of the doctrinal traps is to employ the intuitive and imaginative faculties: to ask, for example, under what circumstances sexual equality could be compatible with the absence of a right to abortion. Another possible approach for feminist constitutional scholars is to proceed from things that we know as women, such as the ways in which society encourages men to initiate sexual activity while making us responsible for preventing or dealing with its consequences.[93] A third innovative approach is to incorporate law's dynamic as well as its static properties by refusing to compartmentalize adjudication: for example, child custody law that asks why new claims made by fathers are recognized more easily than old claims made by mothers, or criminal law that adapts self-defense to the threats perceived by victims of domestic violence as readily to those perceived by men approached by strangers.[94] Other possibilities have yet to be envisioned.

Feminist jurists must give full creative license to the mind. The boundaries between reality and fantasy, between reason and emotion, between perceived and proven fact are as conventional and artificial as the boundaries between neutral and result-oriented jurisprudence, between state and federal power, between consistency and inconsistency. Those rules served purposes which women had little if any part in articulating. A central task of feminist jurisprudence is a willingness to break the rules.

Part I of this book locates the roots of law's maleness in men's division of life into public and private, justice and care, subject and object, rights and responsibility; and in men's assignment of women to specific spheres and duties. This chapter has extended the analysis to law's method as well as its content. Just as women have been stuck in the private sphere, they have been stuck in concrete particulars. Just as the tasks assigned to women have been devalued, so have the ways of knowing which emerge from these tasks. Just as ideology must include both justice and care, epistemology must include both the abstract and the concrete.

But, in epistemology as in ideology, feminists must distinguish between valorizing the work women have had to do and valorizing it as female. The assignment of certain social and intellectual tasks to women to free men from having to do them suggests that the "male" world of the public, the rational, and the abstract may have intrinsic advantages over the "female" world. Society needs both; but women need less of what has been theirs. The breaking up of male monopolies and giving up of female monopolies is equally necessary for another reason. My analysis of one mode of legal reasoning, constitutional interpretation, has shown that the dichotomy between thinking and feeling breaks down in practice. It misrepresents the way people "do law."

This chapter concludes Part I. So far, I have concentrated on constructing a feminist analysis of law and jurisprudence and locating it in the context of others' work. These critiques, including my own, have used women's lives to interpret law. My focus in Part II is the opposite process: I seek to understand how law constructs and interprets women's lives. The next three chapters concentrate on topics crucial to the inequality, vulnerability, and responsibility which are at the core of women's situation. Chapter 8 turns again to conventional theory and feminist critiques to envision a feminist postliberalism.

PART II

WOMEN'S LIVES THROUGH LAW

FIVE

RECONSTRUCTING EQUALITY

FEMINIST CONSTITUTIONAL DOCTRINE

W OMEN'S LIVES do not fit into American constitutional law. Gender is a deviant case, a doctrinal outlier, in the law of equality. Early in this century, *Muller v. Oregon* put sex discrimination outside the scope of equal protection law, placing "woman . . . in a class by herself."[1] As the century ends, woman is still in a special class.

Women's rights cases constitute an exception to almost every generalization which can be made about the Supreme Court in the last fifty years. The Court cared less about individual rights under Chief Justice Warren Burger (1969–86) than under Earl Warren (1953–69)—except for their respective records on women's rights. The Court cared more about precedent during Burger's tenure than during that of either his predecessor or his successor—except for this departure from sixty years of precedent. The Warren Court led a judicial revolution, the Rehnquist Court a counterrevolution, and the Burger Court a holding action—except that the Warren revolution omitted women's rights, the Rehnquist Court has barely touched the constitutional law of sex discrimination, and the Burger Court transformed the meaning of the equal protection clause.

Between 1971 and 1981, the Court revoked the *Muller* license to discriminate. If we examine doctrine alone, it is clear that women won some landmark judicial victories. But these victories have been double-edged and their effects mixed. Between 1981 and 1996, not one woman won a Supreme Court equal protection case on sexual equality. The actual beneficiaries of actual cases include more men than women. And, along with the victories, the Court also ruled that male-only draft registration is permissible, but veterans' preference does not treat women unequally; struck down women-only alimony, while divorce settlements which impoverish ex-wives became more and more common; and allowed single fathers to claim parental rights, while mothers increasingly risked losing their children's custody.[2] Results like these lend support to Nora Ephron's observation that "the major concrete achievement of the women's movement in the 1970s was the Dutch treat."[3]

What Changed?

In 1969, the year Warren Burger took office, *Muller* was still binding precedent. Sex was an "ordinary" or "innocuous" classification, placed on the first "tier," where courts applied "minimal scrutiny": laws were presumed constitutional and upheld if any "rational basis" for them existed.[4] It took sixty-three years for the Court to put the first dent in this doctrine. *Reed v. Reed* labeled an automatic state preference for males an "arbitrary legislative choice," and thus forbidden by even the most permissive reading of the Fourteenth Amendment.[5] In the 1970s, the Court briefly seemed ready to treat sex discrimination like race discrimination: a "suspect classification," presumptively invalid, assigned to the "upper tier" of "strict scrutiny," where laws survived only upon the demonstration of "compelling justification."[6] The justices retreated from that position in 1976, but the resulting compromise did not restore the status quo. *Craig v. Boren* carved out a new class in which to place women by themselves; "classifications by gender must serve important governmental objectives and be substantially related to these objectives."[7]

This "intermediate scrutiny" standard remains the prevailing test in sex discrimination cases. *Craig* is a perfect analogy to *Planned Parenthood v. Casey*, the latest doctrinal statement from the Supreme Court on the one specifically female constitutional right. *Casey* demoted abortion from the "strict scrutiny/compelling justification" tier of protected rights and carved out an intermediate position for it: government may not place an "undue burden" upon the exercise of choice.[8]

The *Craig* rule has resulted in more decisions striking down sex discrimination than the *Muller* rule did. On the other hand, claimants have lost under the intermediate scrutiny standard nearly as often as they have won. But the *Craig* test does not tell students of constitutional law many of the things we would like to know. Who has benefited from the rulings? What have they gained? Who really wins, and who loses? Why? And what difference does it make?

Who Benefits?

From 1971 to 1996, the Court decided twenty-eight sex discrimination cases under the equal protection provisions of the Fifth and Fourteenth Amendments. *Craig v. Boren*, decided in December 1976, is the ninth case chronologically. In the next seven and a half years, the Burger Court applied the *Craig* standard in seventeen cases.[9] There was a ten-year gap between the 1981 Burger Court case, *Heckler v. Mathews*, and the first Rehnquist court case, *J.E.B. v. Alabama ex rel. T.B.*[10] The most recent ruling, in June 1996, was *United States v. Virginia*, which struck down the Virginia Military Institute's male-only admissions policy.[11]

Of the twenty-eight cases, the claimants won fifteen and lost thirteen. Eight of the fourteen winners were men; one, beer vendor Carolyn Whitener in *Craig*, was suing on behalf of men; the most recent winner, the United States government, was suing on behalf of women; and the remaining five winners were women. More men (eight out of nineteen) than women (five out of eight) won—but more men lost, too. Ten (more than three-fourths) of the losing plaintiffs were male. Women have been more successful in constitutional cases than men have, but there have been more male winners than female winners. Men have instigated most of the sex discrimination cases which have reached the Supreme Court. No matter how we classify *Craig* and *Virginia*, men account for roughly two-thirds of the rulings. The new doctrine has generated more male than female claims. In that sense, constitutional equality has a male bias.

The cases decided after *Craig* display even more striking patterns. The women win one-half or three-fifths of their cases, as opposed to six out of fourteen for the men; but the numbers are so small that the difference must be interpreted cautiously. Fourteen post-*Craig* cases involve men; only four or five involve women. So, while roughly half the women's cases come chronologically before the new test, and half after, more than twice as many cases involving men were decided after *Craig* as before. The ratio of men's cases to women's cases is now better than three to one, rather than two to one. Chronology conveys an even sharper impression. The last sexual equality case brought by a woman before the VMI case was *Kirchberg v. Feenstra*, decided in March 1981—before the first woman justice joined the Court.[12] The next six cases all involved men.[13] The new doctrine of sexual equality has served primarily as a device for men to press their interests.[14]

Does It Matter?

The fact that more men than women win sexual equality cases does not tell us much by itself. We need to know what was won or lost; how important those benefits are; and whose interests ultimately prevailed. We also need an idea of what *might* have been won that has not been. Chapter 2 showed that in family law and criminal law, women's claims are being frustrated while men's claims are accommodated. Is this also true in equal protection law?

Not all victories for men are defeats for women. Two Social Security cases decided in the mid-1970s were brought by men, but they protected women's rights. Both plaintiffs were widowers. After Paula Weisenfeld died in childbirth, her infant son received survivors' benefits. But Stephen Weisenfeld was not eligible for the parents' benefits a widow would have gotten. Leon Goldfarb was ineligible for old-age survivors' benefits because he had not been dependent on his wife, Hannah; a nondependent seventy-two-year-old widow would have received the payments. Both men won, but the Court stressed the interests of women. Paula Weisenfeld "failed to receive for her family the same protection which a similarly situated male worker would have received."[15] Hannah Goldfarb "worked and paid Social Security taxes for 25 years at the same rate as her male colleagues," but "the insurance protection received by the males was broader than hers."[16] *J.E.B. v. Alabama*, which invalidated the use of peremptory challenges to exclude jurors solely on the basis of sex, vacated a child support judgment against a man—but it also keeps defense attorneys from excluding women jurors in rape cases on the assumption that women are more likely than men to sympathize with the victim.[17] The VMI decision was an unambiguous and significant victory for women; it is hard to see how any man had anything to lose but his hubris. Justice Ruth Bader Ginsburg's rhetoric—" 'Inherent differences' between men and women . . . remain cause for celebration, but not for denigration of either sex or for artificial constraints on an individual's opportunity"—leads so inexorably to the ruling that VMI must admit women on an equal basis with men, that the reader can only wonder why it took so long to reach this conclusion.[18]

But some decisions which accept the claims of one sex clearly hurt the other. *Feenstra*, the 1981 woman's case, deprived men of considerable power. It invalidated Louisiana's "head and master" law, which gave husbands unilateral control of jointly owned property. On the other hand, *Caban v. Mohammed* enhanced the rights of unwed fathers at the expense of the mothers, who may no longer give sole consent to their children's adoption, even by their own husbands.

The new doctrine has been useful to women. Several decisions have granted real rights to women and taken real privileges from men. One could even argue that sexual equality *does* demand the imposition of "Dutch treat" policies like gender-neutral spousal support laws, and that the Court erred when it refused to impose upon women the duty to register for the draft in *Rostker v. Goldberg* or penalties for having sexual intercourse with juveniles in *Michael M v. Superior Court of Sonoma County*. After all, is not discrimination against men just as unfair as discrimination against women? Can feminists demand equal rights while refusing to give up privileges?

Laws imposing special burdens on males do indeed violate the principle of sexual equality. But it is not clear that laws discriminating against men do as much damage as those which discriminate against women. Even if it were, sex discrimination is not the only legal form sexual inequality takes. The feminist commitment to sexual equality is premised on the judgment that women's status is inferior relative to that of men, and the evidence overwhelmingly supports that conclusion. Nobody needs to be told that women lag behind men in income, education, employment opportunities, and holding public office. Laws discriminating against men are exceptions to this generalization, exceptions that have little effect on the overall situation. Sexual equality requires changes that benefit women more than it requires the abolition of male obligations.

Feminists can hardly welcome rulings like the victories of William Orr, who reneged on court-ordered alimony payments; his fellow Alabaman, J.E.B., who bucked scientific evidence that put the probability of his fatherhood at 99.92 percent; or Abdiel Caban, who abducted his children—although even the dissenting justices avoided using that verb.[19] After *Orr*, Alabama was under no obligation to make its alimony law gender-neutral (although it did); the state was free to abolish all alimony, as Texas has done.[20] After *Caban*, states could enact custody laws which discriminate between parents on the basis of the closeness of their relationship with their children rather than their sex, or which penalize parental abduction. But a legislature could also respond to the Court's invalidation of a law discriminating between single mothers and single fathers by stripping all single parents of custodial rights—a move which would serve the interest of at least one articulate group, prospective adoptive parents. It is difficult to see how *any* outcome in *Michael M* could help women. Invalidate the law, and a rapist may go free; uphold it, and only male seducers are punished because "only women become pregnant."[21]

Women still have grievances which equal protection law does not reach. Some cases, like the 1979 ruling which upheld veterans' preferences in civil service employment, discounted women's claims on the grounds that only deliberate race or sex discrimination can violate the equal protection clause.[22] This rule essentially allows lawmakers to discriminate as they wish, as long as they have a plausible neutral rationale and are careful about what they say to defend it. Some rulings vindicating men's claims, while not exactly wrong, seem dissonant with our knowledge about the way law disadvantages women.

More men than women use the new constitutional doctrine of sexual equality. More men than women have won constitutional cases before the Supreme Court. The men's overall won-lost record is almost as good as the women's; in fact, the differences are so small, given the number of cases involved, that the men are doing about as well as the women are. The conclusion is inescapable: so far, men have been the primary beneficiaries of the new doctrine of sexual equality. The new sexual equality doctrine does more for men's interests than for women's.

The Male Bias of Constitutional Law

One night we came home from a three-day weekend and
found we had been robbed. Our house was in a shambles, and
"NIGGA" was spray-painted on the walls. The burglars had
poured beer on the pool table and ripped up the felt. They
had broken into my father's trophy case and smashed most of
the trophies. . . . The police came, and after a while they left.
It was then that my parents pulled back their bedcovers to discover that the burglars had defecated in their bed.
(Karen Russell)

[My children] have been called names, have suffered slights
and have experienced first hand the peculiar malevolence that
racism brings out of people. Yet they have never experienced
racial discrimination.
(Shelby Steele)

How, and why, does constitutional adjudication satisfy men's claims while
it shuts out those of women? Any volume of *United States Reports* reveals
a partial answer to this question: far more parties in both decisions and
memorandum cases have male names than female names, even when we
omit the criminal cases. Crude as these figures are, they suggest that the
pool of cases from which the Court selects contains more male than female
petitioners.[23] Do men litigate more than women because they are more
assertive—firm, obstinate, or pigheaded—or because they are wronged
more often? Either explanation is plausible; neither explanation is prov-
able. Men may go to law more often than women because, in general, they
have more money and more free time. Litigation requires both. If litigation
has a man's face, we should not be surprised.

Reading the decisions provides better explanations of the male bias of
constitutional law than counting the names. These explanations lie in aspects of constitutional doctrine which are both prior to and independent
of sexual equality. The cases show that judges do not have to be male su-
premacists to write doctrine which ultimately reinforces male supremacy,
any more than they must be conservatives to reinforce the status quo. They
need only do their job like what they are: lawyers, trained in the habits of
legal thought.

Not all perceived wrongs are actionable wrongs. "I've been screwed,"
however passionately felt, is not the basis for a lawsuit. Potential litigants
must "translate" the harm they suffer into the legal language of grievances
and remedies. The law's vocabulary constrains judicial discourse about

these issues. Equal protection doctrine has constructed the complex, cacophonous, even chaotic material of inequality as it is experienced in this country into the concepts of "discrimination" and "classification." These concepts have subsets like "suspect," "ordinary," "intermediate," "intentional," and so forth. The legal concepts, in their turn, influence the ways we perceive the reality.

The authors of the epigraphs to this section are both black Americans writing about their families. Shelby Steele generalizes: his children have endured racism but not racial discrimination. He implies that calling people names or generally mistreating them is not discriminating against them. Reality does not demand the making of this distinction; but legal language so pervades American culture that it shapes the perceptions even of non-lawyers like this English professor. Karen Russell recounts a specific instance of what Steele calls "peculiar malevolence." A Harvard Law School graduate, she does not try to fit this experience into equal protection language. The episode was part of a pattern of violent acts directed against her family in their white neighborhood with tacit police sanction; but the government's letting white racists attack blacks does not constitute denial of equal protection of the laws.

Equal protection doctrine sorts experiences like Russell's and Steele's into categories, separating those experiences which can be described as instances of official discrimination, of treating A differently from B because of race, from experiences which cannot be so described. The doctrine includes the former and excludes the latter. The doctrine makes relevant any experience which can be described as an instance of official race discrimination, whatever the race of the person suffering it. Equal protection law ranks the harm done to Allen Bakke, whose opportunity to get into medical school was reduced because he was white, as equal to the harm suffered by a minority applicant similarly treated, and, implicitly, as more important than the harm done to the Russell family or the Steele children.[24]

The same legal concepts apply, though less stringently, in sexual equality cases. A person who believes she has been treated unfairly because of race or sex does not have a constitutional case unless she can establish that a racial or sexual classification exists, that the resulting discrimination is deliberate, and that the discriminating is being done by the state, not a private agency. The law's vocabulary constrains the judicial discourse about these issues. And the available doctrinal language fits the claims made by men better than it does those made by women. Too often, "you can't get there (to a constitutional resolution of a woman's claim) from here (a statement of the problem)."

How Doctrine Favors Men

Orr v. Orr, one of the "Dutch treat" cases, illustrates this point. A law which makes ex-husbands, but not ex-wives, vulnerable to court-ordered alimony payments is a deliberate sex-based classification which discriminates against men. As such, this law calls for the intermediate scrutiny described in *Craig v. Boren*; the statute must bear a substantial relationship to an important legislative purpose. The law cannot survive scrutiny under this test.

But in ordinary discourse, we would not understand alimony if we conceptualized it only as "discrimination against men." Women-only alimony is a form of sex discrimination, but it is part of a social context of male supremacy. Marriage has often been necessary for women's economic survival; many women have been unable to earn enough money to meet their needs. Wives (especially women whose marriages are ending now) have often been financially dependent on their husbands. In general, women have less earning power than men. In particular, wives often have less earning power than their husbands because women tend to "marry up"—to marry men who are older and better educated than they—and because wives' job choices are limited by their domestic obligations. The performance of wifely duties frees husbands to do other things, including earning money.[25] Many things that give husbands privileges happen outside the law, not within it.

Every divorce results in an individual settlement agreed on by both parties or arrived at by a judge. On paper, divorce law and child custody law are both gender-neutral and gender-sensitive. The law, in its majesty, allows both male and female investment bankers to leave their families without undue financial loss; but that is not all the law does. Most state laws and the Uniform Marriage and Divorce Act of 1974 permit courts to consider each spouse's contribution to homemaking, child care, and the other spouse's career in awarding support and dividing property.[26] But something happens between the statute books and the court decisions. No researcher has found that no-fault divorce has improved the overall situation of women. Most studies show that men have benefited at women's expense and that child custody decisions increasingly favor fathers over mothers.

Different studies have arrived at different figures, but the findings point in the same direction: the economic status of ex-wives declines relative to that of ex-husbands.[27] The plight of "displaced homemakers," women who have been out of the labor market for decades when their marriages end, has received national attention. While no evidence exists to support Mary Becker's claim that "*Orr v. Orr* has hurt ordinary mothers and wives," the ruling certainly did nothing to help them.[28] Divorce has contributed to the "feminization of poverty" because ex-wives are not always awarded support; even when they are, ex-husbands often fail to pay it; and even when they do, the awards are often inadequate. In the 1980s, less than 15 percent of divorced women got alimony awards, and almost 40 percent of mothers living with children whose fathers were absent got no support awards. For those who were paid support, the mean amount was about twenty-five hundred dollars a year. Governmental efforts to improve support enforcement have effected some improvement in this situation, but the questions being asked have changed and the number getting no support remains large. By 1991, 46 percent of families with a parent living elsewhere (86 percent of which consisted of mothers and children) had binding support orders.[29] Several studies have found that judges give greater weight to legal criteria likely to favor men than to those favoring women in divorce settlements.[30] Viewed in this context, alimony is less a discrimination against men than it is an (inadequate) effort to protect disadvantaged partners when a partnership dissolves. But we can never get at that truth if we limit ourselves to constitutional language. The truth we can get at through the legal language is that laws like Alabama's discriminate against men. The truth we cannot get at is the harm divorce law does to women.

The Court's adherence to what Catharine MacKinnon "affectionately call[s] the stupid theory of equality" suggests that *Orr* may express judicial "indiffer[ence] to whether dominant or subordinate groups are hurt or helped."[31] But we need not agree that discrimination against men is as bad as discrimination against women to reject this particular overbroad and useless discrimination. While the intermediate scrutiny standard is woefully inadequate for cases involving discrimination against women, it has its merits in cases involving discrimination against men. Discrimination against a dominant group is not so grave a matter as discrimination against a subordinate one; but it is grave enough. Sex discrimination against men does not reinforce subordinate status, but it does impose disadvantage because of characteristics the individual could not help and cannot change.[32]

Since decisions about alimony and child custody are made separately in each case, these laws can be gender-neutral. A law providing support for dependent or disadvantaged spouses should result in awards to many women, and few men. It is difficult to disagree with the holding in *Orr*. An affirmative action program which discriminated in favor of women, and thereby against men, might well bear a substantial relationship to an important purpose. But the sex discrimination represented in *Orr* does not.

Caban v. Mohammed has the same relationship to child custody that *Orr* has to divorce. Traditional child custody law is a classic instance of "sex plus" discrimination; the "plus" is marital status.[33] When parents are or have been married to each other, mothers and fathers have equal parental rights; when no marriage has occurred, single mothers had exclusive rights until recently. The New York statute which gave single mothers the right to give unilateral consent for their children's adoption discriminated against single fathers. Like single-sex alimony, these laws disfavor a class composed exclusively of men.

The Court's task in *Caban* was to decide whether "the distinction between unmarried mothers and unmarried fathers . . . [bears] a substantial relation to the State's interest in providing adoptive homes for its illegitimate children."[34] Five justices concluded that the necessary relationship was lacking, because the law erroneously presumed that single fathers were less close to their children than single mothers were. For feminists, it is hard to think of any possible result worth celebrating. As close as the vote was, and as unsympathetic a litigant as Caban is, the facts of the case support the majority's conclusion. The man had lived with his children for several years. Constitutional doctrine can get at the part of child custody law that discriminates against men.[35] But here again, as with alimony, we can only get partway there (to an understanding of child custody law) from here (constitutional doctrine).

The Seneca Falls Declaration of 1848 charged that custody law is "wholly regardless of the happiness of women." The law has undergone two radical changes since then, but the statement is still accurate. Law favored the father in the nineteenth century, and the mother in most of the twentieth. Paternal preference reflected an agrarian society's recognition of the father's economic interest in his children's labor. Maternal preference stemmed not from recognition of the mother's interests but from a shift in priorities from the father to the child. The "tender years" doctrine presumed that young children needed their mothers. Paternal preference put the father first; maternal preference put the child first.[36]

The law favors neither parent now. Custody awards must be made in "the best interests of the child." This neutral standard, applied impartially, might favor the mother. Experts in child psychology generally agree that children's interests are best served by remaining with the adult who has been their primary caregiver. In virtually all families, the mother has been that person.[37] About 90 percent of minor children of divorcing parents stay with their mothers by parental arrangement, whether voluntary or coerced.[38] But fathers who do seek custody win in 35 percent to 70 percent of cases.[39] Judges' rationales for awarding custody to the father often seem to be thinly disguised references to his relative financial superiority (which may give him access to better legal help than the woman can afford). But often the fact that the mother has been the children's primary caregiver throughout their lives goes unremarked.[40]

It is not necessary to valorize care as female—the trap into which too many feminists fall or jump—to perceive the injustice inherent in denigrating care. Chapters 1 and 3 showed that the "ethic of care" arises from the domestic role into which women have been forced. So, also, might a need for continued intimate contact with one's children, greater than their father's emotional need for them in a conventional family. When we commit time, energy, and emotion to intimate relationships, these relationships become increasingly important to our emotional well-being. The care of infants and young children requires vast amounts of time, energy, and emotion. Although children's needs for care diminish as they grow older, their primary caregiver's attachment to them reflects her intense commitment. In most instances, therefore, a mother has a continuing interest in custody of her children. The law has never recognized such an interest.[41]

Mothers have cared for children because society expects them to. Their performance of this essential social function gives them a stake in continued involvement with their children. Specific needs and interests develop around the roles that women must assume. But the same society which assigns these tasks gives no recognition to the human needs arising from them. Women do what they must, and in doing it forge bonds with their children—but law gives these bonds no status at all. It would be difficult to find a clearer example of male bias in law. Yet these grievances almost never become constitutional cases. Why not?

Suppose we try to describe the situation in constitutional terms. Does deliberate sex discrimination exist? Judges are unlikely to invite reversal on appeal by announcing an intention to discriminate on the basis of sex. One way to buttress a claim that a decision maker is discriminatory is to compare several decisions he or she makes over time. But divorce and child custody decisions are made by several hundred different judges in different jurisdictions. Contemporary divorce and child custody law, as applied, work to the disadvantage of women. They reinforce male supremacy. But it is hard to say these things in doctrinal language.

How Doctrine (Almost) Favors Men

The two post-*Craig* cases involving military service further illustrate this disjunction between doctrine and reality. *Personnel Administrator v. Feeney* (1979) upheld civil service veterans' preferences; *Rostker v. Goldberg* (1981) upheld male-only draft registration.[42] The doctrinal symmetry between *Goldberg* and cases like *Orr* and *Caban* is less obvious, but more important, than the different results. Legal discourse conceptualizes male-only draft registration as a sex-based classification that discriminates against men. But thinking about these practices in terms of classification and discrimination is a strangely truncated form of discourse. Judged by the *Craig* test, male-only registration survived because the Court did not need to reach the issue of women's eligibility for military service and combat. *Goldberg* linked the registration requirement to laws restricting combat to men, laws which were not then before the Court. By the mid-1990s, these restrictions were on their way out—thereby undermining the rationale for the decision.

This link between registration and combat helps clarify the context in which compulsory registration must be understood. Combat is, or at least was until Vietnam, a highly valued activity. Drafting men between the ages of eighteen and twenty-six ensured that most warriors were young enough to accept that value without question, and to be relatively unaware of their own mortality. Military service may have derived some of its value for these young men from the fact that only males can fight. Despite the dangers of combat, the majority of warriors survive it without permanent injury. Many veterans have used their experience to get access to education, careers, and public office. Even Vietnam veterans have won Senate seats; and the first nonveteran president since World War II has had some explaining to do. Military service has given warriors competitive advantages over nonwarriors—including women.[43]

Veterans' preference in civil service, the subject of *Feeney*, is one of these benefits. All veterans, male and female, get the preference; but until 1967, the Armed Forces had a 2 percent quota for women. In Massachusetts, where Helen Feeney was kept out of every managerial civil service job in the state by her cohorts who had served in World War II, 98 percent of the veterans were male. By the time the Supreme Court heard her case, the handwriting was on the wall. Two racial cases had held that if a law had a neutral purpose, a disproportionate effect on one race did not render it invalid.[44] *Feeney* applied this principle to sex discrimination. Veterans' preference was valid because its purpose was to encourage and reward military service, not to discriminate against women.[45]

Helen Feeney got screwed. There is no other word for it. She held several management-level positions in state government—something that would have been extremely unlikely for a woman her age working in the private sector—until her job was abolished. Despite her exemplary record and high scores in competitive examinations, she could not get any non-clerical civil service job after that. A state law which favored veterans denied Feeney employment opportunity; the sex ratio of the population of veterans was influenced by a federal policy of deliberate gender discrimination. Yet Feeney's claim went unrecognized.

Policies which reward military service imply that people ought to be rewarded for performing physically dangerous and socially important tasks. But society does not apply this principle consistently. No rewards exist for the risky, important function that only women perform.[46] We have no monuments for women who died in childbirth. We can never get to this insight if we stick to constitutional law.

Nor does equal protection language help us get at the gendered meanings of military service. It is an apparent exception to my argument in this book that women have more responsibility imposed upon them than men do. Military service is an obligation men have kept for other men: not for themselves, since the men writing the laws are not the men who are drafted, but for people like them. The well-documented race and class biases of conscription—not to mention the age bias—support my contention that responsibility is imposed downward. The differences between the ways society treats male and female responsibilities support my thesis that responsibility is gendered. Military service and combat are not devalued the way child care and housekeeping are: they are rewarded and even glorified. Women's work is trivialized; men's work is valorized. And constitutional law is silent.

How Doctrine Shuts Out Women

Pornography provides another example of the distance between constitutional doctrine and institutionalized male supremacy. The familiar feminist argument that "pornography is a discriminatory practice based on sex because its effect is to deny women equal opportunities in society" is absent from American law.[47] The 1984 Indianapolis ordinance drafted by Catharine MacKinnon and Andrea Dworkin, the only legislation ever enacted in the United States containing that phrase, was struck down by the federal courts on First Amendment grounds. The district court opinion evinces more than a little scorn. "Defendants repeat through their briefs the incantation that their ordinance regulates conduct, not speech. They contend (one senses with a certain sleight of hand) that the production, dissemination, and use of sexually explicit words and pictures *is* the actual subordination of women and not an expression of ideas deserving First Amendment protection."[48]

First Amendment doctrine presents no insurmountable barrier to restrictions on pornography. Taken literally, the constitutional language might. But courts have never taken language literally. First Amendment doctrine starts, logically and chronologically, with the assumption that the government may do precisely what the language implies it must not do.[49] The Supreme Court has put several categories of expression outside the scope of the First Amendment; in theory at least, new unprotected categories could be created. The Court has ruled that libel, slander, and "fighting words"—"those which by their very utterance inflict injury"—are not protected speech.[50] It has sustained antidiscrimination laws against First Amendment challenges.[51] It invalidated the only "hate speech" prohibition it has yet judged, but the opinions in *R.A.V. v. City of St. Paul* leave the door open for carefully worded regulation.[52]

The Court has consistently held that obscenity is not part of the expression protected by the First Amendment.[53] The Court has upheld laws restricting communications addressed exclusively to adults, the audience that the feminist argument emphasizes. The case law also states that public morality is a government interest which justifies restrictions.[54] Since *Miller v. California* in 1973, First Amendment law has defined "obscenity" in a way that should include some pornography. Material is "obscene" if it satisfies the following three criteria: "the average person, applying contemporary [local] community standards," finds that its dominant overall appeal is to the prurient interest; if it contains patently offensive descriptions of specific sexual acts; and if, taken as a whole, it lacks serious value. *Miller* listed some types of material a jury might find patently offensive, including representations or descriptions of sexual acts, nudity, excretion, and "lewd exhibition of the genitals."[55] On paper at least, the two categories overlap. To the extent that pornography fits into the category of obscenity, it is censorable. To the extent that it does not fit, a court could still rule that it is yet another category of unprotected speech.

But constitutional doctrine jars with societal practice. While *Miller* appears to permit more government restriction than the rules it replaced, sexually explicit material is more widely available than it was in 1973, not less.[56] A tacit compromise has apparently been struck between the advocates and opponents of restraints. The law regulates sexually explicit material; but the availability of this material happens outside the law. Most adults have access to any material they want. But government, with some cooperation from "private" enterprise, makes an effort to keep sexually explicit material, not just obscenity or pornography, away from children and to keep children out of sexually explicit material. Rating schemes like those used by the Motion Picture Association of America and proposed for television, the "V chip" for television, and "adult book stores" are part of this compromise. It does not work perfectly. Occasional prosecutions directed at mass-circulation magazines violate it; so may video stores and mail-order catalogs. Law is probably no more successful in keeping sexually explicit material away from minors than it is in keeping tobacco and alcohol away from them. However, to the extent that the compromise works, it accommodates the primary concerns of each of the two sides of the *traditional* censorship debate.

But there are now three sides. The newest group of participants in the debate is the antipornography feminists. And the compromise does not come close to addressing their concerns. These feminists would presumably prefer that youth not be exposed to pornography and the attitudes about women it displays. But feminists would not agree, even as a compromise, that it is all right for adults to be exposed to this material. The crucial problem for antipornography feminists is the people who are acting out those attitudes *now*, not those who may do so in the future. Susan Brownmiller wrote in 1975 that "a woman's perspective demands a totally new alignment" on this issue.[57] We are still waiting.

Brownmiller, MacKinnon, Dworkin, and Susan Griffin have all made one or more of the following claims: pornography degrades women; it dehumanizes women by reducing them to the status of sexual outlet; it conveys the impression that women like to be sexually brutalized; it encourages those exposed to it to believe all of these things or to duplicate the treatment of women portrayed therein; or it silences women.[58] This last claim has different meanings to different authors. Griffin appears to mean that pornography stifles women's "real self" by forcing them to impersonate the "false self" which is pornography's image of them. MacKinnon appears to mean that pornography deafens society to women's speech by discrediting women.[59] These statements serve to open a debate, not to resolve it. They are all plausible arguments. We might make any of them ourselves, if we took the antipornography side in a debate.

But would we be likely to say what the Indianapolis city council said?[60] Or define pornography as MacKinnon and Dworkin did in their 1988 Model Ordinance: "graphic sexually explicit materials that subordinate women through pictures or words"?[61] Far from strengthening the argument, the assertion that pornography denies women equal opportunity in society weakens it by inviting, if not demanding, the response "Prove it." The language from the Model Ordinance raises a host of questions in the process of begging one. Why would anyone choose to argue this way? Well, on what other basis could the city council act? It was trying to fulfill its constitutional duty not to deny equal protection of the laws, and to achieve this goal within the constraints of the First Amendment. No wonder the ordinance fell to judicial scrutiny.

Once again, you can't get there from here. Fourteenth Amendment doctrine and First Amendment practice combine to frustrate efforts to make law respond to women's concerns. The feminist argument might gibe with First Amendment law, but it jars with First Amendment practice. But an argument that pornography constitutes legally sanctioned inequality has the merits of presenting a situation where two constitutional rights conflict; the First Amendment case would meet an equal and opposite Fourteenth Amendment case.[62] So the feminists are thrown back on equal protection law, which is inadequate for their argument.

Equal protection doctrine does not address the exploitation and degradation of women. Law "has difficulty grasping harm that is not linearly caused in the 'John hit Mary' sense."[63] Constitutional doctrine is not concerned with unfairness, disadvantage, or exploitation; it does not address the ways in which different social conventions and institutions combine to determine relative status. The law speaks, instead, of intentional classification and discrimination. To speak in these terms presupposes that what is at issue is not the inferior status of women but the classification of people by sex. This underlying premise dictates the conclusion that discrimination against one sex is legally indistinguishable from discrimination against the other. To demand the presence of intent to discriminate implies that the most important feature of a given law is its motive.

The reality of pornography does not fit with the legal terminology. To describe pornography as something that denies women equality in these terms is to force a nonlinear phenomenon into linear language. Equal protection doctrine does not lend itself to making a convincing case against pornography. The law's language does not even allow us to say what it is about pornography that many feminists believe is terribly wrong. If we cannot use the law's language to describe the injury, we cannot use the law to begin to correct the wrong. Doctrine frustrates debate instead of enabling it. Pornography non-law, like divorce law, shows that the inequalities which women suffer cannot be expressed in the language of constitutional discourse as well as men's grievances can be.[64]

The Sources of Doctrine

I have dealt with three components of equal protection doctrine which help explain its male bias: the antidiscrimination principle, the discriminatory intent requirement, and the state action requirement. In order to understand how and why constitutional law evolved in this way, we need to examine the roots of these principles. This history amply supports Roberto Unger's observation that "no one who had mastered . . . all relevant features of American society and culture could have foreseen that equal protection doctrine would have assumed its present form."[65] Two of the three principles were fixed into place by the same Burger Court which made so much new constitutional law in the area of sexual equality. (The exception is the state action doctrine, which goes back much further.) But each of them antedates the tenure of any justice who has participated in this development; each was developed in a legal context far removed from sexual equality. They were in the "repertoire" of legal principles available to judges for use in making decisions. Their use, their popularity, and their effect allow us to question some common unstated assumptions about law and public policy.

Antidiscrimination and Judicial Neutrality

"Reverse discrimination" cases have made much of the fact that the equal protection clause refers to "person" and not "group." This word choice permits the inference that the clause makes discrimination against whites, or men, "just as bad as" discrimination against blacks, or women. In 1995, *Adarand v. Pena* extended this principle to statutory construction; from now on, laws enacting racial preferences will survive only on a showing of compelling justification.[66] But the constitutional language does not demand that conclusion. While it is clear that any and all persons must have equal protection of the laws, it is far from clear what that commodity is.[67]

Does a state deny equal protection when it treats some people differently from others on the basis of race or sex? Or does equal protection permit, if not require, government to act positively to ensure equality? If the first interpretation is correct, it would indeed follow (most of the time) that classifications based on race or sex are unacceptable, no matter whom they affect in what way. But if the clause imposes a positive duty upon government, discriminations which benefit those of unequal status might be permissible (most of the time), while discriminations which burden the advantaged might not matter so much (most of the time). The constitutional language does not help us choose among these interpretations.

We need not adhere to a "jurisprudence of original intention" to consult the legislative history.[68] The Thirty-ninth Congress conducted its debate "almost entirely in terms of grand symbolism—that of the Declaration of Independence in particular—and remarkably little in terms of the specific legal implications of the new amendment."[69] The Radical Republicans who dominated Congress were not at all hesitant to use their power specifically to benefit blacks, as the Freedman's Bureau Bill of 1866 showed. There are also indications that the Republicans thought classification by race, as opposed to discrimination against blacks, was perfectly acceptable; they defended laws barring racial intermarriage in just those terms. The legislative record does not dictate the neutral antidiscrimination reading.[70]

Early Fourteenth Amendment cases distinguished between discrimination against racial minorities and evenhanded classification. The Supreme Court struck down laws barring blacks from jury service, but *Plessy v. Ferguson* gave constitutional sanction to the Jim Crow principle of "separate but equal."[71] The unanimous ruling in 1954 in *Brown v. Board of Education* rejected this principle, striking down de jure school segregation on the grounds that it generated "a feeling of inferiority as to [black children's] status in the community that may affect their hearts and minds in a way unlikely ever to be undone." Separate schools were "inherently unequal" because they were, in fact, premised upon white supremacy and reinforced it.[72]

Brown I gave impetus to a social revolution which has continued to the present day, and which has had an extraordinary equalizing impact upon American society. But the constitutional doctrine of *Brown* got the Court in trouble. The conclusion rests on a questionable interpretation of the facts. Worse, the emphasis on the interests of one racial group appeared to violate the requirement that adjudication "must be genuinely principled, resting . . . on analysis and reasons quite transcending the immediate result that is achieved."[73] When Herbert Wechsler made that criticism of *Brown* in the 1959 Holmes Lectures at Harvard Law School, he spoke for a large segment of the American bar, bench, and academy. Judges listened, and, with the glacial speed typical of jurists, they responded. The effort to ground racial decisions on neutral principles was evident in 1967 in *Loving v. Virginia*, when the Court overturned a state law forbidding racial intermarriage. Chief Justice Earl Warren, again speaking for a unanimous Court, found the law an instance of "the racial discrimination which it was the object of the Fourteenth Amendment to eliminate."[74]

So what has become objectionable is not official endorsement of racism but "racial discrimination." This phrase sounds neutral, more balanced, and generally nicer, as if judges could not bring themselves to acknowledge realities like oppression, subjection, and domination. Yet neither the moderate Burger Court nor the conservative Rehnquist Court made this change. The Warren Court, responding to criticism that it was not judicious enough, established the principle that the law forbids not oppression but classification.

All these conclusions can be made to make more or less sense within prevailing theory and practice. But none of them was inevitable. The prohibition of racial classification is not absolute. Just as free speech doctrine begins with cases upholding government restriction, equality doctrine begins with a decision upholding the internment of Japanese-Americans during World War II.[75] Courts have upheld racial discrimination when the government has convinced them it was really necessary, as in *Korematsu* and its kin,[76] or when the past record of official discrimination is blatant enough to call for compensation, as in the dogma of busing cases and the dicta of reverse discrimination cases.[77]

Regents v. Bakke made clear (by one vote, but that was all that was needed) that the Court meant what it had implied: that there was no principled distinction between discrimination against members of racial minorities and against the white majority. Several decisions at the end of the 1988–89 term resoundingly reaffirmed "our society's deep commitment to the eradication of discrimination based on a person's race."[78] The Civil Rights Act of 1991 negated the statutory decisions, but *Richmond v. Croson* remains binding constitutional precedent.[79] *Adarand v. Pena* applies the antidiscrimination doctrine to civil rights laws; *Shaw v. Reno* and *Miller v. Johnson* did the same to the Voting Rights Act.[80] The sexual equality cases, starting with *Kahn v. Shevin* in 1974, had already made the analogous assumption that discrimination against men was no better or worse than discrimination against women.[81] The neutral principle has been firmly in place, then, since 1978. Dictated by no history, language, or logic, it was the choice of judges alone.

Restraint, Deference, and Legislative Intent

The principle that only intentional race or sex discrimination counts as a denial of equal protection is kin to the neutrality principle: judges made it up, too.[82] The legislative debates offer no guidance on the legal status of the facially neutral policy with an objectionable effect. The constitutional language does not imply that such concepts as due process and equal protection refer to the motives of lawmakers rather than the effects of laws. The term "due process," in particular, had a long history by 1868; it had never meant "freedom from official malevolence." Similarly, in ordinary discourse, "to deny to someone X," whatever "X" is, does not mean exactly what "to want, plan, or intend to deny to someone X" means.

The importance of intent has always been part of the American lawyer's repertoire, available when wanted. Anglo-American criminal law defines many crimes primarily by the purpose attributed to an offender rather than the degree of harm done to the victim. Homicide is murder when done with intent to kill, manslaughter when done without malice. Intent is also important in civil law; several torts, such as libel, include a judgment of intent as a critical element. This emphasis reflects lawmakers' traditional belief (traceable to the Old and New Testaments, among other sources) that individuals' reasons for their actions determine in large part their degree of culpability for those actions. The severity of punishment depends in large part on the actor's intentions.

Intent has not had a secure place in constitutional adjudication. Traditional judicial rhetoric has disavowed any concern with legislative purpose: a typical example is "We cannot cross-examine either actually or argumentatively the mind of [state] legislatures or question their motives."[83] Such statements express the deference to legislatures which judges often claim and sometimes actually show. But intent has had a way of creeping into constitutional deliberations. The justices have been willing to infer intent from consequence when they suspect that lawmakers have used neutral language to mask invidious intentions. Long-standing precedents rejected facially evenhanded policies which were enforced only against members of minorities or were so bizarre that invidious discrimination is the only plausible explanation for them.[84]

Sometimes, judges have probed for intent even when examining laws that appear sensibly written and fairly enforced. Intent has been at the core of establishment clause doctrine since the 1960s: "What is the *purpose* and primary effect of the enactment? If *either* is the advancement or inhibition of religion," the law is invalid.[85] The Burger Court put a final gloss on this test in *Lemon v. Kurtzman*, which established the tripartite standard of secular purpose, secular effect, and minimal entanglement between church and state.[86] The Court reaffirmed its commitment to analyzing purpose in *Wallace v. Jaffree* in 1985.[87] It invalidated Alabama's law requiring "a moment of silence" in school opening exercises because evidence of religious purpose was, so to speak, left lying around. The *Lemon* test does not always require an inquiry into purpose, since the parts of the rule are linked by *and*, not *or*: a law which fails any of the three criteria must fall. A law whose effect is to advance or inhibit religion is unconstitutional no matter what its purpose.

If a neutral law with a religious effect can violate the First Amendment, a neutral law with an unintended discriminatory effect might violate the equal protection clause. But the Court was not willing to subject equal protection cases to the same degree of scrutiny that it applied to establishment clause controversies. Instead, it came close to declaring that neither a racially biased purpose nor a racially biased effect could make a law unconstitutional. *Palmer v. Thompson* was decided in 1971, the same year as *Lemon*. The Court upheld the closing of public swimming pools in Jackson, Mississippi, after a federal court had ordered them desegregated. Although the record contained ample evidence of racist motives, the city won because there was "no action affecting blacks differently from whites."[88] *Washington v. Davis*, five years later, did precisely the opposite of what *Palmer v. Thompson* had done. The Court rebuffed a claim that a verbal skills test for prospective Washington, D.C., police officers denied equal protection because four times as many blacks failed it as did whites. "[We reject] the view that proof of discriminatory racial purpose is unnecessary in making out an equal protection violation."[89]

Palmer and *Davis* are polar opposites; the only continuity seems to be that the government wins and the blacks lose. Together, the cases suggest that any law with a neutral purpose *or* a plausible rationale *or* evenhanded application would stand. The Court applied the same principle to gender discrimination three years later in *Personnel Administrator v. Feeney*.[90] The rule that only intentional discrimination counts is now entrenched. *McCleskey v. Kemp*, decided in 1987, made it clear that the gravity of the interest involved was irrelevant. This decision rejected claims that the death penalty was unconstitutional as applied because a larger proportion of defendants from minority groups, and defendants whose victims were white, got it than did other defendants.[91]

This emphasis on legislative intent fits badly with prevailing constitutional rights doctrine and with constitutional law in general. When the law punishes a criminal, it seems reasonable to link the severity of punishment to the degree of malicious intent. But when a court strikes down a law, the damage done to the legislators who enacted it (even if they are still in office) is minimal compared with that suffered by a losing defendant, criminal or civil. Any damage done to the voters who elected those legislators is even more remote. The harm that judicial review can do in these situations is too slight to warrant this degree of bending over backward to uphold the law.

Cases like *Davis* and *Feeney* send a clear message to lawmakers: you can do anything, as long as you can come up with a reasonable purpose, leave no evidence of an impermissible one, and apply the law regardless of race or sex. Cues like these encourage legislators to make sure that no hint of any intent to discriminate on the basis of race or sex ever gets out. Neutral motives can mask invidious ones because a policy can serve more than one purpose. The veterans' preference law accomplished both the purpose Massachusetts claimed for it and the one Helen Feeney attributed to it.[92]

There is a deeper problem here, an issue familiar from Chapter 3. The Court's emphasis on intent in equal protection doctrine suggests that the judges, like some critics of situation jurisprudence, presume the centrality of free will in human action. This premise leads the Court majority to the conclusion that only the willed consequences of legislative actions matter. The presumption of free will is a common one—the Court certainly did not make *it* up—but it is by no means a universally accepted truth, or even a universally accepted opinion. Philosophical, psychological, and economic determinism, as well as spontaneous order analysis in anthropology, all offer alternatives to free will as explanations of the meanings and consequences of actions. But we need not embrace any of them in order to question whether human purposes are the most important explanations for everything that happens. Anyone who has noticed how, again and again, decisions are made that reinforce the status quo, and how these decisions have innocuous rationales, might be forgiven some skepticism about the primacy of free will. Think, for example, of the following:

- the neoconservative attack on "credentialism" begun in the early 1980s, after women had proven their ability to earn credentials on an equal basis with men, especially when juxtaposed against

- the National Collegiate Athletic Association's decision in the late 1980s to require a minimum score on the Scholastic Aptitude Test for college athletes, in light of the increasing prominence of black athletes in college sports, and the fact that blacks' SAT scores are, on the average, lower than those of whites, or

- the simultaneous emergence in several law firms of the "black review," in which African-American associates undergoing performance evaluations were told they "need to work on their writing," even when they had won awards for it, or

- recommendations in mass-market child care books in the 1970s and 1980s that mothers should breast-feed their infants for as long as a year, or that a mother should refrain from working outside the home until her child starts school, coinciding with the entrance of increasing numbers of women into traditionally male jobs, especially when compared with

- the disapproval of working mothers expressed in the first edition of Dr. Benjamin Spock's *Baby and Child Care*, published in 1946, as men returned from military service to reclaim the jobs women had filled during World War II, or

- the fact that the first man to win first prize in the Pillsbury Bake-Off won the same year the prize was increased to one million dollars.[93]

The actors mentioned here would presumably deny any intention to discriminate against women or minorities. They need not be lying, to us or to themselves, for us to suspect that free will does not tell the whole story, that forces beyond individual control might be at work even if we cannot be sure what these forces are. Nor need we reject free will outright to perceive that the Court, perhaps without realizing it, has chosen among schools of philosophy. Thus, the intent rule represents precisely the kind of choice that judges deny making.

Constitutional Construction and State Action

The idea that the Fourteenth Amendment reaches only state action is almost as old as the amendment itself. The *Civil Rights Cases* of 1883 dealt with the scope of Congress's enforcement power in Section 5 of the Fourteenth Amendment. The Court overturned the public accommodations sections of the Civil Rights Act of 1875. Eight justices chose to read Section 1 of the Fourteenth Amendment narrowly, emphasizing the language of the clause's second sentence: no *state* shall make or enforce . . ., and so forth. The first Justice Harlan was alone in his broad reading of the "substance and spirit" of the Civil War Amendments, whose purpose was "to eradicate" slavery and all its "forms and incidents."[94]

The state action doctrine is no less problematic than the neutral antidiscrimination doctrine or the intent doctrine. The fact that Congress barred racial discrimination in public accommodations as early as 1875, when the Civil War Amendments lay within recent collective memory and while many who had voted for them were still in office, suggests that neither original understanding nor constitutional language bars the extension of the enforcement powers of Section 5 of the Fourteenth Amendment to "private" action. Read with a hundred years' hindsight, the *Civil Rights Cases*, like *Plessy v. Ferguson* or the *Slaughter-House Cases*, suggest that the minority had the better of the argument.[95]

The holding of the *Civil Rights Cases* has, indeed, gone the way of its contemporaries. Congress has used the commerce power to forbid discrimination in the private sector since the 1960s, and state and local governments may forbid discrimination even in clubs and fraternal organizations.[96] But the doctrine of 1883 lives on. While *Shelley v. Kraemer* negated restrictive covenants in the 1940s by extending the definition of state action to include court enforcement of private agreements, *Moose Lodge v. Irvis* narrowed the doctrine in the 1970s by failing to find state action in liquor licenses or sumptuary laws.[97] The state action requirement evinces the unquestioning acceptance of the public-private distinction that much feminist jurisprudence rejects.

The translation of the real claims of real people into the language of deliberate classification and discrimination is traceable to legal principles—neutrality, intent, and state action, to be exact—which have no direct connection with sexual equality and exist independently of it. Yet the application of these principles weakens the constitutional guarantee of sexual equality. These doctrinal developments leave the impression that some hidden historical hand is at work even with respect to the Court itself. The institution which presumes the centrality of free will in theory may refute its own premise in practice.

Conclusion

The 1970s found the Supreme Court, like the rest of American society, struggling with gender issues. Years before the Equal Rights Amendment was defeated, the Court had arrived at a compromise between the patriarchal ideas society had rejected and the egalitarian ideas it was not ready to embrace. The era of "protective" restrictions on women and family law based on "old notions" of sex roles was over. Women may well be the only disadvantaged group to have fared better in the Burger Court than in the Warren Court.

But the Court has not had occasion to apply its new doctrine to a claim initiated by a woman since 1981. The next six cases were originated by men. Although women have a marginally better won-lost record than men do, more men than women have won cases. So far, the new rules have served men's interests better than they have those of women. This record is particularly disturbing because women continue to suffer injustices which are imposed, or at least sanctioned, by law. These injustices remain impervious to adjudication.

Analysis of actual and hypothetical cases reveals the ways in which the language of constitutional doctrine favors men. Expressing the complex, entropic reality of divorce, child custody, military service, and pornography in the kind of language of which constitutional cases are made writes the men's claims in and shuts the women's claims out. The law's indifference to claims arising from women's responsibility for child rearing is matched by its solicitude for claims arising from men's responsibility for warmaking. Equal protection doctrine is dominated by the demand for neutrality, the reliance on the intent of lawmakers, and the distinction between public and private conduct, rather than by the effects of laws or the severity of injuries. These rules are the creation of courts alone; they are dictated by no tenet of constitutional interpretation. These rules come from decisions which, for the most part, have nothing to do with sexual equality. The rules are products of the ways lawyers and judges think about things. They are so independent of the issues raised by the cases that the results might not have differed much if the Court had declared sex a suspect classification or if the ERA had been ratified.

The demand for neutrality, a demand that influenced so many critiques of the landmark *Brown* decision, constitutes a rejection of result-oriented jurisprudence in favor of judicial impartiality. The idea is that results should depend on principles, not preferences. Yet neutral principles, consistently applied, will ultimately reinforce the status quo. If the central idea is that law must concern itself with the disadvantaged (the idea of *Brown I*), decisions may well disturb the balance of power, the patterns of domination and subjection that prevail in society. But if the central idea is that race or sex discrimination is unacceptable (the idea of *Loving, Bakke,* and *Craig*), sooner or later the doctrine will lose its power to initiate change.

This neutralization occurs partly because the advantaged will bring cases; suing is one of many things that advantage enables you to do. But the neutralization has a more complex cause. White supremacy and male supremacy are not neutral institutions. They are institutions of subjection and domination. They consist of power relationships. They are about results. To the extent that adjudication demands neutrality, it is inherently conservative. A search for judicial principles may, in the end, amount to result-oriented jurisprudence.

The reliance on purpose at the expense of effect follows logically from the self-restraint, the presumption of legislative good faith, that judges claim to possess. But why is equal protection the only area of constitutional law in which purpose is given this primacy? By presuming that these laws are the result of conscious choices, thereby choosing free will over other explanations of human action, the Court takes a more activist role than it realizes. Similarly, the state action requirement ensures that court decisions will not disturb the existing division between what happens within the law and what happens outside it.

These judicial choices may doom efforts to create racial and sexual equality. The courts themselves may be part of a dialectic that reinforces the existing power structure. The powerful do not win all the time; but they win often enough, and when necessary. So the constitutional doctrine of sexual equality supports the status quo: male supremacy. Perhaps supporting the status quo is what judges do best. The sexual equality cases are not the only examples of neutralized doctrine. For instance, a "free speech" doctrine which begins by asking when government may restrict speech is likely to result in victory for government censorship at least some of the time.

No one has better described the role of the bench and bar than Alexis de Tocqueville did in 1832: "By birth and interests a lawyer is one of the people, but he is an aristocrat in habits and taste; so he is the natural liaison between aristocracy and people, and the link that joins them." Lawyers and judges, "naturally strongly opposed to the revolutionary spirit and to the ill-considered passions of democracy," mediate between the powerful and the crowd of noisy, demanding litigants.[98] In 1941, Attorney General (later Justice) Robert Jackson wrote, "Never in its entire history can the Supreme Court be said to have for a single hour been representative of anything except the relatively conservative forces of its day."[99] At that time, the Court's "entire history" consisted of just over 150 years. Presumably, Jackson's conclusion would not have surprised Tocqueville.

In retrospect, the Warren Court appears to be an exception to the general rule. A critical majority on that Court was committed to certain results: protecting the disadvantaged, the disenfranchised, the powerless. Because of those commitments, the Court was able, most notably in *Brown I*, to break out of the traditional mold of judicial behavior and categories of judicial thinking, and create new law. In a sense, the Court may have rejected its determined role, without, perhaps, realizing just what it was doing.

Many who welcomed the result of *Brown I* criticized its reasoning. The Court was able to rest its new doctrine on more balanced principles, and those principles have led to a doctrine of sexual equality which benefits those who need it least. The Burger Court may have restored the traditional moderation to the judicial role, relying on precedents and principles which limit the possibilities of change. The Rehnquist Court appears to have assumed the task the Burger Court began, of returning the Court to its appointed place in American society. The more feminists learn about law, the more difficult it becomes to distinguish between principled and result-oriented jurisprudence. In the previous chapter, I called on feminist jurists to give full creative license to the mind, to begin with a willingness to break the rules. This chapter's examination of the constitutional law of sexual equality has moved from general theory of why law might be male-biased to specific analysis of how one area of law stays male-biased. This analysis demonstrates both the consequences of feminists' unreflective acceptance of aspects of conventional doctrine and the reconstructive potential of feminist critique.

Each of the three ruling principles of equal protection doctrine has a counterpart in contemporary feminist jurisprudence. The neutral antidiscrimination principle incorporates the same liberal notion character jurists tend to accept: the idea that law is not an instrument of domination but one of consensus. Law does not oppress; it just makes mistakes in achieving the consensus. For feminist character theory, law's mistake consists in leaving out women's voices; for equal protection doctrine, law's mistake consists in choosing the wrong bases for classification. Neither group seriously considers the possibility that law's purpose has been to subjugate: to put a subordinate group at the service, if not the mercy, of a dominant group.

Likewise, the intent principle evinces the same unreflective premise of free will that allows feminists like Mary Dunlap and Suzanne Rhodenbaugh to read Catharine MacKinnon wrong. For critics of situation jurisprudence, emphasis on women's oppression denies their agency; for the Supreme Court, human agency is the primary factor in determining the constitutional meaning of equal protection law.

Only in considering the state action doctrine do we find feminist jurists leading the way out of the trap. The doctrine of *Civil Rights Cases, Shelley,* and *Moose Lodge* presumes the public-private distinction which feminist theorists criticize. The Fourteenth Amendment, as interpreted, does not reach what happens outside the law—even though the law allows these things to happen. So a woman impoverished by divorce or deprived of her children has no case against the court persuaded by her husband's high-priced lawyer; a disabled child has no case against the public school which allows her classmates to ridicule her; Karen Russell's family has no case against the town which allowed whites to harass them; and Joshua DeShaney has no case against the bureaucracy which let his father beat him almost to death.[100] Feminists' skeptical approach to the public-private distinction permits us to question these results of the state action doctrine; the implications go far beyond women's issues.

By encouraging the breaking of rules, feminist jurisprudence also allows us to breach the traditional regional and topical boundaries in order to extend the scope of equal protection doctrine. Family law has belonged to the states; but the courts' combined receptivity to new claims brought by fathers and indifference to those of mothers should become a constitutional issue. Criminal law has belonged to the trial courts; but their selective revision of the law of self-defense should be subjected to equal protection scrutiny. This chapter reinforces the lesson of Part I that a feminist jurisprudence must accept nothing and question everything.

SIX

RECONSTRUCTING RIGHTS

FEMINIST REPRODUCTIVE FREEDOM

ROE V. WADE confounded the expectations of ideologues and the predictions of experts.[1] Its right to reproductive choice did not survive the Reagan-Bush years intact, but it did survive. Even as *Planned Parenthood v. Casey* allowed states to discourage abortion, the Supreme Court plurality reaffirmed "*Roe*'s concept of liberty in defining the capacity of women . . . to make reproductive decisions."[2] While no branch of the national government seems eager to make abortion more convenient, neither have the states rushed to make it less available. A marginally pro-choice Democratic president and an uneasily antichoice Republican Congress lurch toward deadlock on the issue.

One ruling by seven justices helped put two presidents in office for three terms and dominated the selection of hundreds of judges whose influence will extend long into the twenty-first century. Although Ronald Reagan and George Bush could not make good on their promise to get *Roe* overruled, their electoral success was a measure of the public anger this decision has aroused and of its political failure. Although the right to choose abortion survived the twelve years' war, the narrowness of the pro-choice victory and the Rehnquist Court's weakening of the constitutional right are measures of the judicial disdain *Roe* has aroused and of its doctrinal failure. In twenty years, *Roe* and its successors failed to reach the audiences to which they were addressed.

A majority of Americans may or may not agree with the Court's abortion decisions. Abortion is the pollsters' ultimate puzzle. No one really knows how most people feel about it; findings seem to depend on how any given study phrases the questions. In the late 1990s, experts and pundits inform us that a new consensus has emerged which favors discouraging but not banning abortion—essentially the position taken by the plurality in *Casey*—and hint that it would be nice if the outliers would shut up and go away.[3] But people with intense opinions on the abortion issue will not yield to any centrist consensus, real or illusory. The Court failed to convince opinionated Americans to separate moral from legal questions. Even legal scholars who support abortion rights have found *Roe* useless, at best, in defending their positions.[4]

Apparently, something is wrong with *Roe* and its progeny. I agree with virtually every commentator on these opinions that they contain serious defects. But I suspect that the Court did the best it could with what it had. *Roe v. Wade*'s failure to ground the right of reproductive choice in constitutional doctrine may have been due to defects in the doctrine rather than defects in the opinion. This doctrine is the product of two hundred years of intellectual activity carried on by the half of the human race which does not bear children. While *Roe v. Wade* was the work of seven men, it represented an abrupt departure from the law's conventional way of constructing gender and human reproduction. That departure, long overdue, made *Roe* hard to defend with conventional constitutional arguments—and, I suspect, had far more influence on *Roe*'s critical reception than imperfections in the arguments had. A successful defense of a constitutional right to reproductive choice must go beyond the conventional roots of constitutional interpretation. It must face the gender issues which the Court sidestepped.

"This Right of Privacy": *Roe v. Wade* and Constitutional Theory

Roe v. Wade evinces a great deal of work but not much hard thinking, collegial discourse, or collective deliberation.[5] Justice Harry Blackmun's majority opinion is fifty pages long and crammed with references not only to legal documents but to medical, historical, philosophical, and theological authorities. But the opinion does not indicate appreciation of the complexity of these issues. What *Roe* says raises questions which go unanswered about privacy and personhood. What *Roe* leaves unsaid begs questions which need answers about law and about women.

Privacy and Personhood

The core of *Roe* consists of two propositions with which the Court has little apparent difficulty. The first is Blackmun's statement that "this right of privacy, whether it be founded in the Fourteenth Amendment's concept of personal liberty" or "in the Ninth Amendment's reservation of rights to the people, is broad enough to encompass a woman's decision whether or not to terminate her pregnancy."[6] This conclusion could not resolve the case by itself. Since no constitutional right is absolute, government may infringe rights when a compelling justification to do so exists. If the fetus is a human being from the moment of conception, the right to abortion would therefore become nugatory.[7] But Blackmun's research demonstrated to the majority's satisfaction that no consensus on fetal status has ever existed in our society. Thus, *Roe*'s second proposition: "that the word 'person,' as used in the Fourteenth Amendment, does not include the unborn."[8] Neither of these propositions is obviously true on its face. Each raises a crucial question. First, why does the constitutional right to privacy include the right to choose abortion? Second, if society has never resolved the question of the status of the fetus, why cannot a state decide that human life begins at conception? *Reproductive Health Services v. Webster*, decided sixteen years after *Roe*, ruled that a legislature may write this conclusion into law, but even after *Casey* it remains unclear what this policy entails.[9]

"This right of privacy" came from a 1965 case, *Griswold v. Connecticut*. This decision overturned a uniquely obsolescent law banning the use of contraceptives. Justice William O. Douglas's plurality opinion declared that, although the Constitution recognizes no specific right of privacy, it contains a "zone of privacy" created by "penumbras, emanating" from several provisions of the Bill of Rights. These provisions include the First Amendment, which protects privacy of association; the Third Amendment's prohibition of quartering of soldiers in the home; the Fourth Amendment's protection against unreasonable searches and seizures; the Fifth Amendment's self-incrimination clause; and the Ninth Amendment's reference to unenumerated "rights . . . retained by the people." A married couple's right to use birth control resided within this zone of privacy. The result of *Griswold* was far more welcome than its doctrine. Douglas's opinion, with its perambulation through the constitutional text and its reference to "the sacred precincts of marital bedrooms," confused privacy with autonomy, enforcement with proscription, and listing with thinking.[10]

The decision provoked widespread criticism from law professors, and it remains useful for honing the analytical and critical skills of students. But subsequent cases indicate that the Court settled the issue to its own satisfaction in 1965. While *Griswold* never became a blank-check precedent, later decisions extended the right to use contraceptives to single individuals and to minors without provoking much wrath.[11] *Casey* reaffirmed the principle that "our law affords constitutional protection to personal decisions . . . concerning not only the meaning of procreation but also human responsibility and respect for it."[12] *Roe* was one in a series of cases which built on the same vulnerable precedent.

The right to privacy is far from being the only constitutional doctrine which rests on flawed judicial reasoning. The need to command a Court majority, and the fallibility of the human mind, ensure that jurisprudence will strive for perfection rather than attain it. But *Griswold*'s recognition of a right to privacy does not entail *Roe*'s extension of this right to the abortion decision. That conclusion bore a heavy burden of justification.

The differences between contraception and abortion are at least as obvious as the similarities. There is a perceptible logical relationship between contraception and the guarantees invoked in *Griswold*: the Third and Fourth Amendments, which protect private space, and the self-incrimination clause of the Fifth Amendment, which protects private information. But abortion is not private—not yet, anyway. It requires the cooperation of medical professionals. So even if one accepts Douglas's argument in *Griswold*, its application to abortion must be demonstrated rather than assumed.

Roe needed a stronger defense than *Griswold* for another reason. The widespread public support for the right to use birth control that existed in 1965 cushioned the reaction to *Griswold*. Eight years later, opposition to abortion was widespread enough and intense enough to ensure that *Roe* would get maximum critical scrutiny. The only other occasion where extending the privacy doctrine would have gotten the Court into controversial territory was *Bowers v. Hardwick*, the 1986 homosexual rights case; here, the Court refused to extend *Griswold*.[13]

A persuasive argument for the right to abortion might have defused *Roe*'s second unanswered question. If a woman's right to privacy includes the right to end a pregnancy, public support for a problematic definition of life cannot constitute a compelling interest in abridging the right. Therefore, the state cannot force people to act as if human life begins at conception. Those who believe abortion is murder may be beyond persuasion on this point. But the Court failed even to mount a convincing argument for the rights of people who do not share this opinion.

Blackmun's argument for extending the privacy right to cover abortion relied on the harmful consequences of unwanted pregnancy: "specific and direct harm medically diagnosable," "a distressful life and future," "psychological harm," "the distress, for all concerned, associated with an unwanted child," and "the problem of bringing a child into a family already unable, psychologically and otherwise, to care for it."[14] Even an unfriendly critic conceded that "having an unwanted pregnancy can go a long way toward ruining a woman's life."[15] But government interferes with our freedom and imposes burdens on us all the time. If a right to abortion exists, there must be better reasons than that unwanted pregnancy is rough. So are paying taxes, getting drafted, losing the old family home to make room for a super-highway, and any number of burdens that government can impose on us. Since *Roe* does not effectively distinguish unwanted pregnancy from other burdens human beings must bear, the Court's refusal to let legislatures decide the issue of fetal status is not persuasive.

Rights and Gender

Like *Lochner v. New York*, *Griswold* enacted a "theory which a large part of the country does not entertain."[16] What *Lochner* was to social Darwinism, *Griswold* is to liberalism—as Justice Hugo Black's dissent implies.[17] While reliable evidence of the degree of popular support for liberal theory is lacking—as with abortion, it seems to depend on how you phrase the question—the idea that a constitutional right to abortion is implied by the widely shared beliefs of Americans did not gain much acceptance. The privacy cases go even further than some liberal philosophers do. Unlike John Stuart Mill, *Griswold* and its successors do not base the liberty they recognize on a distinction between self-regarding and other-regarding actions.[18] Instead, less like Mill than like Jefferson in the Declaration of Independence, the cases posit rights which are not qualified by a requirement that their exercise be innocuous. Moreover, *Griswold*, *Roe*, and *Casey* treat as settled an issue on which Mill argued and Jefferson was silent. The decisions apply rights theory to women.

What these cases leave unsaid is as problematic as what they say. The birth control cases give little indication that the ability to control one's fertility has a greater impact on women's lives than on men's. Even *Roe*, despite its emphasis on "the detriment that the State would impose upon the pregnant woman," aims for neutrality. In early pregnancy, "the abortion decision and its effectuation must be left to the medical judgment of the pregnant woman's attending physician" (who is always "he").[19] But in *Casey*, Justice Sandra Day O'Connor wrote, "The destiny of the woman must be shaped to a large extent on her own conception of her spiritual imperatives and her place in society."[20] This is how liberal theory construes *man's* destiny. But it is not the way American law has construed woman's reality.

Rights theory was generated by men and derived from male experience.[21] The theory's origins do not, by themselves, make the theory invalid for women (see Chapter 2). But the question of whether, how, and to what extent rights theory applies to women has never been settled, not even among feminists. *Roe* unambiguously brings women within the scope of rights theory. Women, like men, have a "zone of privacy" which the state may not invade. *Roe* and *Casey* do not argue in favor of this proposition; they take it for granted. For the Court to treat women's inclusion in the system of constitutional rights as a proposition so basic that it is beyond debate reflects a much stronger commitment to sexual equality than discussing the proposition would have. Comparing *Roe* and *Casey* with the Court's opinion in *Craig v. Boren* or the plurality opinion in *Bakke* will illustrate this distinction.[22] But the assumption that liberal theory applies to women was no more popular than the assumption that liberal theory is embedded in the Constitution: less so, probably, given the fact that *Roe* coincided with the antifeminist backlash which defeated the Equal Rights Amendment.[23]

Law and Nature

The privacy cases' use of political theory is not their only innovation. These decisions reverse—in fact, they upend—the conventional relationship between law and reproduction. The fact that women bear children is not the *cause* of male supremacy, any more than dark skin was the cause of slavery. But childbearing has provided a convenient rationale for unequal treatment: how can we treat women like men when they are so obviously different from men? American jurisprudence has invoked women's reproductive function to justify depriving them of freedom ("protective" labor legislation, as in *Muller v. Oregon*); subjecting them to coercion (involuntary sterilization, as in *Buck v. Bell*); and burdening them with duties ("fetal protection" policies, like the one overturned in *United Auto Workers v. Johnson Controls*).[24] Less often, law has used women's childbearing capacity to justify restrictions on men, as in *Michael M v. Superior Court of Sonoma County*.[25]

As Chapter 7 will show, these different policies presume different relationships among women, children, and the state. But they all use nature (women's reproductive function) to justify law (usually, restrictions on women). The privacy cases do exactly the opposite. The story *Griswold*, *Roe*, and *Casey* tell is one in which law allows people to control nature's effects. Chapter 4 showed that the idea of *men* mastering nature is embedded in the conventional epistemology of liberal discourse. But, until the privacy cases, the relationship between women and nature, as constructed by law, has been the other way around. And *Roe* does not notice what it has done.

No wonder *Roe* generated so much public opposition and so little scholarly support. The Court made assertions it failed to defend; it reversed the conventional legal relationship between women and their reproductive function, and between law and nature; it endorsed a political theory that many Americans reject; and it doubled the population to whom that theory applied. *Roe v. Wade* rested on shaky foundations indeed.

The academic reaction to the decision was vehement. Scholars made all these criticisms, and more, and made them persistently. One prominent critic was Louis Lusky, a "ghostwriter" of liberal judicial activism; as a law clerk, he drafted Footnote Four of *United States v. Carolene Products*, the basis for heightened judicial protection of individual rights.[26] Now, with palpable anger, he wrote, "The Justices have given serious cause for suspicion that they have come to consider the Court to be above the law." John

Hart Ely, an advocate of both judicial activism and legalized abortion, called *Roe* "a very bad decision. It is bad because it is bad constitutional law, or rather because it is *not* constitutional law and gives almost no sense of an obligation to try to be." Richard Epstein declared, "*Roe v. Wade* is symptomatic of the analytical poverty possible in constitutional litigation." Even Laurence Tribe, who defended the ruling, insisted that "interest-balancing of the form the Court pursues fails to justify any of the lines actually drawn." The opinion did not earn the approval of the Supreme Court's critics circle.[27]

What We Know as Women

Twenty years later, the effects of time, postmodernism, and Title IX on the legal profession have sensitized us to the subtext: *John* Ely, *Louis* Lusky, *Richard* Epstein. The critical chorus, like the court it criticized, sang in the lower registers only. The jurisprudential debate over *Roe* reminded me of an opinion I encountered in writing a book on protective labor legislation. In 1910, the Illinois Supreme Court wrote, "It is known to all men—and what we know as men we cannot be ignorant of as judges—that woman's physical structure and the performance of maternal functions place her at a great disadvantage in the battle for life."[28] The conclusion, long since discredited, is less interesting than the prologue. What we know as *men*, indeed. If there are things men know as men, what things might women know as women?

While there is no unanimous feminist position on abortion, most women who label themselves feminists support legalized abortion, and most women who oppose legalized abortion do not label themselves feminists. In general, feminists seem to recognize that a commitment to women's rights entails a commitment to reproductive choice.[29] But feminist scholars have been as critical as any other group of *Roe* and its ideological under-pinnings.

Character jurists have questioned the premises of liberalism and its com-mitment to negative rights. Robin West's argument that liberal legal theory is untrue for women partly because they bear children, and Carol Gilligan's thesis that women's ethical orientations value relationships over rights, dis-pute a proposition that *Roe* assumes to be true.[30] Other feminist critics of liberalism have made similar arguments. Elizabeth Fox-Genovese is dis-turbed by a similarity between the right to abortion and a "right to the male model of individualism," while Jean Bethke Elshtain deplores *Roe*'s "militant notion of privacy that undercuts any serious political claims launched from a moral point of view by deploying a notion of tolerance construed as the insistence that the private opinions of others can exert no claims over us."[31] Situation jurists found *Roe* at best an inadequate guarantee for women, and at worst a dangerous trap for them. Wendy Brown, for instance, questioned the rights orientation embedded in the decision: "Insofar as rights are inherently *protective, defensive* and *isolating*, these are three things that women-as-reproducers do not need more of."[32] Catharine MacKinnon warned that protecting women from the state might leave them more vulnerable to private power: "The availability of abortion removes the one remaining legitimized reason that women have had for refusing sex besides the headache."[33] These feminists' commitment to reproductive choice has not led them to accept the Court's argument for a right to abortion.

Part I of this book suggested that a chorus which sang in the upper as well as the lower registers might arrive at its conclusions by different routes: make different arguments (or argue in different ways, or do something other than argue); reason from those things known to women which may not be known to men (or not in the same way); and order priorities in ways more responsive to women's experience.

Recomposing for Women's Voices: Feminism and Choice

Having argued that feminist jurisprudence must be willing to break the rules of conventional legal reasoning, I now violate at least two of them. I rely in part on imagination: the "what if?" approach, with its ventures into fantasy. I employ this device because personal opinions, unlike arguments, do not always lend themselves to the conventional modes of intellectual analysis. All too often, the answer to "why?" is "because." But asking "What would have to change for me to change this opinion?" springs the trap of "why?" and "because."

Another unconventional aspect of my argument is its flouting of the conventional strictures against emotion, opinion, and result-oriented jurisprudence.[34] I let my own feelings and experiences into the analysis. I start from a prerational conviction that sexual equality entails the right to reproductive choice. But, I submit, the combination of analysis and opinion is a virtue, not a defect, of this scholarship. A predisposition in favor of one side of an issue does not require rigid determination to keep this opinion out of one's argument, nor does such a bias inevitably skew the results of one's scholarship. Instead, such a conviction can lead to an effort to discover any core of truth the opinion might have.

A common objection making connections between constitutional law and personal opinion goes something like this: "Yes, but the opponents of choice feel as deeply as you do, and you object to *their* reasoning from their feelings." A second problem is that "we"—the writers and readers of jurisprudence—are not typical of all women. We are educated, middle-class professionals.[35] These attributes may be particularly salient and divisive in the debate over reproductive choice. Many of us fit Kristin Luker's description of the typical pro-choice activist: a woman with a college education, a professional career, and no more than two children.[36] My doctorate, university professorship, and child-free status constitute an almost perfect fit with Luker's model. A third difficulty with grounding a case for a constitutional right to choice in women's experiences is that no common opinion unites either those who share these experiences or those who lack them. Neither women nor men agree among themselves. Luker found that most activists on both sides were women. Since she wrote, in the 1980s, more male antichoice activists have become prominent. But public opinion polls show no clear, consistent differences between men and women on this issue.[37]

These problems do not doom my enterprise to defeat. The parallel between pro-choice and antichoice reasoning from opinion is inexact. To my knowledge, pro-choice advocates have not tried to force anyone to act against her prerational conviction that abortion is morally wrong. But the other side tries to force people to act in conformity with its beliefs.[38] The relative homogeneity of feminist scholars, and their differences from most women, need not sentence us to silence; even middle-class women professionals have added dimensions to the constitutional debate which the middle-class *men* professionals who have dominated it have not provided. The third problem is the most serious. An effort to construct woman-centered arguments for choice must deal with the woman-centered arguments against choice which already exist, and I do so. But basing a case for choice on distinctively female knowledge and experience does not require that the argument be acceptable to all or most women.

The fact that a group of people share similar experiences does not mean that all the members of the group must draw the same conclusions from the experiences. The lack of consensus among women, even among feminists, about reproductive rights challenges the feminist scholar even as it frustrates her. The arguments of self-styled "pro-life feminists" provide a starting point for my efforts to construct theory. Anyone may call herself anything she chooses; there is no English Academy of Political Language. But analysis reveals that the arguments of the pro-life feminists are incompatible with the principle of sexual equality. I then ask if we can envision circumstances under which these two positions could be reconciled. Out of these elements, I work toward a feminist theory of reproductive rights.

Who Decides?

The arguments made by antichoice feminists fall into two general categories. They assert, first, that the fetus is human. But their positions on fetal status are indistinguishable from those of antichoice authors who do not label themselves feminists. Sharon Long, a former national officer in Feminists for Life and volunteer counselor with Birthright, asks, "If an individual woman has to kill her child to get ahead, what does 'getting ahead' mean?" Sydney Callahan admits she does not know "why I'm committed to those tiny little dots of nothing that an embryo is."[39] Compare this rhetoric to the following excerpts from essays published in the center-to-left print media since 1989: "We should not be permissive concerning the taking of human life"; "I have always been convinced that the term 'unborn child' is a genuine description of material reality"; "we already know . . . that abortion is the eradication of human life"; and, from a feminist, "how . . . can I square a recognition of the humanity of the fetus, and the moral gravity of destroying it, with a pro-choice position?"[40] Opponents of choice are as free as anyone else to act upon their feelings, and proponents of choice are free to feel as much agony as they wish, but these writers offer no convincing arguments for imposing those feelings upon others.

Roe v. Wade found "the difficult question of when life begins" unanswerable.[41] Hindsight, medical advances, and ongoing debate allow us to regret that the Court framed the question as it did. The reproductive process is extraordinarily complex, the question of fetal status has no clear answer, and the resolution of the abortion issue need not depend upon the status of the fetus.[42] But woman-centered analysis suggests a different question to answer.

To answer Blackmun's "difficult question" by proclaiming that life begins "at conception" is useless, for several reasons. First, " 'life' does not begin; it is passed on" from a live sperm and a live ovum. Therefore, the beginning of life cannot be equated with fertilization (the joining of sperm and egg, producing a zygote), with implantation (when the former zygote, now a blastocyst, attaches to the uterine wall), with "viability" (the stage of gestation when the fetus can live outside its mother's body), or with birth. Second, the term "conception" has no precise meaning. Dictionaries define it, unhelpfully, as "becoming pregnant." Third, there is no "at." Fetal development consists not of changes occurring at any "identifiable 'moment,' " as the preposition implies, but of gradual stages and processes.[43]

Even if life does not "begin" at any point, we can still debate whether or not the fetus is a person. Opinions, informed and otherwise, range from denial of any humanity before birth to the position that human life is pres-

ent by the time a woman has confirmed her pregnancy. Most of these solutions rest on notions of what it means to be human that are not universally
accepted and have been widely criticized. Yes, a fetus may look like an
infant already born, but no more so than a doll or a puppy dressed in baby
clothes; yes, "the fetus is biologically determined by its genetic code," but
so is every cell in the human body.[44] None of these facts make a fetus a
human being, because we have no clear, shared definition of what a human
being is.[45]

Even if the fetus is human, it need not follow that the pregnant woman
has a duty to keep that person alive. Judith Jarvis Thomson's hypothetical
dying violinist who can survive only if connected to another person's body
for nine months is perhaps the best-known example of this sort of argument.[46] Thomson's ventures into science fiction have provoked more attacks on her mode of argumentation than challenges to her conclusion that
no one would posit a legal obligation to cooperate in such a situation.[47] But
her argument does not require reliance on fantasy. Restrictive abortion
laws impose obligations on pregnant women which are qualitatively different from, and more onerous than, any which the law routinely imposes on
anyone else. Real-life situations exist—donating blood, for example—in
which people can save others' lives at little risk to their own. The law does
not force people to do so—not even for members of their own families.[48]
Eileen McDonagh argues "that the key issue in the abortion debate is not
what the fetus 'is,' but rather what it 'does'. . . . If the fetus is a human life
under state protection, then when it intrudes on a woman's body without
her consent, the state must allocate public resources to stop the fetus to
the degree that the state stops private parties from intruding on others."[49]

Roe juxtaposed the woman's privacy interests to the state's interest in
preserving "potential human life."[50] The Court gave priority to the woman
over the state because no societal agreement existed on what was being
preserved. This emphasis on society's failure to decide the status of the
fetus implies that the power to resolve that question belongs to the state:
it could decide (but has not) what the entity inside the woman's body is
and determine her obligations in the light of that definition. Yet it makes
equally good sense to start from the viewpoint of the individual pregnant
woman. How does she think and feel? What does she do?

A woman faced with an unwanted pregnancy does not inevitably place
what Justice Byron White's dissent calls her "convenience" ahead of "the
continued existence and development of the life or potential life that she
carries."[51] Millions of women have chosen not to have abortions since 1973.
Apparently, women themselves have a wide range of ideas of what is inside
their bodies, of relationships with that entity, and of notions of their responsibilities to it. Some women, however unwelcome their pregnancies
are, never consider abortion; others decide against it. Women who do abort

react in different ways: with indifference, numbness, anger, grief, guilt, or relief.[52] Why not trust pregnant women, rather than allow the state to impose its own definition? Why not presume that it is the woman, by aborting or going to term, who decides to make the fetus human? This is obviously a liberal argument, but the position it articulates is also a feminist one. It grants the power to confer humanity to the mother, not to the state, to experts, or to vocal segments of the population, however passionate their beliefs.

This position has powerful implications for the abortion debate. If humanity is conferred by the mother, the important prepositions are "inside" and "outside," not "at." The rationale for prohibiting abortion after "viability" disappears. The premise that the mother confers humanity also means that abortion can be a positive good rather than a tolerated right; it can be the best solution to some unwanted pregnancies. The position which can be summarized as "adoption, not abortion"—argued by George Bush in the second debate in the 1988 presidential campaign—loses its force if we presume that the mother decides if and when the fetus is human.[53] The reverse side of these arguments is that a pregnant woman who believes she is carrying a baby, not a fetus, must not be forced into abortion.

One answer to the question In the absence of agreement, why may not a state act on the presumption that human life begins at conception? is "Because the state is (1) legislating nonsense, by ignoring facts, or (2) substituting its own fiat for the insights of women's own experience, or (3) arbitrarily singling out pregnant women to impose upon them burdens imposed on no one else." We know the state may legislate morality, but may it legislate unreason?[54]

In Whose Interests?

The second argument stressed by antichoice feminists is that a right to abortion is antithetical to the genuine, permanent interests of women. The assertion that the unborn deserve equal consideration with the born depends not only on an unreflective and unexamined premise that the fetus is human but also on a specific idea of what is good for women. This argument relies partly on theses familiar from character jurisprudence. Sydney Callahan invokes Carol Gilligan's work to argue that the pro-choice position is "a betrayal of feminism, which has built the struggle for justice on the bedrock of women's empathy." For Callahan, abortion rejects "a responsible commitment to the loving nurture of specific human beings" in favor of "male aggression and destruction."[55] But her reference to "women's biologically unique capacity and privilege" gives the game away.[56] To describe as "unique" an ability shared with roughly half the world's adult population and with the females of numerous other animal species is, to say the least, rhetorical excess. The fact that this exaggeration is common in discourse about reproductive freedom should not desensitize the critical feminist reader to the possibility that it masks something fishy. The words "capacity and privilege" suggest that Callahan is fudging. Something you *can* do is a capacity; something you *may* do is a privilege; something you *must* do is a duty. This formulation turns something only women (and no men) can do into something any pregnant woman must do; this imperative becomes a unilateral duty. If a capacity shared by virtually all women entails duties men do not share, women are not equal to men. "Pro-life feminism" is not feminism at all.

The fact that men may have duties women do not share, like military service, does not make this inequality go away. Three factors vitiate the comparison between motherhood and military service. First, as Chapter 5 showed, military service has carried with it privileges as well as risks. But even if society attached privileges to motherhood, the analogy would not hold. The second important difference between these two functions is that military service has never been the presumed duty of virtually all men, as childbearing has been for women. There is no draft now, and there has not been one since 1973. Conscription was in effect for a total of thirty-nine years of United States history: from 1940 to 1973, during World War I (1917–18) and during the Civil War (1861–65). When the draft did exist, only men within certain age-groups were subjected to it. Finally, the analogy presumes that men and women are basically equal, so that discrimination against one sex is just as bad as discrimination against another. But the thesis of this book has been that women do not enjoy equal status with men except in the narrowest literal sense. Therefore, women-only burdens violate sexual equality in a way that men-only burdens do not. The draft never relegated men to a general position of gender inferiority, where they were continually vulnerable to obligations women did not share.[57]

Several feminist critics of *Roe v. Wade* find its theoretical premises hostile to women for reasons that not entail single-sex obligations.[58] Character theory's ethic of care can provide support for an antichoice position. The decision to destroy the fetus rather than to make it human could be interpreted as choosing an ethic of autonomy over Gilligan's "ethic of nurturance, responsibility, and care," choosing rights over the "womanly duties" Sara Ruddick associates with "maternal thinking," or choosing abstract justice over Nel Noddings's "affective human response."[59] But the positions of prominent character theorists and feminist critics of liberalism range from silence to ambivalence to forthright defense of choice. Neither Gilligan nor Ruddick commits herself in print to any position on reproductive choice. However, Gilligan's chapter on the decision to continue or terminate an unwanted pregnancy shows that the choice of abortion can be consistent with the highest level of an ethic of care and responsibility; the accounts of Gilligan's subjects cast serious doubt on Callahan's assertion that abortion represents a choice of aggression over nurturance. Jean Bethke Elshtain and Elizabeth Fox-Genovese disapprove of abortion and criticize *Roe* without going so far as to advocate recriminalization.[60] For Noddings, "our attention should go to those already existing beings with whom we can establish a positive relation."[61] Robin West bases her defense of choice on her thesis of women's material connection to human life: "Women need the freedom to make reproductive decisions not merely to vindicate a right to be left alone, but often to strengthen their ties to others."[62] A defense of reproductive choice grounded in women's obligations to serve others ominously echoes defenses of protective labor legislation on the grounds that it gave women more time to serve their families.[63] But, whatever the merits of this argument, it is one of several against reasoning from character theory to an antichoice position. Not only would rejecting rights leave women at the mercy of people who *do* value rights; but ethical theorists are able to separate *legal* rights from *moral* choices.

Some pro-life feminist arguments read less like character jurisprudence than like situation jurisprudence. Sydney Callahan asserts that legalized abortion reinforces rather than alleviates women's disadvantages vis-à-vis men and society. "Traditionally, many men have been laggards in assuming parental responsibility and support for their children; ironically, ready abortion, often advocated as a response to male dereliction, legitimizes male irresponsibility and paves the way for even more male detachment and lack of commitment."[64] Sharon Long questions the priorities of pro-choice feminists. "Keeping teens unpregnant may help a few individuals, but it will do nothing to change the basic structure of the ghetto."[65] Juli Loesch, whose statement that abortion allows men to "use a woman [and] vacuum her out" was quoted in Chapter 3, has worked with both Feminists for Life and Operation Rescue.[66] Loesch's vulgarization of intercourse is the reverse image of Callahan's idealization of childbirth. It requires no great skill with the English language to reduce pregnancy and childbirth to the kind of crude physical violation that Loesch makes of sex. If intercourse is men using women, forced abortion is surely no worse than forced pregnancy followed by forced childbirth. But the discourse is one-sided, in tone if not in content. Harsh, reductionist language is acceptable in referring to sex, but not to reproduction.

Tone aside, these authors have got something right. *Roe v. Wade* offers no protection to the woman who cannot pay for an abortion, cannot find a qualified professional to perform it, needed help in preventing the pregnancy in the first place, or wants the baby.[67] It is scant help to a woman to have the right to an abortion if—as the law decreed until very recently—her husband has the right to demand her sexual services. Evidence confirms MacKinnon's and Loesch's suspicions that some women are coerced into abortions they do not want.[68] Situation theorists' distrust of the privacy doctrine leads back from *Roe* to *Griswold*, with its emphasis on the marriage relationship. Feminist scholars have found other ways to characterize marriage than "sacred," "enduring," and "noble." For instance: "Underlying all family law principles in the American legal system is the concept of the privatized, closed family system. . . . The 'hands off' principle functions to increase the control of the more powerful party in an institution such as marriage."[69]

But not only; and not quite. First of all, *Griswold, Eisenstadt v. Baird, Roe,* and *Casey* apply to women outside marital or quasi-marital relationships. Second, the privatized family system presumed by American law also presumed that only one partner in the marriage had rights. The rulings on birth control and abortion make the partners more nearly equal by removing any doubt over whether the right to control fertility extends to women.[70] Men's rights are dangerous for women; women's rights are not. The antichoice feminists are right to insist that, in the absence of enforceable claims upon men and upon society as a whole, choice only makes women more nearly equal to men, not truly equal. But the fact that a right to abortion is inadequate to ensure women's reproductive freedom not does not make legalized abortion bad in itself. "A right to privacy looks like an injury got up as a gift" because the law's definition of "right" is so narrow and men's advantages over women so powerful.[71]

Loesch and Callahan move from the accurate insight that legal abortion allows men to behave badly to the dubious assumption that forbidding abortion would make men behave better. While abortion does increase men's sexual access to women, recriminalizing abortion would not decrease men's access in general—only (maybe) their temporary access to individual women. While "you didn't have to have the kid" expresses a familiar attitude, men have never needed an excuse to leave child care to women. Does anyone seriously believe that men would be taking more responsibility in the 1990s if the Court had ruled differently in 1973?

Sharon Long's argument presupposes that poverty is the primary motivation behind the choice of abortion. Would women who choose to abort have their babies if they had more money? In general, affluent women do not bear more children than poor women. The evidence is overwhelmingly to the contrary, at least in industrial societies: as standard of living rises, fertility declines. A similar inverse relationship exists between female fertility and education. The more choices a woman has, the fewer children she bears.[72] And no wonder. Money might make a difference in a woman's first pregnancy; but what about her fourth, or seventh, or ninth? A little of women's unique capacity and privilege seems to go a long way.

Pro-choice feminists cannot casually dismiss the moral questions raised by Callahan's argument that "all human life is interdependent and in need of nurturing protection, especially from its progenitors and kin, whatever our stage of achieved maturity or present access to power or resources; valid rights arise from need."[73] But the antichoice feminists do not distinguish between moral and legal questions. Forbidding abortion would impose obligations to these helpless unborn only upon their mothers. The antichoice feminists should follow their own advice about priorities. Easing the burdens of mothers is an important goal. Making women unpoor rather than unpregnant, and redistributing responsibility for children, would improve women's material situation much more than access to abortion does. But recriminalizing abortion would make women's situation worse, not better. Policy changes which would improve women's situation cannot be accomplished in time to relieve the burdens of a woman who is now pregnant. Like the ethicists of care, the antichoice feminists have an ethic of obligation for women only.[74]

So far, "pro-life feminists" have not succeeded in making an even minimally feminist case against legalized reproductive choice. Indeed, much of what they say reinforces the pro-choice feminist position. There is nothing antifeminist about arguing that relieving poverty or redistributing responsibility is more important than abortion rights. But feminists are justified in questioning anyone's claim to be both an opponent of abortion rights and a proponent of sexual equality.

What If . . . ?

One way to formulate a feminist case for the right of reproductive choice is to ask: Under what circumstances would a commitment to women's rights be compatible with, or even demand, a *rejection* of the right to abortion? Thinking about what conditions might reduce feminist support for reproductive choice can help illuminate those circumstances which make choice so important.

Suppose, for instance, that "the burdens that the State would impose upon the pregnant woman by denying her this choice altogether" did not attend motherhood: that, instead, to be a mother was to have significant tangible privileges, to have a claim on others for support, to have partner, family, and community share one's responsibilities.[75] Suppose men and women took equal responsibility for child care in the home; that good, reliable child care was readily available outside the home; that health care for mothers and infants was free; and that childbearing and parenting leaves were granted to all workers. Suppose, further, that here, as in Europe, the state subsidized all custodial mothers, single or married, employed or unemployed. Or, imagine a "mothers' preference," similar to "veterans' preference," that would confer employment advantages upon those who perform this valuable public service. Any of these changes might induce some women who now choose abortion to have their babies instead. But where my "imaginary" policies actually exist, they have accompanied the right of choice rather than replacing it. And none of these reforms would eliminate the physical burdens of pregnancy, or the possibility of accidental conception.

Since this exercise is an imaginative one, we need not restrict our hypothetical circumstances to those that are now capable of realization. Suppose, for example, that no woman could become pregnant more than once in her life, so that an abortion would prevent her from ever becoming a mother. Would we then oppose abortion? Feminists do not agree among themselves about the significance of motherhood in a woman's life. Very few feminists either reject motherhood forever, for everyone, and under all circumstances or deny that in the real world women have valid reasons not to bear children.[76] Many, perhaps most, feminists believe that, if the choice was not coercively structured and where the consequences Justice Blackmun mentions did not attend motherhood, some women would become mothers and some would not. But a few feminist writers seem to doubt that, under ideal conditions and with free choice, a woman would renounce motherhood.[77] Even these feminists might be reluctant to force their views on other woman to the extent of denying them the choice to remain child-free. (After all, we do accept a woman's right to voluntary sterilization.) But if a woman could get pregnant only once in her life, the costs to her of legal abortion might outweigh the gains. Again, fantasy helps clarify reality. For most women, most of the time, the supply of fertility far exceeds the demand. Choosing to terminate a pregnancy rarely entails renouncing parenthood. A woman who seeks an abortion can anticipate becoming a mother in the future, if she is not one already. The use of words like "unique," "valuable," and "privilege" to describe childbearing capacity obscures the fact that fertility lacks one attribute which makes us value things: scarcity.[78]

Suppose we revise the last fantasy. Birth control essentially "locks" a person's fertility. What if we had to "unlock" it instead? Suppose a man and woman could not become parents unless they both underwent some purposeful procedure at some time prior to and separate from sexual intercourse. Or suppose we could control fertility by a technique similar to biofeedback. Suppose, further, that after conception our fertility locked itself up again. If we had to intend *to* conceive rather than *not* to, a woman who chose to end a pregnancy under these circumstances might be accused of trying to renege on an agreement. But only the woman suffers the physical consequences of pregnancy and childbirth. These can be harsh, without threatening her life or long-term health. A woman who chose to get pregnant might feel that she had not grasped the physical consequences of this decision and that, therefore, her decision was not an informed one. Or her circumstances might change; the child's father might renege on his part of the bargain.

No imaginative exercise can leave out the obvious: suppose men, not women, became pregnant? It would be selfish of women to deny men the right to terminate pregnancies. But it certainly would not threaten *women's* autonomy if abortion were forbidden. Or suppose that both men and women could bear children.[79] The absence of reproductive choice would not put women at a disadvantage. But it would restrict everyone's freedom. Women would be less able to fight for their rights. Reproductive choice would be no less necessary for women in this situation than freedom of expression is now. However, feminists do not agree about freedom of expression (witness the debate over pornography), so there is no reason to conclude that they would agree about reproductive choice if both sexes were equally vulnerable to pregnancy.

If women could not conceive unless they chose to, and *if* their partners had to make a similar choice, and *if* motherhood conferred benefits instead of burdens, could we make a feminist case against abortion? Any such argument would jar with the reality that situations can change after pregnancy in ways that make motherhood burdensome even in these Utopian circumstances. True, there might be fewer abortions. Feminists might not have to devote so much energy to defending this right. Still, we seem to be left with the conclusion that the only circumstances in which a ban on abortion would be compatible with women's rights are those in which men bore and raised children.

Rights, Needs, and Conventional Theory: Regrounding Jurisprudence

> A focus on "rights" ignores *needs*.
> *(Barbara Katz Rothman)*

> Valid rights arise from need.
> *(Sydney Callahan)*

The authors quoted in these epigraphs both identify themselves as feminist scholars. Rothman supports legalized abortion, while Callahan opposes it. While their policy positions are mutually contradictory, their theoretical positions are ultimately reconcilable. Rothman assesses; Callahan prescribes. Rothman juxtaposes rights and needs; Callahan tries to reconcile them. Rothman articulates a familiar feminist critique of rights theory; Callahan provides the basis of a feminist response to this critique which ultimately undercuts her own argument.

Rothman's statement, and its converse, are true, at least within the intellectual tradition of *Roe v. Wade*. This tradition recognizes two sources of rights. The standard theory that feminists challenge grounds rights in one's status as an autonomous individual: rights are part of what it means to be human. This idea, associated with Locke and Jefferson, provoked a critique that I call elsewhere an "antitheory." Nineteenth-century defenders of slavery, like John C. Calhoun, insisted that rights must be earned: "liberty . . . is a reward reserved for the intelligent, the patriotic, the virtuous and the deserving."[80]

Theory and antitheory, contradictory on paper, coexist in law. Some rights arise from entitlement; others are earned. Sometimes we confuse the two; Social Security, for example, is an "entitlement" program consisting mostly of payments for which eligibility is earned through worker participation.[81] Thus, we recognize both entitlement and desert as sources of rights. But not need. Think again of Heinz's dilemma from Chapter 3: no one suggests that the dying woman has a right to the medicine. People whom liberalism recognizes as having needs tend to lose rights. Think of children (now) and women (formerly). *Muller v. Oregon* asserted—did not imply, *said*—that women's need for protection justified limitations on their rights. Theory and policy set rights and needs in opposition.

And that is precisely Callahan's point. By valid rights, she means positive rights, not just negative rights. By need, she means a condition common to all human beings, not just those the law recognizes as dependent. Her statement, clearly labeled as opinion, may have some, if limited, concrete application.[82] Children have a right to care and support from their parents, as wives once did from their husbands. Children have this right long before they can perform the reciprocal duty of obedience. The same Social Security which provides benefits for workers and their survivors also provides benefits for the disabled. Dependents' rights are, of course, very different from those recognized by Locke, Jefferson, or Calhoun: positive rather than negative, enforceable against other human beings rather than against the state, premised not on autonomy but on its opposite. Still, these are rights, and they accompany need. Does the need thereby create the right?

What happens if parents cannot or will not meet their children's needs? The 1994 election and its aftermath are teaching the poor the brutal lesson that need does not entail rights in American society. Welfare programs that premise entitlement on need are in jeopardy—even grants intended to benefit children, whose share of formal legal rights ranges from partial to nonexistent. Indeed, the limits on children's enjoyment of the negative rights recognized in the Constitution argue against any connection between right and need; surely, people subject to not one but three jurisdictions could use a certain amount of noninterference.[83] The rights of dependents arise not from need but from presumed incompetence—lack of full autonomous human status—and on special relationships: husband-wife once, parent-child still.

The general notion that rights arise from need, an idea whose popularity may be at an all-time low in the 1990s, has never been part of conventional Anglo-American jurisprudence. But neither is it foreign or hostile to our traditions. Franklin Roosevelt was able to include "freedom from want" in his list of basic rights in his 1941 State of the Union address without alienating or even noticeably perturbing his audience.[84] "Freedom from fear" is much more popular at present, though the socially approved means of assuring this right emphasize limitations on the negative rights of the feared rather than recognition of the positive rights of the fearful. The programs of the New Deal and the Great Society gave rise to, and were often defended by, arguments for positive rights; these positions were controversial, but they were publishable.[85] When the Supreme Court refused to recognize a constitutional right to education as a necessary condition for the exercise of specified rights, the vote was not unanimous and the decision did not meet universal approval.[86]

Sydney Callahan's statement that all human life needs protection describes stark reality. In contemporary America, we are not capable of meeting our needs alone. We are vulnerable to our bodies, families, and employers, and at the mercy of the economy. However intelligent and deserving we are, no degree of merit or industry or loyalty or virtue can keep us safe. Women have been and remain especially vulnerable to want, as they are to violence. If security against the threat of violence is an end of civil society, as Thomas Hobbes implied long ago, then why not security against destitution?

One obvious difficulty with the idea of deriving rights from need arises from the common human tendency to confuse needs with wants, desires, and preferences, and to confuse our own needs with those of others for whom we claim to speak. Another problem is that some needs are not fulfillable in practice. Human beings need love, for instance, but they cannot will themselves to feel it. The idea of a right to be loved collides with this contradiction. But accepting in principle the possibility of need-based rights does not require us to accept any particular need-based claim, or even to endorse the whole modern welfare state. Suspicion about positive rights based on need does not preclude recognition of negative rights like the right to reproductive choice.

Conventional theory incorporates a jurisprudence of the person that makes a sharp distinction between the competent and the incompetent, the autonomous and the nonautonomous, the independent and the dependent. Entitlement to ordinary rights precludes recognition of need; recognition of need abrogates enjoyment of rights. Sydney Callahan and other antichoice feminists recognize the connection between rights and needs in principle; but they restrict these rights to the unborn and impose correlative duties only upon the mothers of the unborn. Why shouldn't need create rights for women against men and society?

Needs, Nature, and Selective Vulnerability

> [Women] can get all the rights in the world—the right to vote, the right to go to school—and none of them means a doggone thing if we don't own the flesh we stand in, if we can't control what happens to us, if the whole course of our lives can be changed by somebody else that can get us pregnant by accident, or by deceit, or by force. So I consider the right to elective abortion, whether you dream of doing it or not, the cornerstone of the women's movement . . . because without that right, we'd have about as many rights as the cow who is brought to the bull once a year.
>
> *(A pro-choice activist interviewed by Kristin Luker)*

> You made your choice in bed.
> *(Male counterdemonstrator, Los Angeles, March 1986)*

This assertion, with its evident woman-hatred, refutes itself. Women have not always been able to choose to have intercourse. Rape is an everyday occurrence. Men's power over women in intimate relationships can extend to sex. Until recently, American law gave husbands the right to sexual access to their wives. It appears true (although the Census Bureau does not collect this sort of information) that men are more likely than women to initiate sex. Part I of this book showed (as if it needed showing) that women who differ greatly from one another share an understanding of sex as something men do to them.[87]

But what about women who have sex with men because they want to, who enter into relationships that are truly consensual? Accepting these women's accounts of their lives does not weaken the case for reproductive choice. In a relationship where one partner dominates the other, the subordinate partner loses rights. In a relationship between equals, both partners give up rights. Is it likely that *any* lover, male or female, in an ongoing relationship may consistently exercise "the right to say no"? Even when women have sex because they want to, is it fair that two people face such different consequences for performing the same act? We do not normally presume that people are responsible for all foreseeable consequences of their actions. The choice made in bed is rarely the choice to become pregnant. There is no reason why women's vulnerability to pregnancy entails responsibility to avoid it. It could follow equally well that the partner immune from risk has the duty to protect the partner vulnerable to risk.

No woman, no matter how autonomous in her sexual relations or how conscientious in her avoidance of risk, can protect herself against both pregnancy and physical harm from contraceptives. No reversible method of birth control is both universally safe and universally reliable. The method which comes closest, a combination of spermicide and condom, requires the man's cooperation. Condoms are used, or at least bought; the sale of condoms increased even after the birth control pill was marketed in the 1960s. But three popular reversible contraceptive methods—the birth control pill, the intrauterine device, and Norplant—are used by women. While these methods have lower failure rates than the barrier methods, the first two carry a demonstrable risk of complications—for the woman only.[88] In 1994, researchers found that Norplant, touted as the perfect contraceptive, was more difficult and more dangerous to get out of a woman's arm than to put in.

There are only two safe, foolproof ways for a woman to prevent pregnancy: undergoing sterilization or avoiding genital heterosexual intercourse. The right to abortion, therefore, is a necessary condition for a woman's enjoyment of the substantive rights granted her by law: not only the rights to vote or go to school, but the fundamental autonomy which American law grants to human beings—to determine her own destiny and to establish intimate relationships.

Women, Men, and Collective Responsibility

A whole bunch of people think it's the woman's own fault. You know, she should have said no. She shouldn't have gotten herself pregnant. I have yet to hear anyone say, "He should not have had sex with her." Have you ever heard them say the man should have said no, or ever read it or that's the solution? It's a woman's problem.
(Minette Doderer)

Don't you think that the irresponsible behavior of men is caused by women?
(Pope John Paul II when told that about two hundred thousand women die every year from self-induced abortions)

Nature, public policy, and economic disadvantage are not the only forces which make women's fertility a source of inequality. Men, individually and collectively, help create and sustain the inequality. They do so by having sex without using birth control, by not sharing child care, by not maintaining households with their children's mothers, and by refusing financial responsibility. This inequality will persist as long as men refuse to change, no matter what the government does or what technological advances are made. Men do not constitute a community which teaches its members about their moral obligations. Men are far more likely to offer moral instruction to women than to other men.

George Bush's "adoption, not abortion" sermonette in the 1988 presidential campaign is one classic example of this selectivity. Bush's successor, Bill Clinton, has taken a similar approach. When he says that "abortion should be safe, legal, and rare," he is discouraging women from getting abortions, not encouraging men to make them unnecessary. In 1994, he urged junior high students "not to have a baby until you're old enough to take care of it, until you're married." Since an estimated two-thirds of teenage mothers are impregnated by men over twenty, and almost three-fourths of mothers under fourteen are rape victims, Clinton would seem to have targeted the wrong audience.[89] By late 1998, the Monica Lewinsky scandal and revelations that Clinton had lied under oath had destroyed his claim to moral leadership.

The abortion rights debate displays the confusion of situation and situated that I discussed earlier in the book.[90] Since women get pregnant, women constitute the problem; since women constitute the problem, changes in women's behavior must constitute the solution. Politicians try to limit women's alternatives by condemning both abortion and single motherhood. Some contemporary advocates of welfare reform recommend placing the children of destitute mothers in orphanages or even putting them up for adoption without parental consent. These proposals threaten the proletariat with the loss of its *proles*.[91] At least one feminist, Naomi Wolf, appears to take seriously the claim of prospective adoptive parents of a right to the unborn children of reluctantly pregnant women. This claim gives new meaning to the concept of alienated labor.[92] Yet no one lectures men, who have the power to prevent pregnancy, single motherhood, child loss, and abortion.

In absolving men while exhorting women, public officials follow the culture's lead. Compare, for example, the mass-circulation magazines targeted at men with those targeted at women. "Women's magazines" contain masses of advice about marriage, child care, child rearing, family nutrition, balancing job and home responsibilities, and every imaginable aspect of the wife-mother role. The advertising in the ostensibly gender-neutral *Parents* is clearly aimed at a female market. "Men's magazines" range from *Esquire* and *Gentleman's Quarterly*, which stress popular culture, to *Playboy*, whose name is its market, to *Penthouse* and *Hustler*. And then there are always *Argosy*, *True Detective*, and *Soldier of Fortune*. The checkout counter at the supermarket confronts a woman with volumes of advice and exhortation in the ordinary course of grocery shopping. When men perform this chore, they find *Time*, *Newsweek*, *Sports Illustrated*, and *TV Guide* nestled among publications obviously not meant for them.

Women may get more of these secular sermons directed at them than men do because women represent a larger audience. Imagine the reaction to a publisher who tried to start *Working Father* magazine. But here it is difficult to separate cause from effect.[93] Women (including feminist theorists) advise, urge, and exhort one another. Women who exhort and admonish men (except, to some extent, mothers of young sons) invite accusations of "male-bashing," "extremism," and worse. The weight of moral as well as physical responsibility for the unborn falls almost exclusively upon women. Men have power over sexual expression; women have responsibility for its consequences. Men have often been free to refuse even financial responsibility for their children. Society provides little help for the mothers of young children: no guaranteed living wage, no subsidy, little available child care or health insurance, minimal enforcement of support awards. And a pervasive system of socialization and exhortation reinforces this distribution of duty and immunity. If "the pregnant woman can never be isolated in her privacy," nature and society combine to isolate her in her calamity.[94] She has full responsibility for the consequences of sex, but she does not have the right to decide whether or not to let the fetus become a person. Once again, women are excluded from only half of liberal theory.[95]

What's That Got to Do with Constitutional Law?

None of this lengthy exercise in imagination and analysis reads like constitutional interpretation. The explanation for this difficulty lies partly in the narrow, positivist contemporary notion of what constitutes acceptable constitutional discourse. Before the Civil War, some abolitionists persistently argued that slavery was unconstitutional, despite what appeared to others to be the clear import of the constitutional text and contemporaneous Supreme Court opinions which ruled just the opposite. These activists' arguments, such as the claim that slavery was unconstitutional because it violated the principles of the Declaration of Independence, were anchored in no specific constitutional provision. Today, anyone who made arguments like these would be accused of reading the Constitution to enact natural law principles, or of writing her own views into law. But that accusation is a product of our preferred modes of adjudication, not a universal truth.

True, fantasy—recognized as such, anyway—has never been a part of court opinions, but it has been a part of political theory for a long time.

Consider, for example, the social contract theory of Hobbes's *Leviathan* or Locke's *Second Treatise on Government*. Intellectual historians agree that the "state of nature" contractarians posit is not to be taken literally; it can be read as asking the reader to imagine what life would be like without civil government. Plato's cave, Hobbes's state of nature, and Rawls's veil of ignorance are not meant literally. They are imaginary constructs that illuminate reality. So does counterfactual reproduction.

If data about the effects of long hours upon health and safety were permissible topics for the "Brandeis briefs" of the early labor legislation cases, there is no reason why data about reproductive physiology, contraception, child care, social expectations, and financial responsibility do not belong in constitutional argument. Indeed, the Brandeis briefs themselves contained the sort of information about women's disproportionate responsibility for domestic work and child care which is an essential component of any defense of reproductive freedom.[96]

These facts do not fit easily into constitutional discussions; but again, why not? The constitutional doctrine that we now have, that is accessible to us for interpretive use, did not emanate automatically and inevitably from the text. Instead, it is the product of choices made and accepted by judges. These choices have been shaped and directed by the lawyers arguing before the judges, and by the bench, bar, and academy which react to the judges' work. Other arguments, other choices, might have produced different doctrine. Since these judicial choices have been made in a context that is almost exclusively male, it is possible that women lawyers, judges, and scholars would have affected the development of doctrine in other directions, had they been equal participants in the dialogue.[97]

A woman-centered constitutional doctrine of reproductive rights can usefully draw on the doctrine we have now. The *Griswold* privacy doctrine has its defects, but relying on several provisions of the Constitution rather than a single clause is not among them. There is no reason to exclude multiple-clause interpretation from the permissible techniques of constitutional adjudication. The case for abortion rights becomes stronger if we move beyond the Bill of Rights. To the extent that laws restricting abortion are premised on the belief that the fetus is a person, these laws raise serious due process and equal protection questions. So grounded, the laws do not even bear a rational relationship to a legitimate public purpose. The same restrictions subvert equality by imposing upon pregnant women obligations unique in both degree and kind; no other class of people is burdened with similar duties toward other human beings. To the extent that restrictive laws are based upon considerations other than the status of the fetus, the constitutional difficulties remain. In discussing the abortion issue within the context in which sexual relations, pregnancy, and childbearing take place in American society, I have described a situation of inequality. Men—at least, those men who have political power—restrict the choices that only women have to make. Those few women who become lawmakers operate within structures designed and still controlled by men.

This inequality is even more manifest in private life. Again, men can refuse responsibility for birth control and child rearing. If women's resulting burdens, fully sanctioned by public policy, are not both involuntary servitude and denial of equal protection, then what are they?[98] Even if men assumed equal responsibilities, we can hardly imagine a society which had established sexual equality within the family denying women freedom in that way. An approach to interpretation which considers the Thirteenth and Fourteenth Amendments as well as the Bill of Rights offers real possibilities in establishing a constitutional right to reproductive choice.

Conclusion

Privacy doctrine writes the liberal theory of negative rights into the Constitution and presumes that this liberalism includes women. These ideas are not propositions about which general agreement exists in American society, even among feminists. This chapter has defended judicial activism, liberalism, and their application to women. It has also made clear that *if* liberalism includes women, it must include the right to reproductive choice. A woman cannot protect herself from unwanted motherhood without this right; a woman cannot be a liberal subject unless she can protect herself from unwanted motherhood. The rights to confer humanity on a fetus inside one's body and to act on that decision are necessary, whether or not they are sufficient, conditions for autonomy. The controversy over *Roe* and its successors is yet another indication of the fact that women have never really been part of liberalism.

This chapter has discussed several feminist authors who are leery of liberal principles, especially when applied to abortion rights. Critics like Sydney Callahan and Elizabeth Fox-Genovese, who reject liberal principles in favor of commitment to care and nurturance, confuse the legal with the moral. Worse, by presuming unilateral female obligations, these scholars violate the principle of sexual equality they claim to accept. But other critiques steer liberalism and feminism in important directions. Wendy Brown's and Barbara Katz Rothman's concerns that recognizing individual rights may serve as an excuse for overlooking individual needs suggest the possibility of a feminist grounding of rights in needs—to join, not to replace, the liberal grounding of rights in personhood and the conservative grounding of rights in merit. Juli Loesch's and Catharine MacKinnon's

warnings that legalizing abortion may aggravate women's sexual vulnerability underscore the limits of negative rights as guarantees of sexual
equality. These conclusions arise not from women's ways of knowing but
from what we know as women. A liberal feminism clarifies the elusive distinction between the born and the unborn. A feminist postliberalism can
resolve the apparent contradiction between rights and needs.

SEVEN

RECONSTRUCTING RESPONSIBILITY

FEMINIST FETAL PROTECTION

T HE 1960S AND 1970S brought a radical departure from the traditional jurisprudence of human reproduction. All three branches of the national government took part in effecting this change. Supreme Court decisions like *Griswold*, *Eisenstadt*, and *Roe* used law to enhance women's control over their reproductive functions instead of using women's reproductive functions to justify restrictive law. In 1964, Congress rendered *Muller v. Oregon* obsolescent by prohibiting sex discrimination in employment. In 1979, the bureaucracy did the same for *Buck v. Bell* with regulations governing the use of public funds for sterilization.[1]

But the old jurisprudence of reproduction is far from dead. Even as society began to accept the idea that women bear rights, powerful forces promoted new restrictions premised on the fact that women bear children. "Fetal protection" policies have been ubiquitous in the 1980s and 1990s. Fetal rights advocates posit what Ron Beal calls "a woman's duty to protect her embryo-fetus, from the point of conception." Beal concedes—indeed, he proclaims—that recognizing such a duty "will have tremendous implications for the women of this country and how they conduct their everyday lives."[2]

Fetal Protection and Gendered Thinking

Fetal protection policies include several kinds of regulations. Employment restrictions limiting women's exposure to substances harmful to fetuses thrived from the late 1970s to the early 1990s. Civil courts have heard lawsuits to force pregnant women to undergo procedures such as cesarean sections or fetal surgery, and lawsuits by children against mothers for prenatal damage. Lifestyle restrictions—the use of criminal law or civil judgments to prohibit pregnant women from using drugs or alcohol—-comprise a fourth type of fetal protection rule.[3] One law professor supports such mandatory medical treatments as the force-feeding of anorexic pregnant women. A professor of medicine exhorts every woman to "consider herself pregnant on the first day her period is due and avoid exposure to anything that has been implicated in birth defects." A third scholar-advocate posits a maternal duty not only to refrain from causing harm but to prevent harm—even though not all birth defects are preventable.[4]

Like the old "protective" labor laws to which they are often compared, fetal protection policies exemplify what Sally Kenney calls "gendered thinking." They presume "that if women are different from men," society "can treat them less favorably."[5] How much less favorably? Expectant fathers have already sought court orders imposing restrictions on their pregnant former wives or lovers; what would happen in ongoing relationships? Some hospitals have won court orders for cesarean sections and blood transfusions; could physicians, spouses, or families do the same? Would the "friends of the fetus" who challenged abortion laws in the 1970s reemerge as litigants? Inquisitive strangers—who apparently feel free to approach pregnant women—might serve as volunteer enforcers. Some already have; in 1991, a pregnant woman in Seattle made the national news when a restaurant refused to serve her a daiquiri.

Pregnant women could face oppressive intrusion into their lives even if they abstained from alcohol, drugs, or tobacco. How would these policies be implemented? Presumably, enforcement would require blood and urine testing. Once a month, the conventional schedule for medical appointments during the first eight months of a low-risk pregnancy, is not often enough to monitor use. Perhaps weekly tests would be required, adding one more chore to a pregnant woman's life, at either her expense or that of her insurance carrier (and, therefore, at everyone's expense). These tests would insult innocent women by effectively presuming their guilt.

Much expert opinion agrees that some, most, or all fetal protection policies have two serious defects: they're not legal and they won't work. None of these rules has gained a secure place in American law, and one has been invalidated outright. The Supreme Court's unanimous decision in *United Auto Workers v. Johnson Controls* in March 1991 struck down workplace restrictions under Title VII of the Civil Rights Act of 1964.[6] Between 1985 and 1992, at least 167 women had been prosecuted for delivering drugs to a minor (through the umbilical cord), child abuse, or (where the infant died) homicide. Most of these prosecutions ended with courts' dismissing charges or overturning convictions, usually on the grounds that existing statutes do not apply to these situations. In April 1997, the Wisconsin Supreme Court ruled that the state had acted wrongfully in detaining Angela M.W., a pregnant woman who had tested positively for cocaine. But in October, the South Carolina Supreme Court upheld Cornelia Whitner's conviction and eight-year prison sentence for child neglect after she gave birth to a baby boy who tested positive for cocaine. Nothing prevents a legislature from enacting criminal laws which explicitly punish pregnant women; but only Florida had done so by 1995.[7] The legality of forced treatment has been problematic since the ruling in *Matter of A.C.* that a cancer patient should not have been subjected to a cesarean section that neither she nor the baby survived.[8] As yet, no prenatal damage suits against mothers have succeeded, although some courts have ruled that parental immunity is no bar to such a suit.[9]

The only puzzling part of *Johnson Controls* was why it took nine years to strike down the company's rule. No reasonable construction of Title VII can turn fetal protection into a "bona fide occupational qualification reasonably necessary to the normal operation of that particular business or enterprise."[10] The final decision in *A.C.* conforms both to every compassionate impulse and to the established legal principles governing an adult's right to refuse treatment and a parent's control over her child's medical care. Judicial rulings that drug and alcohol use by pregnant women were not included in the original statutory definitions of child abuse or passing drugs to a minor seem reasonable. But legislatures are free to enact new laws or to amend old ones. Who knows what a Congress and president loudly committed to "family values" might do?

There is no reason to suppose that lawmaking will be inhibited by doubts about the effectiveness of these policies. Federal and state statute books abound with laws—especially criminal laws—that don't do what they are supposed to do. Any judgment about whether fetal protection policies "work" depends on what the purpose of these rules is. Advocates of criminal sanctions maintain that pregnant drug and alcohol users will seek help if they are threatened with prosecution. Some have, but no one knows how many women simply stop getting prenatal care. The threat of punishment may have protected some identifiable infants from addiction in utero, but there is no evidence that it has reduced the instance of birth defects. At any rate, "help," in the form of treatment for addiction, is rarely available for pregnant women. The practical difficulties that attend implementation of fetal protection policies have been extensively documented.[11]

So fetal protection policies probably won't work—if their purpose is to protect fetuses. But if their purpose is to coerce women, they could work very well indeed. Analysis of these restrictions shows that coercing women is not only their probable result but the only tenable explanation of their purpose. Katha Pollitt has called fetal rights "a new assault on feminism," but this criticism does not go far enough.[12] The assault is a multifaceted attack on several feminist gains: improved employment opportunities, increased social freedom, and dramatic advances in obstetrical practice inspired by a woman's consumer rights movement. Fetal protection policies threaten *all* women—pregnant or not, prospectively pregnant or not, vulnerable to pregnancy or not.

I Can Get Angry

Human beings and their emotions will not stay out of the fetal protection debate. Media accounts tend toward the individual and the dramatic. Audience reactions tend to be passionate. Michael Dorris constructs a powerful argument for the incarceration of pregnant drinkers from the life of his adopted son, Abel. "Conceived and grown in an ethanol bath," Abel "live[d] each day in the act of drowning" until he was killed in an automobile accident at twenty-three.[13] Dorris's argument deserves consideration on its merits, independently of common knowledge about the life of its author. But later accusations that Michael Dorris sexually abused one or more of his daughters, and his suicide in April 1997, call into question his fitness as a moralist. No charges were proved, and the informal rules of academic discourse put the private lives of public commentators off limits as subjects of analysis. But Dorris's history, like the scandals surrounding President Clinton, raises the possibility that other self-appointed authorities may be throwing stones from glass houses and encourages skepticism about people who tell us what to do.

The story of Angela Carder, who lived only three years longer than Abel Dorris, has an equal power to arouse emotion. Carder, a long-term cancer survivor, was hospitalized in her sixth month of pregnancy with an inoperable lung tumor. She and her doctor wanted to try chemotherapy and radiation, even at the cost of the baby's life. But the hospital gave up on her, withheld treatment, and successfully sought a court order for a cesarean section. The infant girl lived for two hours; Carder died in coma two days later.[14]

Fetal protection is an emotional issue because it involves relations of mother and child, doctor and patient, worker and employer, state and individual. Since all of us are or have been part of these dyads, we cannot keep our particular, concrete selves out of our research. Scholars could not duplicate the detached stance of what Joan Williams calls "traditional Western epistemology" even if they wanted to.[15] The self I bring to this debate further complicates this mix of issues and perspectives. As a woman with a birth defect, I embody both the target of coercion and the result this coercion seeks to prevent. I combine a total opposition to fetal protection restrictions with the certain knowledge that not having a birth defect is better than having one. My reactions to the debate on fetal protection are informed by this perspective.

The title of Ron Beal's article—" 'Can I Sue Mommy?' "—conveys an impression of young litigants as whiny brats.[16] The double message is jarring: oppressive substance and flippant style; expounding a legal duty to prevent birth defects while trivializing the standpoint of people with birth defects. The title's casual indifference expresses an attitude familiar from public discourse as well as personal experience. Birth defects have always been with us; but public support for the rehabilitation of disabled people originated in response to war injuries rather than congenital ones. From time to time, advocacy of amputation or disfigurement as forms of criminal punishment surfaces in public discourse; the debate has not included consideration of how the deliberate linking of physical anomaly with legal criminality might affect those of us who acquired visible defects by accident.[17] The cartoon in which a poor woman fears that "war on poverty" means "they're going to shoot me" reminds us that it may not be easy to tell the difference between the situation and the situated.[18]

Rights, Responsibility, and Reproductive Choice

The experience of Bree Walker, a newscaster who inadvertently became a newsmaker, illustrates this familiar (con)fusion of situation and situated. Walker, who has a congenital, hereditary deformity of hands and feet, is coanchor of the evening news show at KCBS-TV in Los Angeles. She has achieved extraordinary success in a profession notorious for its emphasis on physical appearance. Her first child, a daughter, was born with the same condition. In 1991, Walker, visibly pregnant with her second child, was anchoring the show with her husband, Jim Lampley. A local radio talk show host criticized her decision to bear a child whose risk of inherited disability was so high. "Is it fair to the child?" Jane Norris asked her listeners. What Walker and Lampley thought was a family decision ended up in the national news. "I felt terrorized," said Walker, whose son did inherit the disability.[19]

Yet at roughly the same time—while the future of *Roe v. Wade* was in doubt and legalized abortion was the focus of bitter public controversy— "designer babies" became a taunt hurled at women who sought abortions when medical tests revealed fetal defects. Some disability rights activists share these fears that parents will treat unborn children like consumer goods.[20] (Bree Walker's critics, by contrast, seemed to expect her to treat human parenting like animal breeding.) Opponents of reproductive choice would deny women the freedom to prevent birth defects. But fetal protection restrictions, and demands that carriers of genetic defects refrain from conceiving, make women responsible for doing so. Once again, women have an asymmetrical place in conventional jurisprudence.

Selective solicitude abounds in the fetal protection debate. Proponents prefer restrictions on women to other means of protecting the unborn and publicize the effects of prenatal exposure to toxic substances in isolation from other factors that might contribute to fetal damage. The fetal rights movement seems to care more about some women than about others: to try to keep all women out of certain jobs while refusing the requests of actual pregnant workers for accommodations and concessions; to show greater concern with toxic exposure in occupations which civil rights laws have opened to women than in the female job ghetto or, for that matter, the home; to ignore any disproportionate impact restrictions may have on poor and/or minority women.[21]

These charges have been well documented elsewhere. My experience has sensitized me to yet another set of contradictions. The possibility of birth defects justifies laws depriving women of personal rights. But the fact of birth defects is not even a big enough deal to make an author curb his wit. Society's concern with child nutrition peaks before birth; parents do not face sanctions for a child's diet after birth. When these inconsistencies are added to the equation, the impression grows that fetal protection is primarily and secondarily, directly and indirectly, deliberately and inadvertently, an instrument of women's subjection.

The fetal protection movement abuses and misuses knowledge, power, and theory. All three become weapons against women. First, the fetal protection debate ignores what we have learned in this century about sexual equality, about doctor-patient relationships, and about the limits of expert knowledge. Second, the controversy shows how limited is the American repertoire of resources and solutions to public problems. Our fondness for criminal punishment combines with sex-role stereotypes to restrict the range of policy choices to those sanctioning women. Third, the controversy is a concrete illustration of the inadequacy of conventional jurisprudence to speak to women's lives.[22] This jurisprudence has furnished powerful intellectual weapons to the advocates of exclusion and restriction. Finally, the fetal protection issue reveals the limited ability of recent feminist theory to repulse, let alone to anticipate and prevent, these threats to women.

Knowledge Against Women: Fetal Rights, Maternal Wrongs, Official Choices

One reason—only one—that fetal protection policies have become a political issue is the cumulative effect of important breakthroughs in medical knowledge in the last generation. This knowledge provides an occasion for, though not a cause of, new restrictions. As late as 1960, expert opinion held that the placenta acted as a barrier between the fetus and any substance which entered a pregnant woman's body. The thalidomide tragedy of the 1960s and the discovery of the carcinogenic properties of the drug DES initiated a slow process of professional learning that has reversed this assumption. Experts now believe that anything absorbed by the mother can cross the placenta.[23] In the 1980s and 1990s, medical advances which made fetal surgery possible and lowered the gestational age at which infants could survive after birth encouraged doctors to try to force pregnant women to undergo cesarean sections or permit fetal surgery.

During the 1960s and 1970s, evidence mounted that benzene, lead, radiation, and other toxic substances threatened the health, safety, and fertility of perhaps twenty million workers and their children.[24] While no one has so far identified any children with serious birth defects attributable to their mothers' exposure to toxic substances at work, the harmful prenatal effects of nicotine, alcohol, and addictive street drugs have been documented.[25] The association between maternal smoking and prematurity and low birth weight has been known for years. By the mid-1980s, enough knowledge existed about the fetal effects of alcohol that pregnant women were advised to abstain completely—a significant change in obstetrical practice.[26] By 1989, when Michael Dorris's memoir was published, it was common knowledge that children whose mothers drink heavily during pregnancy may get fetal alcohol syndrome (FAS) or the less serious fetal alcohol effect (FAE). The symptoms, which can take years to appear, include mental retardation, poor memory, learning disabilities, and facial abnormalities.[27] An increase in the use of cocaine, especially the highly addictive "crack," in the 1980s and 1990s led to the "crack-baby myth." Infants born to addicted mothers might "shake so badly they rub their own limbs raw." By 1995, experts could not distinguish the congenitally addicted children from the nonaddicted; but the movement to punish drug-using mothers continues.[28]

The response to these developments may have been an accident of timing. Things might have been different, I suppose, during the New Deal of the 1930s or the Great Society of the 1960s. The government that created jobs, strengthened organized labor, and established old-age insurance might have encouraged business and labor to cooperate to make the workplace safer as the National Industrial Recovery Act brought them together to establish codes of fair competition, and found ways to bring new knowledge to the poor and isolated the way the Tennessee Valley Authority brought them electricity. The government that founded Medicare, Medicaid, Head Start, and the Job Corps might have emphasized detoxification, education, rehabilitation, and employment opportunities. Then again, these were not periods of high feminist consciousness; coercing women might have seemed the easiest and cheapest route for busy, committed governments. At any rate, increases in medical knowledge have coincided not with commitments to social welfare but with the exhaustion of the War on Poverty, followed by four successive presidential administrations too preoccupied with self-destruction to give much thought to reform, followed by the "Reagan Revolution." By the 1970s, the strongest tool industry had to protect workers and children was prohibition. By the 1980s, the only tool society had left was the criminal sanction.

Globe Union, a manufacturer of batteries in Owosso, Michigan, insti-
tuted a biological "monitoring" and medical "surveillance" program in
1969 for employees exposed to lead. Globe Union spent about fifteen million dollars in efforts to reduce toxic exposure, but by 1977, a year before
it was bought by Johnson Controls, the company began focusing on fetal
damage. It recommended that women who were planning a family not
work in high-risk jobs, and it required all women employees to attest that
they had been advised of the risks.[29]

At about the same time, the American Cyanamid plant in Willow Island,
West Virginia—long a depressed economic area which offered few decent
blue-collar jobs—forced five women employees to undergo sterilization
and transferred two others out of high-exposure jobs; the Occupational
Health and Safety Administration ruled against the sterilized workers on
the grounds that their decision stemmed from factors beyond the company's control.[30] The Olin Corporation went even further, effectively
banning all women from high-exposure jobs.[31] In 1982, Johnson Controls
(the Wisconsin-based corporation which had bought Globe Union) did
the same.

The idea of using criminal law to keep pregnant women from smoking,
drinking, or using drugs got on the public agenda in the mid-1980s. When
Dr. Warren Bosley of Grand Island, Nebraska, addressed the 1984 annual
meeting of the American Academy of Pediatrics, he attracted little attention with his proposal that any woman "who refuses to stop smoking during
pregnancy" be charged with child abuse. No major newspaper carried the
story.[32] So far, no woman has been prosecuted for smoking. But Bosley's
idea has been applied to the use of other harmful substances. Prosecuting
drug-using mothers was a logical extension of both the prevailing antidrug
sentiment and greater public awareness of the fetal dangers of the mid-
1980s. Between 1987 and 1991, there were about sixty criminal proceed-
ings against mothers for substance abuse in nineteen states and the District
of Columbia.[33] Accounts exist of women on Indian reservations being
locked up during their pregnancies. In at least one case, a husband obtained
a court order preventing his estranged pregnant wife from drinking or
taking drugs.[34]

Subjecting mothers to criminal penalties requires considerable creativity.
Nothing prevents a prosecutor from charging a pregnant or postpartum
woman with using cocaine or any other illegal drug. But the penalties for
drug use are so light, in practice, that the deterrent value of such accusations is negligible. Since alcohol is legal, pregnant drinkers cannot even be
prosecuted to this extent. Bosley's suggestion, prosecution for child abuse,
is one alternative. Another is to charge women with passing drugs or alcohol to a minor—the unborn child, through the umbilical cord. That was
the State of Florida's accusation against Jennifer Johnson in 1989. So far,

no woman so accused has gone to prison, although there are sentences under appeal now.[35] But legislatures have the power to make drug or alcohol use criminal.

How have such coercive policies gotten on the public agenda? Pregnant women are now routinely advised to abstain from alcohol, drugs, and tobacco.[36] Bars, bottles, packages, and labels carry warnings targeted at pregnant women. The surgeon general's report in 1988 warned about the fetal hazards of alcohol. These recommendations stem from two recognized facts. First, no use of these substances, however minimal, has been proven safe. Second, demonstrated associations exist between all of these substances and fetal damage. Advising pregnant women not to drink, smoke, or use drugs is, therefore, good medical practice. But we usually do not jump quite so fast from "People shouldn't do X" to "X should be illegal." At any rate, the following statements are also correct. First, there is no proof that any amount of alcohol or drugs, however small, will harm the unborn child.[37] Second, professional opinion is not always superior to lay opinion.

Pregnant women who ingested forbidden substances have produced healthy babies. One of the two children born to the women prosecuted for cocaine use in "caring" Muskegon County was affected; the other was not.[38] Any halfway competent researcher confronted with results like these would suspect the existence of intervening variables. Ordinary observation supports the statement of a character in a novel about alcohol and marijuana use during pregnancy: "A little was fine and a lot was bad."[39]

"Pregnancy is a time when women should be conservative with their bodies," one pediatrician told a reporter.[40] Is pregnancy also a time when women should be obedient? If that were true, medicine would have to roll back the clock thirty years. The 1960s and 1970s saw dramatic changes in obstetrical practice. These changes include revisions in recommended weight gain during pregnancy; decreases in the use of medication during labor, combined with increased use of nonmedical techniques of pain control such as Lamaze breathing; reduction in the use of the lithotomy position for delivery; the end of routine pubic shaving; routine encouragement rather than routine discouragement of breast-feeding; fewer episiotomies; and the presence at childbirth of people selected by the mother. The motivating force behind these changes was a consumer movement led and organized by obstetrical patients.[41]

The lessons which apparently were not learned from this consumer movement are, first, that patients sometimes know more than doctors do, and, second, that expert knowledge is imperfect. Doctors learned from their patients that much of what they thought they knew in the 1950s and 1960s was incorrect or incomplete. But the 1970s and 1980s brought a significant increase in the proportion of babies delivered by cesarean section—a method which effectively deprives the mother of input into decision making.[42] Hospitals have even gone to court, in at least fifteen cases between 1981 and 1987, to get permission to perform this operation against the mother's wishes. The hospitals won in thirteen cases, but only ten of these operations actually took place. The other three mothers had successful vaginal deliveries before the orders could be carried out—a fact that does not increase the reader's faith in medical judgment.[43]

There is an ironic linkage between the current fetal protection movement and the obstetrical reform movement. Women activists were instrumental in drawing attention to findings that substances given to the mother affect the fetus.[44] One result was the increased use of natural childbirth and a decline in reliance on medication. Now, the advocates of fetal protection policies are turning this knowledge back on women. The use of knowledge as a means of social control is not without precedent. In 1954, Margaret Mead reviewed the contemporary literature on child development. At that time, experts recommended a degree of maternal involvement so intense as to effectively bar the mothers of young children from all other sustained activity. Finding the data insufficient to support these theories, Mead perceived in them "a new and subtle form of antifeminism in which men—under the guise of exalting the importance of maternity—are tying women more tightly to their children than has been thought necessary since the invention of bottle feeding and baby carriages."[45]

Although the responsibility for the fetal rights movement is shared by both sexes, we need not believe in an antifeminist conspiracy among corporations, the medical establishment, and government to suspect that something similar to what Mead described is happening now. Male supremacy does not need deliberate reinforcement; like racism, it is powerful enough to reinforce itself.

Power Against Women: The Mother, the Child, and the State

The juristic roots of the fetal protection debate are deep and tangled. The echo of *Muller v. Oregon* is hard to miss, and few commentators have.[46] The detective who called prosecuting pregnant cocaine users "a form of caring" evinces an attitude similar to that professed, and sometimes actually held, by supporters of the old "protective" laws.[47] Like protective legislation, fetal protection policies apply to women whether or not they are relevant to these women's lives. Oregon enacted its ten-hour law at a time when 80 percent of wage-earning women were single and few mothers worked outside the home.[48] The Olin Corporation's fetal vulnerability rule, adopted in 1978, barred all women of childbearing age from jobs involving exposure to known or suspected abortifacient or teratogenic agents. "Childbearing age" was between five and sixty-three.[49]

Both the old and the new policies represent specific, and similar, choices among possible approaches to social problems. *Lochner v. New York*, which invalidated general hours laws, effectively forced progressive activists to limit their definition of the problem to one involving women workers.[50] But even after *Lochner*, reformers could have done some or all of the following things: prohibit sex discrimination in employment, encourage unionization, or facilitate access to birth control. Instead, employment discrimination was state and corporate policy, while the last two alternatives were actively discouraged, sometimes by criminal charges.

Contemporary fetal protection advocates had a wider range of choices than early social feminists had. They could have defined exposure to toxic substances as a problem affecting all workers and their children, born and unborn; but they chose to concentrate on fetal damage. Even then, the discovery that the placenta does not protect the fetus from toxic substances absorbed by the mother could have spurred efforts to detoxify the workplace, to privatize the freedom to set personal priorities rather than the responsibility to prevent fetal damage, to promote alcohol and drug education, and/or to make treatment and rehabilitation more available. But in the 1970s, as in the 1900s, the eventual remedies represented two specific kinds of choices. First, they were what William Ryan calls exceptionalistic as opposed to universalistic: they sought to change individual behavior rather than institutional arrangements.[51] Second, they were gender-specific; they consisted of restrictions on women.

Moreover, fetal protection policies are as selective in their application as the old laws eventually became. Although the earliest protective policies covered jobs held almost exclusively by women, within ten years after *Muller* these laws were keeping women out of (better paid) "men's" work. In 1969, a federal appeals court ruled that Title VII negated all "protective" legislation remaining on the books.[52] The adoption of exclusionary workplace policies in the 1970s coincided with efforts by the federal government to open well-paying, traditionally male blue-collar jobs to women. The Equal Employment Opportunity Commission and the Office of Civil Rights were putting considerable pressure on employers to hire women for these jobs. Fetal protection rules were not adopted in mostly female occupations. The electronics industry, a heavy user of benzene, had no fetal protection rules; and hospitals installed waste gas scavenging systems in operating rooms only after the wives of male workers began having miscarriages.[53] Even though the unions, once on the side of men against women, now took the side of women against employers, the recent fetal protection rules reserved high-paying blue-collar jobs for men—just as labor laws once kept women out of traditionally male jobs.

Fetal Protection and the Legacy of Buck

Muller is not the only ancestor of fetal protection jurisprudence. *Buck v. Bell*, which upheld the compulsory sterilization of an allegedly "feeble-minded" woman whose mother and daughter were allegedly likewise afflicted, has a claim to equal parentage. As *Muller* is the product of the Progressive movement, *Buck* is the product of the "eugenics" movement. *Muller* casts the state as the protector of the mother-child unit, while in *Buck* the relationship between state and family is adversarial. Sterilization is one of those "sacrifices" demanded of "those who already sap the strength of the State[,] . . . in order to prevent our being swamped with incompetence." Much fetal protection rhetoric echoes Justice Holmes's pronouncement that "three generations of imbeciles are enough."[54] A law professor tells pregnant women, "Your right to abuse your own body stops at the border of your womb." The same detective who spoke of "a form of caring" says, "If the mother wants to smoke crack and kill herself, I don't care. Let her die, but don't take that poor baby with her."[55] The new twist is that fetal protection law posits an adversarial relationship between mother and child. Instead of state and family together (*Muller*) or state against family (*Buck*), fetal protection has the state taking the child's side against the mother. Yet "that poor baby" loses its claim on our solicitude once it is born and becomes a sapper of the state's strength.

Fetal Protection and the Conservative Revolt

One obvious difference between protective labor legislation and fetal protection policies pertains to the political contexts that produced them. The history of women's labor legislation is part of the history of Progressivism, the first American political movement to look to government as a solver of social problems. Contemporary workplace and lifestyle restrictions belong to an era of conservative reaction against "big government," from Progressivism to the New Deal to the Great Society. This "counterrevolution" promises to limit the government's power over individual and corporate activity. But these strikingly different political eras share a preference for solving problems by means of restrictions on women. This shared predilection is one reason I doubt that the official response to the discovery of the toxic workplace and the permeable placenta would have been much different in the 1930s or 1960s from what it has been since. The use of power against women unites eras and administrations which have little else in common. Analysis of the historical differences between the two sets of policies reveals still greater similarities.

Derivative Responsibility and the Criminal Law

So reformers tried to improve the health of workers and their families by reducing women's working hours; eugenicists tried to improve the national gene pool by rendering certain women incapable of reproduction; and the fetal rights movement seeks to protect the unborn by limiting women's freedom. To this extent, the fetal protection movement is the heir of the Progressive and eugenics movements. But one feature of fetal protection policies represents an abrupt departure from these traditions: its (real, potential, or promised) use of criminal sanctions against women.

Such a recommendation may strike a responsive chord for reasons other than sexism. The United States leads the world in proportion of inhabitants incarcerated. (We used to be third, before the collapse of the Soviet Union and the democratization of South Africa.) Thirty years of public opinion polls suggest that this high rate conforms to popular will. Support for punishment as a solution to crime has steadily increased since the 1960s. A society in which ever larger majorities urge ever harsher sentences for ever growing categories of offenses may be receptive to efforts to make more behavior criminal. The usual direct targets of this public sentiment are men, especially young men, especially young black men. The indirect harm done to women by incarcerating members of their families is obvious, but the direct threat to women may not be. The movement for using the criminal law to impose lifestyle restrictions on women (supposedly only on pregnant women, but who wants to bet on it?) coincides with efforts both to punish women for the behavior of others and to excuse men for criminal behavior by making women responsible.

Criminal law seems to be struggling to create a doctrine of derivative responsibility. Some states punish parents for the crimes committed by their children, or reduce welfare benefits for the parents of habitual truants. These ostensibly gender-neutral policies are enforced against custodial parents, usually mothers. The case of Shirley Draper of San Marcos, Texas, shows that derivative responsibility can even extend to relationships between adults. Draper had custody of her two daughters; her ex-husband, Gregory Cook, had visitation rights. When the girls and their father were killed in an automobile accident in September 1994, his blood alcohol content tested at 0.22 (more than twice the legal limit). Draper was charged with injury to a child and endangering a child because she let the girls leave with their father. Cook, who had a record of drunk driving offenses, had an ignition-disabling device on his car; Draper knew one of the girls would have to blow into it before Cook could start the engine. Representatives of Mothers Against Drunk Driving compared Draper to Susan Smith, the South Carolina mother who drowned her two sons in 1994. Three indictments against Draper have been quashed or withdrawn as "too vague," but the official effort to punish her continues. In June 1997, a grand jury indicted her for the fourth time. She faces life imprisonment.[56] Any lawyer knows that a custodial parent who tries to prevent a noncustodial parent from exercising visitation rights is putting herself at legal risk. Everybody knows that a woman who tries to restrain a drunken man is putting herself at considerable *physical* risk. Maybe Shirley Draper should have called the police—but "should have" has the benefit of hindsight.

Derivative responsibility can, and has, inculpated women; but it can also exculpate men. Consider the crime of rape, legally reclassified as a form of "sexual assault": a man having sexual intercourse with a woman by force and without consent. More often than not, law and public opinion presume that rape prevention is women's responsibility. In 1989, a jury in Fort Lauderdale, Florida, acquitted a man who had raped a woman at knifepoint because "she asked for it" by wearing a short skirt.[57] This verdict contradicts the law, since the use of a weapon constitutes force.[58]

Law does not distinguish between stranger rape and acquaintance or "date" rape. But the trial and acquittal of William Kennedy Smith in Palm Beach, Florida, in 1991 found many commentators eager to make the distinction. Patricia Bowman was criticized for drinking alone in the bar where she met Smith and for accompanying him to the Kennedy estate. One letter to the *New York Times Magazine* advised women to "date in the way that people with common sense drive their cars—defensively and sober."[59] This advice echoes the familiar "lock your doors and don't go out alone at night" approach to rape prevention; but its potential impact is more severe. Whatever the merits of sobriety, a defensive approach to human relationships is not a healthy psychological strategy.

Even some feminists have embraced this gender division of responsibility. Camille Paglia and Katie Roiphe urge women to concede that "no" does not always mean "no," to examine the nuances of their own behavior rather than to blame men.[60] Erica Jong is on their side. "Sex *is* terrifying," she writes, "full of uncontrollable darkness and illogic that it is far easier to suppress. Easier to scream *Rape!* than admit complicity in desire."[61] Jong is of course wrong: *easy* to call the police, to go to the hospital when all you want is to wash, to tell your friends that their friend is a rapist? But suppose we temporarily concede, for the purpose of argument, that these authors are right about people not always meaning exactly what they say. What follows? If a man takes "no" to mean "no," there will be no sex on that occasion. So what? A woman frustrated often enough might learn to name her desires herself and communicate them to others. Would that be a gain or a loss? To whom?

When we compare these attitudes toward crimes against women to the increasing use of criminal sanctions on women, the notion of derivative responsibility emerges as the common theme. Because women are responsible, we punish them for drinking while pregnant or for not preventing their children's deaths at the hands of their drunken father. Because women are responsible, we do not hold men accountable for violent sexual acting out or for exposing their children to danger. By selective exculpating and inculpating, society uses criminal law to reinforce women's disproportionate vulnerability and responsibility.

Theory Against Women: Fetal Rights and Conventional Jurisprudence

I have argued throughout this book that much feminist theory consists of responses to a standard or conventional jurisprudence which contains embedded as well as articulated premises. The jurisprudence of fetal rights provides further evidence that such a theory, while hardly a monolith, can be said to exist "out there": that theorists refer, implicitly or explicitly, to a set of assumed premises that need not be defended. The juristic arguments for fetal protection policies can be divided into two overlapping but distinguishable categories. The scholars I quoted early in this chapter make a positive case for fetal protection: they assert a maternal obligation to protect the unborn. The negative case for fetal protection policies asserts that these policies either are not inconsistent with or must override certain conventional principles. Both the positive and negative arguments rely on elements of standard theory.

The Positive Case for Fetal Protection: Rights and Choices

Margery Shaw and John Robertson—professors, respectively, of medicine and law—have created a jurisprudence of fetal protection. Robertson is the advocate of force-feeding, forced treatment, and forced abstinence quoted earlier; Shaw is the advocate of self-imposed presumptive pregnancy. Both ground their arguments in what Robertson calls "contingent legal personhood." The status of the fetus as person is contingent upon the woman's decision not to abort; once a woman decides to bear a child, the state has a compelling interest in protecting the unborn which justifies restrictions on its mother's freedom. "While the right to abortion recognized in *Roe v. Wade* means that a woman has no legal duty to ensure that a fetus is born alive, this does not necessarily preclude the law from imposing on the woman who does go to term, a duty to assure that the fetus is born as healthy as possible."[62] This "duty of care" doctrine holds that the woman's exercise of her right to continue her pregnancy imposes upon her the duty to promote "the health and well-being" of the child.[63]

On its face, an argument that *Roe v. Wade* entails a private duty of care is no more persuasive than an argument that the Twenty-first Amendment entails a public duty to treat alcohol addition. But the duty of care doctrine is a more familiar type of idea. It is a specific expression of the general notion that rights carry responsibilities. This platitude may be a good moral maxim, if something of a tautology: what does it mean to say we should exercise our rights according to our own notion of responsibility? As a legal rule, it asserts that we must exercise our rights in conformity with some official notion of responsibility (a notion familiar from the former Soviet Union).[64] It is a huge step from a moral duty of care for a child one decides to bear to a legal obligation to obey all medical advice (as Robertson implies); or a duty to impose prospective restrictions on oneself in the face of any possibility of pregnancy (as Shaw asserts); or a duty to prevent the unpreventable (as Deborah Mathieu argues).[65] The individual rights recognized in American law entail correlative duties; for instance, the individual's freedom of expression obliges the state not to interfere with the exercise of this freedom. But individual rights have not entailed individual responsibilities. Freedom of expression does not oblige speakers to propose alternative courses of action before criticizing the government's policy; free exercise of religion does not oblige people to make an informed choice for, against, or among; the right to use contraception does not oblige couples to make intelligent decisions about family planning. Why not? Because if these rights had such conditions, they would not be rights at all. Neither would the right to continue or terminate a pregnancy. But Shaw and Robertson propose burdening this right—the only right exercised exclusively by women—with conditions and restrictions unique in American law. Only for women do responsibilities attach to rights. Once again, the liberal asymmetry holds.

This is bad enough, but the difficulties with this argument multiply when we question the premises of the positive case for fetal protection. The duty of care doctrine evokes, though it does not invoke, rational choice theory. Like the Mnookin and Kornhauser article on divorce, Robertson's and Shaw's jurisprudence provides one more illustration of the way the vocabulary of choice and will has become embedded in contemporary discourse.[66] Mnookin's and Kornhauser's divorcing parents choose among possible combinations of money and custody; Robertson's and Shaw's prospective mothers, choosing to bear a child, accept a predetermined set of duties. And, whatever the value of the general theory, grave problems exist with this particular application.

The positive case for fetal protection presumes conditions that do not exist. Abortion is not available to all pregnant woman on demand in the United States. Access is restricted by Medicaid's refusal to pay for most abortions, notification and consent rules for minors, and the scarcity of abortion providers. The increase in violent attacks on abortion clinics by antichoice vigilantes, including five murders between March 1993 and December 1994, further threatens access to abortion.[67] The theory of contingent legal personhood jars with the facts.

Like many opponents of reproductive rights—remember "You made your choice in bed," from Chapter 6—the theory of contingent legal personhood presumes the exercise of will.[68] A woman decides whether or not to have a baby. The difference between Robertson and Shaw and some opponents of choice is that the professors place this decision after rather than before conception. Now, this model of decision making reads like a fairly accurate representation of the way professional, middle-class Americans in the 1990s talk about family planning (at least when they are lucky enough to conceive when they want to). But it is a rigidly time-bound, place-bound, and culture-bound model.

Since addiction weakens will, addicted women are not likely to behave as the model describes. Neither are women in cultures like that of rural Appalachia, where hardly anybody gets an abortion and few even use birth control.[69] In many times and places, even after people have figured out the connection between pregnancy and sexual intercourse, they have believed and continue to believe that God, or nature, sends babies, or that parenthood is something that happens rather than something that human beings plan. The contingent legal personhood model is inappropriate even for the woman who does exercise conscious will. She might be opposed to abortion; the child's father might have input into the decision; or she might follow the wisdom of her body and base a decision on nonrational factors. We may wonder whether *Homo sapiens* can survive if reproduction comes to depend on the choice which the model presumes. Decisions about parenthood, like those about love, sex, marriage, and friendship, have involved a considerable amount of intuition, emotion, chance, and guess. The contingent legal personhood doctrine seeks to impose upon society a culture-specific and limited model of decision making. It is a striking instance of the intellectual imperialism which pervades male-centered jurisprudence.

The vocabulary of agency, will, purpose, and choice permeates defenses of fetal protection. Michael Dorris devotes several pages of his book to a tribal clinic administrator who speaks repeatedly of "abuse," "to ruin somebody else's life," "doing this to our children." Dr. Warren Bosley's smokers "refuse" to stop.[70] According to fetal rights activists, these women choose to ingest chemicals, choose to accept the attendant risks, and choose to continue these habits when they become pregnant. Some may. The woman whose drink order in a Seattle restaurant in 1991 made the national news is an easy target for anger, but she is not typical of the women who have felt the law's force. Investigation reveals mothers no less wretched than their children, women who cannot control their use of drugs or alcohol, women who often seek help and face punishment instead.

Abel Dorris's birth mother lost custody of her son and died of alcohol poisoning in her thirties. Lynn Bremer and Kimberly Hardy, the women arrested for cocaine use in Muskegon County, Michigan, were both addicts.[71] Jennifer Johnson had sought treatment from the Florida officials who testified against her at her trial.[72] Diane Pfannensteil went to a hospital emergency room after her husband beat her, and was subjected to a blood test because an attendant smelled liquor on her breath. She was accused of child abuse because she was legally intoxicated.[73] Expert knowledge bears out the impression conveyed by these cases that fetal damage is more likely the product of addiction than of choice. Tobacco, cocaine, and alcohol are addictive, in varying degrees. The available information about FAS and FAE suggests a general association with levels of drinking which can accurately be described as addictive.[74] Words like "choose," "decide," and "refuse" do not apply to addicts, who, by definition, are *unable* to stop at will. The liberal assumptions of choice, will, and responsibility which undergird the duty-of-care doctrine turn out to be as problematic in application to substance abuse as to family planning.

The Negative Case for Fetal Protection

The misapplication of a deliberate choice model is not the only theoretical failure of fetal rights advocates. What I have called the negative case for fetal protection provides still more evidence of the dangers of imperfect understanding of conventional jurisprudence. Louise Erdrich, a distinguished writer of fiction and the wife of Michael Dorris, wrote the foreword to his book about their FAS-afflicted adopted son. She anticipates that their advocacy of imprisonment for pregnant drinkers

> will outrage some women, and men, good people who believe that it is the right of individuals to put themselves in harm's way, that drinking is a choice we make, that a person's liberty to court either happiness or despair is sacrosanct. I believed this, too, and yet the poignancy and frustration of Adam's life has fed my doubts. . . . After all, where is the measure of responsibility here? Where, exactly, is the demarcation between self-harm and child abuse? Gross negligence is nearly equal to intentional harm, goes a legal maxim. Where do we draw the line?[75]

"Right," "liberty," "responsibility": Erdrich's command of the vocabulary of legal theory equals that of Alan Dershowitz, law professor and defense attorney:

There is a principled distinction between totalitarian intrusions into the way a woman treats her body, and civil libertarian concerns for the way a woman treats the body of the child she has decided to bear. That principled distinction goes back to the philosophy of John Stuart Mill and is reflected in the creed that "Your right to swing your fist ends at the tip of my nose." In the context of a pregnant woman's rights and responsibilities in relation to the child she has decided to bear, the expression might be, "Your right to abuse your own body stops at the border of your womb."[76]

Reading these passages conveys the impression that Western jurisprudence stopped with liberal individualism and John Stuart Mill. (Reading some feminist scholarship can convey a similar impression.) One wonders what it is about *On Liberty* that makes it such a popular reference point, considering how vulnerable the essay is to criticism even from newcomers to the study of political theory. Nevertheless, Dershowitz does explicitly what Erdrich does implicitly; he sets his argument within the context of liberal theory.

The difficulty with "Your right stops at the border of your womb" is that the womb and its contents are inseparable from the body that contains them. It would seem to follow that pregnant women have no rights against state coercion. It may even follow, as it did for Margery Shaw and the Olin Corporation, that no woman who could be or might become pregnant has rights. But Dershowitz's claim that liberal individualism and its prototypical proponent support the case for fetal protection appears at least plausible. Mill's premise that "the only purpose for which power can be rightfully exercised over any member of a civilized community, against his will, is to prevent harm to others" offers no clear protection to the liberty of a pregnant woman vis-à-vis her unborn child.[77]

But no proof exists that any and all consumption of alcohol, drugs, or tobacco by a pregnant woman endangers the unborn child. Consider, again, the woman in the Seattle restaurant. No bystander has grounds to infer that she is creating a risk. We know nothing about how much alcohol she has consumed, how advanced her pregnancy is (except that she is far enough along to "show") or, for that matter, any relevant facts except that she is visibly pregnant and wants a drink. Given the incomplete nature of medical knowledge about fetal damage, and the tendency in the past generation of medical history for patients to be proved right and their physicians proved wrong, I see no way out of the conclusion that, yes, it is the woman's right to choose to ingest these substances—just as it is a mother's right to choose not to follow the latest medical advice about child nutrition, and a worker's right to risk exposure to harmful substances. Liberal rights theory does protect the autonomy of (actually, potentially, possibly, or presumptively) pregnant women. The negative case for fetal protection fails.

Fetal Rights and Feminist Theory: Freedom, Responsibility, and Gender

Does the collapse of the case for fetal protection reveal anything but "the impoverishment of the language of individual rights and the inadequacy of liberal feminism"?[78] If no argument for fetal protection works, must we accept the consequences of toxic exposure? Louise Erdrich urges the advocates of rights to "sit beside the alcohol-affected while they try to learn how to add. . . . Tell them every simple thing they must know for survival, one million, two million, three million times. Hold their heads while they have unnecessary seizures and wipe the blood from their bitten lips. . . . Then go back to the mother, face to face, and say again: '*It was your right.*' "[79]

This argument is powerful on both an emotional and a rational level, even though the reader knows, by this point in the book, that the birth mother is beyond the reach of their admonition. But Erdrich questions only part of conventional theory. While insisting that liberal concepts of individual *freedom* fail, she accepts without question liberal concepts of individual *responsibility*. Similarly, Dershowitz refers to how women *treat* the children *they* have *decided* to bear. This liberal theory overemphasizes "individual" as fatally as it does "responsibility." Both Dershowitz and Erdrich set the issue in terms of rights versus responsibility, freedom versus coercion. *Only* individuals have either rights or responsibilities; individuals have *only* rights to be free of coercion and responsibilities to others. There are no other possible relationships.

Erdrich makes the reader choose between coercing the pregnant drinker and conceding her right to do as she pleases. Those are the choices liberal rights theory provides. But addiction is one problem liberal rights theory cannot deal with. Why are noninterference and prohibition the only possibilities? Could we not say instead, "It was your right to get help for your addiction"? No, because that help is unavailable. Medicaid will not even pay for treatment for pregnant addicts. What about, "It was your right to get an abortion, and then to get treatment, so that you might have healthy babies in the future"? No again. Or what about, "The state has an obligation to protect you from corporations that sell you harmful addictive substances for their own profit"? Of course not. The law has sentenced women to prison for drug use during pregnancy; it has yet to make a tobacco company pay for the damage its products do.[80]

One commentator states, "All children should have the right to begin life free from preventable defects and deformities."[81] This premise is hard to dispute; but what correlative duties does that right entail? A duty to remove toxic substances from the workplace; to provide alcohol and drug rehabilitation; to fund research on birth defects; or to protect pregnant women from domestic violence? No. Only mothers have a duty to prevent birth defects. The proponents of fetal protection call for restrictions on women's rights; even some opponents of these policies, like the author of the article I quoted, call only for maternal education.

We agree that the state has the power to punish. We do not agree that it has a duty to help. That idea is increasingly ridiculed as a silly remnant of obsolescent ideologies. But not even the New Deal or the Great Society recognized entitlements to treatment or to protection from greed. Franklin Roosevelt's vision of "freedom from want" and "freedom from fear" was never realized; as I suggested in the last chapter, the latter freedom leads more readily to calls for tough punishments than for positive rights. Sydney Callahan's argument that "valid rights arise from need" has no place in public debate.[82] This lack, not the combination of "strident language of rights" and "near-aphasia concerning responsibilities" decried by communitarians, is the real "impoverishment of political discourse."[83] Once again, rights must be defended because they are insecure; responsibilities may go unmentioned because they are basic.

However stridently rights are defended, limiting negative rights is a more acceptable solution to almost any given problem than increasing positive rights or limiting institutional powers. Liberal-communitarian hybrids like William Galston and Hillary Rodham Clinton seek to strengthen the family by making divorce harder to get, not by making jobs easier to keep. Conservatives like William Bennett seek to improve moral education by curbing talk shows and rock lyrics, not by making parenting less burdensome or teaching more rewarding.[84] Either we may punish women for ingesting harmful substances during pregnancy, or they have a right to drink, smoke, and use drugs. There are no other possibilities.

Rights discourse often suggests that positive and negative rights are incompatible with and even destructive of each other. Libertarians worry that X's freedom from want may threaten Y's property rights. The "pro-life feminists" I discussed in Chapter 6 fear that recognition of a right to abortion may provide an excuse to deny affirmative governmental assistance. But the issue of fetal protection raises the possibility that negative and positive rights are interdependent: that refusing to guarantee positive rights to assistance may jeopardize negative rights to autonomy. A society which values freedom from birth defects and forecloses the possibility of imposing positive duties on employers and government is left with the sole alternative of restricting the autonomy of women.

None of the foregoing will surprise the student of Western political theory. The idea that the state may punish people who injure others has been a staple of that theory at least as far back as Thomas Hobbes. Acceptance of punishment follows logically from a principle so fundamental to this jurisprudence that it rarely needs to be verbalized: the idea that the protection of persons and property is the central purpose of civil government. Americans differ about what else the state may do, what behavior the state should punish, and how, but we agree that the state *may* punish. The criminal sanction is the bottom line.

Workplace restrictions are the corporate version of the criminal sanction. Like the state, employers use power to prohibit. Unlike the state, they can enforce their rules without resorting to punishment. *Johnson Controls* is a declaration that the choice between what Ruth Rosen calls "the freedom to endanger one's life" and the freedom to forgo a well-paying job belongs to the worker, not the employer. To tell women workers that "decisions about the welfare of future children must be left to the parents who conceive, bear, support, and raise them" provides a "hollow victory."[85] That kind of privatization leads to the absence of child care, parental leaves, and the other policies that would make working parents' lives less burdensome. The reader searches in vain for any suggestion that employers have a duty not to expose their workers to harmful substances, or that women as child bearers have any rights to assistance from society.

The famous sentence from *On Liberty* that I quoted extends the use of the criminal law even as it limits it. To say that society may restrict freedom only to prevent harm to others is like telling Cinderella to be home by midnight. The chances she will stay out that late are at least as good as the chances she will get home that early.[86] The negative case for fetal protection jumps from the principle that the state may limit individual freedom only to prevent harm to others to the position that the state may limit individual freedom whenever others might be harmed—even if limiting freedom is not a good way to prevent harm, or if there is no distinction between what Mill calls self-regarding and other-regarding actions, or if the threatened harm is inadequately understood. Women like Jennifer Johnson and Diane Pfannensteil discover that the state which refuses to extend its hand *to* them will not keep its hands *off* them. The "nanny state" becomes the "bully state."

Asymmetrical Thinking Revisited

How does feminist jurisprudence speak to the issue of fetal protection? Some feminist critiques of fetal rights find conventional jurisprudence more than adequate to discredit fetal protection policies. Wendy Williams and Mary Becker, for example, call on both employers and government to make the workplace safe for prospective parents and their future children.[87] Other feminist critics display various degrees of involvement with and commitment to situation jurisprudence. We have already encountered

Catharine MacKinnon's suggestion that the law protected abortion rights while permitting workplace restrictions because the former increase men's sexual access to women while the latter do not.[88] But this analysis does not explain why law forbids or permits conduct which has no effect on women's heterosexual availability. Sally Kenney's and Cynthia Daniels's studies of concrete cases like *Johnson Controls* and *A.C.* illuminate the woman-blaming, and outright woman-hating, which underlie these policies.[89]

But Part I of this book showed that patriarchal theses can suffer a sex change into something rich and strange called feminist theory. While I know of no defender of fetal protection policies who calls himself or herself a feminist theorist, much of what I call character jurisprudence at best leaves women defenseless against the powerful ongoing threat that the fetal rights movement represents and, at worst, plays right into its hands. There is an ominous similarity, for example, between Alan Dershowitz's assertion that liberal theory excludes pregnant women and Robin West's critique of liberalism's "separation thesis."[90] The similarity between the female "ethic of care" of Carol Gilligan and Nel Noddings and the "duty of care" of Margery Shaw and John Robertson is equally striking. In fact, these works constitute the equivalent of what botanists call "convergent evolution." They all appeared within two years of one another with no evidence of cross-fertilization.[91]

If character jurists have failed to anticipate and repulse the threat of fetal protection, so has at least one of their critics. Shaw's and Robertson's doctrine of contingent legal personhood fits all too neatly with my argument for presuming that humanity is conferred on an unborn child by its mother. While I use that premise to infer rights, Robertson and Shaw use something similar to it to infer duties.[92] Analogous reasoning characterizes the relationship between workplace restrictions and improved job opportunities, and between forced medical treatment and the gains of the women's health movement. A male supremacist system turns new rights into new burdens. When women took responsibility for improving their job opportunities and protecting themselves and their babies, the system "rewarded" them by imposing still more responsibilities.

The fears that Sydney Callahan, Juli Loesch, and Catharine MacKinnon expressed about a backlash to *Roe v. Wade* have materialized in the fetal protection movement.[93] It uses advances in women's freedom as excuses to increase their vulnerability and responsibility. The jurisprudence of fetal protection engages feminist theory in an intellectual jujitsu in which the feminists' own strength becomes a weapon against them. Fetal protection provides yet another illustration of the asymmetrical thinking I discussed in Chapter 3. Power and privilege confer the ability to impose responsibilities on others and refuse them for oneself. A crucial task of feminist theory is to redistribute responsibility: to assign it upward rather than downward, to relinquish it on behalf of women. Men, institutions, and government must be held accountable for what they do and fail to do. Women must refuse to accept new obligations and refrain from imposing them on other women. Feminist jurisprudence must build on its insights about the relationship between law and women's lives to reach outside women's lives.

In Chapter 6, I quoted Wendy Brown's statement that women-as-reproducers do not need more protective, defensive, and isolating rights.[94] This chapter calls Brown's conclusion into serious question. Angela Carder, Bree Walker, and the woman in the Seattle restaurant needed rights. They, and thousands like them, needed society to leave them alone. This conclusion may seem ludicrous with respect to Carder. Surely, she needed help. But is help what she got?

The advocates of coercion would force women to conform to the dictates of medicine and law—two professions whose fallibility has been repeatedly demonstrated—and deny help to women who cannot conform. Is society justified in coercing women, in the absence of any commitment to their welfare or trust in their judgment? Negative rights will not prevent birth defects, any more than they will guarantee women reproductive control or make the workplace safe. But negative rights may be just what women need, as actual, potential, possible, or presumptive reproducers, to protect themselves from law that reflects "the spirit of meanness, not love or kindness."[95] Individual rights and liberal feminism are inadequate for women, but not irrelevant or hostile to them. To say that liberal rights theory is not enough is not to say that it is wrong. A liberalism that includes women as rights-bearing human beings is a necessary component of feminist jurisprudence.

Necessary, but not sufficient. Equal rights with men are not enough to make women equal to men. The last two chapters showed that claims for equal protection and individual privacy are made and answered within a social context of malapportioned rights and duties. This chapter has shown that *Johnson Controls* provides nothing more than a Hobson's choice and that relieving addicted mothers of criminal responsibility does not give them any choice at all. The liberal alternatives of noninterference and prohibition will not help workers exposed to toxic substances, or addicted mothers, or their children. Those objectives call for a whole new theory of government obligation toward the individual.

The recognition of positive rights arising from need would not demand that we prefer them over positive rights arising from autonomy. Why not have both? Why not provide all the help we can, yet agree that, ultimately, a person must be allowed to refuse it? Since coercion is all we have in our repertoire, we have no way of knowing what choices women would make if help were available. We do know that Sweden, where abortion and treatment are available to all, has a high rate of alcoholism and a low rate of

FAS.[96] We know that holding employers accountable for endangering workers and their children need not preclude allowing women to work where they please. The criminal sanction may not always be the appropriate last refuge of the state. Feminist justice may sometimes require the state to help and forbid it to punish.

Conclusion

In Part I, I called upon feminist jurists to break up the male monopoly on justice and give up the female monopoly on care. The first project upends conventional theory by positing women's rights while questioning their responsibilities; the second lays claim to the care and nurturance women have been expected to provide. Applied to reproductive rights and fetal protection, both projects encourage the redistribution of responsibility and challenge some basic assumptions of liberal individualism. These ventures pose popular questions in the 1990s; but my approach is not likely to come up with popular answers. Calls for individual freedom and institutional responsibility are drowned out in the clash between conservatives' pleas for more *individual* responsibility and communitarians' pleas for more individual *responsibility*. Liberals and feminists are in exile. Liberals, disoriented by political defeat, are all but silent in the face of increasing threats to rights. Feminists conduct endless dialogues about gender difference and gendered danger.

My next chapter seeks to resolve this impasse. I combine feminist and liberal theory to construct a feminist postliberalism. I bring that theory into confrontation with the conservative and communitarian voices that dominate American political discourse. My goal is to force feminists to confront mainstream discourse, and mainstream discourse to confront feminism. Finally, I build on the work of these last seven chapters to begin to construct a feminist jurisprudence of the person.

EIGHT

TOWARD A FEMINIST POSTLIBERALISM

THIS BOOK has studied several ongoing debates within feminist scholarship. The participants agree that prefeminist theory is male-biased, that reality is gendered, and that the corrective for implicit male bias is to produce explicit female theory. The important controversies center around gender difference, male dominance, and intellectual method. Feminist scholars have disputed the relative importance of gender difference and male dominance ad infinitum and ad nauseam. But feminist theorists of gender difference have not said much of substance that their pre-, non-, or antifeminist predecessors had not already said, nor have they figured out how to claim the "feminine" without leaving women stuck in it or exiled outside it. Feminist analysts of male dominance tend to conflate it with female dependence, confusing what men do with what women are. Feminist epistemologists distrust traditional modes of learning without either avoiding their characteristic errors or recognizing that these traditions are what attract scholars to scholarship.

Feminist scholars debate one another, to no foreseeable end, while a second set of debates increasingly dominates political and academic discourse. The participants include conservatives, communitarians, "moderates," and increasingly timorous liberals. Most of them accept a premise that President Clinton, to whom the last three labels have been applied, articulated in his 1996 State of the Union address: "The era of big government is over." Most of them are more concerned with balancing the federal budget than with improving the lives of Americans. But, like the feminists, these thinkers have their disagreements. Subjects of dispute include the various roles of state and local governments, institutions, and individuals; the proper balance between individual freedom and individual responsibility; whether religion is a good or bad influence in American life; how to reduce crime; how to conserve natural resources; and questions involving sexuality, reproduction, marriage, and the family.

All of these are feminist issues. Women are less able than men to command an adequate income; more vulnerable to violence, abuse, and exploitation; and more responsible for the young, aged, ill, and disabled. Women are more likely than men to require the state's help at some time in their lives. A smaller, tighter government will make many women's lives harder. Business, crime, religion, and environmental protection, like government, affect women's lives in different ways than they affect men's lives. Feminists do not all agree on any of these issues. In fact, several of them are subjects of dispute in feminist discourse. But this debate is conducted in gender-neutral language. Feminist discourse turns inward, while mainstream political discourse marginalizes feminist concerns. In this final chapter, I attempt to bring feminist theory into the arena of political discourse. A prerequisite for this project is to correct some characteristic errors of feminist theory; a consequence of this project is the possibility of correcting some characteristic errors of contemporary discourse.

I argue in Part I that much contemporary feminist jurisprudence consists of critical responses to an implied conventional or standard theory, similar to but not identical with liberalism. These critiques share a conviction that the standard theory, developed by and for men, is hostile to women. Feminist scholars have had little difficulty finding concrete evidence to support their assertion. The authors I call character jurists have drawn attention to law's consistent devaluing of the essential tasks to which society has assigned women; one instance among many is the refusal of child custody law to recognize that one learns to love a child by caring for it. The authors I call situation jurists have shown how liberal jurisprudence presumes an equality within home and family that does not exist; one instance among many is the refusal of privacy doctrine to recognize men's power over women in relationships.

These failures of conventional jurisprudence to incorporate women's lives are not random occurrences. Male supremacy is as integral a part of the boundaries and dynamics of law as of its content. I have examined ways in which things that happen outside the law make it male, and how law changes in response to men's rather than women's claims. Feminist scholars like Susan Moller Okin and Carole Pateman have convincingly argued that Western political theory presupposes male supremacy and the patriarchal family.[1] The philosophers who wrote of "man" meant adult males. Jurisprudence rationalizes male supremacy; it does not explain it. Law reinforces male supremacy; it did not create it.

The claim that conventional theory is untrue for women has considerable merit. But what feminist theory has failed to do is as crucial as what it has done. The worst errors of feminist jurisprudence stem from an incomplete understanding of the theory it purports to reject. Feminist jurists are hard on liberalism in general, and on individual rights in particular. For character jurists, rights supersede the care and connection so important to women; for situation jurists, rights in men's hands become weapons of female oppression; for feminist scholars with diverse and conflicting views of the world, "abstract rights authorize the male experience of the world."[2]

So far, so good. But this emphasis on the defects of liberalism as applied to women is perplexing. Liberalism has never fully belonged to women, or we to it. The core of liberalism—"not the absence of a substantive conception of the good, but rather a reluctance to move from this conception to full-blown public coercion of individuals"—does not apply to women.[3] When a feminist economist defends a woman's *right* to become a single mother, a communitarian columnist criticizes her for *advising* women to do this.[4] Debate on reproductive rights is indistinguishable from debate on the ethics of abortion; proponents of fetal protection strive to enact medical advice into criminal law. The liberal distinction between "should" and "must," crime and sin, prescription and command, is missing from discourse on women's issues. This distinction, not any concept of what it means to be a human being, is liberalism's real "separation thesis." Robin West got it partly right after all. Liberalism entails a separation thesis which is untrue for women.[5]

This thesis, correctly understood, can serve women well. Presuming that women are liberal subjects helps resolve several of the questions I deal with in this book. Recognizing a pregnant woman's right to decide whether the fetus in her body will become human, or how much medical advice to accept, would not solve all the problems women face, but it would go a long way toward making women autonomous adults. But, despite the obvious advantages to women of distinguishing between the moral and the legal, feminists are reluctant to do this. Feminist jurisprudence does not know Voltaire's distinction between disagreeing with what you say and defending your right to say it. Antipornography feminists confuse opposition with oppression, while feminist defenders of the First Amendment confuse criticism with censorship.[6] Feminists do not know how to agree to disagree. The debate over whether or not women would choose to become mothers under ideal conditions slights the possibility that different women would make different choices.[7] Liberalism cuts people slack. But conventional jurisprudence denies this slack to women, and feminist jurists deny it to one another.

The failure to understand conventional theory's limited application to women is not feminists' only serious mistake. Feminist theorists have committed a common characteristic error of scholarly inquiry; they concentrate on what is said to the exclusion of what goes unsaid. Feminists are not alone in making this error. Communitarians have concluded from the prevalence of "rights talk" in American society that rights are the most important component of conventional theory, that they supersede every other value all the time.[8] It is easy to assume that what is said most often is most important. But Part II of this book has shown how wrong that conclusion is with respect to rights and responsibilities.

Let us concede Mary Ann Glendon her point: the defense of rights is often "strident."[9] It has to be, because there is almost no social problem for which restricting rights is not offered as a solution. Birth defects? Punish women for using drugs or alcohol during pregnancy; don't use Medicaid funds to treat pregnant addicts. Family breakdown? Make divorce harder to get for the parents of young children; don't collect child support payments or build affordable housing. Immorality? Attack rap music, TV talk shows and their respective advertisers; don't restructure the workplace to give parents more time to teach their children morality. Crime? Relax the constitutional restrictions on police and put more people in prison; don't improve the educational system or create jobs. Again and again, we prefer solutions which restrict rights to solutions which enable people to exercise rights. And even that statement puts things too mildly. Punitive discourse is so dominant that it stifles discussion of helpful solutions, while "enabling" refers most often to wives who cover up for alcoholic husbands.

Conservatives, in particular, seem devoted to making life harder for people. Most conservatives believe the era of big government should never have begun. But Patrick Buchanan, their favorite candidate for the 1996 Republican presidential nomination, promised to build a wall along the border between the United States and Mexico to keep out illegal immigrants. Conservatives accuse advocates of corporate responsibility of "letting people off the hook."[10] They attack the government's student loan program (incorrectly) for relieving parents of pressure to save money when their children are young—at a stage in life when family income is low relative to expenses. The message of much conservative rhetoric can be crudely summarized as "We're gonna get you!"

But neither liberals nor communitarians are immune from the call for stringency. President Clinton wants public schools to make students wear uniforms; his emphasis on the connection between school violence and clothing envy suggests he has confused occasion with cause. In March 1996, the commissioner of Social Security asked Congress for $720 million—so her agency might review the cases of people receiving disability benefits. Apparently, the era of big spending is alive and well if you want to stiff the disabled.[11] The "nanny state" (and consider the attitudes embedded in that pejorative term) yields to the "bully state." The conventional theory which feminist jurists question does not privilege rights over responsibility. Rights are so precarious they must be defended; responsibilities are so basic they need not be discussed. Like communitarians, feminists have failed to understand that conventional theory puts rights on the defensive while taking responsibility for granted.

Responsibilities Talk

This premise of individual responsibility is embedded in the society from which conventional theory emerged. American law presumes that adults are responsible for meeting their basic needs. I have argued that gender "differences" which appear natural are, in fact, contingent on the different ways society has allowed men and women to meet these needs.[12] The fact that responsibility is presumed does not mean it is never talked about; it is, and in ways feminists should ponder. The stories Western culture tells focus on individuals, attributing their successes to things they did right and their failures to things they did wrong. Our folk heroes are people who overcome obstacles; disability and poverty, presented as random occurrences, are staples of this kind of story. Political analysis explains outcomes in terms of what the individuals involved did right or wrong. Institutions, structure, process, and even luck have nothing to do with results. The story of organized labor attributes its decline to internal failure and corruption; the Taft-Hartley Act had nothing to do with it.[13] The story of the Equal Rights Amendment attributes its defeat to Eleanor Smeal's errors or Phyllis Schlafly's acumen; the fact that the constitutional rules militate against the ratification of amendments goes unnoticed.[14] The story of the failed health care plan concentrates on Hillary Rodham Clinton's miscalculations, not on the strength of the forces ranged against the plan.

None of these official stories is absurd (as was, for instance, the idea that Geraldine Ferraro was responsible for the results of the 1984 presidential election). In each instance, the unsuccessful actors made mistakes which influenced the result. But in no case does individual behavior suffice to explain the outcomes; no one can say with confidence that "if X had behaved differently, the outcome would have been different." Structural and institutional influences on outcomes do not become part of the official stories.

No-Fault Downsizing?

People are held accountable. Institutions are not. For the individual, "unemployment" is "the ultimate consequence of bad decisions" (certain exceptions spring to mind, in both directions).[15] But when corporations "downsize"—that is, create unemployment—CEO and owners need not answer to their former employees or to the government. To challenge these decisions is to be unrealistic, to ally oneself with "today's econo-hysterics" who advocate "turning corporations into social service agencies."[16] But many people think it is realistic to ask teenagers to abstain from sex or couples to stay in unhappy marriages. Contemporary "responsibilities talk" is rife with such contradictions.

A useful way to analyze responsibilities talk is to compare two situations which have several features in common: downsizing and divorce. The differences between the two situations may be more obvious than the similarities. While both work and marriage involve mutual self-interest, marriage is an intimate, exclusive relationship and work is not. While both downsizing and divorce involve the termination of a contractual relationship, the two processes tell very different legal stories. In downsizing, the more powerful partner terminates the relationship in its own interests. In American law, no marriage is like this and no marriage ends like this. Since *Kirchberg v. Feenstra*, the spouses are equal partners; since the enactment of no-fault divorce law, the dissolution of marriage takes place by mutual consent.[17] The fact that no-fault divorce was entrenched in fifty states long before asymmetrical marriage law was invalidated by one court may or may not be significant.

But what the law presupposes about marriage may not coincide with the facts. Many marriages are asymmetrical relationships, and many divorces are unilateral decisions. Power may derive from one spouse's, usually the husband's, greater command of resources like income, education, or physical strength; or power may derive according to the famous law of interpersonal relationships, by which the spouse who cares less may exploit the spouse who cares more. When a marriage ends, it is often this same dominant partner who initiates the divorce. "Often" is not "always." Some marriages do end by mutual consent, and others because the subordinate partner gets out. If the divorcing couple has minor children, the analogy works: divorce is the breakup of a family by one or more of its dominant members. One or both parents act in self-interest.

Both a marriage and a job involve a contractual relationship between two parties. If the relationship has been successful, one or both parties has probably given more than the other could demand. We know this happens in marriage. The adage "Marriage is a 50–50 proposition" is often cited by those who reject it in favor of "100–100." The similar extra effort involved in some work relationships may be less obvious and less common. But a 1996 news story about Eastman Kodak's downsizing quotes the daughter of a laid-off senior manager: "In our house, we didn't even use anything that wasn't Kodak, Kodak film, Kodak cameras."[18] IBM's Thomas Watson is reputed to have retained a subordinate whose project had catastrophically failed, on the grounds that IBM had spent two million dollars training him. True or not, the story suggests a reciprocity similar to what I have observed in my own working life. Both downsizing and divorce, as redefined, represent the breakdown of a formal relationship, once important to both parties, because the dominant partner no longer wants it.

Both work and marriage are ostensibly private relationships: most downsizing occurs within the "private" sector, as marriage belongs in the "private" sphere. But these relationships, and their breakdown, illustrate the defects and dangers of the public-private dichotomy. The ramifications of downsizing include not only the obvious economic effects but also equally pernicious social effects. Unemployment leads to decreased spending, which leads to more unemployment, which leads to crime. The relationship between layoffs and family dissolution has been pointed out too often to require elaboration. Downsizing leaves behind a reduced workforce to cope with an unreduced workload; overtaxed employees make errors; inconvenienced customers react with anger and contempt; a surly clientele makes working conditions worse; and a downward spiral of anger, guilt, fatigue, and frustration makes life nastier and more brutish even for those who still have jobs to do and money to spend.[19]

Evaluating the public effects of family dissolution is a difficult task, because the debate has conflated fact with opinion and reality with rhetoric. The following statement from a prominent columnist makes a familiar argument against family breakup: "An avalanche of evidence shows that single-parent kids are way more vulnerable than two-parent kids to all sorts of damage."[20] Much of this evidence consists of studies of single-parent families; lacking a control group, these are useless as support of the quoted statement.[21] Such factors as the extensively documented postdivorce decline in the standard of living for custodial mothers and their children may be significant intervening variables.[22] The critics of divorce have no monopoly on distortion. Parents who want to end their marriages often tell themselves and anyone who will listen that what is good for them is good for their children. Nevertheless, substantial agreement exists among experts that divorce is bad for children.[23]

So both downsizing and divorce represent the termination of legal relationships by one side acting in its own interests, followed by negative social effects. But the discourse surrounding these two forms of dissolution reflects diametrically opposed notions of responsibility and accountability. The mass media rush to excuse the downsizers; thus, a few giant corporations absolve others. "The world is changing"; "there are tides you just can't swim against"; "there is no magic bullet that will make the problem go away."[24] In big business, no one acts: things are, people can't, problems come and go. Free will does not exist for institutions, even though Chapter 5 showed how law excuses them unless they exercise it. This conceptualization of economic trends as irresistible natural forces is similar to the way some of the authors discussed in Chapter 7 perceive male sexuality; workers must protect themselves from downsizing just as women must protect themselves from rape.

ssion hopes couples will improve their prospects of saving
"[30]

t of the American judiciary, I cannot help noticing that the
ric of downsizing and divorce proceeds in ignorance of a core
ntieth-century judicial politics. A single big, strong target may
control than a weak, fragmented one. President Nixon obeyed
e Court's order to turn over incriminating evidence much faster
can schoolteachers took prayer out of their classrooms. But
talk as if millions of couples would be easier to restrict than one
oration. Another difficulty with the parallel rhetoric is that
nship we would make harder to terminate is precisely the one *less*
to regulation. Marriage is not just a relationship of self-interested
involves not only reciprocal rights and duties but love, friend-
sexual attraction, and these cannot be demanded. No perceptive
ould deny that some marriages end for light and transient causes.
her can we deny that people often have good reasons for wanting
ce. Even if children would be better off in a two-parent family, how
an parents be required to sacrifice? Even if parents should
rried for their children's sake, is society justified in turning a moral
l" into a legal "should"? Feminists must insist that society rank
's needs equally with those of children. We must not let the antidi-
faction forget that some marriages end for the same reason some
ges never happen: "Women are much less willing to put up with
equal power relations and division of labor that came with the tradi-
l marriage."[31]

is account of responsibilities talk has suggested that society should
ict the freedom of downsizing employers while maintaining that of
rcing parents. Workers should not be at the mercy of the economy,
must we leave children at the mercy of their parents? No; our inability
emove the causes of divorce does not leave us powerless to control its
cts.[32] But the crucial task of meeting children's needs while preserving
lts' liberty requires us to reexamine another neglected feature of con-
ntional theory: the way responsibility is gendered.

Conventional Jurisprudence and Gender Asymmetry

All people may be responsible, but, to paraphrase *Animal Farm*, some are
more responsible than others. Dominance shows itself in the power to
assign and apportion, to divide human activity into categories and to distribute rights, duties, and dangers along gender lines. Men are let off the
hook, while women are held responsible: for care and nurturance, for birth
control and childbearing, for their behavior toward others and the behavior
of others toward them. Feminist jurists' ignorance of the way the premise

Business executives and ̣
jobs. That is a task for "the e
"the tough, cold, cruel syst
us very well."[25] Once, corpora
by claiming the status of perso.
as human beings. Now, corpora
be part of a neutral, impersonal
ence than the weather. Even the
ment can't suppress" job insecurity
ert Reich called for "corporate res
he would be seen as vilifying corp.
searching.'"[27]

A familiar justification for downsi.
competitive international market: if v
up with unemployment rates as high as
The fact that social safety nets cushio.
Europe, while important to the unempl
ers' position. They may be right, altho
judgment themselves hardly exemplifie
Right or wrong, downsizers do not even h
rationales are accepted at face value. Their
ests as they perceive them goes unchallenge
tion that Congress might enable fired work
ance, no one tries to interfere.[28] People may h
have license. Those who suffer the consequenc
hard enough and the system is allowed to re
better. Things always do, since any self-regula
not everyone benefits. People are made for the e
for people.

If no-fault downsizing is in vogue, no-fault d
decision to dissolve a family which contains minor
more disapproval than the decision to lay off wor.
beyond individual control do not work with divorc
work with teenage sex. In early 1996, a proposal to ab
was introduced in the Michigan legislature. A growin
leaders have proposed restrictions on divorce.[29] Willi
stance, praises the (rejected) 1990 report of Great Brit
sion. This body recommended a mandatory nine-mon
vorces between the parents of minor children. The pare
mediators, would use this delay to decide, in this order,
ture, the property settlement, and financial maintenance.
never be forbidden, but "by encouraging parents to loo.
quences of a family breakup rather than at the alleged caus

it, the commi
the marriage.

As a stude
parallel rhet
lesson of twe
be easier to
the Suprem
than Amer
Americans
huge corp
the relatio
amenable
parties. I
ship. ̣
person w
But neit
to divor
much
stay ma
"shoulc
women
vorce
marri
the u
tiona

T
restr
divc
but
to
eff
ad
ve

of individual responsibility is gendered in our culture leads to the peculiar error of interpretation that I analyzed in Chapter 3. Critics of situation jurisprudence read it wrong. They confuse analysis of women's situation with analysis of their character, so that feminists who expose men's mistreatment of women are accused of denigrating women as passive victims. Situation jurists have difficulty responding to this criticism because they fail to perceive how they are read. The asymmetry of responsibility between individuals and institutions mirrors an asymmetry of responsibility between men and women.

The rhetoric of divorce and downsizing showed how institutions are let off the hook while people are held responsible. Since most downsizers are men, and the exceptions got their power from men and hold it at men's pleasure, corporate license is a gendered issue; it is one more example of men's power to assign roles, rights, and duties and to exonerate as well as to inculpate one another. Chapters 6 and 7 showed how institutions and men are let off the hook while women are held responsible. Heterosexual activity, pregnancy, and child rearing take place in a context where men act freely, while women are expected to deal with the consequences of male initiative. Fetal protection discourse frames the issue as one of women's rights versus women's responsibilities. Business has no responsibility to prevent fetal damage; government need not offer help to the women it is ready to punish.

Children are as vulnerable to their parents' marital situation as women are vulnerable to their reproductive function. Much of the harm divorce does to children is a consequence of the same factor that makes sex and parenthood dangerous for women: *male* irresponsibility. Chapter 5 showed that despite the literal neutrality and evenhandedness of most no-fault divorce statutes, actual outcomes benefit men at the expense of women and children. In divorce settlements, courts tend to base decisions on criteria which favor men rather than which favor women. Support awards tend to be inadequate, and compliance with support orders tends to be incomplete.[33] Divorce impoverishes children financially if they lose one of the family's incomes; it impoverishes children emotionally if they lose one parent.

Law cannot make fathers care about their children. But law can mitigate the effects of male irresponsibility by imposing and enforcing support obligations, just as it could (but does not) make contraception and abortion available or subsidize the burdens of motherhood. Since the mid-1980s, federal and state governments have shown increasing commitment to child support enforcement. By 1996, judges had sent support delinquents to jail, and the federal government had begun to relieve single mothers of the task of collecting support. Government efforts to put its muscle where its mouth is are welcome—if late—but the antidivorce movement threatens to distract attention from a realizable goal of enforcement to an unattainable goal of prohibition. Public discourse casts a problem of male behavior as a gender-neutral problem. Most support delinquents are men; every divorce involves one man and one woman. A solution which coerces both women and men, thus leaving intact the gender asymmetry of rights and responsibilities, is preferred to a solution which would redress the balance and share the burden.

Responsibility floats downhill: from institutions to individuals, from men to women. Power does not include responsibility; power includes the ability to assign responsibility. This asymmetry ensures that society will expect its problems to be solved by those with the least power to do so. People should find work, but employers need not create jobs. Young people should postpone parenthood, and even sex, until marriage, but institutions need not foster social and economic changes that would make the wait worthwhile or the goal feasible. Women faced with unwanted pregnancies should not have abortions, but men need not prevent unwanted pregnancy. These expectations create nice privileges for those who benefit from the status quo. Questioning these expectations in order to subvert the status quo is a necessary task of feminist scholarship. For women to achieve equalilty, responsibility must lie where power lies.

Conventional Jurisprudence Revisited

Jurisprudence presupposes male supremacy, but different types of jurisprudence incorporate male supremacy in different ways. My analysis of what I call conventional or standard jurisprudence has emphasized the ways in which it embeds, encodes, and apportions freedom and responsibility. Conventional jurisprudence and liberalism are kin, but not identical twins. The liberalism of conventional jurisprudence is an asymmetrical liberalism, asymmetrically applied. The "rights" part of liberalism is defended, sometimes stridently, while the "responsibilities" part is presumed. Rights talk has never fully included women, but responsibilities talk has.

The liberalism of conventional jurisprudence confines itself to defenses of negative rights: reproductive choice, for example, but not mothers' subsidies. Conventional theory does not include positive rights, although liberal theory has known about positive rights for at least a century.[34] Conventional theory defends liberalism; it presumes capitalism. Human rights and autonomy are what remain after the claims of ownership are satisfied. Liberalism as we know it (to coin a phrase) is neither subsequent to nor dependent on capitalism as we know it. Liberalism antedates industrial capitalism and has coexisted with socialism. But, if conventional theory is ethically loaded, it is economically driven.

The dominance of capitalism in conventional theory can be seen more clearly if we turn briefly from politics to religion. The American political culture of the late 1990s does not reflect this country's religious diversity. The dominant religious voice in American politics is the "Christian right," which speaks for Christianity about as inclusively as conventional theory speaks for liberalism. The United States lacks the equivalent of the Christian Democratic parties in Europe, which saw the welfare state as an effort to obey Christ's command to help the poor. The Christianity which influences our politics emphasizes heterosexual monogamy, self-discipline, industry, obedience, and traditional gender roles: emphasizes, in other words, those Christian values which are compatible with capitalism. In the United States, capitalism trumps Christianity as it trumps liberalism.

Conventional theory, then, is not so much liberalism as liberalism strained through capitalism. One reason people are held responsible for what happens to them, but institutions are exonerated for what they do, is that institutions are presumed to be homeostatic while people are presumed to exercise free will. One reason women are held responsible for the harm they endure, but men are excused for the harm they inflict, is that the liberal capitalist economy values aggression and exploits vulnerability.

Liberal capitalist economies reward competition as well as aggression. The "better" yields to the "best." American culture is fond of ordinal rankings. Orators declare the United States the best country in the world; pundits like to proclaim, whatever the facts, that "we have the best" educational or health care or political system in the world; and we tend to structure reality as if life were a race in which each runner will come in somewhere from first to last if the official timepiece is fine enough. But few human activities are as orderable as races. Declaring someone "best" makes it easy to incorporate subjective values, including sexism, into the judging. The best man for the job may well be a woman, but usually there is no one best person for the job; a woman is not equal if she must prove she is the best. Structuring reality as a pyramid is more conducive to hierarchy than structuring it as a plane.

Does all this mean that whoever says feminism cannot say capitalism? I do not claim to know whether any capitalism is compatible with sexual equality because I do not know what would remain if the most sexist features of capitalism were altered. I argued in Chapter 3 that society's dependence on aggression makes it difficult to control and vulnerability to it easy to condemn. Can we distinguish between healthy and unhealthy aggression or, for that matter, between being exploited and getting what you have coming to you? Can we differentiate (de facto as well as de jure) between building a better mousetrap than one's neighbor, and raping her? (Even de jure, this distinction was easier to make when rape was the violation of male property rights.)[35] Can we distinguish the imprudence of the sucker from the imprudence of the victim? A society which can accomplish these tasks would make women less vulnerable to aggression and less responsible for their own vulnerability.

This chapter has examined the ability of institutions, including corporations, to impose responsibility downward and reject it for themselves. Suppose government exerted enough control over business to distribute responsibility fairly among people and institutions: would that destroy capitalism or save it? Since experts still do not agree whether the New Deal or World War II saved American capitalism after the Great Depression, history does not provide much guidance in answering questions like these. Redistribution of responsibility is a necessary condition of sexual equality, but what this redistribution would do to the economic system is an unanswerable question at this point.

Furthermore, a belief that sexual equality is incompatible with capitalism does not imply that sexual equality is compatible with any alternative economic system.[36] Both liberalism and capitalism require the existence of the person who, in Nancy Hartsock's phrase, "follows timidly behind, carrying groceries, baby, and diapers"—but Hartsock was writing about Marxism.[37] Socialist governments have not eliminated male supremacy and asymmetrical responsibility, nor do socialist economies dispense with aggression. What capitalism has in common with the feudalism it replaced, with the socialism that Marx expected to replace it, with agrarian and industrial economies, and with liberal and conservative philosophies is male supremacy. Capitalism trumps jurisprudence and theology, but male supremacy trumps capitalism. Why, otherwise, would Americans suddenly become Marxists when debating equal pay, arguing (erroneously) that men need higher pay because they support families, or avoiding the use of capitalist terminology in discussions of reproductive choice?[38] Male supremacy is prior to economic as well as to legal theory. Conventional jurisprudence is "liberal" only with respect to what is left after male supremacy structures the society and "capitalist" only with respect to what is left after male supremacy structures the economy.

This revised understanding of conventional jurisprudence reinforces my conclusion that the malapportionment of autonomy, rights, and responsibilities that characterizes conventional jurisprudence is not compatible with sexual equality. A jurisprudence grounded in women's lives must move from feminism *unmodified* to feminism *modifying* to feminism *revising*. Sexual equality is not compatible with the liberalism or capitalism we have now because they are founded on and yield to male supremacy. When half of humankind is excluded from the creation of theories and systems, what results is not likely to be fair to that half.

Liberalism's rights and autonomy, the freedom it guarantees to do things of which other people may disapprove, are too good to forgo. Excluding women from the full scope of these rights is as great an injury as any that liberalism has inflicted on us. But feminist critics are right to insist that exclusion is not the only injury liberalism does to women and that guaranteeing women rights is not a Utopian solution. Liberalism does not speak to the situation I described in Chapter 1, the "Ellen James Society" of well-fed, relaxed, rested men and hungry, stressed, tired women. Unequal people can have equal rights only on paper; liberalism has never come to terms with inequalities among adults in sexual, family, and work relationships. Liberalism's presumption of free will and consent denies women's vulnerability and responsibility. Individual rights exercised by women may be good for them, but individual rights exercised by people with power over women can oppress them.

For instance, feminists have shown how liberal privacy doctrine protects men's power to trample on the rights of the women in their lives and facilitates their sexual access to women. *Roe v. Wade* recognized a woman's right to decide to end a pregnancy, and that recognition is welcome. But this right compromises her freedom to continue a pregnancy or to refuse sex. The law knows neither compulsory abortion nor forced sex. By invalidating gendered marriage law, *Feenstra* made unenforceable the "conjugal rights" of husbands. But husbands do not need law to give them access, nor is forced sex confined to marriage.

Both character jurists and situation jurists have pointed out that the basic defect of liberal privacy doctrine is not its presumption of equality within relationships but the public-private distinction itself. Conventional theory divides life into "spheres," women are forced into one sphere, and the activities located in that sphere are devalued. Life in the "private" sphere makes women vulnerable to men's power. Women and girls now alive have been socialized into traditional female roles and are expected, to a greater or lesser extent, to adopt them. If they do, they are disadvantaged. If they do not, they are punished. Feminism, revising liberalism, must address women's vulnerability and responsibility. It must recognize the value of what goes on within the "private" sphere at the same time that it liberates women from that sphere. A feminist jurisprudence must put women's lives before the law. It must presume sexual equality as an organizing principle and extirpate, "root and branch," the male supremacy of conventional theory.[39]

A Feminist Postliberalism

"Jurisprudence, after all, is about human beings."[40] The centrality of human beings—not the state, The Good, a deity, an economic system, or a theory of history—is a virtue of both liberal and feminist jurisprudence. But jurisprudence has never been about all human beings. It leaves out the person with the groceries, baby, and diapers. This person, or someone like her, exists everywhere. She must, because the work she does is necessary everywhere. But Western jurisprudence excludes her: specifically, like Aristotle in Book I of the *Politics*; or by omission, like the prefeminist liberals. The baby, equally necessary to the preservation of society, doesn't get in either. Adult males are the human beings jurisprudence is about. It includes women only to the extent that they lead the lives adult males do. I have argued throughout this book that there's nothing wrong with women leading that kind of life. In fact, I differ from several character theorists in suggesting that the realm of rights, justice, and civic activity may be preferable to the realm of care, connection, and concrete particulars. But a theory limited to demanding formal equality with men is destructive of actual equality.

Why? After all, prefeminist liberals—or liberal feminists, for that matter—have two venerable intellectual bulwarks to fall back on, either of which might reassure us that the exclusion from jurisprudence of women's traditional lives really doesn't matter. First, liberalism presumes the exercise of free will; as long as she has freely chosen to lead this life, why worry? Second, the public-private distinction puts homemaking and child rearing outside the scope of jurisprudence; these activities should not be the concern of legal theory. The reasons theory must include this prototypical figure become clear if we examine how liberal feminism can duplicate conventional theory's errors of omission. Early second-wave feminism had its own forgotten women. Bell Hooks, a black feminist author, wrote of *The Feminine Mystique* that "Friedan's famous phrase, 'the problem that has no name,' often quoted to describe the condition of women in this society, actually referred to the plight of a select group of college-educated, middle and upper class, married white women. . . . She did not discuss who would be called in to take care of the children and maintain the home if more women like herself were freed from their house labor and given equal access with white men to the professions." By universalizing "the plight of women like herself," Friedan "deflected attention away from her classism, her racism, her sexist attitudes toward the masses of American women."[41]

Friedan's error of omission was precisely the opposite of that of two other famous liberation manifestos of the 1960s. Martin Luther King's "I Have a Dream" speech of 1963 was full of phrases like "the sons of slaves and the sons of slave owners." The 1962 Port Huron Statement of the Students for a Democratic Society (SDS) surpassed even King in the use of the generic masculine. At any rate, Friedan's attitudes were biased for the same reason and in the same way that conventional theory's exclusion of the home was sexist. The domestic work has to be done. The tasks homemakers perform—providing food, clothing, and shelter, and raising children—meet basic human and societal needs. So do the care and nurturance that are the emotional and affective components of these activities. If middle-class housewives give up full-time homemaking, somebody else must do the essential work they leave behind.

Hooks did not suggest that the husbands of these women would take up the slack. She, and her readers, intuitively grasped that responsibility does not flow from women to men. Hooks's implication, which she hardly needed to spell out, was that domestic work renounced by privileged women would fall on the poor, working-class, and minority women who have historically been stuck with it. Events of the last thirty years have generally vindicated her. While child care centers and fast-food establishments have supplanted Miss Ann's kitchen as the site of underpaid domestic work, Hooks got the essentials right. To the extent that she was wrong, gainfully employed women have continued to do the work themselves.

Women who can get others to do their domestic work have to find these others. Since the pool of available workers consists largely of poor and minority women, women who hire out their home duties act out the racism and classism of their culture. Critiques like Hooks's blame these women for the situation, and blame can be absorbed and internalized as guilt. White, middle-class men are let off the hook once again. So are the men whose partners take on the notorious second shift. The problem that won't go away keeps even privileged women from real equality with men.[42] As long as society assigns these responsibilities to women, and as long as women who give them up have no one but less privileged women to call on, sexual equality is impossible. Jurisprudence must find a different way to be about human beings if it is to include all human beings.

How and whence has conventional jurisprudence of the person become jurisprudence of the adult male? Many theorists have started with a concept of human nature: Hobbes's "desire of power after power," Madison's "diversity in the faculties of man," Mill's individualism, or that basic premise of liberalism mislabeled the "separation thesis." The heroes of Western jurisprudence have been criticized for confusing the universal with the contingent and the essential with the particular. Beyond question, prefeminist liberals confused the human with the male. But so did Marx, who began not with character but with situation. Contemporary liberals have learned from Marx even as they rejected his theory of class struggle. Bruce Ackerman's *Social Justice in the Liberal State*, which I quoted in Chapter 3, begins by asking, in effect, not "What are people like?" but "What does the world look like to a human being?" His answer, that "there can be no escape from the struggle for power," evokes both Marx and Hobbes.[43] I By concentrating on what people need rather than on what they are like, Ackerman builds a more inclusive theory than the early liberals do. He perceives the world much as Hobbes did, but he turns *Leviathan* upside down. I argued in Part I that situation theory gets us closer to understanding women's lives than does character theory: gendered differences in the socially mandated means of meeting these needs provide much better explanations of perceived gender distinctions than do feminist, prefeminist or antifeminist notions of gender difference. What Hobbes attributes to an idea of "human" nature derived from male behavior, Ackerman attributes to human needs men and women share. But few women have been able to meet their needs by struggling for power; they had to be nice, in order to fit into male-dominated households. Ackerman leaves out the work women have to do for self-preservation and the specific dangers women confront.[44] Both Ackerman and Hobbes leave out the maintenance work, the provision of basic needs, that *somebody* must do if all that aggressive behavior is to occur. Whether that aggression is natural, situational, both, or neither, it is an incomplete description of what human life is—and so are the other descriptions that conventional jurisprudence contains.

Feminists have tried to correct the errors of conventional character and situation jurisprudence by starting from women's lives: "the feminine," the "connection thesis," women's "voice," their "ways of knowing." But much of this work substitutes for a partial, exclusive concept of what it means to be a person, an equally limited concept of what it means to be a woman. A concept of humanity may be a trap, but a concept of femininity is a tighter trap. Character feminists have failed to produce theory which is distinguishable from prefeminist theory of gender difference, while situation feminists have failed to make their readers distinguish what is done to women from what women are. Feminist jurists tend to overcorrect for the male bias of conventional jurisprudence, concentrating so hard on women that much of what affects women's lives goes unexamined. So nobody— the ancients, the liberals, the Marxists, *or* the feminists—has yet come up with a concept of what it means to be a human being, a man, *or* a woman which makes equality possible.

Imperative Jurisprudence and Liberal Justice

A comprehensive jurisprudence of the person must go beyond character and situation. What is required—to complement them, not to replace them—is what I call, for want of a better term, imperative theory and jurisprudence. This approach would inquire not what people are like or what the world is like to them but what they and society require for the maintenance of human life and civilization. Imperative theory asks, What has to happen to preserve people and society? What must get done? What can we not do without?

The organizing questions of imperative jurisprudence lead inexorably to the conclusion that the satisfaction of basic human needs and the reproduction of the species are individual and societal necessities. The assignment of responsibility for this necessary work has happened outside the law and prior to jurisprudence. Women are not responsible for all the essential work. Many tasks have belonged to men; one task—defense against aggression—has been almost exclusively men's work; and reproduction is a duty shared by men and women, although men have rarely perceived their contribution as a duty. Nor does conventional jurisprudence exclude all essential functions; it has a great deal to say about commerce and war, for instance. But much traditional women's work consists of essential functions and has been excluded from theory.

Imperative jurisprudence undermines the presumption of will and choice which is at the core of liberalism. True, the maintenance work is not always compulsory. Nor is this work a zero-sum phenomenon; one person's doing less does not always entail another person's doing more. Friedan's observation that "housewifery expands to fill the time available" continues to resonate three decades after she made it.[45] (One could observe with equal accuracy that "national defense expands to spend the money available.") Several years before Friedan wrote, Margaret Mead observed that post–World War II America was the first society in human history to make motherhood a full-time job.[46] And MacKinnon's assertion that the reproductive imperative accounts for only a fraction of the heterosexual intercourse that actually occurs is irrefutable.[47] The danger of confusing the necessary with the desirable, and the desirable with the preferred, is always with us. So, too, are the dangers of conflating one's own needs with others' needs. I have argued that the imperative tasks have not been voluntary for women; performing them has been a requirement for self-preservation. These duties may be voluntary in the sense that some individuals, men, women, or both, choose, with whatever degree of freedom, to perform them. But they are not voluntary for society as a whole. Whether or not I clean my house, somebody has to clean the school, the supermarket, and the hospital. The observable fact that some people can get away with being slobs does not mean that everybody can, everywhere. Whether or not I bear children, somebody must, somewhere. If I do not prepare my own meals or care for any children I do have, someone else has to do those specific jobs.

Imperative jurisprudence explodes the public-private distinction which has proved so dangerous to women, who have gotten stuck on the wrong side of the line. In Chapter 1, I drew an analogy between this dichotomy and a scheme for dividing a cake in which the same people do both the cutting and the choosing. But unless the "private" work is done, there can be no cake at all. The maintenance work is a necessary precondition for the activities theorists love to talk about: the life of the mind, the acquisition of power and property, democratic self-government, and so forth. Somebody has to do the necessary work in order for anyone to be able to do the interesting work. The destruction of the public-private dichotomy has nothing to do with the right of privacy; excellent reasons remain for limiting the power of the state over the individual by establishing "zones" where the state may not enter. But this decision itself is a tacit recognition that the traditionally private does belong in jurisprudence.

The most important contribution of imperative jurisprudence to a feminist postliberalism is to reconcile feminist theory with the aspect of liberalism which has provoked so much feminist criticism: the emphasis on rights. While no one effort to delineate liberal rights theory is accepted as authoritative by all liberal jurists, John Rawls's "principles of justice" probably come as close, and are certainly as well known, as any. First, "each person is to have an equal right to the most extensive total system of equal basic liberties compatible with a similar system of liberty for all"; second, "social and economic inequalities are to be arranged so that they are both: (a) to the greatest benefit of the least advantaged, consistent with the just savings principle" (of intergenerational fairness) and "(b) attached to offices and positions open to all under conditions of fair equality of opportunity."[48]

The generality of Rawls's formulation is one of the greatest difficulties students of political philosophy have had with it; his terms are so broad that they can be used to justify almost any social arrangement. These problems do not disappear in the context of sexual equality, an issue Rawls has been criticized, with justice, for stinting.[49] "Fair" and "benefit" are concepts with ample wiggle room, while "least advantaged" might refer to children as easily as to women. But the organizing questions of imperative jurisprudence do give Rawls's principles a concrete context which mitigates the dangers of abstraction. No rights or liberties can exist unless the essential maintenance work is performed. Liberal principles must, therefore, apply to the assignment of this work. Having to do it is a duty, and immunity from that duty is a privilege. The latter is a liberty, and the former is a denial of equal liberty. Both are "inequalities," in Rawls's sense of the word. Immunity from these responsibilities is a basic liberty, and assignment of responsibilities and immunities alike must conform to the principles of justice.[50]

What we have now—a situation in which men enjoy an immunity from being asked to do maintenance work while the best women can get is a right to say no to it—does not come close to this idea of justice. Rawls's first principle cannot be satisfied simply by extending men's immunity to women the way the Nineteenth Amendment extended the right to vote; no system of liberty could exist for anybody if everybody was immune from responsibility for doing necessary work. But justice requires that no one have a greater immunity or a greater responsibility than anyone else. A woman must have an equal right to say no *and* an equal immunity from being obliged to say yes. Feminist postliberal justice entails forcing responsibility uphill. How can we achieve this goal, which seems in those terms to contradict nature itself?

A rule of strict sexual equality in the division of essential functions would suffice, since everyone would have the same basic liberty and there would be no least advantaged. Such a rule is attractive, not least because it resists the qualifying, hedging, and just plain weaseling out that Rawls's generalities permit. The easiest criticism to make of such a result is that it is "unrealistic" and "unworkable"; but, as I shall argue, the feasibility of the goal depends on how one goes about achieving it. There is, of course, one imperative which cannot be assigned according to this principle. Reproduction requires more of women than of men. But we cannot use the *only* gendered essential function as the organizing principle of the assignment of rights and duties. Childbearing must be the exception, not the generalization. The reason a feminist postliberal justice does not *require* a strictly equal division of labor is not that such a division is impossible, but because the duty to do the work is not the same thing as the work itself. Inequalities can benefit the disadvantaged if those who are burdened with the necessary work can say no, and are rewarded rather than punished for doing the work. Since no man bears children, justice requires that no woman be forced to. Since only women bear children, only a woman can decide how important childbearing is to her; therefore, women must be allowed to bear children. Since some children must get born whether or not women want to bear them, childbearing must become a special contribution which requires compensation instead of what it has always been, the hook on which society retrospectively hangs asymmetrical responsibility.

The principles that apply to childbearing apply with equal strength to the components of that asymmetrical responsibility: the maintenance work of meeting basic human needs and the activities character theorists classify as "care." I argued in Chapter 3 that a feminist jurisprudence must liberate women from assigned roles at the same time that it rewards them for performing assigned activities. The second goal may be easier to achieve than the first. A woman may provide care because she wants to, because she has to, because she feels she must, or some combination of these. Whatever the situation, care is an essential social function. While women should not have exclusive or disproportionate responsibility for care, they deserve credit for providing it. The policy changes which would result from applying principles of justice to care include a rewriting of statutory and constitutional law to give the interests of the primary caregivers of children and the victims of domestic violence parity with those of biological fathers and harassed homeowners.

These changes are within the realm of foreseeable possibility. Other changes would be more subversive and (even) less popular. Suppose we proceed not from a grudging admission that women have a right to bear children but from the fact that birth mothers subject themselves to an arduous, painful, and risky process in order to perform the essential task of reproducing the species. The conclusion follows that motherhood is valuable and should be rewarded. Do we, as a society, believe this? Well, we find it easy to speak, as Justice Holmes did in *Buck v. Bell*, of mothers sapping the strength of the state.[51] But, somehow, to speak of mothers serving state and society carries undertones of "bearing children for the Fuehrer" or "*vous travaillez pour l'armee, madame?*"[52]

Discourse about motherhood as positive contribution would lose its strangeness and its disturbing connotations if we heard it more often. But think of what it would imply. The proposition that motherhood is valuable must hold across race, class, and age boundaries; otherwise, all we would have done is to use women's reproductive functions to oppress some rather than all women. So contemporary America's favorite villain—the young, poor, and unmarried pregnant teenager—is in fact serving society at some risk to herself and deserves help. As a matter of fact, yes. I see no escape from that conclusion. The obvious objection to it is that society doesn't need this service quite so early in these young women's lives. Won't helping them instead of punishing them encourage more teenagers to have babies? Fortunately, solutions to that problem are available. Several Western European countries have more generous mothers' benefits and lower rates of teenage births than the United States does.

What about the other essential goal of feminist jurisprudence: relieving women of their asymmetrical responsibilities? Redistributing responsibility from individual women to individual men looms as an all but impossible task. We already know that neither women nor the state can make men use condoms, change diapers, or cook meals. This social fact does not vitiate any and all efforts at redistributing responsibility. True, no one should recommend or excuse child neglect, or encourage women to refuse to make the coffee, take the minutes, or serve as faculty adviser to the student organization at the cost of her job. "Individual solution" is an oxymoron, but individual initiative is positive energy.

In 1963, Betty Friedan wrote that "every girl who manages to stick it out through law school or medical school, who finishes her M.A. or Ph.D. and goes on to use it, helps others move on."[53] Friedan was right. The women who rejected the feminine mystique made invaluable contributions to sexual equality. This is why every new woman legislator, judge, or cabinet member represents a feminist accomplishment, and why the entry of women into the professions in ever increasing numbers deserves at least one cheer. Today, every woman who refuses to do the traditional women's work, including childbearing, helps others move on. This statement does not contradict what I said earlier about societal imperatives. In fact, my argument puts women in the enviable position of making useful contributions whatever choice they make. If they do, they provide maintenance; if they forbear, they promote change. Men, by contrast, have a choice between contributing to the solution and contributing to the problem.

We know now that what the women professionals of the 1960s did wasn't enough to end male supremacy. One reason individual efforts did not suffice then, and will not now, is the phenomenon Bell Hooks forces us to confront: the likelihood that work abandoned by some women will be taken up not by men but by other, less fortunate women. But, while this downhill flow weakened the impact of individual contributions, it did not negate them. Does any feminist seriously believe that American women would be better off now if *The Feminine Mystique* had never been written? Friedan did not turn her critical scrutiny on herself, the way women and liberals are supposed to do. She looked outward, the way activists and reformers do. She replaced liberal guilt with radical anger. She downplayed the inequalities *among women* in order to emphasize the inequalities *between women and men*. In so doing, she helped create a social movement which did not long remain confined to women like her. The anger Friedan provoked in many minority, lesbian, radical, and working-class readers of her book helped bring about the correction of her errors. Contemporary middle-class professional women who win similar gains should provoke similar healthy, energizing anger.

There remains, however, an additional, compelling reason why individuals' rejection of sex roles is not enough to establish sexual equality even in the remote future. Such a solution only reinforces the inequality against which this book has protested. It assigns the most responsibility to the least powerful and most vulnerable people. Women, individually and collectively, lack the power to distribute tasks equally in every household and every family. But women are members of a self-governing polity. Women can work to redistribute responsibility from individuals to institutions. Women can use law to make themselves less vulnerable to male power and irresponsibility through (to name only a few possibilities) rigorous support enforcement, mothers' subsidies, enhanced employment and educational opportunities, comparable worth, and legal recognition of lesbian relationships. As women gain autonomy outside the home, they will be more nearly equal within it. If men refuse to share the work, they can at least help pay for it through taxes. Women can resist efforts to pass responsibility for product safety from producers to consumers. Women can raise hell when hospitals "outsource" nursing care to patients' families which may or may not exist. (After all, political protest worked with HMOs and postpartum hospital stays.) Women can devote their critical intelligence and analytical skills to deciphering the core domestic political and economic phenomenon of our time: the concentration of more and more resources in fewer and fewer hands, the divorce between power and responsibility, and the subsequent, if not consequent, increase in the vulnerability and responsibility of individuals. By unraveling what has happened since the 1980s, women may begin to understand how to redistribute responsibility.

To work toward such a goal is to buck every viable trend of the late 1990s. The extreme right threatens to become the political center as the center moves to the right. The left, which since the fall of the Soviet Union has no extreme to distinguish itself from, moves to the center or lapses into silence. The Personal Responsibility and Work Reconciliation Act of 1996 is the most comprehensive, but unlikely to be the last, policy change which pushes responsibility downward rather than upward. The policy changes I propose are less popular now than changes like limits on welfare eligibility, which make individuals responsible for finding jobs that do not exist, or restrictions on divorce, which presume gender-neutral irresponsibility in violation of the facts, and would increase rather than reduce men's power over women. My analysis calls for more big government, not less. It calls for government which uses its power on institutions more readily than individuals and on men more readily than women. It commits feminists to perpetual struggle against the dominant political and corporate forces of the day. This is no small thing to ask of a group disproportionately composed of women and liberals, people prone to guilt and timidity, committed more to respecting other people's opinions than to demanding respect for their own, and vulnerable to confusion between change and progress. Feminist postliberalism must remember that majority rule applies to votes, not ideas. If we cannot, yet, change the world, we must keep the world from changing us.

The Future of Imperative Jurisprudence

Character jurisprudence begins by asking, "What are people like?" Situation jurisprudence asks, "What does the world look like to people?" Imperative jurisprudence asks, "What can people and society not do without?" All three questions lead to the conclusion that duty and danger, need and struggle, have been constants in modern Western society. Thomas Hobbes's idea of "man" in the "state of nature" may have been wrong. He may have confused nature with culture; he surely conflated allegory with history. But he understood conditions in his own society. Another famous phrase of his well describes what life in his time and place would have been like without civil government: "solitary, poor, nasty, brutish, and short." Whether because of human nature, capitalist greed, or insufficiently fertile land, Hobbes's England did not promise a safe, secure life to all who sought it. People simply could not protect themselves from violence by their own efforts: not, at least, without creating a state of war. Bruce Ackerman, for his part, may exaggerate the power struggles of modern life. I rather think he does—though my wish may be parent to my thought. But his premise that human beings must strive to meet their needs is unassailable: at least in our own time and place; for that matter, in Hobbes's England and in Madison's and Jefferson's America.

What has changed? The organizing questions of imperative jurisprudence may produce surprising insights. Thinking about what is needed leads to questions about what is not needed. Consider, for example, John Smith's dictum at Jamestown colony in 1607: "He who will not work shall not eat." This maxim, which children learn in school, is not far below the surface of much current debate on welfare policy. It has animated the dismantling of the federal safety net. It is a stern rule, but, like Cinderella's curfew and John Stuart Mill's only purpose for which power can be rightfully exercised, it is two-sided. It implies that he who will work, may eat.[54] As long as the rule excuses those who cannot work, it is fair and sensible in a society which has plenty of work to do and in which the food supply depends on this work. But our society has more than enough food to go around, and not enough work even for everyone able and willing to work. We no longer need everyone's labor. The problem we face is distributing basic resources, not creating them. Can the old rule still work?

The recognition that people cannot protect themselves from violent aggression is an organizing premise of Western political theory. It is time for us to recognize and to name the stark reality of our own society. Not only can we not protect ourselves from violence, we cannot ensure our ability to meet our basic human and societal needs. Throughout history, most women have been unable to earn a living wage. Increasingly, this is true for men as well as women, couples as well as individuals, families as well as couples. In the 1980s, mothers and children became the "new poor." In the 1990s, middle-class couples are becoming the "working poor." A feminist slogan of the 1970s declared, "Most women are a man away from welfare." A similar slogan for the 1990s would have to be "Most people are a pink slip, or an illness, or an accident away from welfare." By the end of the twentieth century, welfare may no longer exist. Even now, industrious, honest, sober, well-disciplined people no longer can be sure if they can support themselves. Women never could be sure.

Feminist postliberal jurisprudence must incorporate as an organizing principle the idea that rights arise from needs as well as from autonomy and desert. Rights and needs can no longer be presumed incompatible.[55] The right to a means of meeting human needs, at the very least, must join the traditional rights of liberal theory. Positive and negative rights must be envisioned as interdependent, not mutually exclusive. Protecting women's negative rights in fact as well as on paper entails recognizing positive rights.

This book has located women's subjection within a system of powers and duties, rights and responsibilities, which makes women responsible for what they do, what other people do, what happens to them, and what happens to others. Women cannot attain equality unless this distribution of responsibilities is equalized. The unfair burdens women bear cannot be eased unless responsibility can be put somewhere else: on men, on institutions, on government, on society. Responsibility must be human as well as female. It must be collective as well as individual.

Conclusion

I began this book in anger and hope. Several years of research, thinking, and writing have strengthened the hope and disciplined the anger. A version of the question Christina Hoff Sommers asks—though not of the answers she provides—has come again and again to my mind.[56] Who *robbed* feminism? Who robbed it of its rightful place in today's crucial controversies? Who robbed it of its aspiration to question everything, and gave it to the glorifiers of gender difference and traditional roles? Who stole away feminism's outward focus and turned its critical scrutiny inward?

Writing this book steered me away from false hopes, as I learned there are some things feminist scholars cannot do. We cannot free the notion of difference from its association with inferiority; we cannot elevate the status of care, nurturance, and domestic work by claiming it as female; we cannot force people to stop confusing male aggression with female passivity. But we can challenge and undermine the distinctions with which male-centered jurisprudence has dismissed our lives: between public and private, between doctrine and result, between rational and emotional, between individual and social. We can just as fairly question the distinctions conventional theory has refused to make: between invidious and ameliorative "discrimination," for instance, or between male and female experiences of the need for "self-defense." We can inquire not how women fit theories but how theories fit women.

It is in hope rather than in anger that I imagine the following scene. A group of men and women gathers in the kitchen to make a pie. There is much conversation and laughter as the fruit is cut, the dough rolled, the ingredients measured. When the pie is in the oven, another group cleans up and puts things away. When the pie is ready, it is placed in the center of a long table. A knife and a serving fork lie beside it, for all those present to serve themselves. As the platter is passed, each person cuts a piece. The portions, while not perfectly equal, are fair. But the first woman to get the pie is besieged by pointing fingers and hectoring voices.

"No, no!" says one group. "You don't need that much," a voice says. Others say, "Shouldn't you stick to fruit, or yogurt?" or "It wouldn't hurt you to go without!" or "You didn't help make the pie. You shouldn't have any." A second group is composed mostly of women. "No, no! We don't want a piece of this pie! We must bake a whole new pie." The hectoring voices drown one another out. With her fair portion, the woman takes her place at the table and speaks in her authentic voice.

NOTES

CHAPTER ONE
INTRODUCTION

1. Bruce A. Ackerman, *Social Justice and the Liberal State* (New Haven, Conn.: Yale University Press, 1980), 1.

2. The sources of the quoted phrases are, respectively, James Russell Lowell and Adam Smith. See Michael Kammen, *A Machine That Would Go of Itself: The Constitution in American Culture* (New York: St. Martin's Press, 1994); Smith, *Wealth of Nations* (1776).

3. Statistics indicate that the incidence of violent crimes against women decreased between 1991 and 1995, but the numbers are still high. The approximately 97,000 rapes reported in 1995 represented the lowest total since 1989; but it was 7 percent higher than in 1985. U.S. Department of Justice, Federal Bureau of Investigation, *1995 Uniform Crime Reports: Crime in the United States*, 13 October 1996, 24. See Fox Butterfield, " '95 Data Show Sharp Drop in Reported Rapes," *New York Times*, 3 February 1997. Because victims do not always report sexual assaults, these figures probably understate the incidence of rape; but there is no reason why underreporting would increase or decrease from 1985 to 1995. Most homicides, by contrast, are reported. FBI data showed that 26 percent of all female murder victims were murdered by husbands or boyfriends; this represents a decrease over the last several years (in the 1980s the figure was around 40 percent). The comparable figure for male victims in 1995 was 3 percent. *Uniform Crime Reports*, 17. See Ann Jones, *Next Time She'll Be Dead: Battering and How to Stop It* (Boston: Beacon Press, 1994), 6–7. The FBI statistics come from data reported by local police departments. The other reliable source is the crime surveys conducted every year by the Bureau of Criminal Justice Statistics. See Kathleen Maguire and Ann L. Pastore, eds., *Sourcebook of Criminal Statistics, 1994* (Washington, D.C.: U.S. Department of Justice, Bureau of Justice Statistics, 1995).

4. See Arlie Hochschild with Anne Machung, *The Second Shift: Working Parents and the Revolution at Home* (New York: Viking, 1989); Alva Myrdal and Viola Klein, *Women's Two Roles*, 2d ed. (London: Routledge and Kegan Paul, 1968).

5. Betty Friedan, *The Feminine Mystique* (New York: W. W. Norton, 1963), chap. 1. This discussion is based on my *Women in American Law: The Struggle Toward Equality from the New Deal to the Present*, 2d ed. (New York: Holmes and Meier, 1996).

6. (New York: E. P. Dutton, 1978), 134–37, 364–421.

7. See Karen Orren, "Metaphysics and Reality in Labor Adjudication," in *Labor Law in America*, ed. Christopher L. Tomlins and Andrew J. King (Baltimore: Johns Hopkins University Press, 1992); Forrest W. Lacey, "Vagrancy and Other Crimes of Personal Condition," *Harvard Law Review* 66 (May 1953): 1203–26.

8. "Compulsory Heterosexuality and Lesbian Existence," in *Blood, Bread, and Poetry: Selected Prose 1979–1985* (New York: W. W. Norton, 1986), 59. See, for

example, Marlene Stein Wortman, ed., *Women in American Law*, vol. 1 (New York: Holmes and Meier, 1985), 22–24.

9. Carol Glassman, "Women and the Welfare System," in *Sisterhood Is Powerful*, ed. Robin Morgan (New York: Random House, 1970), 102.

10. See, for example, Celia W. Dugger, "African Ritual Pain: Genital Cutting," *New York Times* (national edition), 5 October 1996.

11. There are exceptions, like combat, slavery, and membership in certain religious orders. But in general there are limits to the demands employers and supervisors can make on workers.

12. Catharine A. MacKinnon, *Toward a Feminist Theory of the State* (Cambridge, Mass.: Harvard University Press, 1989), 190–91.

13. See Dorothy E. Smith, *The Everyday World as Problematic: A Feminist Sociology* (Boston: Northeastern University Press, 1987), and *The Conceptual Practices of Power: A Feminist Sociology of Knowledge* (Boston: Northeastern University Press, 1990).

14. "Always Well Done," ABC-TV, September 22, 1995.

15. *Blaming the Victim*, revised, updated edition (New York: Vintage Books, 1976).

16. Egon Bittner, "Policing Juveniles: The Social Context of Common Practice," in *Pursuing Justice for the Child*, ed. Margaret K. Rosenheim (Chicago: University of Chicago Press, 1976), 74 (emphasis in original).

17. Heather Ruth Wishik, "To Question Everything: The Inquiries of Feminist Jurisprudence," *Berkeley Women's Law Journal* 1 (Fall 1986): 64–77.

18. See, for example, Susan Bordo, *Unbearable Weight: Feminism, Western Culture, and the Body* (Berkeley: University of California Press, 1993); Susie Orbach, *Fat Is a Feminist Issue* (New York: Berkeley Books, 1988); Naomi Wolf, *The Beauty Myth* (New York: William Morrow, 1991).

19. The respective citations are Carol Gilligan, *In a Different Voice* (Cambridge, Mass.: Harvard University Press, 1982); Nel Noddings, *Caring: A Feminine Approach to Ethics and Moral Education* (Berkeley: University of California Press, 1984); Mary Field Belenky et al., *Women's Ways of Knowing: The Development of Self, Voice, and Mind* (New York: Basic Books, 1986).

20. Drucilla Cornell, *Beyond Accommodation: Ethical Feminism, Deconstruction, and the Law* (New York: Routledge, Chapman and Hall, 1991), 135.

21. MacKinnon, *Feminist Theory*, note 12 above, 52.

22. See MacKinnon, *Feminist Theory*, note 12 above, and *Feminism Unmodified* (Cambridge, Mass.: Harvard University Press, 1987); Nancy Hartsock, *Money, Sex, and Power: Toward a Feminist Historical Materialism* (New York: Longman, 1983).

23. See Chapter 3, "Getting the Reader Right: Situation Theory and Its Critics."

24. See, for example, Christina Hoff Sommers, *Who Stole Feminism? How Women Have Betrayed Women* (New York: Simon and Schuster, 1994); Katie Roiphe, *The Morning After: Sex, Fear, and Feminism on Campus* (Boston: Little, Brown, 1993).

25. See, for example, Stephen L. Carter, *The Culture of Disbelief: How American Law and Politics Trivialize Religious Devotion* (New York: Anchor Books, 1994).

26. Jane J. Mansbridge, *Why We Lost the ERA* (Chicago: University of Chicago Press, 1986), 197.

27. Respectively, *In a Different Voice*, note 19 above; *Feminism Unmodified*, note 22 above, 100.

28. The phrase is Betty Friedan's. See *The Second Stage* (New York: Summit Books, 1981).

29. Respectively, *Rights Talk: The Impoverishment of Political Discourse* (New York: Free Press, 1991); *The Spirit of Community: Rights, Responsibilities, and the Communitarian Agenda* (New York: Crown, 1993), especially 5.

30. James Traub, "The Hearts and Minds of City College," *New Yorker*, 7 June 1993, 43, 48, 42, 46, 53. See also his *City on a Hill: Testing the American Dream at City College* (Reading, Mass.: Addison-Wesley, 1994).

31. "The Other Body," *Ms.*, March/April 1993, 72.

32. Cheryl Marie Wade, letter to the editor, *Ms.*, July/August 1993, 8.

33. Erving Goffman, *Stigma: Notes on the Management of Spoiled Identity* (Englewood Cliffs, N.J.: Prentice-Hall, 1963), 33.

CHAPTER TWO
IS LAW MALE?

1. Catharine A. MacKinnon, *Feminism Unmodified* (Cambridge, Mass.: Harvard University Press, 1987), 37. See Susan Moller Okin, *Women in Western Political Thought* (Princeton, N.J.: Princeton University Press, 1979) and *Justice, Gender, and the Family* (New York: Basic Books, 1989); Carole Pateman, *The Sexual Contract* (Stanford, Calif: Stanford University Press, 1988).

2. See Sandra Harding, *Whose Science? Whose Knowledge? Thinking from Women's Lives* (Ithaca, N.Y.: Cornell University Press, 1991); and Jane Gallop, *Thinking Through the Body* (New York: Columbia University Press, 1988). Other important works are Jean Bethke Elshtain, *Public Man, Private Woman: Women in Social and Political Thought* (Princeton, N.J.: Princeton University Press, 1981); Carol Gilligan, *In a Different Voice* (Cambridge, Mass.: Harvard University Press, 1982); Harding, *The Science Question in Feminism* (Ithaca, N.Y.: Cornell University Press, 1986); and Adrienne Rich, *Of Woman Born: Motherhood as Experience and Institution* (New York: W. W. Norton, 1976), and *On Lies, Secrets, and Silence: Selected Prose 1966–1978* (New York: W. W. Norton, 1979).

3. Deborah L. Rhode, "Feminist Critical Theories," *Stanford Law Review* 42 (February 1990): 617–38, 633.

4. The citations are, respectively, Katharine T. Bartlett, "Feminist Legal Methods," *Harvard Law Review* 103 (February 1990): 832; Catharine MacKinnon, *Toward a Feminist Theory of the State* (Cambridge, Mass.: Harvard University Press, 1989), 84. See also Kimberle Crenshaw, "Demarginalizing the Intersection of Race and Sex," in *Feminist Legal Theory: Readings in Law and Gender*, ed. Katharine T. Bartlett and Rosanne Kennedy (Boulder, Colo.: Westview Press, 1991), 57–80; Elizabeth M. Schneider, "The Dialectic of Rights and Politics: Perspectives from the Women's Movement," *New York University Law Review* 61 (October 1986): 589–652; MacKinnon, *Feminism Unmodified*, note 1 above; Patricia J. Williams, *The Alchemy of Race and Rights* (Cambridge, Mass.: Harvard University Press, 1991).

5. Representative "Crit" scholarship includes Andrew Altman, "Legal Realism, Critical Legal Studies, and Dworkin," *Philosophy and Public Affairs* 15 (Summer

1986): 205–235; Duncan Kennedy, "Form and Substance in Private Law Adjudication," *Harvard Law Review* 89 (June 1976): 1685–1778; Roberto Mangabeira Unger, "The Critical Legal Studies Movement," *Harvard Law Review* 96 (January 1983): 563–675.

6. See, for example, Linda J. Nicholson, ed., *Feminism/Postmodernism* (New York: Routledge, Chapman and Hall, 1990); Jane Flax, *Thinking Fragments* (Berkeley: University of California Press, 1990); and the references cited in these books.

7. Jeffrie G. Murphy, "Marxism and Retribution," in *Philosophy of Law*, ed. Joel Feinberg and Hyman Gross, 3d ed. (Belmont, Calif.: Wadsworth, 1986), 636.

8. *Feminist Theory*, note 4 above, 47–48.

9. *Politics*, I 5 1254b1–32.

10. "Femininity," in *New Introductory Lectures in Psychoanalysis*, trans. James Strachey (New York: W. W. Norton, 1964), 112–35; "Some Psychological Consequences of the Anatomical Distinction Between the Sexes," *International Journal of Psychoanalysis* 7 (January 1927): 133–42; *Three Essays on the Theory of Sexuality* (1905), trans. and ed. James Strachey (New York: Basic Books, 1962).

11. 83 U.S. 130, 140–42 (1872).

12. 208 U.S. 412, 421–23.

13. Ron Beal, " 'Can I Sue Mommy?' An Analysis of Women's Tort Liability for Prenatal Injuries to Her Child Born Alive," *San Diego Law Review* 21 (March 1984): 370.

14. See *Weeks v. Southern Bell*, 408 F. 2d 228 (5th Circ. 1969).

15. For critiques of theories that have this defect, see, for example, Zillah Eisenstein, *The Radical Future of Liberal Feminism* (New York: Longman, 1981); Pateman, *Sexual Contract*, note 1 above.

16. See, for example, Plato, *The Republic*, especially Books V and VI; Locke, *Two Treatises on Government* (1690); Arendt, *The Human Condition* (Chicago: University of Chicago Press, 1958).

17. *The Feminine Mystique* (New York: W. W. Norton, 1963), chap. 5.

18. Gilligan, *In a Different Voice*, note 2 above, 7. Prominent dissenters from Freudian psychoanalytic theory included Karen Horney, "The Flight from Womanhood," *International Journal of Psychoanalysis* 6 (July 1926): 324–39; Clara Thompson, "Cultural Pressures in the Psychology of Women," *Psychiatry* 5 (August 1942): 331–39. For feminist critiques of Freud, see, for example, Nancy Chodorow, *The Reproduction of Mothering* (Berkeley: University of California Press, 1978), chap. 9; Simone de Beauvoir, *The Second Sex*, ed. and trans. H. M. Parshley (New York: Alfred A. Knopf, 1952), chaps. 2, 12; Naomi Weisstein, " 'Kinder, Kuche, Kirche' as Scientific Law: Psychology Constructs the Female," in *Sisterhood Is Powerful*, ed. Robin Morgan (New York: Random House, 1970), 205–20.

19. *Craig v. Boren*, 429 U.S. 190, 199 (1976).

20. See, for example, George P. Fletcher, *A Crime of Self-Defense: Bernhard Goetz and the Law on Trial* (Chicago: University of Chicago Press, 1988), chap. 2.

21. See, for example, Mary Ann Mason, *From Fathers' Property to Children's Rights: The History of Child Custody in the United States* (New York: Columbia University Press, 1995).

22. In a famous 1984 incident, Bernhard Goetz shot and wounded four men who asked him for money on a subway. Charged with attempted murder, he was

convicted of the lesser charge of carrying a concealed weapon. See Fletcher, *Crime of Self-Defense*, note 20 above. In 1993, a jury in Baton Rouge, Louisiana, acquitted Rodney Peairs in the shooting death of Yoshihiro Hattori on October 31, 1992. The Japanese exchange student had been invited to a Halloween party, got the address wrong, and rang Peairs's doorbell. *New York Times*, 25 May 1993. In 1994, Robert Lorenz shot and killed a neighbor who swore at him during an altercation; he was acquitted. Rajiv Chandrasekaran, "Jury Acquits Virginia Man Who Killed Neighbor," *Washington Post*, 9 February 1996.

23. In 1993, two-year-old Jessica De Boer, who is now Anna Schmidt, was removed from the home of her adoptive parents, Roberta and Jan De Boer, and returned to her birth parents, Cara and Dan Schmidt of Cedar Rapids, Iowa. In April 1995, four-year-old Daniel Warburton, who is now Richard Kirchner, was transferred from Kimberly and Robert Warburton to his natural father, Otakar Kirchner. In both cases, the birth mothers had given the children up for adoption and had reconciled with the fathers shortly after the birth. Both men reopened the cases; both adoptions were declared invalid by the respective state courts (Iowa and Illinois). See Lucinda Franks, "The War over Baby Clausen," *New Yorker*, 22 March 1993, 56–73; *New York Times*, 1 May 1995, 20 June 1995; *in re Doe*, 638 N.E. 2d 181 (Ill. 1994).

24. *Leviathan*, ed. Michael Oakeshott (New York: Collier Books, 1962), chap. 11.

25. *On Liberty* (1859), especially chap. 1.

26. Robert H. Mnookin and Lewis Kornhauser, "Bargaining in the Shadow of the Law: The Case of Divorce," *Yale Law Journal* 88 (April 1979): 950–97, 964.

27. "The Emergence of Feminist Jurisprudence: An Essay," *Yale Law Journal* 95 (June 1986): 1375.

28. Harding, *Whose Science?*, note 2 above, 25.

29. Drucilla Cornell, *Beyond Accommodation: Ethical Feminism, Deconstruction, and the Law* (New York: Routledge, Chapman and Hall, 1991), 135.

30. See James Traub, "The Hearts and Minds of City College," *New Yorker*, 7 June 1993, 42–53.

31. *This Sex Which Is Not One*, trans. Catherine Porter with Carolyn Burke (Ithaca, N.Y.: Cornell University Press, 1985), 23–24. See also *Speculum of the Other Woman*, trans. Gillian C. Gill (Ithaca, N.Y.: Cornell University Press, 1985).

32. Elaine Marks and Isabelle de Courtivron, eds. *New French Feminisms* (Amherst: University of Massachusetts Press, 1980), xii.

33. Christine Pierce, "Postmodernism and Other Skepticisms," in *Feminist Ethics*, ed. Claudia Card (Lawrence: University Press of Kansas, 1991), 67.

34. For more Psych-et-Po/*ecriture feminine*, see Hélène Cixous and Catherine Clement, *The Newly Born Woman*, trans. Betsy Wing (Minneapolis: University of Minnesota Press, 1986).

35. Horney, "Flight from Womanhood," and Thompson, "Cultural Pressures," note 18 above. Jacques Lacan's works include *The Four Fundamental Concepts of Psychoanalysis*, trans. Alan Sheridan (New York: W. W. Norton, 1978), and *The Language of the Self: The Function of Language in Psychoanalysis*, trans. Anthony Wilden (Baltimore: Johns Hopkins University Press, 1968). See also Jane Gallop, *Reading Lacan* (Ithaca, N.Y.: Cornell University Press, 1985).

36. For a similar criticism, see Kathy E. Ferguson, *The Man Question: Visions of Subjectivity in Feminist Theory* (Berkeley: University of California Press, 1993), 134. The question I pose may answer itself: "genitallogocentric" theory may appeal precisely because it builds in gender difference.

37. "Jurisprudence and Gender," *University of Chicago Law Review* 55 (Winter 1988): 1–3.

38. *Close to Home: A Materialist Analysis of Women's Oppression*, trans. and ed. Diana Leonard (Amherst: University of Massachusetts Press, 1984), 195.

39. With West, as with Irigaray, I think it is necessary to point out that their work goes far beyond their theories of difference and is nearly always worth reading. See, in particular, West, "The Difference in Women's Hedonic Lives: A Phenomenological Critique of Feminist Legal Theory," in *Women and the Law*, ed. Mary Joe Frug (Westbury, N.Y.: Foundations Press, 1992), 807–25.

40. Chodorow, *The Reproduction of Mothering* (Berkeley: University of California Press, 1978), 1; West, "Jurisprudence," note 37 above, 14–18.

41. *Reproduction of Mothering*, part II. For a thesis similar to Chodorow's which emphasizes social rather than psychoanalytic theory, see Dorothy Dinnerstein, *The Mermaid and the Minotaur* (New York: Harper Colophon, 1976).

42. Ironically, Freudian theory did recognize the importance of age differences in psychosexual development, at least for males. In the Oedipal stage, the boy is doomed to defeat in the struggle for possession of the mother because of the father's superior size and strength. Since father's penis is bigger and stronger, he has the advantage as lover and possessor; since father's entire body is bigger and stronger, he can castrate the son who is his rival. Fearing this punishment, the boy gives up his Oedipus complex, separates from mother, and develops a superego. In abandoning Freud's psychology, object-relations theory also discounted some anatomical facts which he did consider. See Sigmund Freud, "Some Psychological Consequences of the Anatomical Distinction Between the Sexes," note 10 above, and *New Introductory Lectures on Psychoanalysis*, trans. James Strachey (New York: W. W. Norton, 1964); Isaac D. Balbus, *Marxism and Domination* (Princeton, N.J.: Princeton University Press, 1982), chap. 5; Chodorow, *Mothering*, note 40 above, chap. 6.

43. *Feminist Theory*, note 4 above, xi; *Feminism Unmodified*, note 1 above, chap. 2.

44. *Money, Sex, and Power: Toward a Feminist Historical Materialism* (New York: Longman, 1983), 234. For a discussion of MacKinnon's thesis, see Chapter 3, "Situation Theory and Jurisprudence." See also Rhonda Copelon, "Beyond the Liberal Idea of Privacy: Toward a Positive Right of Autonomy," in *Judging the Constitution*, ed. Michael W. McCann and Gerald L. Houseman (Glenview, Ill.: Little, Brown, 1989), 287–314; Elizabeth Schneider, "Dialectic of Rights," note 4 above; Nadine Taub and Elizabeth M. Schneider, "Perspectives on Women's Subordination and the Role of the Law," in *The Politics of Law: A Progressive Critique*, ed. David Kairys (New York: Pantheon Books, 1982), 117–39.

45. See Carol Smart, *Feminism and the Power of Law* (New York: Routledge, 1989), 76–82.

46. See Chapter 1 at note 25.

47. For a critique of this choice of emphasis, see Joan Wallach Scott, *Gender and the Politics of History* (New York: Columbia University Press, 1988), 37–38.

48. See, for example, MacKinnon, *Feminist Theory*, note 4 above, part I.

49. For compatible arguments, see Sally J. Kenney, *For Whose Protection? Reproductive Hazards and Exclusionary Policies in the United States and Britain* (Ann Arbor: University of Michigan Press, 1992), chap. 2; and Judith Butler, *Gender Trouble: Feminism and the Subversion of Identity* (New York: Routledge, 1990).

50. See, for example, the references cited in note 6 above.

51. See, for example, Bartlett, "Feminist Legal Methods," note 4 above; Sandra Harding, "Feminism, Science, and the Anti-Enlightenment Critiques," in *Feminism/Postmodernism*, ed. Nicholson, note 6 above, 83–106, *Science Question*, and *Whose Science?* note 2 above; MacKinnon, *Feminist Theory*, note 4 above, Part II.

52. On race, see, for example, Williams, *Alchemy of Race and Rights*; note 4 above; Mari J. Matsuda, "When the First Quail Calls: Multiple Consciousness as Jurisprudential Method," *Women's Rights Law Reporter* 11 (Spring 1989): 7–10. The literature on sexual preference includes Sarah Hoagland, *Lesbian Ethics: Toward a New Value* (Palo Alto, Calif.: Institute of Lesbian Studies, 1988); Claudia Card, "Intimacy and Responsibility: What Lesbians Do," in *At the Boundaries of Law: Feminism and Legal Theory*, ed. Martha Albertson Fineman and Nancy Sweet Thomadsen (New York: Routledge, Chapman and Hall, 1991), 77–94; and Richard Mohr, *Gays/Justice* (New York: Columbia University Press, 1990). On disability, see, for example, Ynestra King, "The Other Body," *Ms.*, March/April 1993, 72; Anne Finger, "Claiming All of Our Bodies: Reproductive Rights and Disability," in *With the Power of Each Breath: A Disabled Women's Anthology*, ed. Susan E. Browne, Debra Connors, and Nanci Stern (San Francisco: Cleis Press, 1985), 292–309; Sucheng Chan, "You're Short, Besides!" in *Race, Class, and Gender: An Anthology*, ed. Margaret L. Andersen and Patricia Hill Collins (Belmont, Calif.: Wadsworth, 1992), 296–303; Susan Wendell, "Toward a Feminist Theory of Disability," in *Gender Basics: Feminist Perspectives on Women and Men*, ed. Anne Minas (Belmont, Calif.: Wadsworth, 1993), 58–63.

53. *Beyond Accommodation*, note 29 above, 2–3.

54. *When and Where I Enter: The Impact of Black Women on Race and Sex in America* (New York: William Morrow, 1984), 299. See also Bell Hooks, *Feminist Theory: From Margin to Center* (Boston: South End Press, 1984), chap. 1.

55. Friedan, *Feminine Mystique*, note 17 above; Harris, "Race and Essentialism in Feminist Legal Theory," *Stanford Law Review* 42 (February 1990): 585.

56. "Compulsory Heterosexuality and Lesbian Existence," in *Blood, Bread, and Poetry: Selected Prose 1979–1985* (New York: W. W. Norton, 1986), 22. For similar arguments by women of color, see Harris, "Race and Essentialism," note 55 above; Crenshaw, "Demarginalizing," note 4 above; Alice Walker, *In Search of Our Mothers' Gardens* (New York: Harcourt, Brace, Jovanovich, 1983), 371–74. For lesbian perspectives, see, for example, Patricia A. Cain, "Feminist Jurisprudence: Grounding the Theories," in *Feminist Legal Theory*, ed. Bartlett and Kennedy, note 4 above, 263–80.

57. *Beyond Accommodation*, note 29 above, 19. This generalization applies to the racial and class identity of theorists, but it must be qualified with respect to their sexual preference. The reader does not always know that a given writer is heterosexual or that he or she is presuming a heterosexual identity. Unless the theorist makes this presumption obvious (as Robin West does, for example), the reader cannot

justifiably presume that the "Woman" being written about is heterosexual. To do so would be to display the very bias that Cornell criticizes.

58. Matsuda, "First Quail," note 52 above, 9. See also Harding, *Whose Science?* note 2 above.

59. *Feminist Theory*, note 4 above, 121.

60. On class issues, see, for example, Andersen and Collins, *Race, Class, and Gender*, note 52 above.

61. See Elizabeth Fox-Genovese, *"Feminism Is Not the Story of My Life": How Today's Feminist Elite Has Lost Touch with the Real Concerns of Women* (New York: Doubleday, 1996).

62. EEOC, *Guidelines on Discrimination Because of Sex*, 29 C.F.R. Sec. 1604.11 (a) (1985); *Meritor Savings Bank v. Vinson*, 91 L. Ed. 2d 49 (1986).

63. Respectively, *Rabidue v. Osceola Refining Company*, 805 F. 2d 611, 624 (6th Cir. 1986), and *Steiner v. Steamboat Operating Company*, 25 F. 3d 1459, 1461 (9th Cir. 1994); *Ellison v. Brady*, 924 F. 2d 872, 874 (9th Cir. 1991); *Harris v. Forklift Systems*, 114 S. Ct. 367, 369 (1993).

64. *Harris v. Forklift Systems, Inc.*, note 63 above, 370–71.

65. 924 F. 2d 872, 880, 879 (emphasis added).

66. For a different conclusion, see Drucilla Cornell, *The Imaginary Domain: Abortion, Pornography and Sexual Harassment* (New York: Routledge, 1995), chap. 4.

67. Christine Di Stefano, "Dilemmas of Difference: Feminism, Modernity, and Postmodernism," in *Feminism/Postmodernism*, ed. Nicholson, note 6 above, 75. See also Nancy Hartsock, "Rethinking Modernism: Minority vs. Majority Theories," *Cultural Critique* 7 (1987): 187–206.

68. "Race and Essentialism," note 55 above, 604.

69. "White Privilege and Male Privilege: A Personal Account of Coming to See Correspondences Through Work in Women's Studies," in *Race, Class, and Gender*, ed. Andersen and Collins, note 52 above, 70–81.

70. For a similar race- and gender-specific effort to develop theory from the experience of black women, see Patricia Hill Collins, *Black Feminist Thought: Knowledge, Consciousness, and the Politics of Empowerment* (New York: Routledge, Chapman and Hall, 1991).

71. I owe this formulation to a reader for Princeton University Press.

72. Assemblyman William Knight (R-Calif.), quoted in Nina Perales, "A 'Tangle of Pathology': Racial Myth and the New Jersey Family Development Act," in *Mothers in Law: Feminist Theory and the Legal Regulation of Motherhood*, ed. Martha Albertson Fineman and Isabel Karpin (New York: Columbia University Press, 1995), 250–69, 259.

73. See Barbara Dafoe Whitehead, "Dan Quayle Was Right," *The Atlantic*, April 1993, 47–50.

74. See Chapter 7 at notes 13–22.

75. "The Other Body," note 52 above, 72.

76. For confirmation of this point, see the works cited in Chapter 1, note 18.

77. (Berkeley: University of California Press, 1993), 31.

78. See, for example, the references cited in Wendell, "Toward a Feminist Theory," note 52 above.

79. Christopher Lasch, *Haven in a Heartless World: The Family Besieged* (New York: Basic Books, 1977).

80. Critical works on the family include R. D. Laing, *The Politics of the Family and Other Essays* (New York: Pantheon Books, 1971); Alice Miller, *For Your Own Good: Hidden Cruelty in Child-Rearing and the Roots of Violence* (New York: Farrar, Straus and Giroux, 1983), and *Prisoners of Childhood* (New York: Basic Books, 1981). The arguments that Wendy Brown and Catharine MacKinnon make about the way rights doctrine strengthens the power of the stronger partner in marriage apply as well to parent-child relations. See Chapter 3 at notes 50 and 51.

81. The comments of an anonymous reviewer were helpful to me in clarifying this discussion.

CHAPTER THREE
WHAT MAKES LAW MALE?

1. "Difference and Dominance: On Sex Discrimination," in *Feminism Unmodified* (Cambridge, Mass.: Harvard University Press, 1987), 32–45.

2. For example, feminist theorists are critical of liberalism's emphasis on negative rights; but liberalism has known about positive rights for a long time. See Isaiah Berlin, "Two Concepts of Liberty," in *Liberalism and Its Critics*, ed. Michael J. Sandel (New York: New York University Press, 1984), 16–36; T. H. Green, *Lectures on the Principles of Political Obligation, and Other Essays*, ed. Paul Harris and John Morrow (Cambridge: Cambridge University Press, 1986); L. T. Hobhouse, *Liberalism* (1911; New York: Oxford University Press, 1964); John Dewey, *The Public and Its Problems* (Chicago: Swallow Press, 1927), and *Liberalism and Social Action* (1935; New York: Capricorn Books, 1963); John Rawls, *A Theory of Justice* (Cambridge, Mass.: Belknap Press of Harvard University Press, 1971), and *Political Liberalism* (New York: Columbia University Press, 1993); Ronald Dworkin, *Taking Rights Seriously* (Cambridge, Mass.: Harvard University Press, 1977). For a feminist critique of feminist critiques of liberalism, see Linda C. McClain, " 'Atomistic Man' Revisited: Liberalism, Connection, and Feminist Jurisprudence," *Southern California Law Review* 65 (March 1992): 1171–264.

3. Respectively, MacKinnon, "Difference and Dominance," note 1 above; West, "Jurisprudence and Gender," *University of Chicago Law Review* 55 (Winter 1988): 13; Offen, "Defining Feminism: A Comparative Historical Approach," *Signs* 14 (Autumn 1988): 119–57. For difference theory, see also Lucinda Finley, "Transcending Equality Theory: A Way Out of the Maternity and the Workplace Debate," *Columbia Law Review* 86 (October 1986): 1118–82; Suzanna Sherry, "Civic Virtue and the Feminine Voice in Constitutional Adjudication," *Virginia Law Review* 72 (April 1986): 543–616. For dominance theory, see also MacKinnon, *Toward a Feminist Theory of the State* (Cambridge, Mass.: Harvard University Press, 1989).

4. See, for example, Dorothy McBride Stetson, *Women's Rights in the USA* (Pacific Grove, Calif.: Brooks/Cole, 1991), chap. 1; Joan Hoff-Wilson, ed., *Rights of Passage: The Past and Future of the ERA* (Bloomington: Indiana University Press, 1986); J. Stanley Lemons, *The Woman Citizen: Social Feminism in the 1920s* (Champaign-Urbana: University of Illinois Press, 1973); Judith A. Baer, *The Chains of*

Protection: The Judicial Response to Women's Labor Legislation (Westport, Conn.: Greenwood Press, 1978), chaps. 1–3.

5. *Dissemination*, trans. Barbara Johnson (Chicago: University of Chicago Press, 1981), viii (emphasis in original).

6. See, for example, Mary Beard, *Woman as Force in History* (New York: Macmillan, 1949); Gerda Lerner, *The Majority Finds Its Past: Placing Women in History* (New York: Oxford University Press, 1979); Carl Degler, *At Odds: Women and the Family in America from the Revolution to the Present* (New York: Oxford University Press, 1980); Paula Giddings, *When and Where I Enter: The Impact of Black Women on Race and Sex in America* (New York: William Morrow, 1984); Martha Minow, " 'Forming Underneath Everything That Grows': Toward a History of Family Law," *Wisconsin Law Review*, no. 4 (1985): 819–88.

7. See Chapter 2 at notes 47–49.

8. Jean Bethke Elshtain, *Public Man, Private Woman: Women in Social and Political Thought* (Princeton, N.J.: Princeton University Press, 1981), 276 n. 146.

9. Respectively, see, for example, *Goesaert v. Cleary*, 335 U.S. 464 (1948); Phyllis Chesler, *Women and Madness* (New York: Doubleday, 1972); Betty Friedan, *The Feminine Mystique* (New York: W. W. Norton, 1963), chaps. 5–7.

10. Chodorow, *The Reproduction of Mothering* (Berkeley: University of California Press, 1978); Gilligan, *In a Different Voice* (Cambridge, Mass.: Harvard University Press, 1982). See also West, "Jurisprudence and Gender," note 3 above, 1–72.

11. *In a Different Voice*, note 10 above, 2, 151.

12. Ibid., 28, 159. Nona Plessner Lyons, Gilligan's colleague, provides a fuller, more detailed conceptualization of the moralities of justice and of care and response in "Two Perspectives: On Self, Relationships, and Morality," in *Mapping the Moral Domain: A Contribution of Women's Thinking to Psychological Theory and Education*, ed. Carol Gilligan, Janie Victoria Ward, and Jull McLean Taylor (Cambridge, Mass.: Harvard University Press, 1988), 21–48.

13. *In a Different Voice*, note 10 above, 74.

14. See, for example, Barrie Thorne, *Gender Play: Girls and Boys in School* (New Brunswick, N.J.: Rutgers University Press, 1993), 170; Mary Pipher, *Reviving Ophelia: Saving the Selves of Adolescent Girls* (New York: Ballantine Books, 1994).

15. See Carol Gilligan, Nona P. Lyons, and Trudy J. Hanmer, eds., *Making Connections: The Relational World of Adolescent Girls at Emma Willard School* (Cambridge, Mass.: Harvard University Press, 1990), 6–27.

16. "Jurisprudence and Gender," note 3 above, 14, 1–3.

17. See, for example, Drucilla Cornell, *Beyond Accommodation: Ethical Feminism, Deconstruction, and the Law* (New York: Routledge, Chapman and Hall, 1991), chap. 1.

18. A good summary of these criticisms is contained in Rosemarie Tong, *Feminine and Feminist Ethics* (Belmont, Calif.: Wadsworth, 1993), 89–102. Important critiques include Susan Faludi, *Backlash: The Undeclared War Against American Women* (New York: Crown, 1991), 325–32; Kathy E. Ferguson, "Knowledge, Politics, and Persons in Feminist Theory," *Political Theory* 17 (May 1989): 302–14; Harriet G. Lerner, *Women in Therapy* (New York: Harper and Row, 1988), 252; MacKinnon, *Feminism Unmodified*, note 1 above, 38–39; *Feminist Theory*, note 3 above, 52; and her remarks in "Feminist Discourse, Moral Values, and the Law—A Con-

versation," *Buffalo Law Review* 34 (Fall 1985): 11–87, 26–28; Elizabeth M. Schneider, "The Dialectic of Rights and Politics: Perspectives from the Women's Movement," *New York University Law Review* 61 (October 1986): 589–652; Susan Squier and Sara Ruddick, "Review of *In a Different Voice*," *Harvard Education Review* 53 (August 1983): 338–42; Carol Tavris, *The Mismeasure of Woman* (New York: Simon and Schuster, 1992), 83–90; Susan Wendell, "A 'Qualified' Defense of Liberal Feminism," *Hypatia* 2 (Summer 1987): 83; Marcia Westcott, *The Feminist Legacy of Karen Horney* (New Haven, Conn.: Yale University Press, 1986), 141; and Joan Williams, "Deconstructing Gender," in *Feminist Jurisprudence: The Difference Debate*, ed. Leslie Friedman Goldstein (Lanham, Md.: Rowman and Littlefield, 1992), 41–98.

19. Slater, *Earthwalk* (Garden City, N.Y.: Anchor Books, 1974), 26, and *The Pursuit of Loneliness* (Boston: Beacon Press, 1970); Bellah et al., *Habits of the Heart: Individualism and Commitment in American Life* (New York: Harper and Row, 1985).

20. Rheingold, *The Fear of Being a Woman* (New York: Grune and Stratton, 1964), 714 (emphasis in original); Bakan, *The Duality of Human Existence* (New York: Rand-McNally, 1966), 14–15; Lombroso, *The Soul of Woman* (New York: E. P. Dutton, 1923), 5; Erikson, "Womanhood and the Inner Space," in *Identity: Youth and Crisis* (New York: W. W. Norton, 1968), 266. Neither Gilligan nor West cites any of these works.

21. "Jurisprudence and Gender," note 3 above, 50 (emphasis in original).

22. See, for example, Sara Ruddick, *Maternal Thinking: Toward a Politics of Peace* (New York: Ballantine Books, 1990), especially citation below, note 41.

23. *Feminist Theory*, note 3 above, 52.

24. "Knowledge," note 18 above, 304.

25. "Beyond Gender Difference to a Theory of Care," *Signs* 12 (Summer 1987): 644–63.

26. *Feminine and Feminist Ethics*, note 18 above, 90–91.

27. *Price Waterhouse v. Hopkins*, 109 S. Ct. 1775, 1782 (1989). On remand, the federal district court ordered Hopkins's elevation to partnership with back pay, 737 F. Supp. 1202 (D.D.C. 1990). The Court of Appeals affirmed, 920 F. 2d 967 (D.C. Circ. 1990).

28. Tong, *Feminine and Feminist Ethics*, note 18 above, 97.

29. For discussions of this phenomenon, see, for example, Margaret Mead, *Male and Female* (New York: William Morrow, 1949); Alva Myrdal and Viola Klein, *Women's Two Roles*, 2d ed. (London: Routledge and Kegan Paul, 1968); Michelle Zimbalist Rosaldo and Louise Lamphere, eds., *Women, Culture, and Society* (Stanford, Calif.: Stanford University Press, 1974).

30. *Beyond Accommodation*, note 17 above, 3.

31. See above, note 5.

32. *Gender and the Politics of History* (New York: Columbia University Press, 1988), 7.

33. See Chapter 2, notes 29 and 53.

34. *In a Different Voice*, note 10 above, 140–43.

35. Ibid., 74. Gilligan, to her credit, is far more critical of the concept of femininity than are some of the theorists she has influenced. Her description of the highest stage of the ethic of care is telling: women resolve "the conflict *between femininity and adulthood*." Ibid., 97 (emphasis supplied).

36. "Teaching the Classics in Malawi," *New Yorker*, 16 December 1991, 56.

37. See, for example, *In a Different Voice*, note 10 above, 103–5, where Gilligan discusses Erik Erikson's biography of Mohandas Gandhi. Erikson criticizes Gandhi's lack of an ethic of care in his treatment of his wife. Some of the references to "Heinz," passim, also take up this theme.

38. *Caring: A Feminine Approach to Ethics and Moral Education* (Berkeley: University of California Press, 1984), 3, 172.

39. *Public Man*, note 8 above, 333.

40. *"Feminism Is Not the Story of My Life": How Today's Feminist Elite Has Lost Touch with the Real Concerns of Women* (New York: Doubleday, 1996).

41. *Maternal Thinking*, note 22 above, 223–24 (emphasis in original). See also "Maternal Thinking," in *Mothering: Essays in Feminist Theory*, ed. Joyce Trebilcot (Totowa, N.J.: Rowman and Allenheld, 1983), 213–30.

42. *Prisoners of Men's Dreams: Striking Out for a New Feminine Future* (Boston: Little, Brown, 1991), 9–16, 83, 88.

43. D. Kay Johnston, "Adolescents' Solutions to Dilemmas in Fables," in *Mapping the Moral Domain*, ed. Gilligan, Ward, and Taylor, note 12 above, 49–72, 67.

44. "Knowledge," note 18 above, 303.

45. See, for example, Elizabeth Fox-Genovese, *Feminism Without Illusions: A Critique of Individualism* (Chapel Hill: University of North Carolina Press, 1991), chap. 2; Nancy J. Hirschmann, *Rethinking Obligation: A Feminist Method for Political Theory* (Ithaca, N.Y.: Cornell University Press, 1992), chap. 1; Susan Moller Okin, *Women in Western Political Thought* (Princeton, N.J.: Princeton University Press, 1979), and *Justice, Gender, and the Family* (New York: Basic Books, 1989); Carol Pateman, *The Sexual Contract* (Stanford, Calif.: Stanford University Press, 1988).

46. Williams, "Deconstructing Gender," note 18 above, 41.

47. *California Federal Savings and Loan Association v. Guerra*, 107 S. Ct. 683 (1987). This ruling is often referred to as the "Lillian Garland" case. Garland was the employee on whose behalf Mark Guerra, the director of the California Department of Fair Employment and Housing, sued. The American Civil Liberties Union and the National Organization for Women filed amicus curiae briefs in favor of the bank. My argument here asserts that they were wrong. See Judith Baer, *Women in American Law: The Struggle Toward Equality from the New Deal to the Present*, 2d ed. (New York: Holmes and Meier, 1996), 116–19.

48. The leading case is *In the Matter of Baby M*, 537 A.2d 1227 (N.J. 1988). This decision outlawed surrogacy contracts in New Jersey; I know of no state which has a policy anything like the one I suggest. An obvious objection to my proposal is that it would be a disincentive to prospective custodial parents. However, a policy which allows surrogacy but discourages it might be attractive. At any rate, the same difficulties attend conventional adoption; the fact that a birth mother (and increasingly a father) can back off has not rendered the practice unpopular.

49. See Chapter 5 at notes 66–81.

50. "Reproductive Freedom and the Right to Privacy: A Paradox for Feminists," in *Families, Politics, and Public Policy*, ed. Irene Diamond (New York: Longman, 1983), 331.

51. *Feminist Theory*, note 3 above, 190–91.

52. Ibid., 251 n. 2 (emphasis added).

53. Ibid., 150, 174.

54. Ibid., 133, 190, 226.

55. See above, "Justice Reconsidered: Gender Disadvantage and Gender Privilege."

56. The first of MacKinnon's four books published as of 1993 was *Sexual Harassment of Working Women* (New Haven, Conn.: Yale University Press, 1979).

57. Ibid., 133.

58. Respectively, Juli Loesch, quoted in Jason DeParle, "Beyond the Legal Right," *Washington Monthly*, April 1989, 42; *Texas NOW Times*, Summer 1989, 9.

59. Eldridge Cleaver, "Stanford Speech," *Eldridge Cleaver: Post-Prison Speeches and Writings*, ed. Robert Scheer (New York: Random House, 1969), 142–43.

60. *Feminist Theory*, note 3 above, xi.

61. *Feminism Unmodified*, note 1 above, chaps. 11 and 15.

62. The respective citations are to Joan Nestle, in *Powers of Desire: The Politics of Sexuality*, ed. Ann Snitow, Christine Stansell, and Sharon Thompson (New York: Monthly Review Press, 1983), 468–70; and Suzanne Rhodenbaugh in *Michigan Quarterly Review* 30 (1991): 415–22. While Nestle's article is critical of MacKinnon's arguments, it was a direct response not to MacKinnon but to her frequent collaborator, Andrea Dworkin.

63. These phrases come from anonymous reviews of my own work over the years. I have no idea how many readers have made these comments about the articles cited above, note 62, but the comments recur.

64. Fred Strebeigh, "Defining Law on the Feminist Frontier," *New York Times Magazine*, 6 October 1991, 30.

65. *Defending Pornography: Free Speech, Sex, and the Fight for Women's Rights* (New York: Anchor Books, 1995), 111, 117.

66. *Feminism and the Power of Law* (New York: Routledge, 1989), 77.

67. *Beyond Accommodation*, note 17 above, 139. *Jouissance* is a Lacanian term which means both sexual pleasure and union with the Other. See Jacques Lacan, *Feminine Sexuality: Jacques Lacan and the Ecole Freudienne* (New York: W. W. Norton, 1982).

68. "Race and Essentialism in Feminist Legal Theory," *Stanford Law Review* 42 (February 1990): 604.

69. "Feminist Jurisprudence: Grounding the Theories," in *Feminist Legal Theory: Readings in Law and Gender*, ed. Katharine T. Bartlett and Rosanne Kennedy (Boulder, Colo.: Westview Press, 1991), 263–80, 266. See also Wendy Brown, "Consciousness Razing," *The Nation*, 8/15 January 1990, 61–64.

70. *Feminist Theory*, note 3 above, 3.

71. "My Mother," note 62 above, 470.

72. "Feminist Discourse," note 18 above, 75 (emphasis in original).

73. *Of Woman Born: Motherhood as Experience and Institution* (New York: W. W. Norton, 1976), 41.

74. Note 1 above, 306 n. 6.

75. "May I Speak?" note 62 above, 422, 420 (emphasis in original).

76. Ibid., 422 (emphasis in original). Camille Paglia's critique is not autobiographical and does not focus on MacKinnon, but her argument is similar to these. See *Sex, Art, and American Culture* (New York: Vintage Books, 1992).

77. See, for example, Susan Brownmiller, *Against Our Will: Men, Women, and Rape* (New York: Simon and Schuster, 1975). My own knowledge is indirect; I was never raped. I have, however, experienced an attempted rape and several robberies. On each occasion, I briefly felt responsible and sensed that the police held me partly responsible.

78. See Lenore Walker, *The Battered Woman Syndrome* (New York: Springer, 1984). In a later book, Walker suggests that the "victim" label may in fact empower battered women in the same way it empowers victims of random crime. *Terrifying Love: Why Battered Women Kill and How Society Responds* (New York: Harper Perennial, 1989). It is unlikely that learned helplessness and empowerment coexist in the same woman at the same time, but different women may react to abuse in different ways. Nevertheless, the "battered woman syndrome" defense is the one that works, if anything does. See Donald Alexander Downs, *More Than Victims: Battered Women, the Syndrome Society, and the Law* (Chicago: University of Chicago Press, 1996); Adelaide H. Villmoare, "Women, Differences, and Rights as Practices: An Interpretive Essay and a Proposal," *Law and Society Review* 25 (1991): 385–410. For self-defense, see Chapter 2, note 22.

79. Bell Hooks suggests that black women may also tend to regard black men more as "comrades in struggle" than as enemies. *Feminist Theory: From Margin to Center* (Boston: South End Press, 1984), chap. 5. The jurors may well have had just the reverse impression of Nicole Brown Simpson, who was white.

80. Which is not to deny that many opponents of that war had disrespect for the troops, and said so. This fusion reinforces my point, rather than refuting it.

81. Strebeigh, "Defining Law," note 64 above, 53.

82. MacKinnon, *Feminism Unmodified*, note 1 above, 13. See, for example, Tamar Lewin, "Feminists Wonder If It Was Progress to Become 'Victims,' " *New York Times*, sect. 4, 10 May 1992.

83. Mary Louise Fellows and Sherene Razack, "Seeking Relations: Law and Feminism Roundtables," *Signs* 19 (Summer 1994): 1058–61.

84. *Washington Post*, 24 October 1995.

85. Lloyd Weinreb, *Oedipus at Fenway Park: What Rights Are and Why There Are Any* (Cambridge, Mass.: Harvard University Press, 1994), 74.

86. Robin Marantz Henig, review of John A. Byrne, *Informed Consent*, *New York Times Book Review*, 15 October 1995.

87. Faludi, *Backlash*, note 18 above, 349.

88. See, for example, William Ryan, *Blaming the Victim*, revised, updated edition (New York: Vintage Books, 1976). For a feminist critique of excessive attribution of individual responsibility, see Faludi, *Backlash*, note 18 above, chap. 12.

89. Susan Wendell, "Toward a Feminist Theory of Disability," in *Gender Basics: Feminist Perspectives on Women and Men*, ed. Anne Minas (Belmont, Calif.: Wadsworth, 1993), 54.

90. (New Haven, Conn.: Yale University Press, 1980) 1.

91. "Jurisprudence and Gender," note 3 above, 9.

92. One such question concerns its sexism: two active men, one passive woman. This point seems too obvious to require mention; but, unlike most obvious points, it goes unmentioned.

93. Sandra Blakeslee, review of Maggie Scarf, *Intimate Worlds: Life Inside the Family, New York Times Book Review,* 26 November 1995.

94. *Feminist Theory,* note 3 above, 160.

95. *Liberal Purposes: Goods, Virtues, and Diversity in the Liberal State* (Cambridge: Cambridge University Press, 1991), 223.

96. See the works cited in note 4 above, as well as Fox-Genovese, *Feminism Without Illusions,* note 45 above, chap. 7.

97. The reference is to *The Subjection of Women* (1869).

98. For a discussion of minors' rights, see Judith A. Baer, *Equality Under the Constitution: Reclaiming the Fourteenth Amendment* (Ithaca, N.Y.: Cornell University Press, 1983), 162–89.

99. See Marilyn French, *The War Against Women* (New York, Summit Books, 1992), part IV.

CHAPTER FOUR
HOW IS LAW MALE?

1. Walter Ong, "Review of Brian Vickers' *Classical Rhetoric in English Poetry,*" *College English* 33 (February 1972): 615.

2. E. E. Schattschneider, *The Semisovereign People* (New York: Holt, Rinehart, and Winston, 1960), 35.

3. "Feminism and Science," in *Sex and Scientific Inquiry,* ed. Sandra Harding and Jean F. O'Barr (Chicago: University of Chicago Press, 1987), 234.

4. See, for example, Katharine T. Bartlett, "Feminist Legal Methods," *Harvard Law Review* 103 (February 1990): 829–88; "Feminist Discourse, Moral Values, and the Law—A Conversation," *Buffalo Law Review* 34 (Fall 1985): 11–87; Lucinda Finley, "Transcending Equality Theory: A Way Out of the Maternity and the Workplace Debate," *Columbia Law Review* 86 (October 1986): 1118–82; Catharine A. MacKinnon, *Feminism Unmodified* (Cambridge, Mass.: Harvard University Press, 1987), and *Toward a Feminist Theory of the State* (Cambridge, Mass.: Harvard University Press, 1989); Deborah L. Rhode, "Feminist Critical Theories," *Stanford Law Review* 42 (February 1990): 617–38; Ann M. Scales, "The Emergence of Feminist Jurisprudence: An Essay," *Yale Law Journal* 95 (June 1986): 1373–403; Elizabeth M. Schneider, "The Dialectic of Rights and Politics: Perspectives from the Women's Movement," *New York University Law Review* 61 (October 1986): 589–652; Suzanna Sherry, "Civic Virtue and the Feminine Voice in Constitutional Adjudication," *Virginia Law Review* 72 (April 1986): 543–616; Robin West, "Jurisprudence and Gender," *University of Chicago Law Review* 55 (Winter 1988): 1–72.

5. See Leslie Friedman Goldstein, ed., *Feminist Jurisprudence: The Difference Debate* (Lanham, Md.: Rowman and Littlefield, 1992).

6. *Beyond God the Father* (Boston: Beacon Press, 1973), p. 9. See also Susan Griffin, *Woman and Nature: The Roaring Inside Her* (New York: Harper and Row, 1978).

7. See Chapter 2 at notes 31–35.

8. "Feminism and Science," note 3 above, 243. See also *A Feeling for the Organism: The Life and Work of Barbara McClintock* (San Francisco: W. H. Freeman, 1983), and *Reflections on Gender and Science* (New Haven, Conn.: Yale University Press, 1985); and Francis Bacon, *Novum Organum* (1620).

9. Bartlett, "Feminist Legal Methods," note 4 above, 832.

10. "Deconstructing Gender," *Feminist Jurisprudence*, ed. Goldstein, note 5 above, 44–45.

11. *Feminist Theory*, note 4 above, chap. 5.

12. Sandra Harding, *Whose Science? Whose Knowledge? Thinking from Women's Lives* (Ithaca, N.Y.: Cornell University Press, 1991), 119.

13. Dorothy Smith, *The Conceptual Practices of Power: A Feminist Sociology of Knowledge* (Boston: Northeastern University Press, 1990), 19.

14. See Chapter 3, note 18.

15. Mary Field Belenky, Blythe McVicker Clinchy, Nancy Rule Goldberger, and Jill Mattuck Tarule, *Women's Ways of Knowing: The Development of Self, Voice, and Mind* (New York: Basic Books, 1986).

16. Ibid., 101, 229.

17. Respectively, Isabel Marcus, in "Feminist Discourse," note 4 above, 1; *Feminism Unmodified*, note 4 above, 205; Lani Guinier et al., "Becoming Gentlemen: Women's Experiences at One Ivy League Law School," *University of Pennsylvania Law Review* 143 (November 1994): 1–110.

18. For an insightful, though dated, discussion of this method, see Paul Savoy, "Toward a New Politics of Legal Education," *Yale Law Journal* 79 (January 1970): 444–504. Guinier et al., "Becoming Gentlemen," note 17 above, 45–48, suggests that the Socratic method creates a particularly intimidating environment for women.

19. Scott Turow, *One L* (New York: G. P. Putnam's Sons, 1977), 220.

20. Critiques of legal education include Roger Cramton, "The Ordinary Religion of the Law School Classroom," *Journal of Legal Education* 29 (1978): 247–63; Duncan Kennedy, "Legal Education as Training for Hierarchy," in *The Politics of Law: A Progressive Critique*, ed. David Kairys (New York: Pantheon Books, 1982), 40–61; David N. Rockwell, "The Education of the Capitalist Lawyer: The Law School," in *Law Against the People*, ed. Robert Lefcourt (New York: Vintage Books, 1971), 90–104; Andrew Watson, "The Quest for Professional Competence: Psychological Aspects of Legal Education," *University of Cincinnati Law Review* 37 (Winter 1968): 109–65. On sociology of the professions, see, for example, Wilbert E. Moore, *The Professions: Roles and Rules* (New York: Russell Sage Foundation, 1970); Robert Dingwall and Philip Lewis, *The Sociology of the Professions: Lawyers, Doctors, and Others* (New York: St. Martin's Press, 1983).

21. Turow, *One L*, note 19 above, 103.

22. Guinier et al., "Becoming Gentlemen," note 17 above, part II and 59.

23. "The Difference in Women's Hedonic Lives: A Phenomenological Critique of Feminist Legal Theory," in *Women and the Law*, ed. Mary Joe Frug (Westbury, N.Y.: Foundation Press, 1992), 807.

24. American Association of University Women, *The AAUW Report: How Schools Shortchange Girls* (Washington, D.C.: AAUW Educational Foundation, 1992). See also Myra Sadker and David Sadker, *Failing at Fairness: How America's Schools Cheat Girls* (New York: Scribner's, 1994).

25. "Bargaining in the Shadow of the Law: The Case of Divorce," *Yale Law Journal* 88 (April 1979): 950–97, 964.

26. See Chapter 3, "Justice Reconsidered: Gender Disadvantage and Gender Privilege."

27. *Conceptual Practices of Power*, note 13 above, 18–19 (emphasis added). See also *The Everyday World as Problematic: A Feminist Sociology* (Boston: Northeastern University Press, 1987).

28. See Perri Klass, *Baby Doctor* (New York: Random House, 1992), 279.

29. See Gayle Binion, "Toward a Feminist Regrounding of Constitutional Law," *Social Science Quarterly* 72 (June 1991): 218 n. 9.

30. "Deconstructing Gender," note 10 above, 44–47. See also Margaret Jane Radin, "The Pragmatist and the Feminist," *Southern California Law Review* 63 (September 1990): 1699–726.

31. See, for example, Jerome Frank, *Courts on Trial* (Princeton, N.J.: Princeton University Press, 1949).

32. *Earthwalk* (Garden City, N.Y.: Anchor Books, 1974), 26, 33, 155; *The Pursuit of Loneliness* (Boston: Beacon Press, 1970), chap. 3. A decade before Slater, philosopher David Bakan identified women with "communion" and men with "agency." *The Duality of Human Existence* (New York: Rand-McNally, 1966). See chap. 3, note 20.

33. See Chapter 3, note 5.

34. See Chapter 2 at notes 31–36.

35. *Feminist Theory*, note 4 above, 109.

36. "Consciousness Raising," in *Voices from Women's Liberation*, ed. Leslie B. Tanner (New York: New American Library, 1970), 253–54. For a similar criticism of consciousness-raising as a method which is analytical rather than empirical, see Drucilla Cornell, "What Is Ethical Feminism?" in Seyla Benhabib et al., *Feminist Contentions: A Philosophical Exchange* (New York: Routledge, 1995), 75–106, 82.

37. See, for example, Schneider, "Dialectic of Rights," note 4 above; Judith Grant, *Fundamental Feminism: Contesting the Core Concepts of Feminist Theory* (New York: Routledge, 1993), 78–79.

38. See Chapter 6, "Rights, Needs, and Conventional Theory: Regrounding Jurisprudence"; Chapter 7, "Fetal Rights and Feminist Theory: Freedom, Responsibility, and Gender."

39. See Chapter 1, note 27.

40. Sara Ruddick, *Maternal Thinking: Toward a Politics of Peace* (New York: Ballantine Books, 1990), 24.

41. Ibid.

42. That is, the cases I discuss did not require the courts to decide issues of sexual equality. I do not deny that the issues raised by the *DeShaney* and *Cruzan* cases have feminist implications. Of course they do.

43. Respectively, "The Path of the Law" (1897) in *Courts, Judges, and Politics*, 4th ed., Walter F. Murphy and C. Herman Pritchett (New York: Random House, 1986), 22; *An Introduction to Legal Reasoning* (Chicago, University of Chicago Press, 1949), 1.

44. *Reason in Law*, 4th ed. (New York: HarperCollins, 1993), 11.

45. "Feminist Legal Methods," note 4 above, 836.

46. 109 S. Ct. 988 (1989).

47. 110 S. Ct. 2841 (1990).

48. *DeShaney v. Winnebago County Department of Social Services*, 109 S. Ct. 988, 1001–2 (1989); William Glaberman, "Determined to Be Heard: Four Americans and Their Journeys to the Supreme Court," *New York Times Magazine*, 2 October 1988.

49. Glaberman, "Determined," 34.

50. 109 S. Ct. 988, 1011.

51. Ibid., 1007.

52. Ibid., 1012, 1013.

53. *New York Times*, 7 December 1989.

54. 110 S. Ct. 2841, 2851, 2859, 2859, 2863 (1990.)

55. The fact that Justice Sandra Day O'Connor joined the majority opinion does not defeat this argument. Although some feminist scholars (for example, Sherry, "Civic Virtue," note 4 above) have found a "feminine" orientation in her opinions, I reject any notion that the possibility of a feminist jurisprudence must stand or fall on doctrinal differences between either or both women ever to sit on the Supreme Court and their male peers. O'Connor and Ruth Bader Ginsburg are, after all, products of the same legal training as their brethren.

56. *Furman v. Georgia*, 408 U.S. 238, 405, 411 (1972).

57. Anthony Lewis, *Gideon's Trumpet* (New York: Vintage Books, 1964), 120.

58. 110 S. Ct. 2841, 2863.

59. 342 U.S. 165, 172 (1952).

60. 442 U.S. 589, 602 (1979).

61. *Institutionalized Juveniles v. Secretary of Public Welfare*, 459 F. Supp. 30, 38 (E.D. Pennsylvania 1978); *Secretary of Public Welfare v. Institutionalized Juveniles*, 442 U.S. 640 (1979).

62. *Parham v. J.R.*, 442 U.S. 589, 602.

63. 109 S. Ct. 2533, 2548–50, 2552, 2555 (1989).

64. See, for example, Jack W. Peltason, "*Corwin and Peltason's Understanding the Constitution*," 11th ed. (New York: Holt, Rinehart, and Winston, 1988); William W. Crosskey, *Politics and the Constitution in the History of the United States* (1951; reprint, Chicago: University of Chicago Press, 1985).

65. 110 S. Ct. 2841, 2863, 2859.

66. Respectively, Edwin Meese III, "Toward a Jurisprudence of Original Intention," Address to the American Bar Association (July 9, 1985), 6; Robert Bork, *Tradition and Morality in Constitutional Law* (Washington, D.C.: American Enterprise Institute, 1984), 11.

67. *Griswold v. Connecticut*, 381 U.S. 479, 482 (1965). See Hugo L. Black, *A Constitutional Faith* (New York: Alfred A. Knopf, 1969); Learned Hand, *The Bill of Rights* (1961; New York: Atheneum, 1974).

68. Alexander M. Bickel, *The Least Dangerous Branch: The Supreme Court at the Bar of Politics* (Indianapolis: Bobbs-Merrill, 1962), 16. See Ronald M. Dworkin, *Taking Rights Seriously* (Cambridge, Mass.: Harvard University Press, 1977), chap. 5; Walter F. Murphy, James E. Fleming, and William F. Harris II, *American Constitutional Interpretation* (Mineola, N.Y.: Foundation Press, 1986), 23–26.

69. See, for example, H. N. Hirsch, *The Enigma of Felix Frankfurter* (New York: Basic Books, 1981), chap. 5; Bruce Allen Murphy, *The Brandeis-Frankfurter Connection* (New York: Oxford University Press, 1982).

70. It is not clear how this rule applies to judges who are elected, confirmed, or subject to removal by the voters, as most state judges are. So far, American theories of constitutional interpretation have taken the federal courts, whose judges are appointed with permanent tenure, as their reference point. These theories may be in need of substantial revision if they are to apply to all appellate judges.

71. Respectively, Walter F. Murphy, *Elements of Judicial Strategy* (Chicago: University of Chicago Press, 1964); David J. Danelski (1960), "The Influence of the Chief Justice in the Decisional Process," in *Courts, Judges, and Politics*, ed. Murphy and Pritchett, note 43 above, 568–77; Richard Kluger, *Simple Justice* (New York: Vintage Books, 1975), chap. 25; S. Sidney Ulmer, "Earl Warren and the *Brown* Decision," *Journal of Politics* 33 (August 1971): 689–702; Richard M. Neustadt, *Presidential Power* (New York: Wiley, 1960), 32.

72. The respective citations are 320 U.S. 81 (1943); 347 U.S. 483 (1954).

73. Murphy, *Elements of Judicial Strategy*, note 71 above, 46–47 (emphasis in original).

74. Kluger, *Simple Justice*, note 71 above, 683–99. See also Ulmer, "Earl Warren," note 71 above.

75. Rhode, "Feminist Critical Theories," note 4 above, 633. See Chapter 2 at note 3.

76. For example, Alpheus Thomas Mason and Donald Grier Stephenson, Jr., *American Constitutional Law*, 9th ed. (Englewood Cliffs, N.J.: Prentice-Hall, 1990), chap. 2, note 68; Murphy, Fleming, and Harris, *American Constitutional Interpretation*, note 68 above, chap. 2; Ralph A. Rossum and G. Alan Tarr, *American Constitutional Law*, 3d ed. (New York: St. Martin's Press, 1991), chap. 1.

77. These conceptualizations do not present an exhaustive list of possible approaches. Modern texts do not recommend that a judge search for "natural law" principles, although the authors of the Fourteenth Amendment and the abolitionist leaders who influenced several of them thought the Constitution incorporated such principles. Some approaches now on everyone's "list" might not have been included a hundred years ago; original intent, for instance, was not a common mode of interpretation in the nineteenth century.

78. Respectively, Murphy, Fleming, and Harris, *American Constitutional Interpretation*, note 68 above, 297, 299; Rossum and Tarr, *American Constitutional Law*, note 76 above, 10; Sotirios A. Barber, *On What the Constitution Means* (Baltimore: Johns Hopkins University Press, 1984), 35.

79. *A Constitutional Faith*, note 67 above.

80. Meese, "Jurisprudence," note 66 above, 17.

81. Michael Perry, *The Constitution, the Courts, and Human Rights* (New Haven, Conn.: Yale University Press, 1982), 75.

82. "The Sovereignty of Process: The Limits of Original Intention," National Center for the Public Interest, *Politics and the Constitution: The Nature and Extent of Interpretation* (Washington, D.C.: American Studies Center, 1990), 12.

83. Mary E. Hawkesworth, "Knowers, Knowing, Known: Feminist Theory and Claims of Truth," *Signs* 14 (Spring 1989): 536.

84. *The Nature of the Judicial Process* (New Haven, Conn.: Yale University Press, 1921), 12. See also Judith A. Baer, "Reading the Fourteenth Amendment: The Inevitability of Noninterpretivism," National Center for the Public Interest, note 82

above, 69–82; Frank, *Courts on Trial*, note 31 above; Sandra Harding, *The Science Question in Feminism* (Ithaca, N.Y.: Cornell University Press, 1986); *Sex and Scientific Inquiry*, ed. Harding and O'Barr, note 3 above.

85. William H. Rehnquist, "The Notion of a Living Constitution," *Texas Law Review* 54 (May 1976): 706.

86. See Herbert Wechsler, *Principles, Politics, and Fundamental Law* (Cambridge, Mass.: Harvard University Press, 1961).

87. "Feminist Legal Methods," note 4 above, 862.

88. Bob Woodward and Scott Armstrong, *The Brethren* (New York: Simon and Schuster, 1979), 15.

89. *The Critical Legal Studies Movement* (Cambridge, Mass.: Harvard University Press, 1986), 50.

90. See Chapter 6.

91. Stephanie Mencimer, "Playing in the Shadows," *Washington City Paper*, 22 March 1996, 22–32, 28, 31.

92. See Chapter 5 at notes 47–64.

93. See Chapter 6, "Rights, Needs, and Conventional Theory: Regrounding Jurisprudence."

94. See Chapter 2 at notes 20–23.

CHAPTER FIVE
RECONSTRUCTING EQUALITY

1. 208 U.S. 412, 421 (1908).

2. The draft registration case is *Rostker v. Goldberg*, 453 U.S. 57 (1981); the veterans' preference case is *Personnel Administrator v. Feeney*, 442 U.S. 256 (1979); and the alimony case is *Orr v. Orr*, 440 U.S. 268 (1979). On divorce, see, for example, the sources cited below, note 30. On the rights of single fathers, see below at notes 33–41; Lucinda Franks, "The War over Baby Clausen," *New Yorker*, 22 March 1993, 56–73; *New York Times*, 1 May 1995, 20 June 1995; *in re Doe*, 638 N.E. 2d 181 (Ill. 1994). The 1981 case is *Kirchberg v. Feenstra*, 450 U.S. 455.

3. *Heartburn* (New York: Alfred A. Knopf, 1983), 81.

4. A discussion of equal protection doctrine can be found in any constitutional law textbook, or in Judith A. Baer, *Women in American Law*, 2d ed. (New York: Holmes and Meier, 1996), 31–36.

5. 404 U.S. 71, 76 (1971).

6. *Frontiero v. Richardson*, 411 U.S. 677 (1973).

7. 429 U.S. 190, 197.

8. 112 S. Ct. 2791, 2819 (1992). *Roe v. Wade*, 410 U.S. 113, 153, 164 (1973) spoke not of women's rights but of the rights of pregnant women *and physicians*. I call the right to abortion "specifically" (not "exclusively") female because it is the only right the exercise of which requires a female subject.

9. Since 1971, the Court has also decided on different grounds several cases that are pertinent to sexual equality. These cases include *Roe v. Wade*, 410 U.S. 113 (1973), *Reproductive Health Services v. Webster*, 109 S. Ct. 3040 (1989), and *Planned Parenthood of Southeastern Pennsylvania v. Casey*, 112 S. Ct. 2791 (1992); cases involving various penalties on pregnancy, *Cleveland Board of Education v. LaFleur*, 414 U.S.

632 (1974), *Geduldig v. Aiello*, 417 U.S. 484 (1974), and *Turner v. Department of Employment Security*, 423 U.S. 44 (1975); one case on jury service, *Taylor v. Louisiana*, 419 U.S. 522 (1975); cases upholding civil rights laws against First Amendment claims, for example, *Pittsburgh Press v. Human Relations Commission*, 413 U.S. 376 (1973), and *Roberts v. U.S. Jaycees*, 468 U.S. 609 (1984); one case affirming, without opinion, a lower court decision which invalidated a feminist-sponsored antipornography ordinance on First Amendment grounds, *Hudnut v. American Booksellers' Association*, 106 S. Ct. 1172 (1986); and one case rejecting the due process claim of a natural father, *Michael H. v. Gerald D.*, 109 S.Ct. 2333 (1989). Since the Court did not invoke sex discrimination doctrine in deciding these cases, I exclude them from the analysis. I also exclude the many cases involving federal civil rights laws.

10. Respectively, 464 U.S. 728 (1984); and 114 S. Ct. 1419 (1994).

11. 116 S. Ct. 2264 (1996).

12. 450 U.S. 455.

13. *Michael M. v. Superior Court of Sonoma County*, 450 U.S. 464 (1981); *Rostker v. Goldberg*, 453 U.S. 57 (1981); *Mississippi University for Women v. Hogan*, 458 U.S. 718 (1982); *Lehr v. Robertson*, 463 U.S. 248 (1983); *Heckler v. Mathews*, note 10 above; and *J.E.B. v. Alabama ex rel. T.B.*, note 10 above.

14. Lower court rulings which rely on these precedents do not appreciably alter this picture. While the federal cases decided through 1993 involve women more often than men, state cases (and there are more of them) present the opposite pattern. The women's federal success record was about 50–50 through 1988, and improved to 75–25 (with a total of eight cases) from 1989 to 1993. The few male litigants have lost, with three somewhat ominous exceptions. *Bachur v. Democratic National Party*, 666 F. Supp. 763 (D. Md. 1987), invalidated the segment of the "equal division rule" which limited the number of convention delegates of one sex which any voter could select in the primary. *Michigan Road Builders Association v. Milliken*, 834 F. 2d 583 (6th Cir. 1987), overturned a state law providing for contract set-asides to women under the intermediate scrutiny rule, on the grounds that no evidence of past discrimination existed. The Ninth Circuit made just the opposite ruling about a similar program (*Associated General Contractors of California v. San Francisco*, 813 F. 2d 922 [1987]). *Lamprecht v. FCC*, 958 F. 2d 382 (D.C. Cir. 1992) invalidated a policy giving preference to women owners in granting licenses for radio stations. In 1989, I examined appellate court rulings in the five largest states—California, Texas, New York, Florida, and Pennsylvania—which contained about 35 percent of the country's population. From *Craig* to 1989, the state cases convey the impression that the primary beneficiaries of the new doctrine, especially in the two largest states, have been single fathers. They do not always win, but they account for a large share of the cases. See, for example, *In re Baby Girl M*, 688 P. 2d 918 (Cal. Sup. Ct. 1984); *Michelle W v. Ronald W*, 703 P. 2d 88 (Cal. Sup. Ct. 1985); *In the Matter of Andrew Peter H.T.*, 100 N.Y. App. Div. 2d 585 (1984); *Matter of Anthony F*, 121 N.Y. Misc. 2d 592 (Family Court, Bronx County, 1983); *Matter of Adoption of Doe*, 524 So. 2d 1037 (Fla. App. 5 Dist. 1988); *Matter of Raquel Marie X*, 150 N.Y. App. Div. 2d 23 (1989). Since 1990, there is no discernible pattern to the subject matter of the cases. All three cases brought by women resulted in victory for the plaintiffs; the men won six cases and lost one. The most striking feature of the cases brought since 1990 is how very few there are: eleven federal, ten state.

15. *Weinberger v. Weisenfeld*, 420 U.S. 636, 645 (1975).

16. *Califano v. Goldfarb*, 430 U.S. 199, 208 (1977).

17. See note 10 above.

18. 116 S. Ct. 2264, 2276 (1996).

19. The respective case citations are *Orr v. Orr*, 440 U.S. 268 (1979); *J.E.B. v. Alabama ex rel. T.B.*, 114 S. Ct. 1419 (1994); *Caban v. Mohammed*, 441 U.S. 380 (1979).

20. Ala. Civ. App. 1979.

21. In my opinion, *Orr*, *Caban*, and *J.E.B.* were rightly decided, but *Michael M* was not. See below, "How Doctrine Favors Men." But few feminists assign high priority to abolishing spousal support and child custody laws which favor women. It is easy to think of possible claims whose satisfaction would enhance equality far more than *Orr* and *Caban* did. *J.E.B.* abolished a practice—excluding prospective jurors on the basis of sex—which is reasonably evenhanded in its effects. For instance, prosecutors may not exclude male jurors in rape cases, but neither may defense attorneys exclude women. The solution Justice O'Connor proposes in her concurring opinion—to apply the ruling only to the government—seems to me to be even worse for women than an outright ban; far more women are victims than criminals. On balance, I think the decision was correct, because it forbade action based on "invidious, archaic, and overbroad stereotypes about the relative abilities of men and women" (opinion of the Court, slip opinion, p. 2).

22. *Personnel Administrator v. Feeney*, note 2 above.

23. Collecting more precise data is not feasible. The Supreme Court Database, Phase II, lists all cases between 1953 and 1993, but it does not consistently report the gender of litigants.

24. *Regents of the University of California v. Bakke*, 438 U.S. 265 (1978).

25. The scholarly literature on division of labor within marriage is voluminous. See, for example, Jessie Bernard, *The Future of Marriage* (New York: World Publishing, 1972), chaps. 7 and 8; Caroline Bird, *Born Female: The High Cost of Keeping Women Down*, rev. ed. (New York: David McKay, 1973), 2; Philip Blumstein and Pepper Schwartz, *American Couples* (New York: William Morrow, 1983), 53–59, 139–46; Julia A. Ericksen, William L. Yancey, and Eugene P. Ericksen, "The Division of Family Roles," *Journal of Marriage and the Family* 41 (May 1979): 301–13; Arlie Hochschild with Anne Machung, *The Second Shift: Working Parents and the Revolution at Home* (New York: Viking, 1989); Gayle Rubin, "The Traffic in Women: Notes on the Political Economy of Sex," in *Toward an Anthropology of Women*, ed. Rayna Rapp Reiter (New York: Monthly Review Press, 1975), 157–210; *The 1985 Virginia Slims American Women's Opinion Poll* (Storrs, Conn.: Roper Center, 1985), 93, Table 6.8.

26. See Baer, *Women in American Law*, note 4 above, 141–46; Susan Faludi, *Backlash: The Undeclared War Against American Women* (New York: Crown, 1991), 24.

27. Lenore Weitzman, *The Divorce Revolution* (New York: Free Press, 1986), found that after divorce the economic status of ex-wives fell by an average of 73 percent, while ex-husbands experienced a rise of 42 percent. Weitzman's interpretation of her data, derived from sample surveys, has been subjected to considerable criticism. Therefore, her statistical findings cannot be accepted as valid; but other studies support her conclusion that divorce has impoverished many women and

children. For example, contemporaneous data from the Panel Study of Income Dynamics put women's average decline at 33 percent. Saul D. Hoffman and Greg G. Duncan, "What *Are* the Economic Consequences of Divorce?" *Demography* 24 (November 1988): 641–45. Some commentators have suggested that California's equal distribution rule skewed Weinstein's results. But California, where over 10 percent of the U.S. population lives, can hardly be considered anomalous; even if it could, a study from the country's third-largest state suggests that different policies can produce similar results. Marsha Garrison, "Good Intentions Gone Awry: The Impact of New York's Equitable Distribution Law on Divorce Outcomes," *Brooklyn Law Review* 57 (Fall 1991): 621–754. Studies of other states report similar patterns; for example, Jean M. Gerval and Carelle Muellner Stein, "Spousal Support in Minnesota: Where Are We Going?" *Minnesota Family Law Journal* 6 (March/April 1993): 29–39; Heather Hammer, "The Economic Impact of Divorce in Hawaii," Preliminary Report to the Hawaii Supreme Court on Gender and Other Fairness Issues, 1993. The most recent study I found reported that the decline in ex-wives' standard of living, relative to that of ex-husbands, was greatest at the high and low ends of the economic spectrum. Joyce Arditti, "Women, Divorce, and Economic Risk," *Family and Conciliation Courts Review* 35 (January 1997): 79–89.

28. "Prince Charming: Abstract Equality," in *Feminist Jurisprudence: The Difference Debate*, ed. Leslie Friedman Goldstein (Lanham, Md.: Rowman and Littlefield, 1992), 111.

29. *Child Support and Alimony: 1985 Supplemental Report*, Current Population Reports, Special Studies, Series P-23, No. 154, U.S. Bureau of the Census, Tables A, C, and H; *Statistical Abstract of the United States*, 1996, Table No. 604. See also Office of Child Support Enforcement, *Giving Help and Support to America's Children: Handbook on Child Support Enforcement* (1996), 13; these data indicate that 56 percent of the over eleven million families with a *parent* living elsewhere have legally binding support orders.

30. For example, the references cited above, note 27; Terry Arendell, *Mothers and Divorce* (Berkeley: University of California Press, 1986); Renee Cherow-O'Leary, *State-by-State Guide to Women's Legal Rights* (New York: McGraw-Hill, 1987), 11; Lois Greenwood-Audant, "The Internalization of Powerlessness: A Case Study of the Displaced Homemaker," in *Women: A Feminist Perspective*, ed. Jo Freeman, 2d ed. (Palo Alto, Calif.: Mayfield, 1979), 264–81; Ruth Sidel, *Keeping Women and Children Last: America's War on the Poor* (New York: Penguin Books, 1996); Judith S. Wallerstein and Joan Kelly, *Surviving the Breakup: How Children and Parents Cope with Divorce* (New York: Basic Books, 1980); Judith S. Wallerstein, *Second Chances: Men, Women, and Children a Decade After Divorce* (New York: Ticknor and Fields, 1989).

For reservations about these findings, see Faludi, *Backlash*, note 26 above, 19–27; Martha Fineman, "Implementing Equality," *Wisconsin Law Review*, no. 4 (1983): 789–887; Herbert Jacob, "Another Look at No-Fault Divorce and the Post-Divorce Finances of Women," *Law and Society Review* 23 (1989): 95–115. All of the cited figures come from sample surveys; they are reliable to the extent that any such data are reliable. Faludi and Jacob argue that the evidence does not show that women do worse after divorce "reform" than they did before. This observation is accurate; complaints about women's postdivorce situation go back to the 1920s. See Baer, *Women in American Law*, note 4 above, 136–41. But the huge increases in the divorce rate in this century make the class of ex-wives larger than it has ever been.

31. *Only Words* (Cambridge, Mass.: Harvard University Press, 1993), 98.

32. For a discussion of these issues, see Judith A. Baer, *Equality Under the Constitution: Reclaiming the Fourteenth Amendment* (Ithaca, N.Y.: Cornell University Press, 1983), chaps. 5 and 10.

33. See *Phillips v. Martin-Marietta*, 400 U.S. 542 (1971).

34. 441 U.S. 380, 391 (1979).

35. In a series of cases beginning with *Stanley v. Illinois*, 405 U.S. 645 (1972), the Court has considered equal protection claims from single fathers. Abdiel Caban and Peter Stanley, who gained the right to apply for custody of his children when their mother died, were the only victors. See, for example, *Quilloin v. Walcott*, 434 U.S. 246 (1978); *Lehr v. Robertson*, 463 U.S. 248 (1983). Like *Caban*, these cases involved natural fathers who sought to veto the adoption of their children by their stepfathers; but Leon Quilloin and Jonathan Lehr lost. *Fiallo v. Bell*, 430 U.S. 787 (1977), upheld a section of the federal immigration laws which discriminates in favor of the children of single mothers who are U.S. residents. *Parham v. Hughes*, 441 U.S. 347 (1979), upheld a wrongful death law which allowed the children of single mothers, but not single fathers, to sue.

Traditionally, single mothers had exclusive parental duties as well as rights. A single father was not even considered a parent in common law. Until recently, a single father had no legal obligation in this country unless the mother won a "paternity suit" against him by convincing a court that the defendant was the child's father. Since proving that any man is the father of a particular child was all but impossible until the advent of DNA testing (and remains quite expensive), this kind of litigation has not been a common or effective means of obtaining child support. The Family Support Act of 1988 does oblige single fathers to provide support, contingent on acknowledgment or court finding of paternity. See Baer, *Women in American Law*, note 4 above, 40–45,146–47.

Until the 1970s, the general rule was that single fathers had no legal right of access to their children, even when they made support payments. The only exceptions consisted of six state court decisions awarding visitation rights to individual fathers. See Norman Gardner Tabler, Jr., "Paternal Rights in the Illegitimate Child: Some Legitimate Complaints on Behalf of the Unwed Father," *Journal of Family Law* 2 (1971): 231–54.

36. See Baer, *Women in American Law*, note 4 above, 150–59; Nancy Polikoff, "Gender and Child Custody Determinations: Exploding the Myths," in *Families, Politics, and Public Policy*, ed. Irene Diamond (New York: Longman, 1983), 183–202; Rena Uviller, "Fathers' Rights and Feminism: The Maternal Presumption Revisited," *Harvard Women's Law Journal* 1 (Spring 1978), 107–21.

37. See, for example, David L. Chambers, "Rethinking the Substantive Rules for Custody Disputes in Divorce," *Michigan Law Review* 83 (December 1984): 480–569; *Garska v. McCoy*, 278 S.E. 2d 357 (W.Va. Sup. Ct. 1981).

38. See Polikoff, "Gender and Child Custody," note 36 above; Marianne Takas, *Child Custody* (New York: Harper and Row, 1987).

39. See Polikoff, "Gender and Child Custody," note 36 above, and "Why Mothers Are Losing: A Brief Analysis of Criteria Used in Child Custody Determinations," *Women's Rights Law Reporter* 7 (Spring 1982): 234–43; Weitzman, *Divorce Revolution*, note 27 above, 233; Lenore Weitzman and Ruth Dixon, "Child Custody Awards: Legal Standards and Empirical Patterns for Child Custody, Support, and Visitation After Divorce," *University of California, Davis, Law Review* 12 (Summer 1979): 471–521.

40. See, for example, Chambers, "Rethinking," note 37 above; Phyllis Chesler, *Mothers on Trial* (New York: McGraw-Hill, 1986); Martha Fineman and Anne Opie, "The Uses of Social Science Data in Legal Policymaking: Custody Determinations at Divorce," *Wisconsin Law Review*, no. 1 (1987): 107–58; Polikoff, "Gender and Child Custody" note 36 above, and "Why Mothers Are Losing," note 39 above; Uviller, "Fathers' Rights," note 36 above; Weitzman, *Divorce Revolution*, note 27 above, 310–18; *Salk v. Salk*, 393 N.Y. 2d 84 (New York Court of Appeals 1975).

41. See Baer, *Women in American Law*, note 4 above, 157–59; Chambers, "Rethinking," note 37 above, 541–44; John Bowlby, *Attachment and Loss*, vol. 3 (New York: Basic Books, 1980).

42. See note 2 above.

43. For a provocative analysis of the relationship between combat and masculinity, see Judith Hicks Stiehm, *Bring Me Men and Women* (Berkeley: University of California Press, 1981), especially 288–304.

44. *Washington v. Davis*, 426 U.S. 229 (1976); *Arlington Heights v. Metropolitan Housing Development Corporation*, 429 U.S. 252 (1977).

45. Note 2 above.

46. See, for example, Christine A. Littleton, "Reconstructing Sexual Equality," *California Law Review* 75 (July 1987): 1279–337.

47. Indianapolis Code Sec. 16–3, 16–17 (1984).

48. *American Booksellers Association v. Hudnut*, 598 F. Supp. 1315, 1316 (S.D. Ind. 1984) (emphasis in original). See also *Hudnut v. American Booksellers' Association*, 771 F. 2d 323 (7th Circ. 1985); 106 S. Ct. 1172 (1986). Canada's obscenity law prohibits "undue exploitation of sex, or of sex and any one or more of the following subjects, namely, crime, horror, cruelty, and violence." Martin's Criminal Code, 1993, S. 163 (8). In *Butler v. R.*, the Canadian Supreme Court unanimously upheld the conviction of the owner of a pornography store under this law. The opinion stressed the right to "the equal protection and equal benefit of the law . . . without discrimination based on race, national or ethnic origin, colour, religion, sex, age or mental or physical disability" guaranteed in Article 15 of the Charter of Rights and Liberties over Article 2's guarantee of "freedom of thought, belief, opinion and expression," on which Butler had based his case. "If true equality between male and female persons is to be achieved, we cannot ignore the threat to equality resulting from exposure to . . . violent and degrading material." 2 W.W.R. 577, 609 (1992). See MacKinnon, *Only Words*, note 31 above, 97–105.

49. *Schenck v. United States*, 249 U.S. 47 (1919); *Gitlow v. New York*, 268 U.S. 652 (1925); *Dennis v. United States*, 341 U.S. 494 (1951); *Brandenburg v. Ohio*, 395 U.S. 444 (1969); *Texas v. Johnson*, 109 S. Ct. 2533 (1989).

50. *Chaplinsky v. New Hampshire*, 315 U.S. 568, 572 (1942). But in *Gooding v. Wilson*, 405 U.S. 518, 524 (1972), the Court narrowed the definition to "words that

have a direct tendency to cause acts of violence by the person to whom, individually, the remark is addressed." On libel, see *New York Times v. Sullivan*, 376 U.S. 254 (1964).

51. For example, *Pittsburgh Press v. Human Relations Commission*, 413 U.S. 376 (1973); *Roberts v. U.S. Jaycees*, 468 U.S. 609 (1984).

52. 112 S. Ct. 2538 (1992).

53. The first Supreme Court ruling on obscenity was *Roth v. United States*, 354 U.S. 476 (1957).

54. The prevailing standard for obscenity was established in *Miller v. California*, 413 U.S. 15, and *Paris Adult Theater I v. Slaton*, 413 U.S. 49 (1973). Special restrictions on the sale of sexually explicit material to minors were upheld in *Ginsberg v. New York*, 390 U.S. 629 (1968). *Osborne v. Ohio*, 495 U.S. 103 (1990), sustained a law prohibiting the possession of pornographic photographs of children.

55. 413 U.S. 15, 24.

56. See Donald Alexander Downs, *The New Politics of Pornography* (Chicago: University of Chicago Press, 1989), chap. 1.

57. *Against Our Will: Men, Women, and Rape* (New York: Simon and Schuster, 1975), 441.

58. See MacKinnon, *Feminism Unmodified* (Cambridge, Mass.: Harvard University Press, 1987), part III; *Toward a Feminist Theory of the State* (Cambridge, Mass.: Harvard University Press, 1989), chap. 11; *Only Words*, note 31 above; Brownmiller, *Against Our Will*, note 57 above, 437–45; Dworkin, *Pornography: Men Possessing Women* (New York: Perigee Press, 1981); Griffin, *Pornography and Silence: Culture's Revenge Against Nature* (New York: Harper and Row, 1981).

59. Griffin, *Pornography and Silence*, note 58 above, 206; MacKinnon, *Only Words*, note 31 above, chap. 1; *Feminist Theory*, note 58 above, 197–207.

60. See above, note 47.

61. See Andrea Dworkin and Catharine A. MacKinnon, *Pornography and Civil Rights: A New Day for Women's Equality* (Minneapolis, Minn.: Women Against Pornography, 1988); MacKinnon, *Only Words*, note 31 above, 22.

62. See MacKinnon, *Only Words*, note 31 above, chap. 3.

63. MacKinnon, *Feminist Theory*, note 58 above, 206.

64. I do not mean to imply endorsement of MacKinnon's and Dworkin's position on pornography. Their views are not shared by all woman jurists—in fact, the district judge was Sarah Evans Barker—or even by all feminists. The point is, rather, that here is an example of a claim to equality with which current doctrine cannot adequately deal.

65. *The Critical Legal Studies Movement* (Cambridge, Mass.: Harvard University Press, 1986), 50. See Chapter 4, at note 89.

66. U.S. Sup. Ct., No. 93–1841.

67. For a valuable analysis with a different focus, see Timothy J. O'Neill, "The Language of Equality in Constitutional Order," *American Political Science Review* 75 (September 1981): 626–35. See also John Brigham, *Constitutional Language* (Westport, Conn.: Greenwood Press, 1978).

68. Edwin Meese III, Address to the American Bar Association, 9 July 1985, 15.

69. Alfred H. Kelly, "Clio and the Court: An Illicit Love Affair," *Supreme Court Review* 1965: 119–58, 134.

70. See Baer, *Equality Under the Constitution*, note 32 above, chap. 4.

71. 163 U.S. 537 (1896). The rulings on jury service are *Strauder v. West Virginia*, 100 U.S. 3, and *ex parte Virginia*, 100 U.S. 339 (1880).

72. 347 U.S. 483, 495.

73. Herbert Wechsler, "Toward Neutral Principles of Constitutional Law," in *Principles, Politics, and Fundamental Law* (Cambridge, Mass.: Harvard University Press, 1961), 5.

74. 388 U.S. 1, 11.

75. *Korematsu v. United States*, 323 U.S. 214 (1944).

76. See also *Hirabayashi v. United States*, 320 U.S. 81 (1943).

77. On busing, compare *Swann v. Charlotte-Mecklenberg*, 402 U.S. 1 (1971), *Keyes v. School District No. 1, Denver, Colorado*, 413 U.S. 189 (1973), and *Milliken v. Bradley*, 418 U.S. 717 (1974). On reverse discrimination, compare *Regents v. Bakke*, note 24 above, and *City of Richmond v. J.A. Croson*, 448 U.S. 469 (1989).

78. *Patterson v. Mclean Credit Union*, 109 S. Ct. 2363, 2371. See also *Wards Cove Packing v. Atonio*, 109 S. Ct. 2115; *Martin v. Wilks*, 109 S. Ct. 2180.

79. See note 77 above.

80. Respectively, note 66 above; 509 U.S. 630 (1993); U.S. Sup. Ct., No. 94–631.

81. 416 U.S. 351.

82. See Gayle Binion, " 'Intent' and Equal Protection: A Reconsideration," *Supreme Court Review* 1983: 397–457.

83. *Goesaert v. Cleary*, 335 U.S. 464, 468 (1948).

84. See *Yick Wo v. Hopkins*, 118 U.S. 356 (1886); *Gomillion v. Lightfoot*, 364 U.S. 339 (1960).

85. *School District of Abington Township v. Schempp*, 374 U.S. 203, 222 (1963) (emphasis added).

86. 403 U.S. 602 (1971).

87. 472 U.S. 38.

88. 403 U.S. 217.

89. 426 U.S. 229, 245 (1976). See also *Arlington Heights v. Metropolitan Housing Development Corporation*, note 44 above.

90. See above at notes 42–46.

91. 481 U.S. 279.

92. There was, in fact, some evidence of deliberate intent to discriminate on the basis of sex. When the legislature enacted the preference in 1943, it exempted any position "especially calling for women": i.e., low-paying clerical work. Ignored by the majority, this fact was emphasized by the dissenters. 442 U.S. 256, 283–85.

93. For the neoconservative position, see George Gilder, *Wealth and Poverty* (New York: Basic Books, 1980), 145–52; for the "black review," Mona Harrington, *Women Lawyers: Rewriting the Rules* (New York: Alfred A. Knopf, 1994), 125–26; for child-rearing practices, see Lendon Smith, *Feed Your Kids Right* (New York: McGraw-Hill, 1979), 223, and Amy Bjork Harris and Thomas A. Harris, *Staying OK* (New York: Harper and Row, 1985), 227–30; on "working mothers," see Benjamin Spock, *The Common Sense Book of Baby and Child Care* (New York: Duell, Sloan, and Pierce, 1946), 484–89. Kurt Wait's victory in the 1996 Bake-Off is described in "Taking the Cake," *U.S. News and World Report*, 11 March 1996, 16.

94. 109 U.S. 3, 35–36.

95. Respectively, note 71 above; 83 U.S. 394 (1873).

96. The leading commerce clause case is *Heart of Atlanta Motel v. United States*, 379 U.S. 241 (1964), upholding Title II of the 1964 Civil Rights Act under the commerce clause. State and local antidiscrimination provisions were upheld in *Roberts v. U.S. Jaycees*, 468 U.S. 609 (1984); *Rotary International v. Rotary Club of Duarte*, 107 S. Ct. 940 (1987); and *New York State Club Association v. City of New York*, 108 S. Ct. 2225 (1988).

97. Respectively, 334 U.S. 1 (1948); 407 U.S. 163 (1972).

98. *Democracy in America*, trans. George Lawrence, ed. J. P. Mayer (New York: Doubleday, 1969), 266, 264.

99. *The Struggle for Judicial Supremacy* (New York: Alfred A. Knopf, 1941), 187.

100. See above at notes 23–24; Chapter 4 at notes 44–52.

CHAPTER SIX
RECONSTRUCTING RIGHTS

1. 410 U.S. 113 (1973.)

2. 112 S. Ct. 2791, 2812 (1992).

3. Barbara Hinkson Craig and David M. O'Brien, *Abortion and American Politics* (Chatham, N.J.: Chatham House, 1993), chap. 7. See also Elizabeth Adell Cook, Ted G. Jelen, and Clyde Wilcox, *Between Two Absolutes: Public Opinion and the Politics of Abortion* (Boulder, Colo.: Westview Press, 1992); Karen O'Connor, *No Neutral Ground? Abortion Politics in an Age of Absolutes* (Boulder, Colo.: Westview Press, 1996).

4. See, for example, Sotirios A. Barber, *On What the Constitution Means* (Baltimore: Johns Hopkins University Press, 1984), chap. 5; Catharine A. MacKinnon, "Privacy v. Equality: Beyond *Roe v. Wade*," in *Feminism Unmodified* (Cambridge, Mass.: Harvard University Press, 1987), 93–102; Michael Perry, *Morality, Politics, and Law* (New York: Oxford University Press, 1988), 175–76; Laurence H. Tribe, *Constitutional Choices* (Cambridge, Mass.: Harvard University Press, 1985), 243–45, and *Abortion: The Clash of Absolutes* (Cambridge, Mass.: Harvard University Press, 1992).

5. See Bob Woodward and Scott Armstrong, *The Brethren* (New York: Simon and Schuster, 1979), 229.

6. 410 U.S. 113, 153 (1973).

7. While this conclusion follows in contemporary legal doctrine, it is not dictated by any logical rule or moral principle. See below at notes 39–54.

8. *Roe v. Wade*, 410 U.S. 113, 158 (1973). The entire holding was much more complicated than this, and is no longer in effect. *Roe* ruled that maternal health was a sufficient justification for state *regulation*, beginning with the second "trimester" of pregnancy. State interest in "potential human life" did not justify a ban on abortion until the last trimester, when the fetus could survive outside the mother's body. While a general prohibition in the third trimester was permissible, the state had to permit exceptions where the mother's life or health was threatened. 410 U.S. 113, 160. The Court implicitly rejected the trimester framework in *Webster v. Reproductive Health Services*, 492 U.S. 490 (1989), and explicitly did so in *Planned Parenthood*

v. Casey (1992), note 2 above. While the "undue burden" test has replaced the division into trimesters, the state still must permit abortion throughout pregnancy to save the mother's life.

9. 492 U.S. 490, 506–7.

10. 381 U.S. 479, 484, 486.

11. For post-*Griswold* decisions, see *Bowers v. Hardwick*, 106 S. Ct. 2841 (1986); *Eisenstadt v. Baird*, 405 U.S. 438 (1972); *Carey v. Population Services International*, 432 U.S. 678 (1977).

12. 112 S. Ct. 2791, 2807 (1992).

13. See note 11 above.

14. 410 U.S. 113, 153 (1973).

15. John Hart Ely, "The Wages of Crying Wolf: A Comment on *Roe v. Wade*," *Yale Law Journal* 82 (April 1973): 920–49, 923.

16. *Lochner v. New York*, 198 U.S. 45, 75 (1905).

17. 381 U.S. 479, 507–27 (1965).

18. *On Liberty* (1859).

19. 410 U.S. 113, 153, 164 (1973; emphasis added). Physicians' denying women requested medical treatment is not without precedent. Until the 1970s, the American College of Obstetrics and Gynecology recommended that its members perform voluntary sterilizations only on women whose age, multiplied by the number of living children they had, equaled at least 120. Sterilization was available to any adult male on request. See Lucinda Cisler, "Unfinished Business and Birth Control," in *Sisterhood Is Powerful*, ed. Robin Morgan (New York: Random House, 1970), 245–88; Boston Women's Health Collective, *Our Bodies, Ourselves*, rev. ed. (New York: Simon and Schuster, 1976), 11–12. Physicians and hospitals are no longer the primary providers of abortions. By 1985, 83 percent of abortions were performed in clinics by other trained medical personnel such as nurses. However, not all women have ready access to clinics; in fact, in many parts of the country clinics are few and far between. In Bryan-College Station, Texas, for instance, a community of slightly over one hundred thousand people and the site of a major university, no facility performs elective abortions, nor does any insurance plan pay for them. In 1998, the local Planned Parenthood clinic announced plans to build such a facility, but it has not yet been completed. The restricted availability of abortion in many parts of the country is documented in Lisa Belkin, "Women in Rural Areas Face Many Barriers to Abortions," *New York Times*, 11 July 1989. See Faye D. Ginsburg, *Contested Lives* (Berkeley: University of California Press, 1989), 3; Boston Women's Health Collective, *The New Our Bodies, Ourselves*, updated edition (New York: Simon and Schuster, 1992), chap. 17. Parental involvement laws restrict minors' access to abortion; restrictions on Medicaid funding limit access to all women dependent on public funds, minors or not. Deborah Haas-Wilson, "The Impact of State Abortion Restrictions on Minors' Demand for Abortions," *Journal of Human Resources* 31 (Winter 1996): 140–58, estimates that parental involvement laws decrease minors' demand for abortion by 13 to 25 percent, and restrictions on Medicaid funding by 9 to 17 percent.

20. 112 S. Ct. 2791, 2807 (1992).

21. See Chapter 1.

22. Respectively, 429 U.S. 190 (1976); 438 U.S. 265 (1978).

23. See Susan Sterett, "Review of Gerald Rosenberg, *The Hollow Hope*," *Women and Politics* 14 (1994): 111–12.

24. The respective citations are 208 U.S. 412 (1908); 274 U.S. 200 (1927); 111 S. Ct. 1196 (1991).

25. Chapter 5 at note 19.

26. 304 U.S. 144, 152, note 4 (1938).

27. Respectively, Lusky, *By What Right? A Commentary on the Supreme Court's Power to Revise the Constitution* (Charlottesville, Va.: Michie, 1975), vii; Ely, "Wages," note 15 above, 926, 937 (emphasis in original); Epstein, "Substantive Due Process by Any Other Name: The Abortion Cases," *Supreme Court Review* 1973: 184; Tribe, "Toward a Model of Roles in the Due Process of Life and Law," *Harvard Law Review* 87 (November 1973): 5.

28. *Ritchie v. Wayman*, 244 Ill. 509, 520 (1910). The book is Judith A. Baer, *The Chains of Protection: The Judicial Response to Women's Labor Legislation* (Westport, Conn.: Greenwood Press, 1978).

29. Feminists are divided on the morality of abortion, both in general and in particular specific situations: when the fetus has a genetic defect, for instance, or if it is the "wrong" sex. See Kristin Luker, *Abortion and the Politics of Motherhood* (Berkeley: University of California Press, 1984); Rosalind Petchesky, *Abortion and Woman's Choice* (New York: Longman, 1983), 326–63; Linda Bird Francke, *The Ambivalence of Abortion* (New York: Random House, 1978). On the status of potentially disabled infants, see Anne Finger, "Claiming All of Our Bodies: Reproductive Rights and Disability," in *With the Power of Each Breath: A Disabled Women's Anthology*, ed. Susan E. Browne, Debra Connors, and Nanci Stern (Pittsburgh: Cleis Press, 1985), 292–307; Laura Hershey, "Choosing Disability," *Ms.*, July/August 1994, 26–32; and Rayna Rapp, "The Ethics of Choice," *Ms.*, April 1984, 97. On the sex of the fetus, see "Another Modest Proposal," *In These Times*, 17–23 May 1989, 5.

30. West, "Jurisprudence and Gender," *University of Chicago Law Review* 55 (Winter 1988): 1–72; Gilligan, *In a Different Voice* (Cambridge, Mass.: Harvard University Press, 1982). See Chapter 2 at notes 36–39; Chapter 3, "Man's Separation, Woman's Connection: The Different Voice."

31. Respectively, *Feminism Without Illusions: A Critique of Individualism* (Chapel Hill: University of North Carolina Press, 1991), 82; *Public Man, Private Woman: Women in Social and Political Thought* (Princeton, N.J.: Princeton University Press, 1981), 313.

32. "Reproductive Freedom and the Right to Privacy: A Paradox for Feminists," in *Families, Politics, and Public Policy*, ed. Irene Diamond (New York: Longman, 1983), 332–38, 335 (emphasis in original).

33. "Privacy vs. Equality," note 4 above, 99.

34. See Chapter 4.

35. For a discussion of these problems, see Chapter 2 at notes 58–61.

36. *Abortion and the Politics of Motherhood*, note 29 above, 194–97.

37. Craig and O'Brien, *Abortion and American Politics*, note 3 above.

38. A better analogy with the position of a pro-choice advocate who proceeds from opinion to scholarship is a Jesuit scholar, like John T. Noonan, who mounts an intellectual argument for the humanity of the fetus. See his "An Almost Absolute Value in History," in *The Morality of Abortion*, ed. John T. Noonan (Cambridge,

Mass.: Harvard University Press, 1970), 1–59; and "How to Argue About Abortion," in *Contemporary Issues in Bioethics*, ed. Tom L. Beauchamp and LeRoy Walters (Enrico, Calif.: Dickenson, 1978), 210–17. If either of us is wrong, it is because our arguments do not hold up, not because of who we are.

39. Pamela Erens, "Anti-Abortion, Pro-Feminism?" *Mother Jones*, May 1989, 46 and 47, respectively.

40. Respectively, Laurence E. Lynn, Jr., "Now, I'm Against Abortion," *New York Times*, 26 March 1989, sect. 4; Christopher Hitchens, "Minority Report," *The Nation*, 24 April 1989, 546; Jason De Parle, "Beyond the Legal Right," *Washington Monthly*, April 1989, 29; Naomi Wolf, "Our Bodies, Our Souls: What the Pro-Choice Movement Must Learn to Say," *The New Republic*, 16 October 1995, 26, 33.

41. 410 U.S. 113, 159 (1973).

42. A comprehensive discussion of reproductive physiology is found in Leslie F. Goldstein, "Examining Abortion Funding Policy Arguments: An Attempt to Recast the Debate," *Women and Politics* 5 (Summer/Fall 1985): 44–51. Efforts to resolve the issue of fetal status include Baruch Brody, "On the Humanity of the Fetus," in *Contemporary Issues in Bioethics*, ed. Beauchamp and Walters, note 38 above, 229–40; Bernard Nathanson, *Aborting America* (Garden City, N.Y.: Doubleday, 1979); Noonan, "An Almost Absolute Value," note 38 above; Mary Anne Warren, "On the Moral and Legal Status of the Fetus," in *Bioethics*, ed. Beauchamp and Walters, 217–18; Ruth Macklin, "Personhood and the Abortion Debate," in *Abortion: Legal and Moral Perspectives*, ed. Jay Garfield and Patricia Hennessey (Amherst: University of Massachusetts Press, 1984), 81–102.

43. See Goldstein, "Examining Abortion Funding," note 42 above, 41–51.

44. Brody, "On the Humanity of the Fetus," note 42 above.

45. See, for example, Roger Wertheimer, "Understanding the Abortion Argument," *Philosophy and Public Affairs* 1 (Fall 1971): 67–95.

46. "In Defense of Abortion," in *Rights, Restitution, and Risk* (Cambridge, Mass.: Harvard University Press, 1986), 1–19.

47. See, for example, Philip Abbott, *The Family on Trial* (University Park: Pennsylvania State University Press, 1981), 138; Baruch Brody, "Thomson on Abortion," *Philosophy and Public Affairs* 1 (Spring 1972): 335–40; John Finnis, "The Rights and Wrongs of Abortion," *Philosophy and Public Affairs* 2 (Winter 1973): 117–45; Goldstein, "Examining Abortion Funding," note 42 above, 58–59 n. 11; Noonan, "How to Argue About Abortion," note 38 above.

48. See, for example, Michael Tooley, "Abortion and Infanticide," *Philosophy and Public Affairs* 2 (Fall 1972): 37–65; Donald H. Regan, "Rewriting *Roe v. Wade*," *Michigan Law Review* 77 (August 1979): 1569–646; Cass R. Sunstein, "Neutrality in Constitutional Law (With Special Reference to Pornography, Abortion, and Surrogacy)," *Columbia Law Review* 92 (January 1992): 1–52; Joel Feinberg, "The Moral and Legal Responsibility of the Bad Samaritan," in *Philosophy of Law*, ed. Joel Feinberg and Hyman Gross, 4th ed. (Belmont, Calif.: Wadsworth, 1991), 579–91. Four states, Vermont, Minnesota, Massachusetts, and Hawaii, have duty-to-rescue ("good Samaritan") statutes; none of these apply to situations where rescue puts the bystander at risk.

49. *Breaking the Abortion Deadlock: From Choice to Consent* (New York: Oxford University Press, 1996), 173.

50. 410 U.S. 113, 159 (1973).

51. *Doe v. Bolton*, 410 U.S. 179, 222 (1973).

52. See, for example, Boston Women's Health Collective, *New Our Bodies, Ourselves*, note 19 above, chap. 17.

53. It is cruel to urge a women faced with an unwanted pregnancy to select what counselors agree is the most difficult and painful of her three basic choices: to bear a child and surrender it. The context and timing of Bush's exhortation made it particularly callous. Joel Steinberg was then on trial (and was later convicted) for the murder of his illegally adopted daughter, Lisa—a blatant lesson to any birth mother of the inherent risks of surrender, even without the frequent presence of Lisa's natural mother, Michelle Launders, on national television. In the 1990s, it is considered inappropriate to mention Steinberg (or Joan Crawford, another excellent argument against giving up one's child for adoption) in the context of the abortion debate. See Christina Crawford, *Mommie Dearest* (New York: William Morrow, 1979). This account of the abuse inflicted on the author by her adoptive mother, the film star, has been corroborated by impartial witnesses. But the memoir received extensive criticism and, in some circles, became a joke. If we presume that the mother confers humanity on the fetus, it becomes unnecessary to invoke worst-case scenarios in order to defend the choice of abortion.

54. Barber, *Constitution*, note 4 above, 139, makes a related argument: that abortion laws are based on "the mere wants, resentments, and religious beliefs of those who control the government." Most opponents of choice deny that their position has a religious basis. We may have to take their statements at face value, more or less, but Barber's point is not without validity.

55. "Abortion and the Sexual Agenda: A Case for Prolife Feminism," in *Abortion and Catholicism: The American Debate*, ed. Patricia Beatty Jung and Thomas A. Shannon (New York: Crossroad, 1988), 128–38, 133.

56. Ibid., p. 137.

57. Nevertheless, I think it is clear that a male-only draft is incompatible with sexual equality as defined in American law. The most recent precedent does not really deny this; *Rostker v. Goldberg*, 453 U.S. 57 (1981), upheld male-only *registration* because of regulations barring women from *combat*. These regulations were not challenged in that case and no longer exist.

58. For historical perspective and a wide variety of positions, see Rachel Mac-Nair, Mary Krane Derr, and Linda Naranjo-Huebl, eds., *Prolife Feminism: Yesterday and Today* (New York: Sulzburger and Graham, 1995).

59. Respectively, Gilligan, *In a Different Voice*, note 30 above, chap. 2, note 6; Ruddick, *Maternal Thinking: Toward a Politics of Peace* (New York: Ballantine Books, 1990), chap. 2, note 32; Noddings, *Caring: A Feminine Approach to Ethics and Moral Education* (Berkeley: University of California Press, 1984), chap. 2, note 30.

60. See Gilligan, *In a Different Voice*, note 30 above, chaps. 3 and 4; Ruddick, *Maternal Thinking*, note 59 above; Elshtain, "Reflections on Abortion, Values, and the Family," in *Abortion: Understanding Differences*, ed. Sydney Callahan and Daniel Callahan (New York: Plenum Press, 1984), 47–72; Fox-Genovese, *"Feminism Is Not the Story of My Life": How Today's Feminist Elite Has Lost Touch with the Real Concerns*

of Women (New York: Doubleday, 1996), 229–33. My comments apply to statements these scholars have made in writing, not in person.

61. *Women and Evil* (Berkeley: University of California Press, 1989), 153.

62. "Taking Freedom Seriously," *Harvard Law Review* 104 (November 1990): 84–85. West's defense of legalized abortion is interesting as a clarification of one possible connection between an ethic of care and a right to reproductive choice, but I find her argument less than persuasive. Her defense of reproductive choice echoes the defense of labor legislation in the Brandeis briefs in the working hours cases. These briefs defended hours limitations for men because, inter alia, they gave workers time to educate themselves; hours limitations for women were supported because they gave women more time for domestic duties. See Baer, *Chains of Protection*, note 28 above, chaps. 2 and 3; Brief for Defendant in Error, *Bunting v. Oregon*, 243 U.S. 426 (1917); Josephine Goldmark, *Fatigue and Efficiency* (New York: Charities Publications Industries, 1912), part II. West makes a similar argument: women must be given a break so they can better serve others.

63. See Baer, *Chains of Protection*, note 28 above, chaps. 2–4.

64. "Abortion and the Sexual Agenda," note 55 above, 136.

65. Erens, "Anti-Abortion," note 39 above, 46.

66. Chapter 3, at note 58; Erens, "Anti-Abortion," note 39 above, 46–47.

67. Justice Potter Stewart's opinion in *Harris v. McRae*, upholding the ban on Medicaid funding of abortions, is a clear example of the limits of liberal rights theory. "Although government may not place obstacles in the path of a woman's exercise of her freedom of choice, it need not remove those not of its own creation. Indigency falls in the latter category." 448 U.S. 297, 316 (1980).

68. See, for example, Don Sloan with Paula Hartz, *Abortion: A Doctor's Perspective, A Woman's Dilemma* (New York: Donald I. Fine, 1992). Young, poor, or disabled women are especially vulnerable to pressure from physicians, parents, and lovers. See Susan E. Davis, *Women Under Attack: Victories, Backlash and the Fight for Reproductive Freedom* (Boston: South End Press, 1988); John D'Emilio and Estelle B. Freedman, *Intimate Matters: A History of Sexuality in America* (New York: Harper and Row, 1988). On disabled women, and women carrying potentially disabled infants, Anne Finger, "Claiming All of Our Bodies," note 29 above, 305, reports instances of medical professionals putting pressure on disabled women to abort. Employers may also coerce employees. See Nadine Brozan, "Abortion Urged, Jail Officers Say," *New York Times*, 24 May 1989. I know of no cases of inmates forced to have abortions, but the possibility is present.

69. Respectively, 381 U.S. 479, 486; Nan D. Hunter, "Women and Child Support," in *Families, Politics, and Public Policy*, ed. Diamond, note 32 above, 203–19, 204.

70. The Supreme Court has invalidated spousal consent requirements for abortion (*Planned Parenthood v. Danforth*, 428 U.S. 52 [1976]), and a spousal notification requirement (*Planned Parenthood v. Casey*, 112 S. Ct. 2791 [1992]).

71. MacKinnon, *Feminism Unmodified*, note 4 above, 100.

72. See, for example, R. J. Herrnstein, "IQ and Falling Birth Rate," *Atlantic Monthly*, May 1989, 72–76.

73. Letter to the editor, *Mother Jones*, July 1989, 6. Callahan was writing in response to a letter from me, criticizing statements quoted in Erens, "Anti-Abortion," note 39 above.

74. See Chapter 3 at notes 29–37.

75. *Roe v. Wade*, 410 U.S. 113, 153 (1973).

76. Those who do include Shulamith Firestone, *The Dialectic of Sex* (New York: Bantam Books, 1970); Jeffner Allen, "Motherhood: The Annihilation of Women," in *Mothering: Essays in Feminist Theory*, ed. Joyce Trebilcot (Totowa, N.J.: Rowman and Allenheld, 1983), 315–30.

77. Feminists who regard motherhood as a value-neutral choice include Robin Morgan, *Going Too Far* (New York: Random House, 1977); Gloria Steinem, *Outrageous Acts and Everyday Rebellions* (New York: Holt, Rinehart, and Winston, 1983). Simone de Beauvoir, *The Second Sex*, trans. by H. M. Parshley (New York: Alfred A. Knopf, 1952), 456–97; and Martha Gimenez, "Feminism, Pronatalism, and Motherhood," in *Mothering*, ed. Trebilcot, note 76 above, 287–314, emphasize what Gimenez calls the "compulsory nature of parenthood," 288. Feminists who seem reluctant to conclude that women might freely choose not to become mothers include Sylvia Ann Hewlett, *A Lesser Life* (New York: William Morrow, 1986); Germaine Greer, *Sex and Destiny* (New York: Harper and Row, 1984); and possibly Adrienne Rich, *Of Woman Born: Motherhood as Experience and Institution* (New York: W. W. Norton, 1976), 253–57.

78. I emphasize the words "in general." This statement is not meant to sound callous, though I fear it may. Fertility is precious to those who lack it. But I think the debate over reproductive choice has been distorted by refusal to recognize the fact that most people have far more chances to become parents than they need or want.

79. Consider, for example, the situation constructed by Ursula LeGuin in her science fiction novel *The Left Hand of Darkness* (New York: Ace Books, 1969), 89–97. All human beings in the mythical "Gethen" are asexual except during phases known as "kemmer," similar to estrus (heat) in certain mammals. During kemmer, they are both aroused and fertile, and are either male or female. Hence, "the mother of several children may be the father of several more."

80. *A Disquisition on Government*, in Richard K. Cralle, ed., *The Works of John C. Calhoun*, vol. 1 (Columbia, S.C.: A. S. Johnson, 1851), 52. See Judith A. Baer, *Equality Under the Constitution: Reclaiming the Fourteenth Amendment* (Ithaca, N.Y.: Cornell University Press, 1983), 65–67.

81. See, for example, *Weinberger v. Weisenfeld*, 420 U.S. 676 (1975); *Califano v. Goldfarb*, 430 U.S. 199 (1977); *Califano v. Webster*, 430 U.S. 313 (1977); Chapter 5 at notes 15–16.

82. See above, note 73 and accompanying text.

83. See Baer, *Equality Under the Constitution*, note 80 above, chap. 7.

84. 6 January 1941. *The Public Papers of F. D. Roosevelt*, vol. 9, 663; reprinted in Henry Steele Commager, ed., *Documents in American History*, vol. 2, 7th ed. (New York: Appleton-Century Crofts, 1963), 446–49.

85. See, for example, Charles A. Reich, "The New Property," *Yale Law Journal* 73 (April 1964): 733–87, and "Individual Rights and Social Welfare: The Emerging Legal Issues," *Yale Law Journal* 74 (March 1965): 1245–57. For a critique, see Mi-

chael B. Levy, "Liberty, Property, and Equality: Critical Reflections on the 'New Property,' " in *The Liberal Future in America: Essays in Renewal*, ed. Philip Abbott and Michael B. Levy (Westport, Conn.: Greenwood Press, 1985), 127–47.

86. *San Antonio Independent School District v. Rodriguez*, 411 U.S. 1 (1973); Baer, *Equality Under the Constitution*, note 80 above, chaps. 5 and 10.

87. See Chapter 3, note 58.

88. Boston Women's Health Collective, *The New Our Bodies, Ourselves*, note 19 above, 260, 264, 275, 279–92.

89. Mike Males, "Why Blame Young Girls?" *New York Times*, 29 July 1994. The statistics come from studies conducted by the National Center for Health Statistics and the Alan Guttmacher Institute. In 1995, a Guttmacher Institute study of women who gave birth in 1988 revealed that almost 80 percent of the fathers of babies born to mothers between fifteen and seventeen were over eighteen. *New York Times*, 6 August 1995, sect. 4.

90. See Chapter 3, "The Situation and the Situated."

91. The Greek *proles*, children, is the root word of "proletariat." Members of the proletariat were people who had nothing but their children.

92. "Our Bodies, Our Souls," note 40 above, 28–29.

93. I have dealt with these issues briefly in "On Feminism and Ethics," *Women and Politics* 5 (Summer/Fall 1985): 1–5.

94. *Roe v. Wade*, 410 U.S. 113, 159 (1973). My statements are obviously generalizations. Sources of evidence to support them include Boston Women's Health Collective, *The New Our Bodies, Ourselves*, note 19 above, 220–262; Philip Blumstein and Pepper Schwartz, *American Couples* (New York: William Morrow, 1983); Arlie Hochschild with Anne Machung, *The Second Shift: Working Parents and the Revolution at Home* (New York: Viking, 1989); Lenore Weitzman, *The Divorce Revolution* (New York: Free Press, 1986).

95. See Chapter 3, "Women and Men, Rights and Responsibility: Asymmetrical Thinking."

96. In these last two paragraphs, I have drawn on my own previously published work. See *Equality Under the Constitution*, note 80 above, 38–56; *Chains of Protection*, note 28 above, 42–135.

97. See Timothy J. O'Neill, "The Language of Equality in Constitutional Order," *American Political Science Review* 75 (September 1981): 626–35.

98. See Andrew Koppelman, "Forced Labor: A Thirteenth Amendment Defense of Abortion," *Northwestern University Law Review* 84 (Winter 1990): 480–535.

CHAPTER SEVEN
RECONSTRUCTING RESPONSIBILITY

1. In *Weeks v. Southern Bell*, 408 F. 2d 228 (5th Circ. 1969), a federal court of appeals ruled that Title VII of the Civil Rights Act of 1964 preempted state protective labor legislation. In 1979, the Department of Health, Education, and Welfare (now Health and Human Services) forbade sterilization without consent. See Judith A. Baer, *The Chains of Protection: The Judicial Response to Women's Labor Legislation* (Westport, Conn.: Greenwood Press, 1978), chap. 5; *Women in American Law: The*

Struggle toward Equality from the New Deal to the Present, 2d ed. (New York: Holmes and Meier, 1996), 187–88.

2. " 'Can I Sue Mommy?' An Analysis of Women's Tort Liability for Prenatal Injuries to Her Child Born Alive," *San Diego Law Review* 21 (March 1984): 362. See also Katha Pollitt, " 'Fetal Rights': A New Assault on Feminism," *The Nation*, 26 March 1990, 409–18.

3. The Supreme Court overturned workplace restrictions in *United Auto Workers v. Johnson Controls*, 111 S. Ct. 1196 (1991). In *Matter of A.C.*, 573 A. 2d 1235 (D.C. Circ. 1990), reversing *In re A.C.*, 533 A. 2d 611 (D.C. Circ. 1987), an appellate court ruled that a woman could not be forced to accept medical treatment. On prenatal damage suits, see Beal, "Mommy," note 2 above. For a general treatment of these issues, see Cynthia R. Daniels, *At Women's Expense: State Power and the Politics of Fetal Rights* (Cambridge, Mass.: Harvard University Press, 1993). On forced medical treatment, see "Developments in the Law—Medical Technology and the Law," *Harvard Law Review* 103 (May 1990): 1556–84; Janet Gallagher, "Prenatal Invasions and Interventions: What's Wrong with Fetal Rights," *Harvard Women's Law Journal* 10 (Spring 1987): 9–58; Nancy K. Rhoden, "The Judge in the Delivery Room: The Emergence of Court-Ordered Caesareans," *California Law Review* 74 (December 1986): 1951–2030; *Application of Jamaica Hospital*, 491 N.Y.S. 2d 898 (Supreme Court, Special Term, Queens County, 1985); *Crouse Irving Memorial Hospital v. Paddock*, 485 N.Y.S. 2d 443 (Supreme Court, Onondaga County, 1985); *Jefferson v. Griffin Spalding County Authority*, 247 GA 86, 274 S.E. 2d 457 (Ga. Sup. Ct. 1981).

4. Respectively, John A. Robertson, "The Right to Procreate and in Utero Fetal Therapy," *Journal of Legal Medicine* 3 (September 1982): 357–58; Margery Shaw, "Constitutional Prospective Rights of the Fetus," *Journal of Legal Medicine* 5 (March 1984): 73; Deborah Mathieu, "Respecting Liberty and Preventing Harm: Limits of State Intervention in Prenatal Choice," *Harvard Journal of Law and Public Policy* 8 (Winter 1985): 48–55. See also "Maternal Substance Abuse: The Next Step in the Protection of Fetal Rights?" *Dickenson Law Review* 92 (Spring 1988): 691–715; Robertson, "Procreative Liberty and the Control of Conception, Pregnancy, and Childbirth," *Virginia Law Review* 69 (April 1983): 405–64.

5. *For Whose Protection? Reproductive Hazards and Exclusionary Policies in the United States and Britain* (Ann Arbor: University of Michigan Press, 1992), 2.

6. *United Auto Workers v. Johnson Controls*, note 3 above.

7. Daniels, *At Women's Expense*, note 3 above, chap. 4; Tamar Lewin, "Detention of Pregnant Woman for Drug Use Is Struck Down," *New York Times*, 23 April 1997; *International Herald Tribune* (Frankfurt), 31 October 1997.

8. *Matter of A.C.*, note 3 above.

9. See Beal, " 'Can I Sue Mommy?' " note 2 above; *Grodin v. Grodin*, 102 Mich. App. 396, 301 N.W. 2d 869 (1980); *Stallman v. Youngquist*, 125 Ill. 2d 267, 531 N.E. 2d 355. (1988.)

10. Note 3 above; 42 U.S.C. Sec. 2000e 703(e) (1964).

11. See, for example, Gallagher, "Prenatal Invasions," note 3 above; "Pregnancy Police: The Health Policy and Legal Implications of Punishing Pregnant Women for Harm to Their Fetuses," *New York University Review of Law and Social Change*

16 (1988): 277–319; Barbara Katz Rothman, *Recreating Motherhood* (New York: W. W. Norton, 1989).

12. "Fetal Rights," note 2 above.

13. Michael Dorris, *The Broken Cord* (New York: Harper and Row, 1989), 264, and chap. 10.

14. *In the Matter of A.C.*, 533 A. 2d 611 (D.C. Circ. 1987). This decision was vacated in 1988, reheard *en banc*, and reversed, *In re A.C.*, 573 A. 2d 1235 (D.C. Circ. 1990). See above, note 3. See Susan Faludi, *Backlash: The Undeclared War Against American Women* (New York: Crown, 1991), 430–43; Sarah Burns, "Notes from the Field: A Reply to Professor Colker," *Harvard Women's Law Journal* 13 (1990): 189–206.

15. "Deconstructing Gender," in *Feminist Jurisprudence: The Difference Debate*, ed. Leslie Friedman Goldstein (Lanham, Md.: Rowman and Littlefield, 1992), 44–45.

16. Beal, " 'Can I Sue Mommy?' " note 2 above, 362, 370 (emphasis in original). The title may have been chosen by an editor, not the author; but it is difficult to believe that a student-edited publication would impose a title on a professor over his objections.

17. Little support for these forms of punishment exists among criminal justice experts in the West, even those who advocate severe and painful punishments. See, for example, Graeme R. Newman, *Just and Painful* (London: Macmillan, 1983), chap. 2; Ernest van den Haag, *Punishing Criminals* (Lanham, Md.: University Press of America, 1991), chap. 17.

18. See Chapter 3, "The Situation and the Situated."

19. Steven A. Holmes, "Radio Talk About TV Anchor's Disability Stirs Ire in Los Angeles," *New York Times*, 23 August 1991; *New York Times*, 30 August 1991.

20. See Laura Hershey, "Choosing Disability," *Ms.*, July/August 1994, 26–32.

21. See, for example, Jean Bethke Elshtain, "If You're an Addict, It's Now a Crime to Give Birth," *The Progressive*, December 1990, 26–28; Jan Hoffman, "Pregnant, Addicted—And Guilty?" *New York Times Magazine*, 19 August 1990; Robert H. Blank, *Fetal Protection in the Workplace: Women's Rights, Business Interests, and the Unborn* (New York: Columbia University Press, 1993), chaps. 7 and 8; Suzanne Daley, "Born on Crack and Coping with Kindergarten," *New York Times*, 7 February 1991; Joseph Losco, "Fetal Rights and Feminism," in *Feminist Jurisprudence*, ed. Goldstein, note 10 above, 231–62; Pollitt, " 'Fetal Rights,' " note 2 above; Dorothy E. Roberts, "Punishing Drug Addicts Who Have Babies: Women of Color, Equality, and the Right of Privacy," *Harvard Law Review* 104 (May 1991): 1419–82; Michael J. Wright, "Reproductive Hazards and 'Protective' Discrimination," *Feminist Studies* 5 (Summer 1979): 302–9. The argument that rules affecting women are in fact designed to protect men from competition has its roots in the history of protective legislation. See Baer, *Chains of Protection*, note 1 above, chaps. 3 and 4; *Goesaert v. Cleary*, 335 U.S. 462 (1948). However, the unions, which once sided with men against women, now side with women against employers. The contradictions embedded in workplace policies are explored in Kenney, *For Whose Protection?* note 5 above, chap. 6; Andrea Hricko with Melanie Brunt, *Working for Your Life: A Woman's Guide to Job Health Hazards* (Berkeley, Calif.: Labor Occupational Health Program, 1976), chaps. 3 and 4; Jeanne Mager Stellman, *Women's Work*,

Women's Health: Myths and Realities (New York: Pantheon Books, 1977); Jeanne M. Stellman and Susan M. Daum, *Work Is Dangerous to Your Health* (New York: Vintage Books, 1973).

22. See Chapter 3 at notes 1–6.

23. See, for example, Suzanne Arms, *Immaculate Deception* (San Francisco: San Francisco Book Company/Houghton Mifflin, 1975); Dorris, *Broken Cord*, note 13 above.

24. See, for example, Wendy Chavkin, "Occupational Hazards to Reproduction: A Review Essay and Annotated Bibliography," *Feminist Studies* 5 (Summer 1979): 310–25; Hricko, *Working for Your Life*, note 21 above; Rosalind Petchesky, *Abortion and Woman's Choice: The State, Sexuality, and Reproductive Freedom* (New York: Longman, 1983), chap. 9; Donna M. Randall and James F. Short, Jr., "Women in Toxic Work Environments: A Case Study of Social Problem Development," *Social Problems* 30 (April 1983): 410–34; Wendy W. Williams, "Firing the Woman to Protect the Fetus: The Reconciliation of Fetal Protection with Equal Employment Opportunity Goals Under Title VII," *Georgetown Law Journal* 69 (February 1981): 641–704.

25. There have been cases of infants born to exposed mothers who had abnormally high blood levels of lead at birth. For instance, at least one baby born to a Johnson Controls worker between 1979 and 1983 had tested above thirty micrograms per cubic meter. But there is no evidence that these babies suffered serious permanent effects. *United Auto Workers v. Johnson Controls*, 886 F. 2d 871, 876–77 (7th Circ. 1989).

26. See Dorris, *Broken Cord*, note 13 above; Elisabeth Rosenthal, "When a Pregnant Woman Drinks," *New York Times Magazine*, 4 February 1990; Pollitt, "Fetal Rights," note 2 above; Rothman, *Recreating Motherhood*, note 11 above.

27. Dorris, *Broken Cord*, note 13 above; Rosenthal, "Pregnant Woman," note 26 above.

28. Elshtain, "If You're an Addict," note 21 above, 26; Hoffman, "Pregnant, Addicted," note 21 above; Katharine Greider, "Crackpot Ideas," *Mother Jones*, July/August 1995, 54.

29. *United Auto Workers v. Johnson Controls, Inc.*, note 3 above, and 886 F. 2d 871 (7th Circ. 1989).

30. *Secretary of Labor v. American Cyanamid*, OSHRC Docket No. 79–5762, p. 10 (1979).

31. *Wright v. Olin Corporation*, 697 F. 2d 1172, 1182 (4th Circ. 1982).

32. "Doctor Calls Pregnant Smokers Child Abusers," *Chapel Hill (N.C.) Newspaper*, 28 March 1984, 4.

33. Isabel Wilkerson, "Court Backs Woman in Pregnancy Drugs Case," *New York Times*, 3 April 1991.

34. Respectively, Dorris, *Broken Cord*, note 13 above, chap. 10; Mary Grabar, "Sending Women to Jail Is Not the Answer," *The Progressive*, December 1990, 24.

35. Hoffman, "Pregnant, Addicted," note 21 above.

36. See sources cited above, note 26.

37. This fact, by itself, does not refute an argument for criminal sanctions against pregnant users. After all, driving while intoxicated is a crime even though many people do so without getting into automobile accidents. This analogy is inexact,

however, for two reasons. First, it is driving with a certain level of alcohol in one's body, not driving after drinking, which is illegal. Second, laws making substance use a serious crime only for pregnant women, and for all pregnant women, amount to status offenses; they punish being, not just doing.

38. The charges against Bremer were dismissed. Her daughter was placed in foster care after birth, but Bremer got her back. See Hoffman, "Pregnant, Addicted," note 21 above. For other instances, see Pollitt, "Fetal Rights," note 2 above.

39. Marge Piercy, *Small Changes* (New York: Fawcett Crest, 1973), 390.

40. Rosenthal, "Pregnant Woman," note 26 above, 61.

41. See, for example, Arms, *Immaculate Deception*, note 23 above; Boston Women's Health Collective, *The New Our Bodies, Ourselves*, updated and expanded edition (New York: Simon and Schuster, 1990); Sheila Kitzinger, *The Complete Book of Pregnancy and Childbirth*, revised and expanded (New York: Alfred A. Knopf, 1989); Barbara Seaman, *Free and Female* (New York: Fawcett Crest, 1972).

42. See Nancy Wainer Cohen and Lois J. Estner, *The Silent Knife: Caesarean Prevention and Vaginal Birth After Caesarean* (South Hadley, Mass.: Bergin and Garvey, 1983).

43. See "Developments in the Law"; Gallagher, "Prenatal Invasions"; and Rhoden, "Judge in the Delivery Room," all cited at note 3 above.

44. See especially Boston Women's Health Collective, *Our Bodies, Ourselves*, and Seaman, *Free and Female*, note 41 above.

45. "Some Theoretical Considerations on the Problem of Mother-Child Separation," *American Journal of Orthopsychiatry* 24 (July 1954): 477.

46. See, for example, Mary E. Becker, "From *Muller v. Oregon* to Fetal Vulnerability Policies," *University of Chicago Law Review* 53 (Fall 1986): 1219–1273; Kenney, *For Whose Protection?* note 5 above, chaps. 1 and 6; Williams, "Firing the Woman," note 24 above.

47. Detective Sergeant Al Van Hemert, quoted in Hoffman, "Pregnant, Addicted," note 21 above, 34. On protective labor legislation, see Baer, *Chains of Protection*, note 1 above, chaps. 1–3.

48. U.S. Bureau of the Census, *Women in Gainful Occupations, 1870 to 1920*, Monograph No. 19 (Washington, D.C.: U.S. Government Printing Office, 1929), 77.

49. *Wright v. Olin Corporation*, note 31 above.

50. 198 U.S. 45 (1905).

51. *Blaming the Victim*, revised, updated edition (New York: Vintage Books, 1976), chap. 1. See Chapter 1 of this book at note 15.

52. See Baer, *Chains of Protection*, note 1 above, chaps. 3 and 4; *Bosley v. McLaughlin*, 236 U.S. 385 (1915); *Radice v. New York*, 264 U.S. 292 (1924); *Goesaert v. Cleary*, 335 U.S. 464 (1948). The Title VII case is *Weeks v. Southern Bell*, note 1 above.

53. See Becker, "Fetal Vulnerability Policies," note 46 above; Wright, "Reproductive Hazards," note 21 above, 304; works by Kenney, Hricko, and Stellman, notes 5 and 21 above.

54. 274 U.S. 200, 207 (1927).

55. Respectively, Alan M. Dershowitz, "Drawing the Line on Prenatal Rights," *Los Angeles Times*, 14 May 1989; Hoffman, "Pregnant, Addicted," note 21 above, 34.

56. *New York Times*, 13 November 1994; *San Antonio Express-News*, 28 February 1996; *Bryan-College Station Eagle*, 15 June 1997.

57. *New York Times*, 22 and 25 June 1985.

58. But Florida later became the first state to ban the use of the "dress" defense in rape cases. New York enacted a similar law in 1994.

59. Letter from Herbert Tarr, 9 June 1991.

60. See Paglia, *Sex, Art, and American Culture* (New York: Vintage Books, 1992); Roiphe, *The Morning After: Sex, Fear, and Feminism on Campus* (Boston: Little, Brown, 1993).

61. *Fear of Fifty: A Midlife Memoir* (New York: HarperCollins, 1994), 317 (emphasis in original).

62. Robertson, "Right to Procreate," note 4 above, 352. See also his *Children of Choice: Freedom and the New Reproductive Technologies* (Princeton, N.J.: Princeton University Press, 1994); Shaw, "Constitutional Prospective Rights," note 4 above.

63. Respectively, Pollitt, "Fetal Rights," note 2 above; Shaw, "Constitutional Prospective Rights," note 4 above, 116.

64. "Enjoyment by citizens of their rights and freedom must not be to the detriment of the interests of society or the state." Article 39, Constitution of the Union of Soviet Socialist Republics. See Adamantia Pollis, "Liberal, Socialist, and Third World Perspectives on Human Rights," in *Toward a Human Rights Framework*, ed. Peter Schwab and Adamantia Pollis (New York: Praeger Publishers, 1982), 1–26.

65. See works cited above, note 4.

66. Mnookin and Kornhauser, "Bargaining in the Shadow of the Law: The Case of Divorce," *Yale Law Journal* 88 (April 1979): 964. See Chapter 2 at notes 26–27; Chapter 4 at note 25. For a general treatment of the popularity and influence of rational choice in political science, see Reid Cushman, "Rational Fears," *Lingua Franca*, November/December 1994, 42–54.

67. See, for example, Lisa Belkin, "Women in Rural Areas Face Many Barriers to Abortion," *New York Times*, 11 July 1989; Boston Women's Health Collective, *The New Our Bodies, Ourselves* note 41 above; Faye D. Ginsburg, *Contested Lives* (Berkeley: University of California Press, 1989). The last year for which the federal government has statistics is 1994. The Centers for Disease Control and Prevention reported that 1.2 million abortions were performed that year; about 21 in every 1,000 women between age fifteen and twenty-four had an abortion. These numbers are the lowest since 1976. Experts attribute the decline both to the increased availability of contraception and to the increased concentration of abortion services in urban areas. *New York Times*, 5 January 1997.

Contingent legal personhood cannot be dismissed as unrealistic where access to abortion is guaranteed: for example, in Canada, Britain, the Netherlands, and Scandinavia. But, since most of these countries require parental consent, the doctrine would be inapplicable to pregnant minors.

68. See Chapter 6 at notes 87–88.

69. See Maureen A. Flannery, "Simple Living and Hard Choices," in *Before the Law: An Introduction to the Legal Process*, ed. John J. Bonsignore et al., 4th ed. (Boston: Houghton Mifflin, 1989), 54–60.

70. Respectively, *Broken Cord*, note 13 above, 163–70; "Doctor," note 32 above.

71. Wilkerson, "Court," note 33 above. See Hoffman, "Pregnant, Addicted," note 21 above.

72. Grabar, "Jail," note 34 above, 22.

73. Tamar Lewin, "Drug Use During Pregnancy: New Issue Before the Courts," *New York Times*, 5 February 1990.

74. See Dorris, *Broken Cord*, note 13 above; Rosenthal, "Pregnant Woman," note 26 above.

75. Dorris, *Broken Cord*, note 13 above, xvii. Abel Dorris is called "Adam" in the book.

76. "Drawing the Line," note 55 above.

77. John Stuart Mill, *On Liberty* (1859), chap. 1.

78. Ruth Rosen, "What Feminist Victory in the Court?" *New York Times*, 1 April 1991.

79. Dorris, *Broken Cord*, note 13 above, xviii (emphasis in original).

80. On 17 February 1995, Judge Okla B. Jones 2d of the U.S. Eastern District of Louisiana ruled that a consortium of sixty law firms could sue seven tobacco companies for punitive damages for addicting smokers and concealing the fact that cigarettes are addictive. The defendants included American Tobacco Company, the R. J. Reynolds Tobacco Company, the Brown & Williamson Tobacco Corporation, Philip Morris, Liggett & Myers Inc., the Lorillard Tobacco Company, and the United States Tobacco Company. *New York Times*, 18 February 1995. In March 1996, Liggett settled with the consortium. The company agreed to comply with proposed federal regulations of tobacco products and to fund programs to help people quit smoking. *Washington Post*, 13 March 1996.

81. "Maternal Liability: Courts Strive to Keep Doors Open to Fetal Protection—But Can They Succeed?" *John Marshall Law Review* 20 (Summer 1987): 747–68, 767.

82. Letter to the editor, *Mother Jones*, July 1989, 6.

83. Mary Ann Glendon, *Rights Talk: The Impoverishment of Political Discourse* (New York: Free Press, 1991), x, xi.

84. Respectively, Galston, *Liberal Purposes: Goods, Virtues, and Diversity in the Liberal State* (Cambridge: Cambridge University Press, 1991), 286; Clinton, *It Takes a Village: And Other Lessons Children Can Teach Us* (New York: Simon and Schuster, 1996); Bennett, *The Book of Virtues* (New York: Simon and Schuster, 1993).

85. "What Feminist Victory?" note 78 above; *UAW v. Johnson Controls*, note 3 above, 1207.

86. For an interesting twist on the story, see Eric Berne, *What Do You Say After You Say Hello?* (New York: Grove Press, 1972), 230–43.

87. Respectively, "Firing the Woman" note 24 above; "From *Muller v. Oregon* to Fetal Vulnerability Policies," note 46 above; see also Note, "Getting Beyond Discrimination: A Regulatory Solution to the Problem of Fetal Hazards in the Workplace," *Yale Law Journal* 95 (January 1986): 577–98.

88. *Toward a Feminist Theory of the State* (Cambridge, Mass.: Harvard University Press, 1989), 226. See Chapter 3, note 54.

89. Respectively, *For Whose Protection?* note 5 above; *At Women's Expense*, note 3 above.

90. West, "Jurisprudence and Gender," *University of Chicago Law Review* 55 (Winter 1988): 1–72.

91. See Chapter 3 at notes 37–38. The citations are, respectively, Gilligan, *In a Different Voice* (Cambridge, Mass.: Harvard University Press, 1982); Noddings, *Caring: A Feminine Approach to Ethics and Moral Education* (Berkeley: University of California Press, 1984); and the articles cited above, note 4.

92. See Chapter 6, "Who Decides?"

93. See Chapter 6, notes 64–74 and accompanying text.

94. "Reproductive Freedom and the Right to Privacy: A Paradox for Feminists," in *Families, Politics, and Public Policy*, ed. Irene Diamond (New York: Longman, 1983), 335 (emphasis in original).

95. Rothman, *Recreating*, note 11 above, 97.

96. Pollitt, "Fetal Rights," note 2 above.

CHAPTER EIGHT
TOWARD A FEMINIST POSTLIBERALISM

1. See Okin, *Women in Western Political Thought* (Princeton, N.J.: Princeton University Press, 1979), and *Justice, Gender, and the Family* (New York: Basic Books, 1989); Pateman, *The Sexual Contract* (Stanford, Calif.: Stanford University Press, 1988).

2. Catharine A. MacKinnon, *Toward a Feminist Theory of the State* (Cambridge: Harvard University Press, 1989), 248.

3. William Galston, *Liberal Purposes: Goods, Virtues, and Diversity in the Liberal State* (Cambridge: Cambridge University Press, 1991), 89.

4. John Leo, "On Society: Where Marriage Is a Scary Word," *U.S. News and World Report*, 5 February 1996, 22.

5. "Jurisprudence and Gender," *University of Chicago Law Review* 55 (Winter 1988): 1–72.

6. For the former, see Catharine A. MacKinnon, *Feminism Unmodified* (Cambridge, Mass.: Harvard University Press, 1987), part III; for the latter, Nadine Strossen, *Defending Pornography: Free Speech, Sex, and the Fight for Women's Rights* (New York: Anchor Books, 1996), chap. 1.

7. See Chapter 6 at notes 76–77.

8. See Mary Ann Glendon, *Rights Talk: The Impoverishment of Political Discourse* (New York: Free Press, 1991); and Amitai Etzioni, *The Spirit of Community: Rights, Responsibilities, and the Communitarian Agenda* (New York: Crown, 1993).

9. *Rights Talk*, note 8 above, x.

10. Chester Finn, "New Paradigm Seminar: Reframing Family Values," Woodrow Wilson International Center for Scholars, Washington, D.C., 20 November 1995.

11. Robert Pear, "U.S. Seeks to Review More Disability Cases," *New York Times*, 19 March 1996.

12. See Chapter 1, "Duty and Danger: Woman's Condition"; Chapter 3, "Care and Coercion: The Roots of a Female Ethic."

13. See Thomas Geoghegan, *Which Side Are You On? How to Be for Labor When It's Flat on Its Back* (New York: Farrar, Straus and Giroux, 1991).

14. See Judith A. Baer, *Women in American Law: The Struggle Toward Equality from the New Deal to the Present*, 2d ed. (New York: Holmes and Meier, 1996), chap. 2.

15. Alan Wolfe, "The Feudal Culture of the Postmodern University," *Wilson Quarterly* 20 (Winter 1996): 60.

16. James K. Glassman, "Far from Doomsday," *Washington Post*, 5 March 1996.

17. 450 U.S. 455 (1981). See Chapter 5.

18. Rick Bragg, "Big Holes Where the Dignity Used to Be," *New York Times*, 5 March 1996.

19. I know. I have been guilty of being an angry customer myself.

20. Leo, "Marriage," note 4 above.

21. These studies include, most notably, a longitudinal project directed by Judith S. Wallerstein. See Wallerstein and Joan Kelly, *Surviving the Breakup: How Men, Women, and Children Cope with Divorce* (New York: Basic Books, 1980); Wallerstein, *Second Chances: Men, Women, and Children a Decade After Divorce* (New York: Ticknor and Fields, 1989).

22. See Chapter 5 at notes 26–30; Ruth Sidel, *Keeping Women and Children Last: America's War on the Poor* (New York: Penguin Books, 1996), chap. 2.

23. Some of these experts have good feminist credentials. See, for example, Mary Pipher, *Reviving Ophelia: Saving the Selves of Adolescent Girls* (New York: Ballantine Books, 1994), chap. 7; Okin, *Justice*, note 1 above, 4, 162–69, 182–83. For analysis of a substantial body of relevant literature, see Barbara Dafoe Whitehead, "Dan Quayle Was Right," *The Atlantic*, April 1993, 47–50.

24. Allan Sloan, "The Hit Men," *Newsweek*, 26 February 1996, 44–48.

25. Former Senator William Proxmire (D-Wisc.), explaining his opposition to the Chrysler bailout of 1979. See James McGregor Burns, Jack W. Peltason, and Thomas E. Cronin, *Government by the People*, bicentennial edition, 1987–89, national, state, and local edition (Englewood Cliffs, N.J.: Prentice-Hall, 1987), 540.

26. Robert J. Samuelson, "The Politics of Self-Pity," *Newsweek*, 26 February 1996, 50.

27. David E. Sanger and Steve Lohr, "A Search for Answers to Avoid the Layoffs," *New York Times*, 9 March 1996.

28. Samuelson, "Politics of Self-Pity," note 26 above.

29. See Chapter 7 at note 84.

30. *Liberal Purposes: Goods, Virtues, and Diversity in the Liberal State* (Cambridge: Cambridge University Press, 1991), 286.

31. Kristin Luker, *Dubious Conceptions: The Politics of Teenage Pregnancy* (Cambridge, Mass.: Harvard University Press, 1996), 159.

32. "There are two methods of curing the mischiefs of faction: the one, by removing its causes; the other, by controlling its effects." *Federalist*, No. 10 (James Madison). "Light and transient causes" comes from Thomas Jefferson's Declaration of Independence.

33. For example, Terry Arendell, *Mothers and Divorce* (Berkeley: University of California Press, 1986); Renee Cherow-O'Leary, *State-by-State Guide to Women's Legal Rights* (New York: McGraw-Hill, 1987), 11; Lois Greenwood-Audant, "The Internalization of Powerlessness: A Case Study of the Displaced Homemaker," in *Women: A Feminist Perspective*, ed. Jo Freeman, 2d ed. (Palo Alto, Calif.: Mayfield,

1979), 264–81; Sidel, *Keeping Women and Children Last*, note 22 above; Wallerstein and Kelly, *Surviving the Breakup*, and Wallerstein, *Second Chances*, note 21 above. For discussion of these studies, see Chapter 5 at note 30.

34. See references cited in Chapter 3, note 2.

35. See Susan Brownmiller, *Against Our Will: Men, Women, and Rape* (New York: Simon and Schuster, 1975).

36. Some prominent feminist scholars do reject capitalism as incompatible with feminism. See, for example, Zillah Eisenstein, *The Radical Future of Liberal Feminism* (New York: Longman, 1981); Nancy Hartsock, *Money, Sex and Power: Toward a Feminist Historical Materialism* (New York: Longman, 1983); Alison M. Jaggar, *Feminist Politics and Human Nature* (Totowa, N.J.: Rowman and Allanheld, 1983).

37. *Money, Sex and Power*, note 36 above, 234.

38. See Baer, *Women in American Law*, note 14 above, chap. 3.

39. *Keyes v. Denver School District No. 1*, 413 U.S. 189, 221 (1973).

40. West, "Jurisprudence and Gender," note 5 above, 1.

41. *Feminist Theory: From Margin to Center* (Boston: South End Press, 1984), 1, 2.

42. See Baer, *Women in American Law*, note 14 above, 318–19; Chapter 1 of this book at note 4.

43. (New Haven, Conn.: Yale University Press, 1980), 1.

44. See Chapter 1, note 1; Chapter 3 at notes 90 and 91.

45. *The Feminine Mystique* (New York: W. W. Norton, 1963), chap. 10.

46. "Some Theoretical Considerations on the Problem of Mother-Child Separation," *American Journal of Orthopsychiatry* 24 (July 1954): 471–83.

47. See Chapter 3 at note 54.

48. *A Theory of Justice* (Cambridge, Mass.: Belknap Press of Harvard University Press, 1971), 302. For the "just savings principle," see 284–93.

49. See, for example, Okin, *Justice*, note 1 above, chap. 5.

50. Rawls himself might deny this. In a later work, he limits the reach of his concept of justice as fairness to the political realm. But my argument here that no acceptable jurisprudence can exclude activity essential to the maintenance of society undermines his implied distinction. See Rawls, *Political Liberalism* (New York: Columbia University Press, 1993); Susan Moller Okin, "Review," *American Political Science Review* 87 (December 1993): 1010–11.

51. 274 U.S. 200, 207 (1927).

52. "Are you working for the army?" A Frenchwoman said this to the poet Adrienne Rich, the mother of three sons, during the Vietnam War. See *Of Woman Born: Motherhood as Experience and Institution* (New York: W. W. Norton, 1976), 11.

53. *Feminine Mystique*, note 45 above, 374–75.

54. And she? For any society, the assumption that most women worked is a much safer bet than the assumption that they got enough food. But historians have documented women's hard work in the colonies; their nutritional needs were met at least to the extent they were able to do their work, to bear children, and to recover from childbearing.

55. See Chapter 6, "Rights, Needs, and Conventional Theory: Regrounding Jurisprudence."

56. *Who Stole Feminism? How Women Have Betrayed Women* (New York: Simon and Schuster, 1994).

Berger, Brigitte, and Peter L. Berger. *The War over the Family: Capturing the Middle Ground*. Garden City, N.Y.: Doubleday, 1983.

Berger, Raoul. *Government by Judiciary: The Transformation of the Fourteenth Amendment*. Cambridge, Mass.: Harvard University Press, 1977.

Bernard, Jessie. *The Future of Marriage*. New York: World Publishing, 1972.

Bickel, Alexander M. *The Least Dangerous Branch: The Supreme Court at the Bar of Politics*. Indianapolis: Bobbs-Merrill, 1962.

Bird, Caroline. *Born Female: The High Cost of Keeping Women Down*. Rev. ed. New York: David McKay, 1973.

Black, Hugo L. *A Constitutional Faith*. New York: Alfred A. Knopf, 1969.

Blumstein, Philip, and Pepper Schwartz. *American Couples*. New York: William Morrow, 1983.

Bordo, Susan. *Unbearable Weight: Feminism, Western Culture, and the Body*. Berkeley: University of California Press, 1993.

Bork, Robert H. *Tradition and Morality in Constitutional Law*. Washington, D.C.: American Enterprise Institute, 1984.

Boston Women's Health Collective. *The New Our Bodies, Ourselves*. Updated edition. New York: Simon and Schuster, 1992.

Brigham, John. *Constitutional Language*. Westport, Conn.: Greenwood Press, 1978.

Brownmiller, Susan. *Against Our Will: Men, Women, and Rape*. New York: Simon and Schuster, 1975.

Butler, Judith. *Gender Trouble: Feminism and the Subversion of Identity*. New York: Routledge, 1990.

Butler, Judith, and Joan W. Scott, eds. *Feminists Theorize the Political*. New York: Routledge, Chapman, and Hall, 1992.

Card, Claudia, ed. *Feminist Ethics*. Lawrence: University Press of Kansas, 1991.

Cardozo, Benjamin N. *The Nature of the Judicial Process*. New Haven, Conn.: Yale University Press, 1921.

Carter, Lief. *Reason in Law*. 4th ed. New York: HarperCollins, 1993.

Carter, Stephen L. *The Culture of Disbelief: How American Law and Politics Trivialize Religious Devotion*. New York: Anchor Books, 1994.

———. *Reflections of an Affirmative Action Baby*. New York: Basic Books, 1991.

Cherow-O'Leary, Renee. *State-by-State Guide to Women's Legal Rights*. New York: McGraw-Hill, 1987.

Chesler, Phyllis. *Mothers on Trial*. New York: McGraw-Hill, 1986.

Child Support and Alimony. 1985 Supplemental Report. Current Population Reports, Special Studies, Series P-23, No. 154. United States Bureau of the Census, 1985.

Chodorow, Nancy. *The Reproduction of Mothering*. Berkeley: University of California Press, 1978.

Cixous, Hélène, and Catherine Clement. *The Newly Born Woman*. Trans. Betsy Wing. Minneapolis: University of Minnesota Press, 1986.

Clinton, Hillary Rodham. *It Takes a Village: And Other Lessons Children Can Teach Us*. New York: Simon and Schuster, 1996.

Cohen, Nancy Wainer, and Lois J. Estner. *The Silent Knife: Caesarean Prevention and Vaginal Birth After Caesarean*. South Hadley, Mass.: Bergin and Garvey, 1983.

Collins, Patricia Hill. *Black Feminist Thought: Knowledge, Consciousness, and the Politics of Empowerment*. New York: Routledge, Chapman and Hall, 1991.

BIBLIOGRAPHY

BOOKS

Abbott, Philip, and Michael B. Levy, eds. *The Liberal Future in America: Essays in Renewal.* Westport, Conn.: Greenwood Press, 1985.

Ackerman, Bruce A. *Social Justice in the Liberal State.* New Haven, Conn.: Yale University Press, 1980.

———. *We the People.* Cambridge, Mass.: Belknap Press of Harvard University Press, 1991.

American Association of University Women. *The AAUW Report: How Schools Shortchange Girls.* Washington, D.C.: AAUW Educational Foundation, 1992.

Andersen, Margaret L., and Patricia Hill Collins, eds. *Race, Class, and Gender: An Anthology.* Belmont, Calif.: Wadsworth, 1992.

Arendell, Terry. *Mothers and Divorce.* Berkeley: University of California Press, 1986.

Aristotle. *The Politics.*

Arms, Suzanne. *Immaculate Deception.* San Francisco: San Francisco Book Company/Houghton Mifflin, 1975.

Baer, Judith A. *The Chains of Protection: The Judicial Response to Women's Labor Legislation.* Westport, Conn.: Greenwood Press, 1978.

———. *Equality Under the Constitution: Reclaiming the Fourteenth Amendment.* Ithaca, N.Y.: Cornell University Press, 1983.

———. *Women in American Law: The Struggle Toward Equality from the New Deal to the Present.* 2d ed. New York: Holmes and Meier, 1996.

Balbus, Isaac D. *Marxism and Domination.* Princeton, N.J: Princeton University Press, 1982.

Barber, Sotirios A. *On What the Constitution Means.* Baltimore: Johns Hopkins University Press, 1984.

Bartlett, Katharine T., and Rosanne Kennedy, eds. *Feminist Legal Theory: Readings in Law and Gender.* Boulder, Colo.: Westview Press, 1991.

Belenky, Mary Field, Blythe McVicker Clinchy, Nancy Rule Goldberger, and Jill Mattuck Tarule. *Women's Ways of Knowing: The Development of Self, Voice, and Mind.* New York: Basic Books, 1986.

Bell, Derrick. *And We Are Not Saved: The Elusive Quest for Racial Justice.* New York: Basic Books, 1987.

———. *Faces at the Bottom of the Well: The Permanence of Racism.* New York: Basic Books, 1992.

Bellah, Robert N., Richard Madson, William M. Sullivan, Ann Swidler, and Steven M. Tipton. *Habits of the Heart: Individualism and Commitment in American Life.* New York: Harper and Row, 1985.

Benhabib, Seyla, Judith Butler, Drucilla Cornell, and Nancy Fraser. *Feminist Contentions: A Philosophical Exchange.* New York: Routledge, 1995.

Benjamin, Jessica. *The Bonds of Love: Psychoanalysis, Feminism, and the Problem of Domination.* New York: Pantheon Books, 1988.

Bennett, William. *The Book of Virtues.* New York: Simon and Schuster, 1993.

Congressional Globe. 1866.

Cook, Elizabeth Adell, Ted G. Jelen, and Clyde Wilcox. *Between Two Absolutes: Public Opinion and the Politics of Abortion.* Boulder, Colo.: Westview Press, 1992.

Cornell, Drucilla. *Beyond Accommodation: Ethical Feminism, Deconstruction, and the Law.* New York: Routledge, Chapman and Hall, 1991.

———. *The Imaginary Domain: Abortion, Pornography and Sexual Harassment.* New York: Routledge, 1995.

Crosskey, William W. *Politics and the Constitution in the History of the United States.* 1951. Chicago: University of Chicago Press, 1985.

Daly, Mary. *Beyond God the Father.* Boston: Beacon Press, 1973.

Degler, Carl N. *At Odds: Women and the Family in America from the Revolution to the Present.* New York: Oxford University Press, 1980.

Delaney, C. F., ed. *The Liberalism-Communitarianism Debate.* Lanham, Md.: Rowman and Littlefield, 1994.

Delphy, Christine. *Close to Home: A Materialist Analysis of Women's Oppression.* Trans. and ed. Diana Leonard. Amherst: University of Massachusetts Press, 1984.

Denfield, Rene. *The New Victorians.* New York: Warner Books, 1995.

Derrida, Jacques. *The Archeology of the Frivolous.* Trans. John P. Leavey, Jr. Lincoln: University of Nebraska Press, 1973.

———. *Dissemination.* Trans. Barbara Johnson. Chicago: University of Chicago Press, 1981.

———. *Of Grammatology.* Trans. Gayatri Chakravorty Spivak. Baltimore: Johns Hopkins University Press, 1976.

———. *Positions.* Translated and annotated by Alan Bass. Chicago: University of Chicago Press, 1981.

———. *Spurs/Eperons.* Trans. Barbara Harlow. Chicago: University of Chicago Press, 1978.

———. *Writing and Difference.* Trans. Alan Bass. Chicago: University of Chicago Press, 1978.

Dewey, John. *Liberalism and Social Action.* 1935. New York: Capricorn Books, 1963.

———. *The Public and Its Problems.* Chicago: Swallow Press, 1927.

Dingwall, Robert, and Philip Lewis. *The Sociology of the Professions: Lawyers, Doctors and Others.* New York: St. Martin's Press, 1983.

Di Stefano, Christine. *Configurations of Masculinity: A Feminist Perspective on Modern Political Theory.* Ithaca, N.Y.: Cornell University Press, 1991.

Donnelly, Jack. *Universal Human Rights in Theory and Practice.* Ithaca, N.Y.: Cornell University Press, 1989.

Dorris, Michael. *The Broken Cord.* New York: Harper and Row, 1989.

Downs, Donald Alexander. *More Than Victims: Battered Women, the Syndrome Society, and the Law.* Chicago: University of Chicago Press, 1996.

Dworkin, Andrea. *Pornography: Men Possessing Women.* New York: Perigee Press, 1981.

Dworkin, Ronald. *Law's Empire.* Cambridge, Mass.: Belknap Press of Harvard University Press, 1986.

———. *Taking Rights Seriously.* Cambridge, Mass.: Harvard University Press, 1977.

Eisenstein, Zillah. *The Color of Gender: Reimaging Democracy.* Berkeley: University of California Press, 1994.

Eisenstein, Zillah. *The Female Body and the Law*. Berkeley: University of California Press, 1988.

———. *The Radical Future of Liberal Feminism*. New York: Longman, 1981.

Elshtain, Jean Bethke. *Democracy on Trial*. New York: Basic Books, 1995.

———. *Public Man, Private Woman: Women in Social and Political Thought*. Princeton, N.J.: Princeton University Press, 1981.

Ephron, Nora. *Heartburn*. New York: Alfred A. Knopf, 1983.

Epstein, Cynthia Fuchs. *Women in Law*. 2d ed. Champaign-Urbana: University of Illinois Press, 1993.

Erikson, Erik H. *Identity: Youth and Crisis*. New York: W. W. Norton, 1968.

Estrich, Susan. *Real Rape*. Cambridge, Mass.: Harvard University Press, 1987.

Etzioni, Amitai. *The Spirit of Community: Rights, Responsibilities, and the Communitarian Agenda*. New York: Crown, 1993.

———, ed. *Rights and the Common Good: The Communitarian Perspective*. New York: St. Martin's Press, 1995.

Faludi, Susan. *Backlash: The Undeclared War Against American Women*. New York: Crown, 1991.

Ferguson, Kathy E. *The Man Question: Visions of Subjectivity in Feminist Theory*. Berkeley: University of California Press, 1993.

Fine, Michelle, and Adrienne Asch, eds. *Women with Disabilities: Essays in Psychology, Culture, and Politics*. Philadelphia: Temple University Press, 1988.

Fineman, Martha Albertson, and Isabel Karpin, eds. *Mothers in Law: Feminist Theory and the Legal Regulation of Motherhood*. New York: Columbia University Press, 1995.

Fineman, Martha Albertson, and Nancy Sweet Thomadsen, eds. *At the Boundaries of Law: Feminism and Legal Theory*. New York: Routledge, Chapman and Hall, 1991.

Fish, Stanley. *Doing What Comes Naturally: Change, Rhetoric, and the Practice of Theory in Literary and Legal Studies*. Durham, N.C.: Duke University Press, 1989.

Flax, Jane. *Thinking Fragments*. Berkeley: University of California Press, 1990.

Fletcher, George P. *A Crime of Self-Defense: Bernhard Goetz and the Law on Trial*. Chicago: University of Chicago Press, 1988.

Flexner, Eleanor. *Century of Struggle*. Rev. ed. Cambridge, Mass.: Belknap Press of Harvard University Press, 1970.

Fox-Genovese, Elizabeth. *"Feminism Is Not the Story of My Life": How Today's Feminist Elite Has Lost Touch with the Real Concerns of Women*. New York: Doubleday, 1996.

———. *Feminism Without Illusions: A Critique of Individualism*. Chapel Hill: University of North Carolina Press, 1991.

Frank, Jerome. *Courts on Trial*. Princeton, N.J.: Princeton University Press, 1949.

French, Marilyn. *The War Against Women*. New York: Summit Books, 1992.

Freud, Sigmund. *Three Essays on the Theory of Sexuality*. Trans. and ed. James Strachey. New York: Basic Books, 1962.

Friedan, Betty. *The Feminine Mystique*. New York: W. W. Norton, 1963.

———. *The Second Stage*. New York: Summit Books, 1981.

Gaard, Greta, ed. *Ecofeminism: Women, Animals, Nature*. Philadelphia: Temple University Press, 1993.

Gallop, Jane. *Reading Lacan*. Ithaca, N.Y.: Cornell University Press, 1985.

———. *Thinking Through the Body*. New York: Columbia University Press, 1988.

Galston, William A. *Liberal Purposes: Goods, Virtues, and Diversity in the Liberal State*. Cambridge: Cambridge University Press, 1991.

Giddings, Paula. *When and Where I Enter: The Impact of Black Women on Race and Sex in America*. New York: William Morrow, 1984.

Gilder, George. *Wealth and Poverty*. New York: Basic Books, 1980.

Gilligan, Carol. *In a Different Voice*. Cambridge, Mass.: Harvard University Press, 1982.

Gilligan, Carol, Nona P. Lyons, and Trudy J. Hanmer, eds. *Making Connections: The Relational World of Adolescent Girls at Emma Willard School*. Cambridge, Mass.: Harvard University Press, 1990.

Gilligan, Carol, Janie Victoria Ward, and Jill McLean Taylor, eds. *Mapping the Moral Domain: A Contribution of Women's Thinking to Psychological Theory and Education*. Cambridge, Mass.: Harvard University Press, 1988.

Ginsburg, Faye D. *Contested Lives*. Berkeley: University of California Press, 1989.

Glendon, Mary Ann. *Rights Talk: The Impoverishment of Political Discourse*. New York: Free Press, 1991.

Goffman, Erving. *Stigma: Notes on the Management of Spoiled Identity*. Englewood Cliffs, N.J.: Prentice-Hall, 1963.

Gornick, Vivian. *Women in Science: 100 Journeys into the Territory*. Rev. ed. New York: Simon and Schuster, 1990.

Grant, Judith. *Fundamental Feminism: Contesting the Core Concepts of Feminist Theory*. New York: Routledge, 1993.

Green, T. H. (1879–80). *Lectures on the Principles of Political Obligation and Other Essays*. Ed. Paul Harris and John Morrow. Cambridge: Cambridge University Press, 1986.

Griffin, Susan. *Pornography and Silence: Culture's Revenge Against Nature*. New York: Harper and Row, 1981.

———. *Woman and Nature: The Roaring Inside Her*. New York: Harper and Row, 1978.

Grimshaw, Jean. *Philosophy and Feminist Thinking*. Minneapolis: University of Minnesota Press, 1986.

Hand, Learned. *The Bill of Rights*. 1961. New York: Atheneum, 1974.

Haraway, Donna J. *Simians, Cyborgs, and Women: The Reinvention of Nature*. New York: Routledge, Chapman and Hall, 1991.

Harding, Sandra. *The Science Question in Feminism*. Ithaca, N.Y.: Cornell University Press, 1986.

———. *Whose Science? Whose Knowledge? Thinking from Women's Lives*. Ithaca, N.Y.: Cornell University Press, 1991.

Harding, Sandra, and Jean F. O'Barr, eds. *Sex and Scientific Inquiry*. Chicago: University of Chicago Press, 1987.

Harrington, Mona. *Women Lawyers: Rewriting the Rules*. New York: Alfred A. Knopf, 1994.

Harris, Amy Bjork, and Thomas A. Harris. *Staying OK*. New York: Harper and Row, 1985.

Hartsock, Nancy. *Money, Sex, and Power: Toward a Feminist Historical Materialism.* New York: Longman, 1983.

Hawkesworth, M. E. *Beyond Oppression: Feminist Theory and Political Strategy.* New York: Continuum, 1990.

Hirsch, H. N. *The Enigma of Felix Frankfurter.* New York: Basic Books, 1981.

Hirschmann, Nancy J. *Rethinking Obligation: A Feminist Method for Political Theory.* Ithaca, N.Y.: Cornell University Press, 1992.

Hobbes, Thomas. *Leviathan.* (1651). Ed. Michael Oakeshott. New York: Collier Books, 1962.

Hobhouse, L. T. *Liberalism.* Introduction by Alan P. Grimes. (1911). Oxford: Oxford University Press, 1964.

Hochschild, Arlie Russell. *The Time Bind: When Work Becomes Home and Home Becomes Work.* New York: Metropolitan Books, 1997.

Hochschild, Arlie, with Anne Machung. *The Second Shift: Working Parents and the Revolution at Home.* New York: Viking, 1989.

Hooks, Bell. *Ain't I a Woman? Black Women and Feminism.* Boston: South End Press, 1981.

———. *Feminist Theory: From Margin to Center.* Boston: South End Press, 1984.

Hull, Gloria T., Patricia Bell Scott, and Barbara Smith, eds. *All the Women Are White, All the Blacks Are Men, but Some of Us Are Brave.* Old Westbury, N.Y.: Feminist Press, 1982.

Irigaray, Luce. *Speculum of the Other Woman.* Trans. Gillian C. Gill. Ithaca, N.Y.: Cornell University Press, 1985.

———. *This Sex Which Is Not One.* Trans. Catherine Porter with Carolyn Burke. Ithaca, N.Y.: Cornell University Press, 1985.

Jackson, Robert H. *The Struggle for Judicial Supremacy.* New York: Alfred A. Knopf, 1941.

Jaggar, Alison M. *Feminist Politics and Human Nature.* Totowa, N.J.: Rowman and Allanheld, 1983.

Jaggar, Alison M., and Susan R. Bordo, eds. *Gender/Body/Knowledge: Feminist Reconstructions of Being and Knowing.* New Brunswick, N.J.: Rutgers University Press, 1989.

Kammen, Michael. *A Machine That Would Go of Itself: The Constitution in American Culture.* New York: St. Martin's Press, 1994.

Kanowitz, Leo. *Women and the Law: The Unfinished Revolution.* Rev. ed. Albuquerque: University of New Mexico Press, 1969.

Keller, Evelyn Fox. *A Feeling for the Organism: The Life and Work of Barbara McClintock.* San Francisco: W. H. Freeman, 1983.

———. *Reflections on Gender and Science.* New Haven, Conn.: Yale University Press, 1985.

Kenney, Sally J. *For Whose Protection? Reproductive Hazards and Exclusionary Policies in the United States and Britain.* Ann Arbor: University of Michigan Press, 1992.

Kittay, Eva Feder, and Diana T. Meyers, eds. *Women and Moral Theory.* Totowa, N.J.: Rowman and Littlefield, 1987.

Kitzinger, Sheila. *The Complete Book of Pregnancy and Childbirth.* Revised and expanded. New York: Alfred A. Knopf, 1989.

Kluger, Richard. *Simple Justice.* New York: Vintage Books, 1975.

Kuhn, Thomas S. *The Structure of Scientific Revolutions*. 2d ed. Chicago: University of Chicago Press, 1970.

Lacan, Jacques. *The Four Fundamental Concepts of Psychoanalysis*. Trans. Alan Sheridan. New York: W. W. Norton, 1978.

———. *The Language of the Self: The Function of Language in Psychoanalysis*. Trans. Anthony Wilden. Baltimore: Johns Hopkins University Press, 1968.

Lasch, Christopher. *Haven in a Heartless World: The Family Besieged*. New York: Basic Books, 1977.

———. *The Minimal Self: Psychic Survival in Troubled Times*. New York: W. W. Norton, 1984.

Levi, Edward H. *An Introduction to Legal Reasoning*. Chicago: University of Chicago Press, 1949.

Lewis, Anthony. *Gideon's Trumpet*. New York: Vintage Books, 1964.

Luker, Kristin. *Abortion and the Politics of Motherhood*. Berkeley: University of California Press, 1984.

———. *Dubious Conceptions: The Politics of Teenage Pregnancy*. Cambridge, Mass.: Harvard University Press, 1996.

MacIntyre, Alasdair. *After Virtue*. 2d ed. Notre Dame, Ind.: University of Notre Dame Press, 1984.

MacKinnon, Catharine A. *Feminism Unmodified*. Cambridge, Mass.: Harvard University Press, 1987.

———. *Only Words*. Cambridge, Mass.: Harvard University Press, 1993.

———. *Sexual Harassment of Working Women*. New Haven, Conn.: Yale University Press, 1979.

———. *Toward a Feminist Theory of the State*. Cambridge, Mass.: Harvard University Press, 1989.

MacNair, Rachel, Mary Krane Derr, and Linda Naranjo-Huebl, eds. *Prolife Feminism: Yesterday and Today*. New York: Sulzburger and Graham, 1995.

Marks, Elaine, and Isabelle de Courtivron, eds. *New French Feminisms*. Amherst: University of Massachusetts Press, 1980.

Mason, Alpheus Thomas, and Donald Grier Stephenson, Jr. *American Constitutional Law*. 9th ed. Englewood Cliffs, N.J.: Prentice-Hall, 1990.

Mason, Mary Ann. *The Equality Trap: Why Working Women Shouldn't Be Treated Like Men*. New York: Simon and Schuster, 1988.

———. *From Father's Property to Children's Rights: The History of Child Custody in the United States*. New York: Columbia University Press, 1995.

McCorvey, Norma, with Andy Meisler. *I Am Roe: My Life*, Roe v. Wade, *and Freedom of Choice*. New York: HarperCollins, 1994.

McDonagh, Eileen L. *Breaking the Abortion Deadlock: From Choice to Consent*. New York: Oxford University Press, 1996.

McGlen, Nancy E., and Karen O'Connor. *Women's Rights: The Struggle for Equality in the Nineteenth and Twentieth Centuries*. New York: Praeger, 1983.

McPherson, C. B. *The Political Theory of Possessive Individualism*. Oxford: Clarendon Press, 1962.

Midgley, Mary. *Can't We Make Moral Judgements?* New York: St. Martin's Press, 1991.

Mill, John Stuart. *On Liberty*. 1859.

Minnich, Elizabeth Kamarck. *Transforming Knowledge*. Philadelphia: Temple University Press, 1990.

Mitchell, Juliet. *Psychoanalysis and Feminism*. New York: Pantheon Books, 1974.

——. *Woman's Estate*. New York: Pantheon Books, 1971.

Moi, Toril, ed. *French Feminist Thought*. New York: Basil Blackwell, 1987.

——. *The Kristeva Reader*. New York: Columbia University Press, 1986.

Moore, Wilbert E. *The Professions: Roles and Rules*. New York: Russell Sage Foundation, 1970.

Murphy, Bruce Allen. *The Brandeis-Frankfurter Connection*. New York: Oxford University Press, 1982.

Murphy, Walter F. *Elements of Judicial Strategy*. Chicago: University of Chicago Press, 1964.

Murphy, Walter F., James E. Fleming, and William F. Harris II. *American Constitutional Interpretation*. Mineola, N.Y.: Foundation Press, 1986.

Neustadt, Richard E. *Presidential Power*. New York: Wiley, 1960.

Newman, Graeme R. *Just and Painful*. London: Macmillan, 1983.

Newman, Katharine. *Declining Fortunes: The Withering of the American Dream*. New York: Basic Books, 1993.

Nicholson, Linda J., ed. *Feminism/Postmodernism*. New York: Routledge, Chapman, and Hall, 1990.

Nielsen, Joyce McCarl, ed. *Feminist Research Methods*. Boulder, Colo.: Westview Press, 1990.

The 1985 Virginia Slims American Women's Opinion Poll. Storrs, Conn.: Roper Center, 1985.

Noddings, Nel. *Caring: A Feminine Approach to Ethics and Moral Education*. Berkeley: University of California Press, 1984.

O'Brien, Mary. *The Politics of Reproduction*. Boston: Routledge and Kegan Paul, 1981.

——. *Reproducing the World: Essays in Feminist Theory*. Boulder, Colo.: Westview Press, 1989.

Okin, Susan Moller. *Justice, Gender, and the Family*. New York: Basic Books, 1989.

——. *Women in Western Political Thought*. Princeton, N.J.: Princeton University Press, 1979.

Paglia, Camille. *Sex, Art, and American Culture*. New York: Vintage Books, 1992.

——. *Sexual Personae: Art and Decadence from Nefertiti to Emily Dickinson*. New Haven, Conn.: Yale University Press, 1990.

Pateman, Carole. *The Disorder of Women: Democracy, Feminism and Political Theory*. Stanford, Calif.: Stanford University Press, 1989.

——. *The Sexual Contract*. Stanford, Calif: Stanford University Press, 1988.

Pearsall, Marilyn, ed. *Women and Values: Readings in Recent Feminist Philosophy*. 2d ed. Belmont, Calif.: Wadsworth, 1993.

Peltason, Jack W. *Corwin and Peltason's "Understanding the Constitution."* 11th ed. New York: Holt, Rinehart, and Winston, 1988.

Perry, Michael. *The Constitution, the Courts, and Human Rights*. New Haven, Conn.: Yale University Press, 1982.

Piercy, Marge. *Small Changes*. New York: Fawcett Crest, 1973.

Plato. *The Republic*.

Ragland-Sullivan, Ellie. *Jacques Lacan and the Philosophy of Psychoanalysis.* Champaign-Urbana: University of Illinois Press, 1986.

Rasmussen, David, ed. *Universalism vs. Communitarianism: Contemporary Debates in Ethics.* Cambridge, Mass.: MIT Press, 1990.

Rawls, John. *Political Liberalism.* New York: Columbia University Press, 1993.

———. *A Theory of Justice.* Cambridge, Mass.: Belknap Press of Harvard University Press, 1971.

Raymond, Janice G. *Women as Wombs: Reproductive Technologies and the Battle over Women's Freedom.* New York: HarperCollins, 1993.

Rhode, Deborah L. *Justice and Gender: Sex Discrimination and the Law.* Cambridge, Mass.: Harvard University Press, 1989.

———, ed. *Theoretical Perspectives on Sexual Difference.* New Haven, Conn.: Yale University Press, 1990.

Rich, Adrienne. *Blood, Bread, and Poetry: Selected Prose 1979–1985.* New York: W. W. Norton, 1986.

———. *Of Woman Born: Motherhood as Experience and Institution.* New York: W. W. Norton, 1976.

———. *On Lies, Secrets, and Silence: Selected Prose 1966–1978.* New York: W. W. Norton, 1979.

Robertson, John A. *Children of Choice: Freedom and the New Reproductive Technologies.* Princeton, N.J.: Princeton University Press, 1994.

Rorty, Richard. *Essays on Heidegger and Others.* Cambridge: Cambridge University Press, 1991.

———. *Objectivity, Relativism, and Truth.* Cambridge: Cambridge University Press, 1991.

———. *Philosophy and the Mirror of Nature.* Princeton, N.J.: Princeton University Press, 1979.

Rosenblatt, Roger. *Life Itself: Abortion in the American Mind.* New York: Random House, 1992.

Rossum, Ralph A., and G. Alan Tarr. *American Constitutional Law.* 3d ed. New York: St. Martin's Press, 1991.

Rothman, Barbara Katz. *Recreating Motherhood.* New York: W. W. Norton, 1989.

Ruddick, Sara. *Maternal Thinking: Toward a Politics of Peace.* New York: Ballantine Books, 1990.

Ryan, William. *Blaming the Victim.* Revised, updated edition. New York: Vintage Books, 1976.

Sachs, Albie, and Joan Hoff Wilson. *Sexism and the Law.* New York: Free Press, 1979.

Sadker, Myra, and David Sadker. *Failing at Fairness: How America's Schools Cheat Girls.* New York: Scribner's, Sons, 1994.

Sandel, Michael J. *Democracy's Discontent: America in Search of a Public Philosophy.* Cambridge, Mass.: Belknap Press of Harvard University Press, 1996.

———. *Liberalism and the Limits of Justice.* Cambridge: Cambridge University Press, 1982.

———, ed. *Liberalism and Its Critics.* New York: New York University Press, 1984.

Schattschneider, E. E. *The Semisovereign People.* New York: Holt, Rinehart, and Winston, Inc., 1960.

Schor, Juliet. *The Overworked American: The Unexpected Decline of Leisure*. New York: Basic Books, 1991.

Schwab, Peter, and Adamantia Pollis, eds. *Toward a Human Rights Framework*. New York: Praeger Publishers, 1982.

Seaman, Barbara. *Free and Female*. New York: Fawcett Crest, 1972.

Sellers, Susan. *Writing Differences: Readings from the Seminar of Hélène Cixous*. New York: St. Martin's Press, 1988.

Sidel, Ruth. *Keeping Women and Children Last: America's War on the Poor*. New York: Penguin Books, 1996.

———. *Women and Children Last: The Plight of Poor Women in Affluent America*. New York: Viking, 1986.

Silverman, Hugh J., ed. *Derrida and Deconstruction*. New York: Routledge, 1989.

———. *Postmodernism: Philosophy and the Arts*. New York: Routledge, 1990.

Slater, Philip. *Earthwalk*. Garden City, N.Y.: Anchor Books, 1974.

———. *The Pursuit of Loneliness*. Boston: Beacon Press, 1970.

Sloan, Don, with Paula Hartz. *Abortion: A Doctor's Perspective, A Woman's Dilemma*. New York: Donald I. Fine, 1992.

Smart, Carol. *Feminism and the Power of Law*. New York: Routledge, 1989.

Smith, Barbara, ed. *Home Girls: A Black Feminist Anthology*. New York: Kitchen Table—Women of Color Press, 1983.

Smith, Dorothy E. *The Conceptual Practices of Power: A Feminist Sociology of Knowledge*. Boston: Northeastern University Press, 1990.

———. *The Everyday World as Problematic: A Feminist Sociology*. Boston: Northeastern University Press, 1987.

Smith, Lendon. *Feed Your Kids Right*. New York: McGraw-Hill, 1979.

Smith, Rogers M. *Liberalism and American Constitutional Law*. Cambridge, Mass.: Harvard University Press, 1985.

Snitow, Ann, Christine Stansell, and Sharon Thompson, eds. *Powers of Desire: The Politics of Sexuality*. New York: Monthly Review Press, 1983.

Sommers, Christina Hoff. *Who Stole Feminism? How Women Have Betrayed Women*. New York: Simon and Schuster, 1994.

Spock, Benjamin. *The Common Sense Book of Baby and Child Care*. New York: Duell, Sloan, and Pierce, 1946.

Strossen, Nadine. *Defending Pornography: Free Speech, Sex, and the Fight for Women's Rights*. New York: Anchor Books, 1995.

Takas, Marianne. *Child Custody*. New York: Harper and Row, 1987.

Tavris, Carol. *The Mismeasure of Woman*. New York: Simon and Schuster, 1992.

Thorne, Barrie. *Gender Play: Girls and Boys in School*. New Brunswick, N.J.: Rutgers University Press, 1993.

Tocqueville, Alexis de (1832). *Democracy in America*. Trans. George Lawrence. Ed. J. P. Mayer. New York: Doubleday, 1969.

Tong, Rosemarie. *Feminine and Feminist Ethics*. Belmont, Calif.: Wadsworth, 1993.

———. *Feminist Thought: A Comprehensive Introduction*. Boulder, Colo.: Westview Press, 1989.

———. *Women, Sex, and the Law*. Savage, Md.: Rowman and Littlefield, 1984.

Traub, James. *City on a Hill: Testing the American Dream at City College*. Reading, Mass.: Addison-Wesley, 1994.

Trebilcot, Joyce, ed. *Mothering: Essays in Feminist Theory.* Totowa, N.J.: Rowman and Allanheld, 1983.

Tribe, Laurence H. *Abortion: The Clash of Absolutes.* Cambridge, Mass.: Harvard University Press, 1992.

———. *Constitutional Choices.* Cambridge, Mass.: Harvard University Press, 1985.

Tronto, Joan C. *Moral Boundaries: A Political Argument for an Ethic of Care.* New York: Routledge, 1993.

Unger, Roberto Mangabeira. *The Critical Legal Studies Movement.* Cambridge, Mass.: Harvard University Press, 1986.

———. *Knowledge and Politics.* New York: Free Press, 1975.

van den Haag, Ernest. *Punishing Criminals.* Lanham, Md.: University Press of America, 1991.

Walker, Lenore. *The Battered Woman Syndrome.* New York: Springer, 1984.

———. *Terrifying Love: Why Battered Women Kill and How Society Responds.* New York: Harper Perennial, 1989.

Wallerstein, Judith S. *Second Chances: Men, Women, and Children a Decade After Divorce.* New York: Ticknor and Fields, 1989.

Wallerstein, Judith S., and Joan Kelly. *Surviving the Breakup: How Children and Parents Cope with Divorce.* New York: Basic Books, 1980.

Walzer, Michael. *Spheres of Justice: A Defense of Pluralism and Equality.* New York: Basic Books, 1983.

Wechsler, Herbert. *Principles, Politics, and Fundamental Law.* Cambridge, Mass.: Harvard University Press, 1961.

Weinreb, Lloyd. *Oedipus at Fenway Park: What Rights Are and Why There Are Any.* Cambridge, Mass.: Harvard University Press, 1994.

Weitzman, Lenore. *The Divorce Revolution.* New York: Free Press, 1986.

Williams, Patricia J. *The Alchemy of Race and Rights.* Cambridge, Mass.: Harvard University Press, 1991.

Woodward, Bob, and Scott Armstrong. *The Brethren.* New York: Simon and Schuster, 1979.

Young, Iris Marion. *Justice and the Politics of Difference.* Princeton, N.J.: Princeton University Press, 1990.

———. *Throwing Like a Girl and Other Essays in Feminist Philosophy and Social Theory.* Bloomington: Indiana University Press, 1990.

ARTICLES

Alexander, Caroline. "Teaching the Classics in Malawi." *New Yorker,* 16 December 1991, 53–88.

Arditti, Joyce. "Women, Divorce, and Economic Risk." *Family and Conciliation Courts Review* 35 (January 1997): 79–89.

Auerbach, Judy, Linda Blum, Vicki Smith, and Christine Williams. "On Gilligan's *In a Different Voice." Feminist Studies* 11 (Spring 1985): 149–61.

Baer, Judith A. "The Fruitless Search for Original Intent." In *Judging the Constitution,* ed. Michael W. McCann and Gerald L. Houseman, 49–71. Boston: Little, Brown, 1989.

Baer, Judith A. "How Is Law Male? A Feminist Perspective on Constitutional Interpretation." In *Feminist Jurisprudence: The Difference Debate*, ed. Leslie Friedman Goldstein, 147–71. Lanham, Md.: Rowman and Littlefield, 1992.

———. "Nasty Law or Nice Ladies? Jurisprudence, Feminism, and Gender Difference." *Women and Politics* 11 (1991): 1–31.

———. "Reading the Fourteenth Amendment: The Inevitability of Noninterpretivism." In National Center for the Public Interest, *Politics and the Constitution: The Nature and Extent of Interpretation*, 69–82. Washington, D.C.: American Studies Center, 1990.

———. "What We Know as Women: A New Look at *Roe v. Wade*." *NWSA Journal* 2 (Autumn 1990): 558–82.

———. "Women's Rights and the Limits of Constitutional Doctrine." *Western Political Quarterly* 42 (December 1991): 821–52.

Bartlett, Katharine T., "Feminist Legal Methods." *Harvard Law Review* 103 (February 1990): 829–88.

Beal, Ron. " 'Can I Sue Mommy?' An Analysis of Women's Tort Liability for Prenatal Injuries to Her Child Born Alive." *San Diego Law Review* 21 (March 1984): 325–70.

Becker, Mary E. "From *Muller v. Oregon* to Fetal Vulnerability Policies." *University of Chicago Law Review* 53 (Fall 1986): 1219–73.

———. "Prince Charming: Abstract Equality." In *Feminist Jurisprudence: The Difference Debate*, ed. Leslie Friedman Goldstein, 99–146. Lanham, Md.: Rowman and Littlefield, 1992.

Behuniak-Long, Susan. "Justice Sandra Day O'Connor and the Power of Maternal Legal Thinking." *Review of Politics* 54 (Summer 1992): 417–44.

Binion, Gayle. " 'Intent' and Equal Protection: A Reconsideration." *Supreme Court Review*, 1983: 397–457.

———. "Toward a Feminist Regrounding of Constitutional Law." *Social Science Quarterly* 72 (July 1991): 207–20.

Brennan, William J., Jr. "The Constitution of the United States: Contemporary Ratification." October 12, 1985. Text and Teaching Symposium, Georgetown University, Washington, D.C.

Brown, Wendy. "Consciousness Razing." *The Nation*, 8/15 January 1990, 61–64.

———. "Reproductive Freedom and the Right to Privacy: A Paradox for Feminists." In *Families, Politics, and Public Policy*, ed. Irene Diamond, 322–39. New York: Longman, 1983.

Chambers, David L. "Rethinking the Substantive Rules for Custody Disputes in Divorce." *Michigan Law Review* 83 (December 1984): 480–569.

Colker, Ruth. "An Equal Protection Analysis of United States Public Health Policy: Gender, Race, Age, and Class." *Duke Law Review* 1991: 324–64.

———. "Feminism, Sexuality, and Self: A Preliminary Inquiry into the Politics of Authenticity." *Boston University Law Review* 68 (1988): 217–64.

———. "Conception, Pregnancy, and Birth." *Vanderbilt Law Review* 39 (April 1986): 602–850.

Cramton, Roger. "The Ordinary Religion of the Law School Classroom." *Journal of Legal Education* 29 (1978): 247–63.

Danelski, David J. "The Influence of the Chief Justice in the Decisional Process" (1960). In *Courts, Judges, and Politics*, ed. Walter F. Murphy and C. Herman Pritchett. Fourth edition, 568–77. New York: Random House, 1986.

Delgado, Richard. "Storytelling for Oppositionists and Others: A Plea for Narrative." *Michigan Law Review* 87 (August 1989): 2411–41.

Dershowitz, Alan M. "Drawing the Line on Prenatal Rights." *Los Angeles Times*, 14 May 1989.

———. "The Sovereignty of Process: The Limits of Original Intention." In National Center for the Public Interest, *Politics and the Constitution: The Nature and Extent of Interpretation*, 11–16. Washington, D.C.: American Studies Center, 1990.

"Developments in the Law—Medical Technology and the Law." *Harvard Law Review* 103 (May 1990): 1520–1676.

Dworkin, Ronald M. "Unenumerated Rights: Whether and How *Roe* Should Be Overturned." *University of Chicago Law Review* 59 (Winter 1992): 381–432.

Elshtain, Jean Bethke. "If You're An Addict, It's Now a Crime to Give Birth." *The Progressive*, December 1990, 26–28.

Ericksen, Julia A., William L. Yancey, and Eugene P. Ericksen. "The Division of Family Roles." *Journal of Marriage and the Family* 41 (May 1979): 301–13.

Feinberg, Joel. "Wrongful Conception and the Right Not to Be Harmed." *Harvard Journal of Law and Public Policy* 8 (Winter 1985): 57–77.

Fellows, Mary Louise, and Sherene Razack. "Seeking Relations: Law and Feminism Roundtables." *Signs* 19 (Summer 1994): 1048–83.

"Feminist Discourse, Moral Values, and the Law—A Conversation." *Buffalo Law Review* 34 (Fall 1985): 11–87.

Ferguson, Kathy E. "Knowledge, Politics, and Persons in Feminist Theory." *Political Theory* 17 (May 1989): 302–14.

Fineman, Martha L. "Implementing Inequality." *Wisconsin Law Review*, no. 4 (1983): 789–887.

Fineman, Martha L., and Anne Opie. "The Uses of Social Science Data in Legal Policymaking: Custody Determinations at Divorce." *Wisconsin Law Review*, no. 1 (1987): 107–58.

Finley, Lucinda. "Transcending Equality Theory: A Way Out of the Maternity and the Workplace Debate." *Columbia Law Review* 86 (October 1986): 1118–82.

Flannery, Maureen A. "Simple Living and Hard Choices." In *Before the Law: An Introduction to the Legal Process*, 4th ed., John J. Bonsignore, Ethan Katsh, Peter d'Errico, Ronald M. Pipkin, Stephen Arons, and Janet Rifkin. 54–60. Boston: Houghton Mifflin, 1989.

Fletcher, John C. "The Fetus as Patient: Ethical Issues." *Journal of the American Medical Association* 246 (14 August 1981): 772–73.

Freud, Sigmund. "Femininity." In *New Introductory Lectures in Psychoanalysis*, trans. James Strachey, 112–35. New York: W. W. Norton, 1964.

———. "Some Psychological Consequences of the Anatomical Distinction Between the Sexes." *International Journal of Psychoanalysis* 7 (January 1927): 133–42.

Gallagher, Janet. "Prenatal Invasions and Interventions: What's Wrong with Fetal Rights." *Harvard Women's Law Journal* 10 (Spring 1987): 9–58.

George, Kathryn Paxton. "Should Feminists Be Vegetarians?" *Signs* 19 (Winter 1994): 405–34.

Glassman, Carol. "Women and the Welfare System." In *Sisterhood Is Powerful*, ed. Robin Morgan, 102–15. New York: Random House, 1970.

Goldberg, Susan. "Medical Choices During Pregnancy: Whose Decision Is It Anyway?" *Rutgers Law Review* 41 (Winter 1989): 591–623.

Grabar, Mary. "Sending Women to Jail Is Not the Answer." *The Progressive*, December 1990, 22–24.

Graber, Mark A. "Old Wine in New Bottles: The Constitutional Status of Unconstitutional Speech." *Vanderbilt Law Review* 48 (1995): 349–89.

Greenwood-Audant, Lois. "The Internalization of Powerlessness: A Case Study of the Displaced Homemaker." In *Women: A Feminist Perspective*, 2d ed., ed. Jo Freeman, 264–81. Palo Alto, Calif.: Mayfield, 1979.

Guinier, Lani, Michelle Fine, and Jane Balin, with Ann Bartow and Deborah Lee Stachel. "Becoming Gentlemen: Women's Experiences at One Ivy League Law School." *University of Pennsylvania Law Review* 143 (November 1994): 1–110.

Gutmann, Amy. "Communitarian Critiques of Liberalism." *Philosophy and Public Affairs* 4 (Summer 1985): 308–22.

Haas-Wilson, Deborah. "The Impact of State Abortion Restrictions on Minors' Demand for Abortions." *Journal of Human Resources* 31 (Winter 1996): 140–58.

Harris, Angela. "Race and Essentialism in Feminist Legal Theory." *Stanford Law Review* 42 (February 1990): 581–616.

Harris, William F., II. "Bonding Word and Polity: The Logic of American Constitutionalism." *American Political Science Review* 76 (March 1982): 34–45.

Hawkesworth, Mary E. "Knowers, Knowing, Known: Feminist Theory and Claims of Truth." *Signs* 14 (Spring 1989): 533–57.

Hekman, Susan. "The Embodiment of the Subject: Feminism and the Communitarian Critique of Liberalism." *Journal of Politics* 54 (November 1992): 1098–119.

Hoffman, Jan. "Pregnant, Addicted—And Guilty?" *New York Times Magazine*, 19 August 1990.

Hoffman, Saul D., and Greg J. Duncan. "What *Are* the Economic Consequences of Divorce?" *Demography* 24 (November 1988): 641–45.

Holmes, Oliver Wendell. "The Path of the Law" (1897). In *Courts, Judges, and Politics*, 4th ed., ed. Walter F. Murphy and C. Herman Pritchett, 20–24. New York: Random House, 1986.

Jacob, Herbert. "Another Look at No-Fault Divorce and the Post-Divorce Finances of Women." *Law and Society Review* 23 (1989): 95–115.

Kaufman, Debra Renee. "Professional Women: How Real Are the Recent Gains?" In *Women: A Feminist Perspective*, 3d ed., ed. Jo Freeman, 353–69. Palo Alto, Calif.: Mayfield, 1984.

Kay, Herma Hill. "Equality and Difference: The Case of Pregnancy." *Berkeley Women's Law Journal* 1 (Fall 1985): 1–38.

Keller, Evelyn Fox. "Feminism and Science." In *Sex and Scientific Inquiry*, ed. Sandra Harding and Jean F. O'Barr, 232–46. Chicago: University of Chicago Press, 1987.

Kelly, Alfred H. "Clio and the Court: An Illicit Love Affair." *Supreme Court Review* 1965: 119–58.

Kennedy, Duncan. "Legal Education as Training for Hierarchy." In *The Politics of Law: A Progressive Critique*, ed. David Kairys, 40–61. New York: Pantheon Books, 1982.

Koppelman, Andrew. "Forced Labor: A Thirteenth Amendment Defense of Abortion." *Northwestern University Law Review* 84 (Winter 1990): 480–535.

Littleton, Christine A. "Reconstructing Sexual Equality." *California Law Review* 75 (July 1987): 1279–337.

"A Maternal Duty to Protect Fetal Health?" *Indiana Law Journal* 58 (1983): 531–46.

"Maternal Liability: Courts Strive to Keep Doors Open to Fetal Protection—But Can They Succeed?" *John Marshall Law Review* 20 (Summer 1987): 747–68.

"Maternal Substance Abuse: The Next Step in the Protection of Fetal Rights?" *Dickenson Law Review* 92 (Spring 1988): 691–715.

Mathieu, Deborah. "Respecting Liberty and Preventing Harm: Limits of State Intervention in Prenatal Choice." *Harvard Journal of Law and Public Policy* 8 (Winter 1985): 19–55.

Matsuda, Mari J. "Looking to the Bottom: Critical Legal Studies and Reparations." *Harvard Civil Rights–Civil Liberties Law Review* 22 (Spring 1987): 323–99.

———. "When the First Quail Calls: Multiple Consciousness as Jurisprudential Method." *Women's Rights Law Reporter* 11 (Spring 1989): 7–10.

McClain, Linda C. " 'Atomistic Man' Revisited: Liberalism, Connection, and Feminist Jurisprudence." *Southern California Law Review* 65 (March 1992): 1171–264.

McDonagh, Eileen Lorenzi. "Abortion Rights Alchemy and the U.S. Supreme Court: What's Wrong and How to Fix It." *Social Politics* 1 (Summer 1994): 130–56.

———. "Good, Bad, and Captive Samaritans: Adding-In Pregnancy and Consent to the Abortion Debate." *Women and Politics* 13, no. 3/4 (1993): 31–49.

Mead, Margaret. "Some Theoretical Considerations on the Problem of Mother-Child Separation." *American Journal of Orthopsychiatry* 24 (July 1954): 471–83.

Meese, Edwin, III. "Toward a Jurisprudence of Original Intention." 9 July 1985. Address to the American Bar Association.

Minow, Martha. " 'Forming Underneath Everything That Grows': Toward a History of Family Law." *Wisconsin Law Review*, no. 4 (1985): 819–88.

Mnookin, Robert H., and Lewis Kornhauser. "Bargaining in the Shadow of the Law: The Case of Divorce." *Yale Law Journal* 88 (April 1979): 950–97.

Mossman, Mary Jane. "Feminism and Legal Method: The Difference It Makes." *Australian Journal of Law and Society* 3 (1986): 30–52.

Murray, Pauli, and Mary Eastwood. "Jane Crow and the Law: Sex Discrimination and Title VII." *George Washington Law Review* 34 (December 1965): 232–56.

Nedelsky, Jennifer. "Reconceiving Autonomy." *Yale Journal of Law and Feminism* 1 (Spring 1989): 7–36.

Neff, Christyne L. "Woman, Womb, and Bodily Integrity." *Yale Journal of Law and Feminism* 3 (Spring 1991): 327–53.

Note. "The Creation of Fetal Rights: Conflicts with Women's Constitutional Rights to Liberty, Privacy, and Reproduction." *Yale Law Journal* 95 (January 1986): 599–625.

Note. "Getting Beyond Discrimination: A Regulatory Solution to the Problem of Fetal Hazards in the Workplace." *Yale Law Journal* 95 (January 1986): 577–98.

Offen, Karen. "Defining Feminism: A Comparative Historical Approach." *Signs* 14 (Autumn 1988): 119–57.

Olsen, Frances. "The Family and the Market: A Study of Ideology and Legal Reform." *Harvard Law Review* 96 (May 1983): 1497–578.

———. "Unraveling Compromise." *Harvard Law Review* 103 (November 1989): 105–35.

O'Neill, Timothy J. "The Language of Equality in Constitutional Order." *American Political Science Review* 75 (September 1981): 626–35.

Ong, Walter. Review of Brian Vickers' *Classic Rhetoric in English Poetry. College English* 33 (February 1972): 612–16.

Polikoff, Nancy. "Gender and Child Custody Determinations: Exploding the Myths." In *Families, Politics, and Public Policy*, ed. Irene Diamond, 183–202. New York: Longman, 1983.

———. "Why Mothers Are Losing: A Brief Analysis of Criteria Used in Child Custody Determinations." *Women's Rights Law Reporter* 7 (Spring 1982): 235–43.

Pollitt, Katha. "Are Women Morally Superior to Men?" *The Nation*, 28 December 1992, 799–807.

———. " 'Fetal Rights': A New Assault on Feminism." *The Nation*, 26 March 1990, 409–18.

Posner, Richard A. "Reasoning from the Top Down and from the Bottom Up: The Question of Unenumerated Constitutional Rights." *University of Chicago Law Review* 59 (Winter 1992): 433–50.

"Pregnancy Police: The Health Policy and Legal Implications of Punishing Pregnant Women for Harm to Their Fetuses." *New York University Review of Law and Social Change* 16 (1988): 277–319.

Radin, Margaret Jane. "The Pragmatist and the Feminist." *Southern California Law Review* 63 (September 1990): 1699–726.

Rehnquist, William H. "The Notion of a Living Constitution." *Texas Law Review* 54 (May 1976): 693–706.

Reich, Charles A. "Individual Rights and Social Welfare: The Emerging Legal Issues." *Yale Law Journal* 74 (March 1965): 1245–57.

———. "The New Property." *Yale Law Journal* 73 (April 1964): 733–87.

Rhode, Deborah L. "Equal Protection and Gender Justice." In *Judging the Constitution*, ed. Michael W. McCann and Gerald L. Houseman, 265–286. Boston: Little, Brown, 1989.

———. "Feminist Critical Theories." *Stanford Law Review* 42 (February 1990): 617–38.

Rhoden, Nancy K. "The Judge in the Delivery Room: The Emergence of Court-Ordered Caesareans." *California Law Review* 74 (December 1986): 1951–2030.

Rhodenbaugh, Suzanne. "Catharine MacKinnon, May I Speak?" *Michigan Quarterly Review* 30 (Summer 1991): 415–22.

Roberts, Dorothy E. "Punishing Drug Addicts Who Have Babies: Women of Color, Equality, and the Right of Privacy." *Harvard Law Review* 104 (May 1991): 1419–482.

———. "Social Justice, Procreative Liberty, and the Limits of Liberal Theory: Robertson's *Children of Choice*." *Law and Social Inquiry* 20 (Fall 1995): 1005–21.

Robertson, John A. "Liberalism and the Limits of Procreative Liberty: A Response to My Critics." *Washington and Lee Law Review* 52 (1995): 233–67.

———. "Procreative Liberty and the Control of Conception, Pregnancy, and Childbirth." *Virginia Law Review* 69 (April 1983): 405–64.

———. "The Right to Procreate and in Utero Fetal Therapy." *Journal of Legal Medicine* 3 (September 1982): 333–66.

Rockwell, David N. "The Education of the Capitalist Lawyer: The Law School." In *Law Against the People*, ed. Robert Lefcourt, 90–104. New York: Vintage Books, 1971.

Rosen, Ruth. "What Feminist Victory in the Court?" *New York Times*, 1 April 1991.

Rosenblum, Nancy L. "Civil Societies: Liberalism and the Moral Uses of Pluralism." *Social Research* 61 (Fall 1994): 539–62.

Rosenthal, Elizabeth. "When a Pregnant Woman Drinks." *New York Times Magazine*, 4 February 1990.

Rubin, Gayle. "The Traffic in Women: Notes on the Political Economy of Sex." In *Toward an Anthropology of Women*, ed. Rayna Rapp Reiter, 157–210. New York: Monthly Review Press, 1975.

Ruddick, Sara. "Maternal Thinking." In *Mothering: Essays in Feminist Theory*, ed. Joyce Trebilcot, 213–30. Totowa, N.J.: Rowman and Allanheld, 1983.

Savoy, Paul. "Toward a New Politics of Legal Education." *Yale Law Journal* 79 (January 1970): 444–504.

Scales, Ann M. "The Emergence of Feminist Jurisprudence: An Essay." *Yale Law Journal* 95 (June 1986): 1373–403.

Schneider, Elizabeth M. "The Dialectic of Rights and Politics: Perspectives from the Women's Movement." *New York University Law Review* 61 (October 1986): 589–652.

Shaw, Margery W. "Constitutional Prospective Rights of the Fetus." *Journal of Legal Medicine* 5 (March 1984): 63–116.

Sher, George. "Other Voices, Other Rooms? Women's Psychology and Moral Theory." In *Women and Moral Theory*, ed. Eva Feder Kittay and Diana T. Meyers, 178–89. Totowa, N.J.: Rowman and Littlefield, 1987.

Sherry, Suzanna. "Civic Virtue and the Feminine Voice in Constitutional Adjudication." *Virginia Law Review* 72 (April 1986): 543–616.

Siegel, Reva. "Reasoning from the Body: A Historical Perspective on Abortion Regulation and Questions of Equal Protection." *Stanford Law Review* 44 (January 1992): 261–381.

Stacey, Judith. "On Resistance, Ambivalence and Feminist Theory: A Response to Carol Gilligan." *Michigan Quarterly Review* 29 (Fall 1990): 537–46.

Steele, Shelby. "A Negative Vote on Affirmative Action." *New York Times Magazine*, 13 May 1990.

Strauss, David A. "Abortion, Toleration and Moral Uncertainty." *Supreme Court Review* 1992: 1–28.

Strebeigh, Fred. "Defining Law on the Feminist Frontier." *New York Times Magazine*, 6 October 1991.

Sunstein, Cass R. "Neutrality in Constitutional Law (With Special Reference to Pornography, Abortion, and Surrogacy)." *Columbia Law Review* 92 (January 1992): 1–52.

Tabler, Norman Gardner, Jr. "Paternal Rights in the Illegitimate Child: Some Legitimate Complaints on Behalf of the Unwed Father." *Journal of Family Law* 2 (1971): 231–54.

Taub, Nadine, and Elizabeth M. Schneider. "Perspectives on Women's Subordination and the Role of Law." In *The Politics of Law: A Progressive Critique*, ed. David Kairys, 117–39. New York: Pantheon Books, 1982.

Thomson, Judith Jarvis. "In Defense of Abortion." In *Rights, Restitution, and Risk*, 1–19. Cambridge, Mass.: Harvard University Press, 1986.

Traub, James. "The Hearts and Minds of City College," *New Yorker*, 7 June 1993, 42–53.

Tribe, Laurence H. "The Abortion Funding Conundrum: Inalienable Rights, Affirmative Rules, and the Dilemma of Dependence." *Harvard Law Review* 99 (November 1985): 330–43.

Tronto, Joan C. "Beyond Gender Difference to a Theory of Care." *Signs* 12 (Summer 1987): 644–63.

Ulmer, S. Sidney. "Earl Warren and the *Brown* Decision." *Journal of Politics* 33 (August 1971): 689–702.

Uviller, Rena. "Fathers' Rights and Feminism: The Maternal Presumption Revisited." *Harvard Women's Law Journal* 1 (Spring 1978): 107–21.

Villmoare, Adelaide H. "Women, Differences, and Rights as Practices: An Interpretive Essay and a Proposal." *Law and Society Review* 25 (1991): 385–410.

Watson, Andrew. "The Quest for Professional Competence: Psychological Aspects of Legal Education." *University of Cincinnati Law Review* 37 (Winter 1968): 93–166.

Weitzman, Lenore, and Ruth Dixon. "Child Custody Awards: Legal Standards and Empirical Patterns for Child Custody, Support, and Visitation After Divorce." *University of California, Davis, Law Review* 12 (Summer 1979): 471–521.

Wells, Catharine. "Situated Decisionmaking." *Southern California Law Review* 63 (September 1990): 1727–46.

Wertheimer, Roger. "Understanding the Abortion Argument." *Philosophy and Public Affairs* 1 (Fall 1971): 67–95.

West, Robin. "The Difference in Women's Hedonic Lives: A Phenomenological Critique of Feminist Legal Theory." In *Women and the Law*, ed. Mary Joe Frug, 807–25. Westbury, N.Y.: Foundations Press, 1992.

———. "Feminism, Critical Social Theory and Law." *University of Chicago Law Forum*, no. 1 (1989): 59–97.

———. "Jurisprudence and Gender." *University of Chicago Law Review* 55 (Winter 1988): 1–72.

———. "Taking Freedom Seriously." *Harvard Law Review* 104 (November 1990): 43–106.

Williams, Joan. "Deconstructing Gender." In *Feminist Jurisprudence: The Difference Debate*, ed. Leslie Friedman Goldstein, 41–98. Lanham, Md.: Rowman and Littlefield, 1992.

Williams, Wendy. "Firing the Woman to Protect the Fetus: The Reconciliation of Fetal Protection with Equal Employment Opportunity Goals Under Title VII." *Georgetown Law Journal* 69 (February 1981): 641–704.

Wishik, Heather Ruth. "To Question Everything: The Inquiries of Feminist Jurisprudence." *Berkeley Women's Law Journal* 1 (Fall 1986): 64–77.

GENERAL INDEX

NAMES of parties in court cases are listed only when the person's name does not appear in the case citation. See the Index of Cases for cases listed in the cross-references.

abortion, 9, 56–57, 124–30; and conventional theory, 44; and counter-factual reasoning, 139–41; and equal protection doctrine, 93; and feminist theory, 130–39, 149–50; and fetal protection, 155, 156–67; and fetal status, 133–35; and parental consent, 85; and political discourse, 178; and public opinion, 124, 132; and responsibility, 144–47; and rights theory, 98. *See also* reproductive rights

Ackerman, Bruce, 65, 67, 191–92, 199

affirmative action, 54, 105

Alexander, Caroline, 49–50

alimony, 97, 100–01, 104–7, 224n.21

Allen, Jeffner, 236n.76

Altman, Andrew, 205n.5

American Association of University Women (AAUW), 75

Andersen, Margaret L. 210n.60

Anti-discrimination laws. *See* equal protection doctrine

Arditti, Joyce, 225n.27

Arendell, Terry, 225n.30

Arendt, Hannah, 19, 78

Aristotle, 18–19, 21, 78, 190

Bacon, Francis, 72, 217n.8

Baer, Judith A., 214n.47, 217n.98, 222n.4, 235n.62

Bakan, David, 45, 219n.32

Balbus, Isaac D., 208n.42

Barber, Sotirios A., 234n.54

Barker, Sarah Evans, 228n.64

Bartlett, Katharine T., 82, 90, 93

Beal, Ron, 154, 238n.3, 239n.16

Beauvoir, Simone de, 206n.18, 236n.77

Becker, Mary, 104, 172

Belenky, Mary Field, 73–74

Belkin, Lisa, 231n.19, 242n.67

Bellah, Robert, 45

Bennett, William, 171

Berlin, Isaiah, 211n.2

Bernard, Jessie, 224n.25

biology, gender difference and, 23–26

Bird, Caroline, 224n.25

birth control, 126–28, 138, 140–41, 144–49, 166

birth defects: fetal protection and, 154–56, 170–71; prevention of, 174, 179. *See also* disability

Birthright (pro-life organization), 133

Black, Hugo L., 85–86, 90

Blackmun, Harry J., 83–85, 125–33, 140

Blumstein, Philip, 237n.94

Bordo, Susan, 35–36

Bork, Robert, 90

Bosley, Warren, 158, 167

Bowman, Patricia, 164

Bradley, Joseph, 18

Bremer, Lynn, 168, 241n.38

Brennan, William J., Jr., 83, 85

Brigham, John, 228n.67

Brody, Baruch, 233n.42

Brown, Wendy, 55, 59, 131, 149, 174, 211n.80

Brownmiller, Susan, 111

Brozan, Nadine, 235n.68

Brunt, Melanie, 239n.21

Buchanan, Patrick, 179

Burger, Warren E., 85–86, 97–98, 112, 114, 122

Bush, George, 124, 135, 146, 234n.53

Butler, Judith, 209n.49

Butterfield, Fox, 203n.3

Cain, Patricia A., 59, 209n.56

Callahan, Sydney, 135–39, 141–44

capitalism, 93; and aggression, 20–21, 65–67; and conventional jurisprudence, 66; and moral reasoning, 186–88; and pornography, 56–57

Card, Claudia, 209n.52

Carder, Angela. See *In the Matter of A.C.*; *In re A.C.*

INDEX OF CASES